EXPLOSION IN A PAINT FACTORY

An Autobiography - Volume 1

NICK HOMFRAY

BALBOA.PRESS

A DIVISION OF HAY HOUSE

Balboa Press books may be ordered through booksellers or by contacting:

Balboa Press
A Division of Hay House
1663 Liberty Drive
Bloomington, IN 47403
www.balboapress.co.uk
UK TFN: 0800 0148647 (Toll Free inside the UK)
UK Local: (02) 0369 56325 (+44 20 3695 6325 from outside the UK)

Because of the dynamic nature of the Internet, any web addresses or links contained in this book may have changed since publication and may no longer be valid. The views expressed in this work are solely those of the author and do not necessarily reflect the views of the publisher, and the publisher hereby disclaims any responsibility for them.

The author of this book does not dispense medical advice or prescribe the use of any technique as a form of treatment for physical, emotional, or medical problems without the advice of a physician, either directly or indirectly. The intent of the author is only to offer information of a general nature to help you in your quest for emotional and spiritual well-being. In the event you use any of the information in this book for yourself, which is your constitutional right, the author and the publisher assume no responsibility for your actions.

ISBN: 978-1-9822-8593-7 (sc)
ISBN: 978-1-9822-8592-0 (e)

Print information available on the last page.

Balboa Press rev. date: 06/02/2022

PREFACE

Life is a terminal illness, but it's your choice as to what route
you take towards the inevitable end.

EXPLOSION IN A PAINT FACTORY
A story with a beginning – a middle – but no end . . . as yet.

I made my first appearance in the main ring of this circus that we all call life on the 4th August 1947 in Brum. I can't remember much about it. I must have been there but I couldn't have been very old at the time. Now, on this point, just a note to Birmingham City Council. Where is the blue plaque? I've been back to Brum several times over the years that have followed but I can't see one anywhere ...... cheapskates!! Anyway, enough of wandering off on that tangent. My Mother must have removed me from the clutches of those, no doubt, adoring nurses before I had time to marry any of them. Sorry girls but you can blame the woman that squirted me into this inferno of a life that was to start and unfold as soon as I landed within the walls of the family residence. I wish she hadn't bothered really because the next ten years would leave a lot to be desired as they say. I should have crept into the handbag of one of the maternity nurses a few days earlier before it was too late but it was too late now. My brother Andrew – known as Abb – was already installed in this den of misery because he was older than me and he remained older than me until he died . . . the clever sod!! Then a couple of years later my sister Ellen – known as Fan must have joined the party. I know she arrived after me because she was, and still is, younger than me. Another clever sod. I was surrounded by them. I don't have any enjoyable memories of the time spent with my parents and I doubt Abb or Fan have either. It's never really been spoken about between us because since that time it all went "tits up". We all lost any form of regular contact. In fact Abb and I never saw each other for nearly 50 years. We met again about two years before he died. I have no photographs of any kind, at all, relating to these times, which suits me, because nothing ever happened in this house that was, in anyway, at all, that could be classed as enjoyable. So best forgotten about I think!!

There are a few things I can remember about my time spent with Dad on a "one to one basis". I can recall him trying to teach me how to use a hammer. What a strange memory to hold. Then there was the time that I found a packet of cigarettes which only contained two fags. Now then I took one of these and sneaked off upstairs for a smoke. I think I was eight years old at the time. Anyway, he caught me in the act and proceeded to pick me up and throw me down the stairs. I didn't touch anything on the way down. Not even a small bounce. I was totally airborne until I hit the wall three steps up from the bottom. The really insulting thing about this episode was when he told me that I hadn't been punished for smoking but for being stupid enough to think that he wouldn't notice that one of only two fags was missing.

A regular event, most weekends, was when he used to borrow his sister's car to go and collect 200 or 300 dozen eggs and a quantity of dressed rabbits. He would buy these and then sell them around the pubs. I suppose it was one way of funding his alcoholism. Something that would eventually kill him.

On the odd occasion he'd take me with him. This was all very well until, one day, on the journey home, with a vehicle full of eggs and naked Peter Rabbits, he decided to try and cross a river fording that, even to me as a child, look a bit "iffy". The aforementioned river was obviously not in the best of humours. Anyway the captain of ship was soon to be a captain of a stranded "ship". He threw caution to the wind and went for it . . . oops, wrong decision. First we floated for a while. Then we got caught on some obstruction that was emerging from Davy Jones' locker and our version of The Titanic started to take in water. Luckily it found it's level about a third of the way up the windows. Now "Captain Columbus" managed to extricate himself by forcing the door open enough to push through and reach Terra Firma. He left me alone, shitting myself, in what I assumed was soon to become a watery grave. After what seemed an age "Captain Scarlet" re-appeared with the cavalry in the shape and form of a lady on a horse with a length of rope. They kept chucking the rope to me until I could grab hold of it. Eventually I was pulled out to safety through the partially opened window. What a good job I was small and thin. Needless to say that was the last time he was allowed to borrow my Aunt's car.

Another utterance that found it's way out of this man's alcohol scented mouth was when he was telling me off one day. The phrase "You'll never be as good as your brother". This was a real confidence booster but that was just par for the course I suppose. I have never forgotten it all my life.

I can remember us, as a family, going on holiday to The Norfolk Broads one year but to fuel his need for an alcoholic beverage or ten we always ended up moored near a pub. On one of these occasions I can remember a cow trying to get on the boat. She got as far as getting her front half on. Was that an omen for my life to come I wonder?

4

I can't remember having a pushbike much before I was eight of nine years old but I did have a "buggy" that was propelled by me with the aid of four wheels. The trouble was they were spoked wheels and, one day, a few of the spokes on one wheel broke. I tried to mend them by "sticking" them together with a copious amount of paint. I never was, in any way, going to be a mechanic but it's all I could think of that was capable of sticking. Needless to say it was a case of "exit stage left" for my beloved buggy.

As I write this I am almost seventy three years old and I am still quite dark skinned but, I am now, pale in comparison to what I was as a child. People thought I was a half caste – and to this day I still wonder about that to myself. To continue, I was in the bath one day and Dad came in to check I'd washed behind my ears and my neck. Ah, my neck. This became the subject for his belittling me again. When I was a little fella when I got "suntanned" I turned a sort of mahogany come plum colour. Obviously my neck had succumbed to nature's meteorological influences. Now he tried to remove this "dirt" with a flannel and soap but when this action proved unfruitful it was time to bring in the big guns in the shape of the scrubbing brush that was normally employed to clean the kitchen floor. He got so frustrated when the "dirt" wouldn't come off. All he really succeeded in doing was to make me scream and make my neck very sore . . . what a Wally!!

Another one of his party pieces was to tickle me until I couldn't scream loud enough to try and stop him. I was then and still am extremely ticklish. I've always had the opinion that I could more than likely be tickled to the point of heart failure. What strange behaviour by a man towards his, to all intents and purposes, son.

As I've mentioned earlier my brother Abb got back in touch with me again about two years before he died and we were discussing our childhood. One day Abb said that he thought Dad reckoned that I wasn't his son. This could well be within the realms of possibility because it became clear that my mother never had been the finest example of fidelity available. Abb said he'd been in contact with Dad a couple of times over the years and had asked him what he remembered about me to which he answered "The only thing I can remember about Nick is the day I nearly killed him". Thanks Dad . . . for not a lot really!!

Now let's turn the attention to the other half of this couple that are generally regarded as my parents. Now with the laws of nature the TRUE identity of anyone's paternal lineage can never really be 100% proven but the maternal side is another thing because if a baby emerges from any female's womb then she is 100% the mother. My recollections of time spent with the aforementioned are few and far between. None of them contain much tenderness or caring but I do remember her taking me almost every week to Birmingham Childrens' Hospital for SunRay Treatment. Let me explain. When I was a toddler, and a bit older, I was a very sickly and weak infant for no apparent medical reason. Apparently in such instances, in those day, it was considered that SunRay Treatment was a beneficially treatment. I can remember with great affection my regular stays in hospital. I loved going into hospital to be amongst people who cared for me and showed a degree of tenderness towards me. I still have the vivid memory of two nurses coming round to my bedside and one said to the other "Oh look at those big brown eyes" while smiling at me . . . I WAS IN!!

I always wanted to be in hospital for my birthday but it never materialised. I had to go in one time on the 5th August – one day after my birthday and I was so upset because I'd only missed it by one day. My ambition was to spend Christmas in hospital but that scenario also evaded me.

Now those episodes with the Sunray Treatment would crop up again at a later date when I asked my mother why I was so brown and she said "It's because of the Sunray Treatment". Must have been strong stuff, is all I can say, because I even passed it on to my kids, especially my son Sam.

I can recall being, at home, in a pretty poorly state so one evening I was put into Fan's room to be on my own. My mother came up to say goodnight before she went out to "Chess Club" . . . Hmmmmm. She wasn't the best example of fidelity apparently. I asked her not to go but that request fell on deaf ears.

Memories of my two siblings are few and far between but I can remember Abb taking me to an Air Show at Castle Bromwich Airfield and him insisting that I eat copious amounts of candy floss which I'd never eaten before, and I never have since. Talk about being sick …. Bloody hell!!

Fan was a short dumpy little thing with a bob haircut and a fringe. She used to have ballet lessons. I bet that was a sight for sore eyes at the best of time. I do remember teaching her to read using Noddy books. I used to sit her half way up the stairs and if she got it right she went up a step and if she got it wrong then I put her down a step. If my memory serves me well she learnt to read very quickly. All three of us were in the same shit at this time and things were coming to a head now. The inevitable melt down was on the horizon. Abb went off and joined the Navy at the earliest age possible. I found a new "Mom" and I think Fan stayed with mom for a while. An arrangement that, in the end, also went tits up. I don't think that Mrs Homfray ever got an "A" level or a gold medal in "Mothering". I think they went to London. On a personal point, before I close, on the subject of my parents. All I ever really wanted my Dad to do was to tell me I was a good boy. He only needed to have said this once but he never did.

Something came on T.V. a couple of weeks ago that made me wonder what it must feel like to love, and be loved, by your Mom and Dad. I never had that feeling. I asked Lin and my best mate Rocky Price what it was like and they both said the same thing. That the feeling makes you feel safe and secure. That must have been a nice feeling to have had and I expect Abb and Fan felt the same way I did. Never feeling safe and secure. The situation that arose between me and my siblings meant that we didn't communicate for decades.

I mentioned earlier that as a toddler I was very dark skinned and extremely thin. I must have looked like a Twiglet with a pair of big brown eyes welded on top. Now, later on in life a story has been told to me. When I was a toddler at home, as a form of amusement, I was stripped off and a Terry Towel nappy was put on. They would then sit me cross-legged on the floor and call me "Gandi". I should be so lucky. Those little episodes must have happened very early on because I have no conscious memory of them but I am assured that it did happen.

Enough of all this twilight and sad world. Let's look through another door. The door that led to my refuge. My place of safety and security with no fear. My Nan and Grandad's house. The residence of a certain Mr HORACE GENGE and his good Lady AMANDA ALAMANDA GENGE. Their home was the place where my sun began to shine. I used to stay with them most week-ends and sometimes for longer. I know Abb came

Grandad:- My childhood best friend and mentor.

as well, at times, and I think Fan did as well but I was the chosen one
of the three of us siblings. I know this because I was the one that Nan
and Grandad took on holiday every year to Barmouth in Wales. I can
vividly remember riding on Peter Pan's themed childrens' round-a-bout
where all the seats were characters from Peter Pan. I always insisted
on riding on Capitain Hook which was a representation of a steam loco
engine and it was black with a bell. You could ring this bell. I spent a
lot of time aboard Captain Hook ringing his bell. Now when it was time
to return home on the coach I can clearly remember closing my eyes and
pretending to be asleep in the hope that when I opened them we really
hadn't gone home but had gone on another holiday instead. Of course
that dream was never realised.

I loved my old Grandad and miss him to this day. He helped me to realise that I could do things to be proud of and to a child that means a lot. He did give the impression of being a miserable old sod. I never saw him smile or laugh. Everything in his world was either black or white. He didn't believe in grey or grey areas but to me he was a God. We both sang off the same hymn sheet. We both loved natural history and doing art. In both our cases it was painting and drawing. He used to show me some of his artwork but the only piece I can really remember was a painting (he only ever painted in sepia as far as I can recall) of a cow lying down. The realism of his milk vein running along her belly was so realistic you felt you could almost touch it. That vision must have burned itself into my mind because I can still picture it today. As I said he didn't seem to be the most jovial man that had ever been born in the history of the world. He was strict . . . very strict . . . but he never raised his voice to me. He didn't have to because I respected him and his knowledge and he'd always encouraged me with what I enjoyed doing. If I did well he'd tell me so, and to me, at that time, to be told you were a "good boy" were the words I had always wanted to hear.

The old boy had a box of "Winsor & Newton" water colour paints and sable and squirrel hair brushes. From time to time I was allowed to use this paint box, on the one absolute condition, that when I'd finished I had to clean it back to the condition it was in when I started and it was immaculate. That rule was chiselled into granite as far as Grandad was concerned!! I used the paper that the butchers used to wrap meat up in those days. I think Grandad must have been well in with the butcher because I used a lot of it. I also used drawing books. I can recall those books had red covers. I can also recall something else connected to those red covered drawing books. I used to practice the art of drawing freehand circles and straight lines – loads of them – under Grandad's judgmental and advisory eye. If I ever did a nice piece of work then he'd let me sign it with my name. That was not an accolade that was to be bestowed readily or often but it did happen from time to time.

When I was in the care of my Nan and Grandad I think I was only ever out on rambles, having nature lessons from the old boy, or drawing and painting or copying out, word for word, the contents of a book called "A Field Guide to British Birds" by R.S.R. Fitter. I seemed to have a love of birds even at that early age and it's never left me. I was absolutely thrilled when, one day, Grandad presented me with a big glass case containing seventeen different stuffed birds. It was delivered by a man on a motorbike and sidecar to Nan and Grandad's house.

Mr Spicer was a very good friend of Grandads. Now Mr Spicer was a taxidermist – a very well respected person in his field so they told me. Even today, as I write this, his work is still highly valued by collectors but he was not only a taxidermist but he also sold birds eggs. My only memory of visiting his shop in Birmingham is that it was situated on a corner right in the middle of the City. I can remember Grandad taking me in and the counter consisted of a run of glass topped, slope fronted, display cabinets. I can picture today the vision of Mr Spicer complete with his bald head and glasses perched on the end of his "beak". Grandad had a big collection of birds eggs that he housed in a very special place. We will come on to it in this little book in a while. I once asked him why he stopped collecting birds eggs. He told me that it was because one day he'd taken a couple of thrushes eggs from a nest and sat down nearby to have a smoke. He noticed the parent bird come back to the nest and scragged it, eggs and all. He never took another birds egg again after witnessing this act.

Sometimes during holidays from school he would take me and sometimes Abb on a journey. This was a trip on the Number 11 bus. This bus was what was called The Outer Circle and it went on a circular route around the outskirts of Birmingham. . This bus took what seemed like enough time to be classed as a day out. Two other days out with Grandad that stick in my mind are the time he took me to the Market in the City that had a really good pet shop and he bought me a tree frog for the princely sum of either 6d or 9d. It was presented by the shopkeeper in a brown, heavy, paper bag. On the way home I discovered that this little amphibian, whose welfare was now my responsibility, had begun to dry out in his paper jail. So I dipped him, bag and all, in a puddle which kept him going until I could get him to the sanctuary of his new home – a glass tank that had also been donated by Nan and Grandad Genge. The other trip I can bring to mind is Grandad taking me on what was to see the only Ginko or Maidenhair tree in a public area anywhere in Birmingham. I could take anyone to the place where this tree lived even today. That is how important it was to this little boy and his beloved Grandad.

The old man's big love was Botany and his garden. Now this garden must have been at least sixty or seventy feet in length with a path up one side. There was a shed at the top where Grandad would spend hours sitting in the doorway on his old canvas beach chair, smoking his pipe and surveying his "estate". This abundance of botanical delights consisted of one hugh rockery with two or three ponds containing newts and fish. The latter he used to feed with broken dog biscuits. A regular happening every year was during the summer school holidays when us three kids stayed at The Genge residence for a couple of weeks. During this time we were tasked to weed this explosion of plant life. Now as far as Grandad was concerned this was a serious business. He made us our own little tools. Little trowels etc and our work was inspected by the Master's critical eye down to the tiniest detail. When he was satisfied we would get paid, probably only a couple of shillings, I suppose, but who cares it was a lesson in life.

The other great attraction to me in the Genge residence was Grandad's specimen room – the magic room in my eyes. This room was crammed and I mean crammed - you could just walk a couple of paces in the middle of it all – with natural history and anthropological curios etc. The prized item in this room was a Lyre Bird's tail which was kept, wrapped in brown paper, behind a cupboard. Every visit to this room was chaperoned by the old man himself. I would be given a small gift on every occasion, not much, say a dried seahorse. I particularly remember receiving a dried Chameleon one day but on other occasions it may have been a bit of Rhino hide or a bird's skull or a few shells or a piece of coral that would be bestowed on me. If I had been really well behaved I was allowed to look at the Lyre Bird's tail but the star prize the "Le Crème de la Crème" was being allowed to actually touch this avian adornment and then back it went cocooned in it's brown paper to it's roost behind the cupboard.

In the living room of the Genge residence was a black piano. I don't think anyone ever played it but it was there. One day the lid was open. It must have been left that way by the piano tuner who I remember was an Albino gentleman with pink eyes. I don't know if the piano was ever tuned because I never heard it utter a note. Now, as I say, the lid was open and lying on the keys was a newspaper cutting from The Birmingham Mail. On it was a picture of Grandad in his room under the caption "The World in One Room". To me, at that time, that's exactly what that room was.

Grandad's spouse went under the title of Mrs Amanda Alamanda Genge. We used to call her "Fat Nan" because she was a dumpy little lady always adorned in the accepted fashion of a working class housewife of the day. At that time this apparel consisted of a knotted scarf worn as a hat and a full length bibbed apron. She had a big fat brown and white dog called BOB and she was obviously trying to create the fattest dog in the entire history of the canine world - all at this poor creature's expense. He looked like a chest of drawers with a bit of brown and white fur stretched over his totally imbalanced frame. His body was perched on top of four clothes pegs with what resembled a tennis ball glued on one end. This appendage housed mainly a mouth that was in constant action most of the time it's host was awake. At the other end of this canine butcher's block, concealed under it's tail, was an orifice that was constantly releasing copious quantities of some foul smelling gas or other. In my eyes Nan's greatest accomplishment was her ability to crochet and read the paper all at the same time. This party piece always amazed me as a child. She would sit on one side of the fire and Grandad on the other with Bob recumbent in between them like a small tropical island. Now Nan's other claim to fame was that she could chatter for England. This at times would get on Grandad's nerves because when he was resident in his chair, complete with his glass of milk and his pipe, he usually had his ear glued to the radio situated about two feet away from him. At times his good woman's chattering would get on his nerves and he'd just look up and utter the immortal words "AMANDA ENOUGH" and that would signal the end of the evening's verbal contact. Both of them were creatures of habit. Nan would go to bed at 8 pm. and Grandad would follow an hour later, without fail, unless there was a boxing commentary on the radio and that meant a late night for the old man.

Grandad had a brother, a brother whose presence and image, I've never forgotten. This was Great Uncle Oscar, an elegant gangly old gentleman, with a domed bald head and a pelmet of grey hair. He wore, what seemed to me, three quarter length trousers, a jacket, waistcoat and tie and the shiniest pair of highly polished tan coloured high boots. When these boots were unveiled in their full glory there was no need for artificial lighting. They didn't just shine, they sparkled. Accompanying Great Uncle Oscar on every visit was a Bulldog that used to sit next to him in his chair. Well it wasn't his chair it was Nan's chair but he used it every time he visited. His sister-in-law (Nan) was exiled to the kitchen and scullery. Now this dog was given a complete beef knuckle bone on every visit. He gnawed and chomped away at it non-stop until all that was left were, may be, a few crumbs and a greasy patch on the carpet. Then, and only then, did Oscar leave with his canine companion. A sure sign that a visit from Great Uncle Oscar was on the horizon was when Nan bought a beef knuckle bone home.

Grandad to me was a man who only dealt in facts. He never drank alcohol so there was no ingredients present in his life to cause him to hallucinate but, for as long as ever I knew him, he insisted that he'd seen fairies!!! He said he'd seen them in a little wooded glen in Barmouth. He used to take me there and show me where he'd seen them but to me they were invisible.

Of course I had a paternal Grandmother but not a Grandad on that side. He died before he had the pleasure of meeting me. Nan was a very skinny little lady with silver hair. I recall that is why she was known as "Thin Nan". Now, she had a hearing problem and was constantly fiddling with her hearing aid. It was regularly emitting strange sounds of various frequencies. She lived with my spinster Auntie Barbara who was an elocution teacher and voice coach. This to me seemed strange because she never helped me with my affliction – stammering. I stammered very badly. Badly enough to make me not want to go anywhere on my own without having a pencil and paper concealed somewhere about my person just in case I needed to say something I was physically incapable of. This problem was the root cause of probably the most humiliating and embarrassing situation in my life. It occurred in Junior School and the teacher, a certain Mr Dowell, asked me a question the answer to which began with the letter "D". The dreaded "D" along with M,N,P,C,K and S were basically out of reach for me at this time. Mr Dowell knew how bad my stammer was and he verbally pummelled me into attempting to say this word. So much so that he got the rest of the class to shout out the answer. All this was just a total piss take on his behalf. This problem never really went away until well after Fleur was born. I had trouble getting my wedding vows out. I remember the dreaded "D" was rampant again. It did become a nuisance as I got older but between us, me and Lin, we managed to work around it so that helped a lot.

At this Junior School I remember we did country dancing. I remember there were five other small children in my class. My partner Jennifer Harding, a lad called Haydn Jolley and his partner Joyce England, and the final couple were Paul Howell and Susan Hare. The school entered us into a competition that was held somewhere near the H.P. Sauce Factory in Birmingham and I can still remember the smell of it. I don't remember how we got on but attending that competition was an escape from reality - if only for one day. I wonder where those other five little people are now?

Before I pull the curtain down on this, my initial introduction to the world, I'd like to relate one more little period that, to this day, I believe was a symptom of what was to come and what was to stay with me all my life right up to now . . . insecurity, sensitivity and lack of self-respect. Let me explain, about a mile or so from where we lived was a wood yard that sold logs by the barrow. Now here was a chance for me (perhaps not consciously at the time) to stick one up 'em as they say. I would go and get a barrow full of logs and push it all the way home. I did this quite regularly but I enjoyed doing it, really enjoyed doing it. I was on my own making my own choices and, I think, looking back on it now, it got me away from being made to feel worthless because I was doing something neither Dad or Abb could do or wanted to do. I was the main man for once, if only for a while. I knew it helped them because they wanted the logs but, it also helped me a lot more, without them realising it. It helped me feel proud and less insecure etc.

Insecurity, in anyone, no matter what age is a really difficult thing to live and cope with. It's like a roller coaster. It forces you to do things that can not only affect you in a negative way but also those around you. It is debilitating because it constantly gnaws away at your mind and consequently your whole being, physical and mental, and in my case it has never stopped. It's just almost constant pressure to please and impress all those you care for.

My second eldest daughter Collette once said to me "Dad, you can't run forever. In the end you'll have to stop". Well I am trying to stop, up to a point, at the time of writing this but I don't think I ever will until it's time to go and sit on Grandad's knee again.

There are many other miserable and grey things that happened in this twilight world in which I was enclosed but I just don't want to go there. The memories aren't really worthy of recollection. The only good thing to come out of it was my time spent with Nan and Grandad Genge. I don't know when any of my natural family died except for Abb. Fan is still alive and she texts me every so often just to see how I'm doing - and

Fat Nan.   I did find out that after Grandad died my mother went and threw all the contents of his beloved room out of the window apparently because he snubbed her in his Will.   Now as far as I know she was the only child out of ten or eleven that survived pregnancy and birth so it stands to reason she'd probably have been a "spoiled child".   She definitely exhibited all the relevant symptoms of being so in later life.

It's time to shut the doors on this cellar as best I can and anyway by the time I was about ten I had a good pushbike, a blue pushbike, a blue pushbike with semi-dropped handlebars and I loved riding it.   Now at this point I had a friend with a bike and we went on rides together.   On one of these excursions my life began to change and change for the better. I would soon be taking my first tentative steps into The Paint Factory.

The time that begins at this point is a bit of a blur but, it now seems to me, that things had changed in my life.   I have no chronologically based recollections of this period.   The time that begins at this point is a bit of a blur but, it now seems to me, that Things just seemed to "happen".   I didn't know how but I did know why.   I just seemed to have "landed" at Auntie Barbara's place.   Abb had gone off and joined the Navy and Fan and Mom had moved in with Nan and Grandad Genge.   It seemed like I was being tossed around like a piece of driftwood in a stormy world with nothing to try and grab hold of to create any semblance of stability.   I still don't know how old I was when all this was going on but I think I must have been at Secondary School.

As I've said earlier Auntie Barbara was a spinster who lived with my paternal Nan but by now her half sister, Auntie Bess had become a widow so she was now resident in this household also.   I remember a regular visitor to this brood of single ladies, was another single lady, a very large women and when I say large I mean LARGE.   She was known as Aunt Ivy and I learnt decades later that her brother was a man called Norman who, at one time, was betrothed to Auntie Barbara but he jilted her.   That is why she lived and died as a spinster.   Another regular visitor to this address was a lady known as "Auntie Audrey".   I didn't, and still don't to this day, know who she was but she seemed to have a "soft spot" for me for some reason.   So much so that she financed an "alternative" treatment for my troublesome – seemingly incurable really, really bad nosebleeds.   This treatment consisted of a trip on a train, with her, to London to be assessed by an eminent herbalist called Sir John Weir.   It is strange how certain events remain in your mind for a lifetime. I can still see now his "surgery". It consisted of a huge entrance hall with a big staircase leading somewhere but I don't remember where. His treatment consisted of a powder that had to be taken daily. These powders arrived in a box in numbered paper wraps and had to be taken in number order. I wasn't allowed to eat anything containing any form of mint. This treatment worked but it must have become unaffordable because the powders stopped arriving and the nosebleeds returned. That is until surgery brought them to their knees and they eventually cleared up and went away. My last real memories of these ladies are Nan reaching her 100th birthday. She always said, when we were kids, that she was going to be 100. I was to her a "little Varmint". She did reach a 100 but I was told she died a few months after she'd reached her target. So far as Auntie Barbara goes, I can remember visiting her years and years later by which time I'd forged my own path in the world. She didn't seem to be in agreement with my life. So much so that she told me that if I didn't change my ways then she wouldn't leave me anything in her Will . . . cheeky cow . . . I didn't and she didn't . . . so what? What you've never had you don't miss – that's what I say. In retrospect I think this was the shittiest period of my life. I'd been cast adrift in the world to find my own way in life with no obvious adult guidance.

At this time I did have two good friends, a certain Master Alan Tinn and a Master Nigel Elwell. Alan Tinn or "Tinny" as we called him was my best mate at Secondary School. Now, myself, Tinny, his elder brother Derek and an older lad called Ernie were the only four kids in the whole school with "a bit of colour". Derek and Earnie were older lads, two or three forms up from me. Tinny and Ernie's main claims to fame were, number 1, he had a tuft of black bristle like hairs growing out of the bridge of his nose and, number 2 , he had an "A" level GCE!! Now, in those days that was some sort of achievement in our world. In today's money, the equivalent would be to prove that Donald Trump has more than one brain cell OR getting an appointment with a G.P. without having to apply by means of a written request carved on a lump of granite and written in Latin. The Tinn brothers were half bred Gurkha boys. Extremely clever half bred Gurkhas boys. Both were into maths, physics and chemistry in a big way. They came from a large, not very well off family so consequently they had the same uniform on the day they left school as they did on the day they started. By the time they were fifteen years old their trousers only reached half way down their shins. Their blazer sleeves ended about six inches away from their wrists and the said garment was adorned with the remnants of four years school dinners but the piece de resistance was the tie. Now, we used our school ties as whips trying to get them to "crack" so naturally, after being subjected to a few years of this kind of treatment, they frayed at the ends. Now, Tinny, with his tie, had taken this habit to the extreme because by the end of his Secondary Education it was just about long enough to go around his neck and conceal the gap in shirt collar. By this time his collar was too small to fasten up with a button. As I mentioned Tinny's main love was physics. Now, when it came to taking exams in this subject, by the time most of the class had written their name on the top of the paper, old Einstein Tinny was going up to the front to get more paper. We lost touch after leaving school but I did later learn that he became a lecturer in his beloved subject at a Canadian University.

As far as any other recollections of my Secondary Education go they consist of three main things Biology, the only subject I was interested in. It was to me what physics was to Tinny but I didn't progress with the subject in the same way . . . well not academically anyway. The second thing was going on a school holiday camping in the Isle of Wight and whilst on this holiday the boys had to take it in turns to cut up the firewood for the stove. Now, this was talking my language. I was good at this point, I'd done it before, a lot, so I was allotted this task for the rest of our time there in camp. Not only did I excel in the woodcutting department but I also got to wear a pair of jeans for the first time in my life. Not my jeans, but a pair lent to me by another lad. The third things that sticks in my thoughts is a girl called Annette Coleman. A pretty little thing with dark hair and blue eyes. I'd started to grow up. Not only had I got a "girlfriend" but I'd also worn my first pair of jeans!!

My other main friend at this time was a lad called Nigel Elwell. Nigel had a brother called Mike. Both brothers were keen cyclists, as I was, by this time. Mike was older than us and I remember being amazed by his ability to put a bike tyre back on a wheel using no tools other than his fingers and thumbs. Nigel and I spent hours out and about on our bikes and we joined a Cycling Club called The Ivy Wheelers. This was based in Castle Bromwich village hall. Being a member of this club enabled us to go out on long club rides most Sundays. Many of these rides were as long as 80-100 miles in a day depending on the time of year and the weather. It also enabled us to take part in Club Time Trials which involved being timed over a set amount of miles and the fastest time was the winner. I remember I did 5 miles in 13 minutes and 48 seconds. I tried to do a 10 mile version on a later date but I failed miserably. It proved a step too far at the time. As I've mentioned Nigel and I spent hours out and about on our bikes. One of these trips was a fishing trip to The Cuttle. A little spot down by the river at Coleshill. This was where the switch to my next life was turned on . . . I was off now, at the beginning of a whole new world and life.

The Cuttle was situated at the bottom of a very steep hill with fields on three sides. The road ran into a very sharp 90 degree bend with a lamppost to warn any motorist of this tangent. It was comprised of two semi-detached "tied" cottages whose gardens ran down to the river. That river bent round to the left and went under a footbridge that accommodated a public footpath. The path then then led from the lane, around a field, and on to Maxstoke Castle. The cottages adjoined a field that was bordered by this footpath and the river. It was a kind of picnic area used by locals and a few visitors from further way. In fact it even had a large wooden shed café that sold drinks, cakes, biscuits and crisps. It was a very popular spot in those days. That is how Nigel and I ended up there one day on a fishing expedition. We set up and started our pursuit of any renegade stickleback or minnow, at the bottom of one of the aforementioned cottages gardens, and waited for any hint of a bite. The sound of "Do you want some floats mate?" disturbed our perceived concentration. We looked up and there, standing against the fence of the garden, was a scruffy little lad, about ten years old, with tousled hair, freckles, khaki shorts and a pair of pumps that had seen better days on his feet. No socks or shirt . . . Meet Billy Carr, the lad who was to become my new "brother" or Billy Whizz as he was later to become known.

This meeting was, what turned out to be, the beginning of some of the happiest years of my life. I gradually started going to The Cuttle at regular intervals, basically every weekend at the time, either by bike or by bus. Billy took me into the cottage to meet his family, his Mom – Mrs Woodcock (I always called her Mrs Woodcock and not "Ma" until a few years ago). I also met his stepdad Frank and his two half-sisters Beryl and Jacqui. Jacqui only being a baby at the time and Beryl a couple of years older. They both turned out, within time, to have waist length platinum blonde hair. This ended up being chopped off to above shoulder length when the daily battle to have it brushed got past being a joke. Mrs Woodcock was (and still is to this day) a short dumpy woman

Frank.   *Frank, Beryl and Jackie at The Cuttle.*

with long hair that she plaited and wrapped up into a bun on top of her head. Frank was, as they say, "built like a brick shit house" with only two fingers and a thumb on his right hand. It seemed to us kids this hand he could use like a vice. I found out years later that the reason Mrs Woodcock took "a shine" to me was because her sister had a son whose father was Maltese. This boy had been killed as a child at about the same age as I was then and, apparently, I was the "spitting image" of this poor boy.   I think Mrs Woodcock thought it was some kind of destiny that I turned up out of the blue. Indeed years and years later I met the boy's Mother and, although Mrs Woodcock had warned her sister how much I looked like her lost boy, the poor woman actually fainted when we met. She fainted even though it had previously been agreed that she must be sitting down at the time I went into the room to meet her . . . Strange thing . . . Fate!!

The Cuttle Cottages, where we lived, comprised of two semi-detached farm worker's tied cottages with large gardens that were bordered by the road, a field, and the river. These dwellings were originally a pair of two up two down places but at some time had had an extension consisting of a small kitchen, an even smaller bathroom and toilet with bedroom above. Thus turning the cottages into 3 bedrooms and two living rooms. The smaller of the downstairs rooms got too damp to be lived in so everything centred around the one room and the kitchen, the latter being just big enough for a cooker, a small table, one chair and a sink which was enough for what was needed and anyway it meant there was only

19

Billy at The Cuttle.

Billy, Beryl and Jackie at The Cuttle.

one room to keep warm and light. The electric light was reserved for the living room and kitchen. The rest was all lit by candles and the only heating was a wood fire. It was a rare occurrence for any coal or coke to cross the threshold.

The cottage also furnished its occupants with a wonderful underground larder with a big stone shelf. The fact the cottage was so close to the river probably meant the ground was kept reasonably cool even though the summer. The larder was accessed by descending two or three stone steps directly from the living room. It was a draughty old

Beryl and Jackie at The Cuttle.

cottage with old plank doors and stone floors but to me it would soon become a place where I could feel safe and cared for . . . HOME . . . a proper home at last.

As I've already mentioned I was soon spending every week-end and all the school holidays with my new family. I used to leave my Auntie Barbara's and Nan's on a Friday night and return on a Sunday. Mother would give me bus fare if I didn't go to Coleshill on my bike and a couple of shillings pocket money which I invariably spent buying sweets for Billy, Beryl and Jacqui because I think I thought it would be a way of showing my appreciation for the kindness and food I was being allowed to share with the family. I helped Frank out with his work as best I could at that age and I absolutely loved every second I spent with him. If I wasn't strong enough or practised enough to contribute much worthwhile then I'd just go with him everywhere. Over the next couple of years, before I was big enough to drive a tractor on my own, I spent hours and hours and hours just sitting on the tractor mudguards, in all weathers. I couldn't have been happier. My Mother always told me I'd wanted to be "a farmer" for as long as she could remember. Maybe that was something she got right after all. I was probably about thirteen or fourteen years old by the time I was strong enough to drive the tractor. (I was still like a little brown stickman) but I had begun to "thrive" by now and practised enough to really do anything that would ease the load on anyone. Of course, in those days, nearly all farm work was done by hand because at that time the "old" farm buildings were still in use and they weren't big enough to accommodate anything much more mechanical than a man and a hand held tool. I couldn't get enough of it. To this very day I can still "smell" the cattle in the sheds and everything that went with that scenario. By now I'd got strong enough to carry a bale of hay (about 56 lbs in those days) on my own. I can recall being sent up the ladder of a winter's evening at feed time to fetch a certain amount of wheat straw bales and ditto oat and barley straw. By then I'd learnt to tell the difference between the three just by touch in the dark. If I got it wrong at any time I was sent back again until I got it right . . . I soon learned. By now I still did not own a pair of wellingtons. I just had strong shoes and wrapped my legs in sacking bound on with baler string but I didn't give a "monkeys" about such a trifling incidental and anyway I'd been given an axe. Frank only ever cut wood up with an axe. He wouldn't entertain using a saw so now I could be even more useful and more of a man. It was a long handled axe with a 2 ½ lb head. I had it for years until I graduated to one with a 4 lb head. Frank's axe had an 8 lb head and he could use it one handed!!! From that day to this I've never been without an axe. Indeed as I write this I have one at the side of the fridge even though to try and use it now would be beyond my capability . . . it's just a strange quirk I've grown up with I suppose . . . A man never knows when he might need an axe.

At the times of year when Frank didn't work at week-ends the main occupation of Billy and I was to play, in the river, up and down the lanes, up and down trees . . . The usual "boys stuff" of the time. At intervals we'd be conscripted into going rabbiting. No gun, no ferrets, just a spade and a long stick. This method was more often than not successful but when it wasn't it was just a case of a lot of digging for no reward. In the back end of the year there were always the pheasants or a duck or two off the river and occasionally the odd moorhen. The only weapons we used were catapults. Frank was a dead shot, and he used 14" square elastic which I could hardly pull back so I used similar elastic but only half the size. Frank always used to tell me that if the worst came to the worst you could always chuck a "Cattie" in the hedge and walk on. A gun was out of the question for two reasons. First, we couldn't afford one and second they were too noisy. Another method the old man used in the winter was a weighted stick which he'd skim across the top of the ground and knock the birds down when they came to feed at the sheep troughs. If you were lucky and quick enough you could get two or three at the same time . . . A bonus and a change from bloody rabbit!!! Basically the only other meat that was affordable was breast of lamb which Mrs Woodcock fried in the pan. On a Sunday she'd bake cakes and corned beef hash pie . . . "White Pie" as my youngest daughter called it and still does call it when her Mom makes it for us. Now Sundays, or at least most Sundays were baking days so Bill and me were chucked out from about nine in the morning until around four in the afternoon. We were sent off with a bottle of home-made lemonade and a sandwich. We just used to wander about anywhere outside of the village. A regular "expedition" was to work our way along the lanes to Maxstoke Priory and back again. A round trip of about five miles but it took us all the time we had been allotted just "pissin about". A regular bit of fun was for Bill to get up a tree on the side of the lane with a pocket full of pebbles. When we heard a vehicle approaching I'd lie down in the lane, with a knife I'd previously pushed into a stick and wedged inside my shirt with the handle sticking out in view of any passing motorist. The idea was that a car would stop, Bill would shower whoever it was with pebbles, and I'd get up and run off but it never worked. All we ever got was a lot of horn tooting and abuse. Imagine trying to do that these days"!! These strolls and excursions were good fun but the "big voyage" was a day spent on "The Island". Now the island was a piece of land probably measuring between one and two acres. This was literally no more than five yards away from the bottom of our garden. It was an island to us because it was surrounded on three sides by the river and on the fourth side by a brook, so, basically it was an island. We'd spend all day just messing about on there. If we could find a bit of old net curtain we'd walk up the river against the flow and just net minnows and sticklebacks which we'd knock on the head, skewer them on a stick and, provided we'd been able to smuggle out a few matches and a bit of paper, we'd light a fire and cook them over that. Not much meat on them, but if you got enough it was O.K. I always thought the minnows tasted a bit like cod . . . who cared anyway ... that's the way it was. At the time The Island and the fun we had in the river was the equivalent of a foreign holiday . . . Little things please little minds I suppose.

The two girls, Beryl and Jackie were, to us two boys, at that age, just two little girls that needed to be made allowances for in our little bubble. Jacqui could be a bit of a little bugger at times. She was attracted to the river like a magnet which wasn't really the healthiest place for a toddler to be unsupervised. It was almost impossible to keep her confined in the garden because, although she couldn't open the gate, she could climb anything. As a last resort, during the Summer, if she was outside on her own we had to tie her up with a rope around the damson tree just to keep her safe. At that age she was a bundle of fun and mischief. In fact one of her favourite pastimes was to have a nappy put on and then Billy and I would push her, across the lino floor of the main room, to each other and shoot her off the step into the kitchen where one of us would catch her. Beryl was a bit more aloof than Jacqui. Anyway she was a bit big to do anything like that with.

The remaining resident of No 1 Cuttle Cottages was a border collie bitch called "Lady". She kept having pups every year but only ever the same dog. Her "suitor" was a Bill who came down from the farm every time she was in season and wait for her on the river bridge. We'd let her go off and they trot "into the sunset" and nine weeks later she'd have her pups under the chair next to the fire. Both Billy and I were allowed to keep a pup each over the period of two or three years. Bill called his dog Buster and I called mine Bruno. I kept him all of his life. What a dog he was, so faithful and clever. He used to run alongside me on my bike when I went to work or anywhere. As I got older and worked on a farm a few miles away and started early in the morning then I'd leave him at home and Mrs Woodcock would let him off mid-morning and he'd come to me at work. If he couldn't find me when he got there then he'd just wait in the shed next to my bike until I turned up. As I said he lived all his life with me and although, as I write this, I've had literally hundreds of dogs he is one of the three or four I've ever owned that were "special".

The farm that our cottage was tied to was owned by the Levi family. The old man Jack, his wife, eldest son Conrad, daughter Julie and youngest Son Mervyn. I remember Jack was a stout old boy with glasses and a hearing aid that he was always fiddling with so that he could tune into you. I always thought it strange that he could hear you drop a coin even though he couldn't hear you speak. He had two other little habits. The first was that he'd come to the back door of his house, open the door, then piddle up the doorpost and then go in again. His other trick was, if he needed a single sheep catching, was to get in his car with Frank, drive across the fields to the sheep, get as close as he could to the one he wanted and then shout "now Frank". This was the signal for Frank to open the car door and throw himself on top of the target ewe. It worked every time, with a bit of luck.

Jack Levi was a well known cattle and sheep dealer with all the animals, including pigs, turning up at the slaughterhouse. During the winter months he'd always buy "reject" fat cattle that were fully grown but not fat enough to be slaughtered. He used to say that "They'd done all their growing, now all they've got to do is to eat, sleep and get fat" . . . a canny old man indeed!!

Today, as I write this, I think how times have changed in farming. More especially farm work. These days everything seems to be done by pushing buttons and relying on machinery and technology. In those days (I am going back to the time in my story) almost everything was done mainly by hand, and by touch, sight and sense. In my eyes those days were more honest and satisfying in many ways. You were "closer" to your work. You smelled of it, you could taste it and feel it and, most of all, appreciate what you'd achieved.

Back in the late 50's and 60's (my most impressionable times) the only concession to mechanisation was basically the horse being replaced by a tractor. Tractor power as opposed to horse power. Otherwise it was as it had been for generations. So far as I can remember the only piece of machinery on the Levi farm that couldn't have been powered by a horse was a tractor mounted, front end loader, that was used to muck out the bigger cattle pens that could accommodate this equipment. Also a silage harvester that was driven by a power shaft direct from the tractor. In fact jumping ahead a few years my best mate Bobbie, who also worked on a farm, and was the same age as me came back from work one night and announced that, on his farm, they'd just got a MUCKSPREADER!!! This was almost unheard of at the time. So much so, that two or three of us lads got on our bikes and cycled off just to go and look at this "gift from the Gods". No more spending hours and hours, in the autumn and winter, spreading muck by hand with a fork from piles that you had previously loaded and unloaded onto and off a trailer, also by hand, and with the same fork. This fork sometime or other you would inevitably stick through your toe or your foot. This was all very well and good but it ruined a perfectly good Wellington. This was akin to losing a week's wages.

Now, to return to the story in chronological order, after my "spouting on" about the old days. I was now probably a good fourteen years old or a little bit younger and had begun to be trusted doing a man's job on my own with no supervision. The three jobs that came into this category, and that have stayed in my mind ever since, were firstly, being allowed and indeed trusted – to ride the "sledge" behind the baler. Let me explain this process. In those days if hay and straw was "baled" then it was all the oblong bales tied with twine that were produced by the baler. This was a machine towed and powered by a tractor. The baler picked up the crop and formed it into bales that were spat out of the back of the aforementioned piece of advanced technology. Now these bales normally were allowed not to weigh less than 40 lb each for straw and 50 lb each for hay – too many light bales used too much baler twine. This weight could be altered by twiddling about with pressure screws that could increase or decrease the density of the end product. The sledge was, as its name suggests, basically a sledge that was big enough to accommodate a man and a stack of 6 or 8 bales. The whole idea was for the man to ride the sledge which was attached and towed directly behind the tractor and within easy reach of the back end of the baler. The man would catch the bales as they came out, stack them, usually in sixes, on the rear of the sledge and flick a trip on the floor with his foot. The stack would slide off. This operation not only saved time when it came to loading the bales on trailers to take in but, it also helped to keep the bales dry if it rained. Now on paper, if you're an adult as opposed to being a fourteen year old boy (who slightly resembled a poster for famine relief at the time) then it was fairly easy job. It was one Sunday in hay time and the men were already occupied so Conrad told me I could "ride the sledge" behind him on the tractor and baler. This was the first time I'd ever done such a job and it couldn't have been a worse time really. The hay contained a lot of clover that made the bales very heavy and the ground was rough. Anyway to cut a long story short I struggled. I think I probably only weighed 5 or 6 stone at this age and, along with the necessary heavier weight of the bales and, trying to balance on the sledge at the same time as stacking these bales I missed a lot of the bales and they were just spat out at random intervals while I was otherwise occupied by trying to do the job properly. Job completed, the field looked as if the bales had been scattered from a helicopter. There were a few stacks of 6 still standing proudly amidst the array of their fellows that had been launched from the sledge incomplete and an assortment of randomly placed single bales. The single bales were the ones I had failed to get a hold on when they had completed their journey through this slave driver of a machine. Anyway I trudged home after my failed excursion into manhood but I just sat and brooded until I just thought "That's it, I'll show 'em". I returned to the scene of my earlier forlorn efforts, re-stacked all the fallen "piss-taking" monuments of roughage and collected up all the "orphaned ammunition" into neat stacks of 6. It took what seemed like hours until finally, with blistered hands and leg and arms and torso that looked like I'd been scrubbed down with a wire wool, I finished. My pride was satisfied. On reflection was this the first real example of what was, and still is, my big problem – stubbornness and pride?

The following Summer dawned and I was then presented and trusted with my next "man's job". This involved riding on the Combine Harvester – always driven by Frank – and "doing the bags". The Levi's didn't own a Tanker Combine. Not many people did back then. In fact I'd never seen one. Instead they had "a bagger" which did the same job as a tanker except that the corn, instead of going into a self- contained tank, and being offloaded mechanically, was riddled and graded inside the machine and expelled through four separate chutes. Two for good corn, one for seconds and the fourth for dust. To "do the bags" involved riding on a platform attached to the side of the combine and facing the four aforementioned chutes. Your job was to wait until one of the good corn bags was full and then flick the latch onto the other chute and while the second bag was filling you had to take the full bag from under the chute, replace it with a new empty bag, and then gather up the neck of the first one, tie it with string and drag it a few feet. You then deposited it on a slide that held three or four full bags which were then released off the slide onto the ground by way of a little trap door at the bottom that you operated by pulling a piece of rope. The only thing that could really go wrong through this process was if you got caught out by somehow not getting rid of the full bag before the one that was filling was ready to go as well. This situation could be remedied by shouting down Frank's ear to "STOP". At times this request was, at odd times, responded to by a hard look or at the worst a "hurry up". In those days all the corn bags were hessian sacks, of varying sizes and thicknesses. These would hold up to between a cwt and in the case of the big old sugar beet bags 2 cwt of wheat. A little less weight for barley and even less of oats. The next job was to get the full bags off the ground and into the dry before they got damp or even worse wet. There were no corn drying machines in our world. These bags were, of course, loaded onto the trailers by hand. Easier if it was two men and anyway I was in no way strong enough to manhandle a cwt bag of corn, three or four feet up onto a trailer. If the bags started to get around 1 ½ cwt each an easy adaption to help in lifting them was to have a man each side of the sack with one hand each on the neck and the other hand on either end of a stout stick, usually an old sledge hammer or axe stale (handle), which was placed at the bottom of the bag.   This was then flipped over using the hands holding the neck. The bottom could then be raised from the ground by lifting up the stick – "a hand on every corner" basically. Any sacks that had been ravaged by rodents at some time or other were just rendered useful again by stuffing the resultant holes with straw.   If and when a slack, rainy day should interrupt proceedings then we would be tasked with darning the most badly affected with baler string. A nice easy job on a rainy day in the summer.

Over both haymaking and corn harvest all the resultant bales were bought in using only manpower apart from when the barns were nearly full to the top. To get these bales up to that height without the aid of a petrol driven elevator would have been, and at times was, not impossible, but awkward and more time consuming. Otherwise everything was moved by hand using only two tined Pitchforks. That's where the name comes from. A fork used to pitch, in the olden days, loose hay or sheaves of corn. Those forks had longer tines than the pitchforks we used in my time. Shorter tines meant it was easier and safer to use them with bales. Easier to put in and easier to release. I never really pitched bales at this age because I just wasn't physically tall enough or strong enough for this job. I was allowed to stack the bales on the trailers. This had to be done using an interlocking and binding pattern because it was thought not to be worth bringing in a load in that wasn't at least seven courses high.   It was a case of woe and behold for the stacker if the load came off. I never had a full load come off but at times the odd back corner or two would decide to liberate itself.

Silage is, and was, the way of storing "green fodder" by storing it in a raw state. Usually in "a clamp". A clamp was basically just a very large area either dug out of the ground or built from railway sleepers lined with empty plastic fertiliser bags. The idea being to keep it all as air tight as possible. This harvest was basically done using a tractor with drawn or mounted implements.   These I was never good enough or old enough to operate, so my job was to just keep driving a tractor up and down on top of the forage to keep it well compressed and as air tight as possible. This was easy enough until the clamp was filled up higher than its surrounding walls and back. This was when things got a "bit iffy" near the edges so this was always left to one of the men to do. At least they'd have been insured if anything should go wrong and the tractor should tip or slide off the whole thing. When all the crop was in the clamp it was sealed on the top and front with plastic sheets and bales of straw or earth . . . "Job done".

Early spring was the time to harrow and roll both the grassland and any spring sown corn. This was a tractor driving job I was allowed to do on my own because it just involved dragging either a set of harrows or a ridged (Cambridge) roll over the ground to ensure a good solid bed for the crop. The only tricky bit was, when rolling in corn, to make sure you didn't go over the same bit of ground too often as this compacted the seed bed too much for it to thrive. This usually occurred on the "headlands. These were either end of the piece where all the turning round took place. I suppose I was about fourteen years old the first time I was trusted to perform this task with no "co-pilot" . . . Was I a proud boy or not??

When the corn harvest was all done and the combine came back into the yard for the winter it was brushed off, and greased up, and the straw walkers cleaned out. The straw walkers were situated at the back of the machine. They consisted of an elevator with what looked like steel sharks teeth on either side. This was the means by which the threshed straw was expelled from the harvester. The trouble was that over the season this elevator collected masses of "barley horns" – the spikey bits on ears of barley. These had to be removed and because of my small stature this was obviously a job that I was "volunteered" to do. Old, heavy duty, hessian socks were laid on top of these "shark's teeth" and I was threaded in to lie on my stomach and clean out all the horns, dust, and sundry bits of debris but I didn't mind. I loved every minute of it all. Of course, of these couple of years I got things wrong but I was never shouted at or scolded. Just shown again how to do what was needed. Luckily I was a quick learner.

The highlight of the spring/summer season came every year at sheep shearing time because once the Levi's ewes and tups had undergone their yearly coiffeur then Frank had his two weeks, yearly holiday, to go off to neighbouring farms to shear their sheep. I went with him to roll the shorn fleeces. This was done in a proper way, in those days, because during that time the fleeces were worth money to the processors who would send out huge hessian sacks. Into these, it seemed, you could have fitted a small car. To bundle the fleece it had to be laid out flat, wool side up. Any twigs or shit removed then the sides folded in towards the middles. They were then rolled up from the neck end to the tail end with enough of it left free to be pulled and twisted into a form of rope which could be wrapped around and tucked under itself . . . Presto!! One rolled fleece thank you very much. Frank always liked to get the sheep hot before shearing because this made the lanolin rise thus making it easier to get the clippers through. A cold sheep never sheared easily. By the end of the two weeks our trousers were that saturated with lanolin that when they got cold they could literally stand up on their own. Afterwards the trousers were never good enough for much else. The lanolin seemed to weaken the fabric. During this shearing holiday we ate well, really well, because the farmers supplied us with food and drink all day long. I'd never seen such posh food particularly when we got to a place owned by a Mr Jack Green. This gentleman had a son called David. It seemed to me the son was a bit up himself. He also had a daughter called Jenny, who was a pretty young thing, a bit older than me. We used to exchange glances across the meal table – daring young things!! Now, this table seemed to me to be like an old fashioned banqueting type. It obviously wasn't but I'd never seen such a big table and it seemed to overflow with all kinds of goodies - sandwiches, cakes, biscuits, pickles. Like a Queen's larder I used to think. Both Frank and I were always invited into the house to share this fare with the Green family. This, back then, was a rare thing for the workers to be invited into the boss mans's house. These two weeks were Frank's yearly "harvest". If I recall, correctly, I think he got paid 1/6d per sheep which meant he could, on a good couple of days, earn as much as he got in a full 48 hours - a week's wages.

Of course, all year round there were two constants. Looking after all the livestock and, in our off time, collecting up enough firewood to start the winter off. Apart from the problem of keeping body and soul together, as far as basic food was concerned, then the other constant thorn in our side was firewood, or the lack of it. As I said we always tried to get a decent stock in store by the time late autumn came around. I can never remember us ever having an inside fire during late spring and summer and no matter how much we'd collected together over the milder months it never turned out to be enough. Sometimes we'd be lucky and old Jack Levi would lend us a tractor trailer for the day and we'd scour the whole farm for anything burnable. These odd days were easy. We could get a trailer load in a day. Much easier than carrying individual boughs etc, on your shoulder sometimes for a couple of miles. It was especially difficult if we had to resort to leaving our farm and "poach" the timber from places we shouldn't have been. The winter of 1962/63 became a particular problem but more of that later. When timber was in real short supply we'd scour a local derelict railway line that, in the past, had been used to transport fuel to the Hams Hall Power Station. On a good day we might scrape together 50 or 60 lb of coal but it wasn't good quality stuff with not a lot of heat in it. Most winter nights would be spent cutting up wood with only axes. It was possible to do it during darkness because right outside the cottage, due to its situation, on a 90 bend, was an electric street light. This was bright enough to illuminate the area that we used to cut up the wood. Frank was "shit hot" with an axe and I was improving by now. Billy never did master it. We'd have competitions to see who could split the most matchsticks. Only one man every won – the old man's axe was as sharp as a razor and because it weighed 8 lbs it was a no contest but, it was fun and good practice to try and beat him. Frank loved his axe. It had been his Grandad's and he'd spend hours and hours sitting on his chair with one eye on the telly, sharpening this axe. Unfortunately his beloved axe head came to a sad end and it was my fault. A mis-judgment that caused it. One day we were splitting a full trunk using two axes and wooden wedges. Frank took the first swipe but the piece of timber in question was reluctant to yield itself easily. Consequently the first strike only rewarded us with a split of a few inches. "Son, put your axe in as close as you can to mine, but stay in the split" came my order of the hour. I struck as hard as I could but I wasn't totally on target. I didn't miss the split but I got too close and the tip of my weapon just caught the top of his axe head where the stale fits in. Because over the years it had been put into so many fires to burn out old broken handles it must have become brittle. I had found the weak spot! I wasn't told off in any nasty way but let's just say I wasn't "flavour of the month" for a few days. He managed "to come into the ownership" of a "new" axe but it was never the same as the old one. He never loved it as he had its predecessor but needs must . . . as they say!!

As I've already said if we were lucky the boss would let us use the tractor and trailer for a day to collect wood. This task and its rewards were shared with our next door neighbour, Jim Bryan, who was the other employee of the Levi farm. Jim was a Herefordshire man. A short, stoutish, little man with a cherry red face, piercing blue eyes with long lashes and a bald head. Whenever his head was liberated from beneath his greasy old flat cap it revealed itself to be as white as the driven snow. He looked a bit like a sherbet lollipop on such rare occasions. His wife, Mary, was I think, a travelling women. Not an ounce of fat on her, weathered leathery skin, hazel eyes, long black hair and a strength of any good man. She'd swing an axe all day long . . . Bless her. They had two children, a lad called Michael and a younger girl called Linda who had inherited her Dad's strikingly blue eyes. Jim's official title was "Stockman" as opposed to Frank's label of a "Tractorman". Jim wasn't the kind of man who would search out work. He only ever seemed to do as much as he needed to do and no more. I think his main love was the pigs. These he swore could see the wind. He honestly believed this and I can recall one day that one old sow had knocked a few bricks out of the wall of her pen. This would only have been enlarged by herself if Jim hadn't managed to secure an old enamel sign over the offending puncture in the brickwork "There you go" he said "She'll stop and read that now!!" On hard ground you could always hear Jim stomping about because he only ever wore hobnailed leather boots and leather gaiters fastened with buckles.

At the age I was now, just between fourteen and fifteen years old, my favourite time of year up at the farm was winter because all the work involved caring for the animals either in the sheds or outside. A lot of the growing cattle and all the sheep were wintered outside and only the beasts that were close to being ready to go were wintered inside. They were either tied up in the old milking sheds or in two decent sized yards and a couple of big pens. On a cold winter's morning or night it was a sight to behold to see the "steam" rising off the backs of these beasts especially the ones tied up in the old milking sheds. Every Sunday evening old Jack Levi would put his hand on every one of them that looked like it might be ready for the inevitable one way trip the following week. He would then mark up which ones, if any, were read to go. They'd be replaced, usually on the same day, by new faces and so it went on. It wasn't Mr Levi's policy to breed many cattle. It was very rare to see a cow and calf on the place but the old sows and boar always lived a full life on the place as long as they kept producing enough pigs to be worthwhile. The ewes were treated the same. Some would be there for years. A lot of sheep went through the farm and a lot were bought in from a farm in Wales that the family had. This place was used as a "staging post" for sheep that had been bought in Wales and waiting to come up to the Midlands to be bred from or fattened on the better grass keep that grew at home.

The farm in Wales was also used to fiddle the sheep subsidies paid by the Government. This was done by moving a certain amount of sheep from Wales to home and vice versa. The double payment could be achieved by taking the sheep either way and, although at home, the sheep had their ears punched to say that the subsidy had been paid on them when these same sheep were taken to Wales and released on the mountain then all the Ministry Official could do was to count them because he couldn't or wouldn't want to get close enough to them to check their ears. Of course this worked both ways. Clean eared sheep counted on the mountain and subsidy granted and then the same sheep transported home for a few days until the subsidy had been granted again and their ears punched . . . A loophole exploited!!

Autumn and winter times back then didn't really ease the workload because a lot of the cattle were inside. Every animal, inside and outside, of course had to be fed twice a day. One of the big jobs that needed to be done to achieve this was to cut and cart the kale. This kale grew to be anything between two and five feet tall with the big stuff managing to achieve a stalk diametre bigger than that of a good jam jar. All this was cut by hand. In our case using a slash hook with a wooden handle taken out. It was then loaded and distributed to the cattle using a hand fork. On wet, frosty or snowy days this was a wet and cold old job. I can't explain in any definitive form how much I enjoyed and soaked up all the time and experiences involved with my first few years spent with my "new family" and "new home" at The Cuttle. I wanted the day to come when I could leave school and put my old weird family life on a back burner. The day when and I could spend all my time feeling that I belonged somewhere. A place where I could grow, without fear, couldn't come quick enough for me now.

Over the few years that had passed since I first arrived on the scene, here, I had gradually befriended four brothers namely, Bob, Ron, Karl and Warren (Wagger) Daniel. They were two sets of twins. Bob and Ron were unidentical and a month younger than me. Karl and Wagger were 100% identical twins who were a year older. They were, I discovered, members of the second biggest family in Coleshill. A family of Mom, Dad and eleven children - nine boys and two girls. The Daniels family were colloquially known as "The Dannies". Old Man Daniel was a tall stringy man with blonde hair who worked at the Lime and Sandpit. He was Northern man who had migrated South in the 30's on The Jarrow Hunger March. Mrs Daniel (Mrs "D") was proper old fashioned well built, bordering on overweight, woman who ruled the roost with a rod of iron. If this strategy failed then the Old Man would be ordered to sort things out which he never failed to do. When he stood up out of his chair, with discipline on his mind, evacuation of the premises by the offending kids was the main aim of the day until he cooled down. The boys were the main culprits but they all knew that, in the end, there was only one boss and that man was the tall blonde headed Northerner!!

These lads helped an old farmer whose land lay across the river from the Levi farm. He was a bachelor man called Brendan Callaghan ... "Bren" to all who knew him. A reasonably tall gent with grey hair and a body that looked like it was made out of gristle and bone wrapped up in leather. He still farmed the old fashioned way with horses although he did own an old Fordson tractor. This was a very temperamental machine that needed at least two week's notice before it would even consider bursting into life. Hence it hardly ever saw the light of day but that was of no heed to the old boy. He knew his horses and they knew him and what and when they needed to do. They were two gelded gentlemen. A grey called Box and a bay called Fox. Box being the more headstrong of the two but Fox was older and wiser and he was bought into action for the more refined tasks.

Old Bren was a strange old boy, hardly ever smiled, a single man living on his own in one of a row of three cottages that he owned on the High Street in Coleshill. A man of sparse needs - no luxuries. His living room contained one old sofa, a wood back chair, a small table set under the window, and a cupboard in the corner. In this cupboard he kept his Fox's Glacier Fruit sweets that people would donate to him. He seemed to live entirely on boiled bacon, bread and butter, potatoes and digestive biscuits washed down with tea – no milk. He had a reputation for being "a tight old sod" which he probably was but who cared. Certainly not us lads. He allowed us to run free over his land in exchange for the Daniel twins giving him a hand when he needed it.

The access to his couple of farm buildings and sheds was through a private tennis club. This, at odd times, was awkward because a couple of the "members" were typical Hoorah Henrys and they seemed to have a problem with me being allowed to pass through their hallowed courts. They took exception to the fact that I was dark skinned and by the time I was fourteen years old my hair, which was coal jet black, had begun to grow into long ringlets. The abuse and snide remarks were a bit upsetting for me and the lads could see it was getting to me. So, unbeknown to me, they "visited" for want of a better word these stuck up idiots one evening . . . No more nasty jibes after that.

Being allowed the free range of Bren's land was handy because the lads had an air rifle and later a bigger gun. I don't know what kind. I never understood the things and still don't today. Anyway, the gun or guns were a useful tool for rabbiting, much easier and quicker than a spade and a pointed stick that I'd got used to. The trouble is, guns are noisy and, when you are rabbiting where you shouldn't be rabbiting, then the noise can end up getting you in trouble. This "trouble", a couple of years, later manifested itself by us five lads ending up in Court for poaching. Frank always said that that was the trouble with guns. I should've listened. It cost us all a fine of £6. each which was nearly three week's wages for a fifteen year old in those days.

As I said earlier Bren farmed in a fashion that was probably a good 30 or 40 years behind the times even compared to the Levi establishment. This fact yielded a yearly cash harvest for us lads, hoeing, and hoeing by hand. Bren always drilled his kale and root crops in rows with a drill that was pre-set to deliver a certain amount of seed at any one time. This resulted in the plants coming up too thick to thrive so they had to be "singled". A process of hoeing out the unneeded plants and just leaving one every few inches. For this we were paid 9d an hour – cash – but that was good money. On a good day a lad could earn almost 10 shillings, or £3. A week. I can remember that one occasion my wage came to a few pence under the £3. and it was only a couple of pence as well. Old Bren was tight old bugger and rather than just giving me the round £3 he hunted high and low for the right change . . . and you had to sign for it!! The "piece work rate" for this job was £8 an acre for singling and £6 an acre for side hoeing. Side hoeing was a simpler process but we didn't get much of that. Instead a middle aged travelling woman called Liz was drafted in and in a good week she could "single" an acre on her own and side hoe even more. With a hoe in her hand she was like "shit off a shovel". I can recall she used to light a fire every lunch-time and put the pan and kettle on, just for her, not for us. We made do with a sandwich or two and pop. These few quid I earned at this time came in handy at home. I'd just keep a couple of shillings for myself and give the rest to Frank and Mrs Woodcock to buy food. I could at last begin to stand on my own two feet properly. I was growing up.

1962 and time to leave school and my old life with my "blood" family completely. My first job was as an apprentice. In those days the word "apprentice" was a substitute for the phrase "child slave labour". Well it was on the farm I was sent to anyway. A farm run by The Hawker family, at Salford Priors, Near Evesham. They were an ignorant bunch who thought a worker's place was down as far as he could be legally pushed. Whilst working for this family I was billeted with a family in the village. A family whose matriarch was a Mrs Green. She ruled the roost, but in a kind way. I was fed well and slept on the sofa in the living room. Memories of this time would rise to the surface years later in my life. Anyway to cut a long, and uninteresting, story short after a couple of months I got fed up with the situation on the farm so I got on my bike and cycled back to The Cuttle. Back to my "new home" "new family" and my dog.

It was now the Autumn of 1962 and I had got myself a job on a smallholding in Shustoke, a village about five or six miles away. A job that was a 5 ½ day week and the wage was £2. Most of this, once again was given to Mrs Woodcock and Frank for my keep. I think I probably kept 10 shillings of it which was enough. I hadn't started smoking then and I hadn't got a girlfriend yet.

This small holding was a family affair supporting the boss Mr Walters, his wife Evelyn, his two sisters Margaret and Gladys and his brother Ivan. Although I'm pretty sure Ivan had a separate means of income because he was rarely seen as he lived in a house a couple of miles away. Anyway, when he did appear the two brothers were always bickering but, Ivan had a van and he could drive – after a fashion. So far the sake of family fortunes a complete fall out was never allowed to occur.

Mr Walters (Norman) the boss was a kind old man with a very bad limp. He had a wonderful singing voice and the ability to breed canaries like no one I've ever seen since. I swear, if he was to have put a pair of canaries in a tin and thrown them up in the air they'd have come down with six or seven chicks. He, and his wife and daughter Yvonne, lived in a cottage down the lane so the only actual "residents" at the holding were the sisters Margaret and Gladys. Margaret worked full time outside with Mr Walters and myself. Gladys spent her time looking after the house. As mentioned earlier Mr Walters had a very bad limp so he couldn't move too fast or with much agility. He therefore got the nickname "Sweater

Walters" in the area but, he said something to me when I started there that I've never ever forgotten and that was "Lad, I'll never ask you to do anything I wouldn't or couldn't do before I got lame". That's stuck with me.

The smallholding consisted of about 50 acres or so in different pieces scattered here there and everywhere. On it were a few cattle, a couple of sows, a house cow, a couple of ponies and a fair few chicken. These were battery hens and cockerels that would be caponised when at the right age and also 50 or 60 turkeys for the Christmas trade. They were the old fashioned Broad Breasted Bronze Turkeys. The white variety were very scarce in those days. Fractious birds, turkeys. Mr Walters always used to tell me that the best way to kill a pen of turkeys was to wait until it got dark and the stand outside the pen and shout. "The silly sods would all die of fright" he used to say. The laying hens production was recorded by marking their individual feed hoppers every time they laid an egg. These were scrutinised every week by either Mr Walters or Margaret and any hens found not to be laying enough were removed. They were killed, plucked and dressed for sale. In the old dairy building, next to the cowshed that had been altered to accommodate the chicken cages, was a mechanical plucking machine. A wonderful piece of kit that was only ever used by the boss himself. The removal of any pin feathers and stubs, using a penknife was one of my tasks. Chicken battery cages in those days weren't cleaned out automatically. It all had to be done by hand. The fowl's droppings were collected on metal trays, one for each cage. These cages housed, usually, only one decent sized bird or two smaller birds. Cleaning the trays just involved sliding them out, scraping them clean into a wheelbarrow with an old wallpaper scraper, and then sprinkling the tray with fresh sawdust. This was at least a weekly job. This I carried on doing for this family every week even after I'd moved on to my next farm up the ladder.

The last of the summer came and went and November was upon us. Mr Walters came out of the house one dreary old morning and presented me with a "grassing hook" and a crook made out of a holly stick. "Come with me lad, I've got a little job for you". Off we went up the lane to a 3 acre field behind his house that had been laid down fallow that year. However it had managed to produce a good crop of muck-weed, probably derived from the chicken muck that had been spread on there. When these weeds die they leave decent sized dead brown stalks that stand aloof above all below them. "You can cut all this lot, then we'll burn it" was the instruction. Imagine asking a young teenager to do such a thing these days!! However, I wasn't bothered, and even if I had been, a boy of my age wasn't allowed to "be bothered". You were just expected to do as you were asked or told to do . . . no problem!!

Christmas and New Year of 1962 saw the arrival of the worst winter in history. Snow, feet deep, and a really bad frost that lasted until the March. At the beginning of this winter getting to work, five miles away, on a pushbike wasn't the easiest thing in the world but after a few days the roads became a lot more navigable to a cyclist due to motors making cleaver pathways. Of course, everything froze solid in the outbuildings especially the water in the chicken pens. That only ran in shallow little troughs in front of the cages. These were basically constantly frozen. Now Margaret took on the mantle of keeping her beloved hens supplied with ample water. This she did by boiling water in the house and distributing it to the hens via a watering can. The image of her doing this has never left me to this day. She was a woman who seemed to be about 70 years old. Not very tall but, very hard working and kind. She seemed to be constantly cocooned in a massive overcoat that almost reached her ankles thus hiding her wellies. She wore a woollen hat pulled right down over her head until it reached the scarf that was wrapped several times around her neck. Her hands protected by at least one pair of gloves. All day long she literally shuffled between the house and the chicken pens whistling gently to herself a never ending , unrecognisable, medley of tunes. Of course, because of the severity of the frost that was busy trying to paralyse all it came across, or so it seemed, by the time dear old Margaret had watered all her hens which were housed in two or three smaller outhouses (apart from the old cow shed) the ones where she'd started her round were once again pecking vainly at ice in their troughs. It just became a never ending job for her. Akin to painting the Forth Bridge I suppose but she just carried on regardless with no thought or sign of anything other than contentment. She loved her hens . . . Bless her!!

The job for every Saturday morning during the winter months was to put enough swedes through the root chopper, again only powered by hand. We would then mix them up with barley meal, bag them up, and put them in the dry so that the beasts had enough food prepared to last until at least Monday morning. Ivan used to come and feed the cattle over this day and a half because Mr Walters was handicapped by his gammy leg. He had enough trouble walking about on good ground never mind on a frozen snow-rutted ice rink as the yard had now become. The best job of the week this winter turned out to be boiling up the pig swill in an old copper wood fired boiler in the yard. A welcoming warm job for an hour or two and much appreciated it was indeed.

I suppose sometime during these bleak months I must have mentioned to Mr Walters that we were struggling to find enough firewood at home due to the depth of snow that was, in most places, a couple or three feet deep all over. He said I could take home any wood I could find on his land. I didn't need telling twice. I got a decent piece of rope that I could attach around any decent length pieces of timber and tie to the saddle stem of my bike. I would tow these home via the lanes. This was a bit further than going via the big road but it was safer I suppose. Mr Walters also donated a dozen eggs every Saturday lunch-time along with my wage. A loving and caring family The Walters, really were, and I visited them regularly ever after with my wife and kids until they all passed away. Every Christmas I gave them a present of a poinsettia plant which, each time, was placed on the kitchen table directly opposite, and usually constantly, open door. Each year the plants thrived for months and months.

The winter and all its strife passed and late spring and summer were knocking on the door. One day Mr Walters came to me and said words to the effect that he could see that I was a keen and willing boy and that I deserved to be given a better chance than he could offer. "I've got you a job on a farm up the road" he said. I was about to get on the second or third rung of the ladder thanks to this dear family who I continued to help for free as long as I was available.

The back end of the year seemed colder than normal and the old weathered plank door that opened straight into the living room at The Cuttle was letting through far more cold draughts than normal. A big heavy old curtain was hung over it but this never seemed to be enough to keep the outside . . . outside. Frank came up with a solution. A distance along the lane the old railway line to Hams Hall crossed the road and on this crossing was the old derelict crossing station. A small brick building that, as I recall, was a two up two down. It must have been used as a residence originally. We had visited these premises in the past for the sole purpose of relieving the property of all its detachable lead that we sold for a few shillings at the time. Inside was an old black upright piano on metal castors. Frank though this would fit nicely and block off the offending draught in our living room so it needed to be liberated and re-sited. This was a task that needed three of us, me, Frank, and Mrs Woodcock. The noise as we trundled this obsolete musical instrument down the lane was horrendous but luckily we had no other properties to pass by and within an hour or two it was installed in its new home It performed its task admirably.

"Things" always had been "tight" but it seemed at this time things got more strained. All us kids were getting bigger and eating more I suppose and although I had just started work and was contributing 30 shillings a week to the family coffers it was still difficult to keep the wolf from the door as they say. One day things took a turn for the worst temporarily, very temporarily. Mrs Woodcock had just enough money left for a jar of jam on a Thursday. This was one day before pay day. She sent Bill on an errand to the shop at the top of the hill to fetch the jam for tea and maybe a bit for the girls' next morning. Off he went and he returned but he returned without jam or money. It seemed he'd seen a pheasant next to the lane and decided to throw the freshly purchased jar of preserve at the said pheasant. Trouble was he missed resulting in no jam, no pheasant either . . . OOPS!!

The Levi farm suffered badly during all this frost, mainly water availability for the stock. The eventual resolution to this was to cut holes in the ice on the river. This was now thick enough to bear the weight of a tractor and trailer loaded with old oil drums. The men filled the drums with buckets of water from the river. They were emptied in the same way. Luckily the pipes to the water troughs in the cattle yards didn't freeze badly due to the heat generated by the stock and the muck housed within but all the cattle that were tied up in sheds and all the pigs had to be hand watered. This chore had to be kept up until a reasonable insulated supply of water could be rigged up to a tap in a warmer corner of one of the cowsheds so that at least eased the burden as long as it worked. At odd times, after a really cold night, then Jack Frost would put things back to square one for a day.

I was lucky in my new job, as I explained earlier, it was only a smallholding and everything could be overcome with relative ease.

Poor old Frank and Jim were still having to cut kale by hand. The severe weather had basically turned the kale into a state resembling not much more than wet rope but it had to be got in. A really cold wet job. So much so that one evening Frank went up to the girls' room, took the orange rubber sheets off their beds, and sat and sewed them together making a rubber waistcoat for himself. This was a step up from tying empty plastic fertilizer bags around himself.

Old Bren carried on regardless all winter, on his own now, because us lads were all at work now. His cattle spent all their lives outside and this winter their coats really grew, especially the calves whose coats must have been a foot long. When they ran their coats looked wonderful wafting about. I say Bren was on his own.... well he was in reality but there used to be an old tramp type man about at the time. This tramp wrapped his head up in bandages and wore a motorcycle crash helmet over this. Bren used to tell us that some mornings he'd see this old boy coming out of the kale, white over with frost. He was sleeping in there. Nobody ever heard this fellow speak, as I knew of, or how he fed himself but he was around for a fair old time. Before, during, and after this really cold weather, roosting in the kale . . . he must have been a hard fellow.

When Frank and I were out on the land of a late afternoon in autumn and winter we'd watch the pheasants going to roost in the trees and where they were. We could then go, after dark, with catapults and hopefully consign a few to "the pot". On a good week we'd manage to claim two or three. One particular incident relating to this subject springs to mind. In fact I've never forgotten it. Neither has Mrs Woodcock to this day. We'd seen this bird come in to roost in a big old Alder tree on the bank of the river a few yards away from the lane. "We'll have him tonight son" the old man said. When darkness came, catapults and good round stones (the river produced a lot of good round stones ideal for the catapults as they tended to fly straighter) loaded into our pockets and off we went. Sure enough, there he was, the future accompaniment to a few potatoes and a drop of gravy. Unfortunately, and unusually, he had perched in an awkward way and in an awkward place. Now, Frank was "shit hot" with a "Cattie" and me, as yet, not as much so. I left it to the Master to fell this avian object of our desires but, as good a shot as he was, the only way he would manage to, at least, bother this bird was to ruffle a few of its wing feathers. Then, horror of horrors, his elastic broke. "Give me your cattie quick" came the order. Just as I passed it to him the aforementioned bird stuck its head out into clear view . . . "Smack!!" A direct hit and down it fell. As dead as a nit into the river. We managed to retrieve it from its watery grave before the current washed it out of reach. Great stuff, pheasant for tea tomorrow. We started to stroll home along the lane when a car's headlights could be seen heading our way. Now, in those days, cars in our lane, in the back end of the year and at night was not a usual sight. "Come here quick son" was a bit of a panicked utterance. Next thing I knew the old man had opened my coat and stuffed this, ice cold, wet, dead and bleeding bird down my shirt. "Just keep walking lad" was the order of the moment. The vehicle came and went. We got home "Get in quick" he said so in I go and just stood in front of Mrs Woodcock and Billy with a dead pheasant stuffed down my shirt and dripping in blood stained river water. That situation is still laughed about to this day.

Before I delve into my new experiences I'd like to convey a classic quote that fell upon my ears one evening in winter of 1962. A lot of evenings Bobby, Dan and I used to go up to old Bren's Cottage and light his fire for him so that he had a warm place to come home to. This was generally around 7 p.m. Anyway, on one such evening one of Bren's tenants, an old man called Mr Johnson, who had spent his whole life on the land, but was now retired, came in just to be nosy. Me and Bobby started going on about how cold it was. To this Mr Johnson pricked up his ears and gave us a look of utter disgust and uttered the immortal phrase . . . "COLD! COLD! You kids don't know what cold is. In 1947 it was so cold the horses were tripping up over the cabbages" . . . a classic, wonderful!!

Time to start my new job. It was on a farm a couple of miles further up the road from the Walters' smallholding. It was called Holliers Farm, run by a certain Mr Ken Alcock. I'd never seen the place or anyone connected with it until I turned up the first morning for work. I was met by Ken. We never called him "Mr Alcock". It turned out in the end that he didn't deserve that kind of respect anyway. I was told that I should be at work every morning by six at the latest. I would work a 48 hour week and get paid £6 a week for doing so. £6. A week!! That was a bloody fortune because I still wasn't 16 years of age. Frank only earned £10. 6 shillings a week and he was a man with a family. Ken was a slightly built bloke. He always wore a collar and tie and a trilby hat that he wore tipped at a jaunty angle and was constantly in wellingtons, no matter what the weather. The thinking behind his addiction to this particular type of footwear would become apparent during the times to come. His wife was an upmarket lady with the name of Alwyn. She had previously married and was the daughter of a hat manufacturing family in Atherstone. She had a son called Christoper who was older then me. The other member of the family was a little girl called Nicola who was the progeny of Ken and Alwyn. A right little bundle of fun and mischief she was too.

It emerged that not long before I started work at Holliers Farm Ken's Dad, John, had "died" in a shooting accident but locally the general consensus of opinion was that he'd actually committed suicide. The Dad, John, had been an extremely proud man, proud of his farm which regularly was awarded the prize for the best farm in Warwickshire but, sadly, his son Ken was cut from a different cloth. A lazy little shit whose main interest in life was a fast car and good looking women. Hence the farm had deteriorated to such an extent, under his management, that the old man had become ashamed of it and his connection with it. A sad story, but apparently true.

This place was a complete eye opener to me. I'd never seen such a big cowshed. A single building that stood twenty four cows each side with a drive through the middle big enough to take a tractor and trailer. This fact alone saved walking many a mile pushing a wheelbarrow. The herd split consisted of twenty four pedigree Ayrshires. These had always been Ken's Dad's pride and joy apparent. It was originally a full herd of forty eight milking Ayrshires but had been diluted by 50% to accommodate Alwyns new toys. These were Jersey cattle, spiteful little sods they could be as well if the fancy took them. An Ayrshire bull lived in a purpose built bull pen at the end of the yard and the Jersey Bull was kept tied up at the far end of the main milking shed. In the early 60's hand milking was basically a thing of the past and had been replaced by machined powered bucket milking. The milk being cooled in different ways using cold water and stored and transported in either 10 or 12 gallon churns. These were collected daily by Midland Counties Dairy lorries. Everything, of course, being "man handled" at this time. The whole dairy cattle operation was overseen by Michael, an ex-German P.O.W who was a man of few words and a fiery temperament. He and Ken hardly ever even acknowledged each others presence unless absolutely unavoidable. It turned out that Michael and Ken's Dad had entered into some form of Government supervised contract that allowed P.O.W'S to stay on after the war if they were employed in agriculture in a full time way but they had to stay on the same farm for a certain amount of years otherwise they would be deported. This arrangement was the driving force behind the situation between Ken and Michael. They just didn't like each other simple as that. Michael left on the day the "contract" came to an end. This explained why I had been given the job here in the beginning. I was drafted in to be Michael's pupil and general "dogs body", as they say, to learn as much as I could so that at least I could manage to achieve the basics by the time for his departure arrived. That turned out to be a significant time in my young life and it laid down the grounding for my future career as a Dairy herdsman. Michael could be a proper hard faced slave driver when the fancy took him but it's the best way to learn. It was then, and it is now, as far as I'm concerned. I'm forever grateful to him. Even today, if I was presented with cows to milk I'd still do it in the same way he ingrained into me getting on for 60 years ago . . . Thank you Michael.

My mentor at the time spoke with a broken German accent and he wasn't the most placid or "laid back" fellow in the history of the world. He seemed strangely addicted, or similar, to cleanliness. He had the most amazing ritual that I'd never seen the like of either before or since. Every time he left or came back on the farm he would strip off to the waist and scrub himself with a hard bristled dairy brush from the waist up. This would happen on average six times a day!! I never asked him why (indeed I don't think anyone ever asked him why) it was just accepted that this is what he did. This pre-occupation carried on into the cowshed. My job for months was to wash the bags (udders) of all those cows that were "in milk". Each beast would be inspected closely by Michael to check for any trace of dirt before he put the machine on to milk them. If any of the cows were found to still bear even the slightest sign of not being as near "lily White" as humanly possible then I was made to wash every one of them again and, this was even if he'd already milked them. Gradually I was allowed to change the top of the milking buckets from a full one and to empty one and carry the full buckets containing 4 gallons to the cooler and bring the empty ones back again. When all was done my job was to wash all the units in troughs of cold and hot water using a variety of hand held brushes and place them all into the steriliser. This was a large steel chest with a screw shut door into which steam was allowed to circulate for about ½ an hour. The door then opened and its contents left to cool until needed again. By the time I'd got used to the idea of earning this £6 a week I realised I'd got enough money left in my pocket, after paying my keep and helping with the family's needs at home, to start smoking and to go to the pictures with my best mate Bobby Dan every so often. As far as Ken was concerned smoking was not banned at work but it was frowned upon by him. Somehow I had come into the possession of a few Players Capstan Full Strength cigarettes which mysteriously vanished at one point but then re-appeared a couple of days later. Overjoyed at my re-acquaintance with my lost "cancer sticks" as Ken used to call them I immediately liberated one. I placed it in my mouth, lit it and took a massive draw on it. Bloody Hell!! It nearly blew my head off. It was like trying to smoke old rancid rope!! Ken was curious to find out if I'd found the fags and if I'd decided to stop partaking in this frowned upon habit . . . turned out that in an attempt to make me stop smoking he'd put the packet of cigarettes in the steam chest so that they got 100% damp without showing any signs of being so. He had then taken them down to his house and dried them out in the stove before putting them back into a place where he knew I'd find them. Needless to say his little prank had no effect other than the original shock of the first inhalation.

Jim Powell was a Welshman in his mid 30's. He was the only other full time worker at Holliers Farm. His main jobs were shepherd and number one tractor driver. His most fascinating skill, it seemed to me back then, was to be able to "brush" a hedge. This meant he could trim natural hedges with a slash-hook to such a precise degree that they wouldn't have looked out of place in the topiary garden of a stately home. At this time all agricultural hedges were trimmed by hand in this way. It was an acquired and hard earned skill to master and one I never really mastered. Indeed when I was made to do it myself I was always told off by the boss for leaving "bird perches". These were small sticks that had been left protruding and looked unsightly. This was usually caused by your hook not being sharp enough. I later found out hedges were always brushed uphill the same way as the growth. This avoided any parts of it being broken off as opposed to being sliced off. I used to watch Jim sharpening his hook. This he did at regular intervals throughout the day and he had to be sure that it was sharp enough to shave hair off his arms. This capability he tested from time to time until he could tell, just by touch, that it was in a good enough and efficient enough state so as to enable him to achieve such a perfect finish to just an ordinary agricultural hedge . . . a job that he took such pride in.

Jim used to check the sheep every morning before he came to the yard but on one occasion he didn't arrive until mid-morning. He'd lost the sheep and couldn't find them anywhere. This was even after spending a couple of hours looking for them, high and low. It turned out that the neighbour Ken had bought them off had been in the night and fetched them back because Ken had failed to pay for them. This habit of the boss being a bad manager of his finances would crop up at regular intervals. An example of this being that whenever he was short of cash he'd get in his car and drive off somewhere on a Saturday morning in the hope that we'd get fed up waiting for him to return to pay us our wages and go home. On odd occasions it would be 3 or 4 p.m. before he returned. He even chased me out of the yard with a riding crop one particular day shouting "Don't come here for money" so that week it was Sunday before I got paid. This ability of his to seem to be permanently in debt made Jim joke that every time a strange car came into the yard and the occupant went into the house then Ken would be hiding under the kitchen table telling Alwyn not to answer the door.

Alongside the dairy herd and the sheep the ducks were the other animal enterprise at the Hollies Farm. Hundreds and hundreds of ducks. All reared outside from about three weeks old. Before that time they were housed in a large shed with access to heaters. It was while Jim and I were working with these youngsters in the shed that, one day, it was revealed why Ken always wore Wellington. All of a sudden he just "appeared" behind us as if from nowhere. We were shocked. Ken just smiled and said "Now you two know why I always wear wellies. It is because they don't make any noise so I can creep up on you and see what you're doing without you knowing I'm on my way" . . . there was method behind his madness!!!

The field where the ducks were kept looked, from a distance, as if it was covered in snow. Just white over with the birds. The birds were slaughtered, plucked and processed on site by a gang of Italian women who, in Ken's eyes, could do no wrong especially a lady called Theresa who he seemed particularly "close to" (for want of a better phrase) but, who knew? According to Ken the only one day in a duck's life that it was totally free of any "pin feathers" was at 8 weeks and 3 days. This was the day they had to be killed, no matter what. Indeed we'd go out and catch and crate the ducks, bring them back into the yard on this specific (as we thought) day. There they would be inspected by the man himself and sometimes he decreed that we'd caught them a day too early and that they couldn't be killed for at least another 24 hours. I think he was usually right – he knew his ducks. The birds were plucked by machines. The first removed all the main feathers and the second one removed all the down. This was achieved by dipping the rough plucked carcasses in hot wax. When this cooled the birds were put through another machine that removed all the waxed down and left them looking as if they'd been polished. Perfectly smooth and clean. They then went on to be dressed and bagged. This duck processing was the most mechanised operation on the whole place, even more so than the cows, because everything else was as it had always been. In my experience everything done by hand, all the muck carting and spreading, all the hoeing, root cutting, hedge brushing, ditch cleaning, thistle cutting dock digging, nettle cutting . . . just everything really. The hay making and corn harvesting was, as ever, all done by manpower apart from the baling and combining. Now Ken's combine harvester had, let us say, "Seen better days". If it went a whole day without a breakdown then that was considered to be a "gift from the Gods". Perseverance was the name of the game back then but most things got done in the end. As explained before, the corn from the combine was put in hessian sacks and carted into the dry this way. Now, a popular cattle feed, back then, and probably even now, was dried sugar beet pulp. This was a by product of the sugar refining industry and in itself was very light in weight. It was shipped in very large sacks so as to enable each parcel to weigh one hundred weight, about 52 kilos in today's money. In those days no bag of anything ever weighed less than 84 lbs – about 40 kilos. Anyway, to get back to these aforementioned sugar beet sacks it was always agreed that they should never be filled more than half full. This was especially so with wheat which weighs very heavy. More than this would be too heavy for any one man to handle. One day, Jim and I thought we'd give it ago and fill one completely full. Bloody hell!! It was heavy. Anyway we managed to get this monster on the trailer along with its more normal sized mates and back to the yard and to the bottom of the granary steps, All the bagged corn was carried up the steps by Jim on his back. Of course, I wasn't big enough or strong enough to achieve this so I just got the bags to the edge of the trailer and on to Jim's back. Nothing unusual about that until it came to the "Goliath" sack. We were standing there looking at this monster and contemplating what to do with it when, Ken, in his usual wellie wearing manner ghosted on to the scene. He snorted an utterance of disgust when we suggested that this beast of a bag of wheat was too heavy to carry up the steps into the granary. Now, these steps consisted of a narrow tread and a high rise at an angle of something

47

around one in two or three with no hand rail to aid any ascent. "Get out of the way you pair just get it on my back and I'll show you how it's done" the boss man snorted. Now this sack of corn, if it weighed an ounce, it weighed 3 cwt – about 150 – 170 kilos – and he did it - he carried this load up this flight of sandstone steps. He did this purely by using the power of his legs because, as I've said, there was no handrail!! Once he'd deposited his load he stood in the granary doorway and crowed "That's how to do it men" before ghosting off in the same manner he'd arrived. We didn't see him at all for the next 2 or 3 days!!

I was old enough now to be allowed to drive a tractor on the road. This, at odd days in the winter came in useful because the farm had land 6 or 7 miles away and the silage for some of the cows winter feed was kept there. A load had to be taken from there to the home farm every two days and sometimes it worked out that I was allowed to drive the tractor there and load the trailer up. Then drive the tractor and trailer home and take it into work next morning. That saved a bit of cycling, at least once a week for a while. It also allowed me to show off and wave to my girlfriend who worked at the kennels en-route. This young lady will come to the fore in my story before too long. Michael, the German cowman, vacated the employ of Ken Alcock. As I said earlier, I was used as a "stop gap" until a new head cowman could be employed and installed in his tied cottage. It turned out this chap was a man called Barry who came from the Isle of Jersey. I can't recall a lot about this fellow except that he was small, a bit like the Jersey cows he'd come to look after and husband. The one thing I do remember was rescuing him from under a hedge where we found him seeking refuge after going missing for a while. He'd gone to check on the heifers that were running with a young Jersey bull. This bull, who like most adolescent post pubescent males, thought he was God's gift to the world and liked to show off in front of his girls. At times he had been known to "push things to the limit" shall we say. We warned Barry about the fact that the young bovine Romeo might well have a poke at him and his response to this well intentioned warning was "You can't tell me anything about Jerseys. I was born and bred there". Off he went and didn't return for a longer than normal time so Jim and I went to look for him. We found him, as I said earlier, taking refuge in the hedge bottom with the bull making sure he stayed there. It was easy enough to get him out. The beast realised he was outflanked and backed off. Luckily Barry wasn't seriously injured but he was well shaken up and a bit scratched and bruised. He had learned that our warning should have been needed. It was revealed at this time that there had been at least two similar episodes with bulls in the preceding years with this herd, the results of which were shown to me. Maybe as a warning because I was beginning to get a bit "headstrong" by now. The first instance was that of a man really badly disfigured who lived on his own in a tiny little cottage that had no windows that could be seen from the road. It turned out that this sad gentleman had, at one time, worked for Ken's dad and had been badly mauled by an Ayrshire bull. To keep him placated Ken's father had supplied him with this dwelling free of charge for the rest of his life as long as he stayed in the shadows and kept his mouth shut. One day, as I was talking to Ken about the danger of taking too many risks with these beasts when he showed me the scars on the two main fingers of his right hand. He then loosened his ever present neck tie and opened his shirt to reveal a single straight scar that went from just below his navel to his breastbone. It turned out that he'd been leading a bull using just these two fingers through the beasts nose ring. Apparently the bull stopped to sniff the air as he was being led across the road. Ken just tweaked his nose and said "Come on lad" and that was the last thing he remembered. It turned out that the bull had pulled free by ripping his ring through Ken's fingers and giving him one good head butt to the torso. It seemed that he had caught the scent of a cow in season down the road and that's where he was going . . . like it or not. In all the time I've spent with cattle I've never really had any really serious incidents with a bull, just the odd face off from time to time. It was really the cows that could do you the damage. The law of averages contributes to the fact. More time is spent in close contact with the girls than was ever spent with a bull. In those days if a cow milked well then she had to be suffered no matter how much she kicked. Probably at least 10% of them were kickers. This habit could be alleviated in various ways but if you'd got a "dyed in the wool" kicker then it was only a matter of time before you felt and saw the results of her spite. Basically a bad kicker was just a spiteful lady. In the years to come it became illegal to sell a cow if you knew she was a bad kicker. I don't think these days health and safety would allow any herdsman to be expected to attend to such an animal.

Times were beginning to change in the dairy cattle industry by the early-mid sixties. Milking parlours and loose yards were beginning to replace the original cow sheds. The main problem with this was the fact that most dairy cows, at this time, still kept their horns. They were no problem, only to the herdsman, who quite often got an unwanted poke in unwelcome places. In fact I can recall Frank telling me one day that when he was a younger man a beast got loose in the shed one day. She got her horn caught under his belt, lifted him off the ground and went on a tour of the building with him still attached to her cranial adornments. He eventually managed to free himself but not until he was a little battered and bruised.

The cattle were tied up all winter and couldn't really do each other any damage but when they started to be wintered in loose yards then injuries to each other did occur . . . either intentional or accidental. The general practice was to remove the horns from all the cattle. Easy enough with the calves as we just burnt the horn buds with a specially adapted, and designed, hot iron but the mature beasts weren't so easy or straightforward. The accepted practice, performed by a vet, ideally, was to inject a local anaesthetic deep into the base of the horn and then baler twine was tied as tight as was humanly possible and as lowdown on the horn as could be achieved. Then once the anaesthetic had taken effect, just cut the horns off with a hacksaw and coat the stub with a good dose of Stockholm Tar. This acted as an antiseptic and fly repellent. This adult de-horning could create a fair bit of blood at times but nothing that couldn't be overcome. Dehorning adult cattle was usually done in the back end of the year when the cattle were already inside and there were fewer, if any, flies about. On the odd occasion a horn would start to re-grow but very rarely. This would result in a very hard and knobbly like protrusion. "A crumpled horn". Usually this wasn't a problem but with the odd cow would realise that this horn could be used like a sledge hammer. She would do just that. A good hit from a crumpled horn generally didn't break the skin but it produced a good bruise and a lot of pain.

Back home things had taken a turn for the worst. Frank had suffered a perforated stomach ulcer and had been rushed into hospital. That meant that he was bringing in no wages for a few weeks. This meant we lived entirely off my wage which meant we were six or seven pounds down each week. To make things worse, one Saturday, on my way home from work I lost my wages somehow. I managed to borrow the £6 off Ronnie Daniel – he was earning more money than me or his twin Bobby, at the time, because he had gone into butchery. That paid better than farm work. Fate was about to smile on the situation at home because the Sunday morning following my tragic loss of wages I was cycling to work early, in the dark, when I felt my bike run over something in the road. It was a wallet!! A wallet with a map of The Isle of Man on the front but better still it contained £10. I really felt that I should immediately return the £6 to Ronnie but I explained the situation to him and he said to pay him back when things had got better. What a gentleman!! That £10 really eased the financial situation we'd found ourselves in.

My journey to and from work took me past a couple of cottages that were right on the side of the road. These cottages had chickens which, from time to time, managed to liberate themselves from their confines and would wander around on the road and peck about under the hedge opposite. Very nice!! One evening I noticed that one of these hens had decided to bed down for the night in this hedge rather than go back home to roost. That was the last time she went to bed anywhere. I waited around for a while until it got a bit darker and she was settled in for the night before I "liberated" her. I Stuffed her up my coat and took her home to meet her end. Chicken for tea everybody . . . nice!!

Whenever Bob and I had a Saturday afternoon off together we'd get on the bus and go into Birmingham. On the way back home we'd sometimes stop off and visit Fat Nan and Grand-dad for an hour. By now Frank was back at work so I had a bit of disposable income and I liked a cake or two. More than the cakes I liked the girl that worked in the Bakers Shop. I'd never bought so many cakes. It was just a chance to ogle at this vision of loveliness but that's as far as it ever got. Soon things were about to change in the girlfriend department. One Saturday Bob and I boarded the bus back from Birmingham, as usual, and as we got on there she was sitting on the seat facing the platform The most beautiful girl I'd ever seen. Long mousy hair and wonderful blue eyes. I was instantly smitten. Love at first sight. Who was this creature, sent from heaven, sitting on my bus and going my way?? Jenny Smith had just entered my life and we would soon become boyfriend and girlfriend.

As I mentioned earlier although I'd left the employ of the Walters family I always tried to give them a hand whenever I could. I used to go one evening a week straight from work, at Ken's place. and clean their chicken cages out for them before I went home. It only took an hour or two and I used to do it as a favour. It came to the time of year when the Walter's cattle had to be Tuberculine tested. This for them was a problem because the cattle had to be manhandled in order for the testing to take place. Obviously they were all too old and weak to be able to do this. Mr Walters said that he had arranged for the Vet to go and do the test at a time that coincided with my dinner break and would I go down and handle the beasts for him. No problem at all. There were only a few of them but the test took a little longer than was anticipated which meant I was late getting back to work. This didn't go down too well with Ken because he and I were steerage hoeing the kale. A steerage hoe was an implement that fitted on to the back of the tractor and did the work of half a dozen people doing the job by hand. This operation needed two people, one to drive the tractor and the other to steer the hoe behind and to keep it in between the rows. My job was to drive the tractor whilst Ken did the hoe steering. Because he was behind and close to the ground he was able to pick up stones and throw them at me without me knowing he'd launched one. Every time he hit me he'd shout. "You won't be fuckin' late again boy!" That's just how it was in those days I suppose.

Jenny and I were now "an item" and I thought she was the only girl in the world. I idolised the ground she walked on. As I sit here writing this at the age of 73 I haven't seen her since my 21st birthday. On this day our paths crossed in the Bull Ring, Birmingham, but I've never forgotten her. What do they say? "First cut is the deepest". She worked as a kennel maid for a man called Reg Wright who owned one, of only two, full working packs of Bloodhounds in England at the time. They were all kept in the working dog way. He had a huge copper boiler in the kennel yard. In this anything and everything was cooked up. Luckily his full time job was as a cattle grader at the markets and slaughterhouses so he had constant access to meat of some sort or another. Because of the exclusiveness of his pack he was invited to appear on the T.V. programme Midlands Today, with a couple of canine companions. I remember watching this and the interviewer posed the question "Tell me Mr Wright is it true that bloodhounds work better in humid conditions because the scent stays closer to the ground?" To which Reg retorted "No!! That's a load of rubbish. Its just that some folks stink more than others!!" Never one to mince his words was Reg. I was at his kennels one Sunday with Jenny and he'd got all the hounds out loose - 12 or 13 couple of them (24 or 26). Now like most working scent hounds they're not the most obedient creatures on earth. They did take a bit of controlling but Reg and his whip and sometimes a horse managed to keep a reasonably acceptable amount of control. At odd times they'd get one over on him and decided to go "on tour" across the fields but he usually got them back without any harm being done. I once asked him what he did if they didn't respond to his commands and his reply was "I shoot the one in front, nobody wants two dozen Bloodhounds rampaging through their garden on a Sunday morning do they?" Apart from his dogs Reg also kept a small flock of sheep and a few cattle. When it came time for the sheep to be sheared he asked Frank if he'd go and do the job for him. Of course I went as well and by now my hair hung in ringlets down to my shoulders. I noticed that during the day Frank and Reg had been giving me strange sideways looks and muttering to each other. I could see what they were planning. They were going to grab me and shear me. We got down to the last couple of ewes left to shear and these two gentlemen, with ill intent on their minds, got too close for comfort so I took off and ran, ran bloody fast, like shit off a shovel . . . Sod you and your sheep Mr Wright!!

Reg was a man a bit stuck in his ways. He didn't have a proper barn on his place to keep his hay so he just built a rick outside. Now he wasn't as good at stacking bales as he was at grading cattle or handling Bloodhounds. The rick would invariably start to slip and lean but his solution to this perennial problem was to place numerous containers of water on the opposite side to the lean - which by now was being supported by an array of timber props. "It'll draw itself back to the water" he always used to say and I don't think he ever had a collapse. Not as I can remember anyway.

Jenny lived with her brother John, her sister Janet, her Mom (her Dad had died) and her Grandfather (Gramps). Now Gramps was to be "the fly in the ointment" as far as our budding romance was concerned. He decided, in his wisdom, that because of what I looked like, and what I did, and what I was, that I wasn't "good enough" for his youngest Grandchild. So it all came down to a "cloak and dagger" relationship. We managed to work our way around things. This was in the days before mobile phones had even been thought of and I didn't know any average person who had a land line. Letters had to be exchanged at times. However Bob and I had joined Coleshill Young Farmers Club so Jenny joined as well. Not much really happened of any significance at the club meetings. The odd visit to different places and quiz nights and things like that. It was more of a club for farmer's sons and daughters than mere farm workers. The annual dance was evening dress and all that crap and rubbing shoulders with a bunch of stuck up wannabes but, it was something to do. Jenny could get out with no problem to attend. She was also allowed out with no questions asked every Tuesday and Saturday night because this was when Coleshill Jazz Club put on live band gigs. It had nothing to do with jazz at all. On a Tuesday it ran from 7.30 p.m. – 10.00 p.m. and on a Saturday from 7.30 p.m. – 10.30 p.m. It cost the princely sum of the equivalent of 15p on Tuesday and 17½ p on Saturday. If the band didn't turn up and records hadn't been played you got your money back. The only drinks that were served were soft drinks. No alcohol whatsoever and at 9 p.m, when the band took a break, a policeman was employed to stand at the entrance with his dog just in case anybody had gone to the Pub in this time and got a bit silly. They weren't allowed back in if so. These two nights were the highlights of our week. I loved dancing and still do to this day but I' not capable anymore. Sometimes Jenny would come up to the town (only one High street, really) on the bus and we'd meet up and just go for walks or sit in the viewing pavilion. It was only occasionally that I could scrape enough money together for us to go into Birmingham. On these occasions subterfuge had to be employed. The bus from Coleshill to Birmingham stopped right outside Jenny's house. Her place was a single house, with a shop attached, in a hamlet of about six or eight dwellings. Right on the end of the drive to the farm where Bob worked so as soon as the bus neared her stop (either way) I had to duck down and hide just in case her Mom or Gramps should be looking out of the window. This fact became quite well known to the bus conductors. So much so, that one evening we got on the bus at the terminal in Birmingham and after a couple of stops the conductor, who luckily was well tuned in to our situation, came dashing up the stairs to warn us that Jen's mother was waiting at the next stop!! Horror of Horrors!! He said to leave it with him and he'd tell her there was something wrong on the upper deck and that no passengers were allowed up there. Luckily it was getting late in the evening so passengers were few and far between. He managed to convince them with the same yarn that he'd spun to Jen's Mom. To go along with this little game Jenny had to stay on the bus (we hid when her Mom got off) go up to Coleshill and go home on the next bus back. That was a close one and I've never forgotten how that bus conductor "Saved our bacon" . . . I wonder if anything like that would ever happen these days? I doubt it.

As I've said money was short but occasionally we could stretch to a night out at the pictures. I remember we went to see the film "Zulu" and she was so concerned about the welfare of the horses during the making of it. She loved her horses and I often drew her a picture of one of her beloved animals as a present. It didn't cost anything and it was the best I could do in those days. Some evenings we would go and visit Fat Nan and Grandad who lived not far from the cinema and sit in their parlour listening to Radio Luxembourg on a transistor radio or "La La Box" as Jen called it. "Our Tune" was 'Little Children' by Billy J Kramer. We thought the lyrics were relevant to our predicament at the time.

Every year a number of Midlands Young Farmers Clubs would hold a rally. This consisted of all the clubs competing against each other in agricultural based competitions. Our club only won two prizes. The first was won by my mate Bob who came top of the tree in the Beef Cattle judging section and I won the milking machine assembly sector. Not one of the snooty farmer sons or daughters won anything. This is why, when I was asked to give a small speech to thank a visiting speaker who had come to our club to give a "lecture" on something or other, I went into a panic. Now, I still stammered really badly and didn't want to embarrass myself in front of everyone present so I refused. "You never do anything for this Club" was the response I got for not wanting to make a fool of myself via my bloody speech impediment. Now, remember Bob and I were the only two members of the Club who'd won anything at the rally the week before. I pointed this out, but it was the opinion of almost all those present that I should still stand up and look like a right idiot in front of everyone. My response to this was to say "You can stick your fucking club up your arses then" and walked out never to return.

Workwise it was time to move on. Ken and his failings in the financial and wages department were getting past a joke now. So, off to pastures new. Jenny had also moved on from Reg Wrights and was now working in a dog grooming parlour in Castle Bromwich. At home the population of No. 1. Cuttle Cottages had expanded. Frank's sister, a heavily pregnant lady called Joan, her husband Pete and their two kids had been made homeless but were on the brink of moving to Australia. Until they departed on their new life they stayed with us. So now there were four adults, six kids and a baby all crammed into this little cottage for a couple of months. To ease the situation I slept on the settee at Bob Daniels house for a few odd nights or two – no problem. The Jazz Club had just revealed that the patron had refused to have The Beatles play live there because he said he would have to charge 5 shillings (25 pence) and that, in his opinion, we (his clientele) wouldn't want to pay that much.

Imagine John, George, Paul and Ringo playing live in a space (a room above the local Co-op "Supermarket") that could barely hold more than 100 kids. That would have been something to tell your children.

By now Mrs Woodcock had got a little part time job at a Greengrocers in Coleshill. The extra cash came in handy. This was just as well, really, because Frank had been given a small asbestos garden shed and an old Hillman van that had been involved in some sort of road accident. It bore the scars to prove it. The idea for the shed was that, once we'd erected it, and put down some concrete on the floor, we would put a few young cockerels in it and grow them on enough to kill and eat. This was fine but for one thing. The river at the end of our garden got quite deep and still at this point and it was a bit of a haven for river rats. Not river voles. Bloody big things they were. Frank said that before he did the floor he'd spread a lot of broken glass down and concrete on top of it. This would, we thought, stop the rats digging up and taking the fowl. This worked for a while but eventually the rodents won. They managed to get through the floor and take the fowl. On the subject of chickens Frank said (before the shed disaster) that I could have a chicken as a pet as long as I paid for it. Enough said . . . I knew of a man who lived in an old cottage two or three miles away who kept bantams. Off I go with a pocket full of change to get myself a chicken. I can recall the gentleman involved had very little hair and wore glasses through which he must have seen me coming because he charged me 3 shillings (15 pence in today's money) for a little bantam hen – the robbing sod!! I've never forgotten his face or where he lived to this day. The little hen managed to stay around for a while. We kept it in a cage at night to keep it safe from the river dwelling bandits but it came to the point that one day we had very little food for ourselves so it ended up surrounded by a few vegetables on the dinner plate. No more chickens in my life for a while. The old Hillman van was a project that hung around for a while. I think mechanically it was pretty good. I had no real interest in it. Mechanics were an alien subject to me, still are really, but I'd do what I could to help. Luckily one of the older Daniel twins, Karl, seemed interested in it all so he helped Frank far more than I did. Indeed, as I write this some fifty odd years later, Karl is still grateful to Frank for getting him interested in mechanics in the first place because that is the career he spent all his working life involved with. H.G.V. mechanics and H.G.V. driving. As I said the old van bore the scars of being involved in some sort of accident. The front end was a lot "the worst for wear". One front wing resembled a bit of screwed up paper but with perseverance the three of us managed to give it a half decent face lift. We used, basically, only a blow torch, a hammer, the back of an axe and a few bits of wood. Alas it only ended up with the scrap-man or somebody else because in no way could we ever afford to put it on the road.

Work wise it was time to move on now. Ken Alcocks strange view of how and when wages should be paid was getting to be a bit of a concern. When I discovered that he hadn't been paying my National Insurance contributions I thought it was the right time to "vacate the premises". I just got another job on a farm a couple or so miles away near Marston Green. Jenny had also moved on from the Bloodhound Kennels and had got a job at a dog grooming parlour a bus ride away at Castle Bromwich. My new boss was a very kindly man named Jack Wright. He had a wife called Audrey and three adopted children. John, Neil and Ellen. So far as his treatment of the staff was concerned he was the polar opposite of Ken Alcock. He bought out tea every breakfast and lunch time. If we were working late he'd feed us at tea time as well. Apart from Jack, who was constantly eating Nuttalls Mintoes (he used to buy them in commercial quantities) the other workers were an older lad called Bob who it turned out had gone to the same school as me. An old boy called George who only stood about 5 feet 4 inches tall. He did a bit of everything. There was a cowman called Bert who was a bit of a miserable old northern bloke who wore a white skull cap, a bit like the pope, at milking time. On the subject of headwear I had taken to wearing a white meat porter's cap that I managed to lodge on my bonce at a nice jaunty angle. I had two or three of these little caps one of which I would wear at all times. In fact I kept a clean "best one" which I wore when I went out anywhere either with Jenny or the lads. "Going out" consisted of either dances two or three times a week, usually always in Coleshill or going somewhere or another and every so often to Water Orton. This was a few minutes bus ride away or a trip to the Cinema a half hours bus ride away every once in a while. Or we would just hang around the High Street, usually near a milk vending machine that was situated on the end of the Church Croft. That was a bit of a focal point in those days because none of us drank alcohol and in any case we weren't old enough to go into a pub. I can recall that one winter a night watchman was installed on the street. He had a canvas shelter, with seats inside, and a coke fired brazier on which he boiled his water to make tea. Bob and I would quite often spend an hour or two chatting to him. He made us tea as well. The only downside was the fumes from the coke fire. They got in your throat and stayed there!!

I was settling in well working for Jack. He was a very understanding and caring sort of chap who kind of took me under his wing. Maybe that was something that spilled over from his attitude towards youngsters. Hence he and his wife adopting their three children. If I did anything wrong he never told me off. He just showed me how to do it in the way he preferred. Fair enough. He was the man who paid the wages after all. Anyway I was loving the fact that I was being given the chance to learn about what I wanted to learn about and being given a bit more responsibility. He farmed two farms about 1 ½ miles apart. My base was the home farm where the milking herd were kept and my main job was to be Bert's sidekick but every other week-end I worked with Jack. This I really enjoyed. He wasn't grumpy like old Bert. The other farm was where little George lived along with his family. His main help on this place was a curly headed man also "vertically challenged" as they say. Just like George but a tiny bit taller. I suppose Roy was in his mid 30's. He may have been short in stature but he was as wide as he was high, and as strong as an ox. This other farm was where all the calves, growing cattle and fat cattle were kept. Between the two farms the milking herd, and all the follow on calves and beasts, were the main enterprise along with a few sows and a boar pig. I can't remember any corn being grown there but I do recall he did grow a few acres of oats one year. This he harvested in the old fashioned way with a binder. This just cut the corn and tied it in sheaves. These were later thrashed and baled in a separate operation. A satellite job that turned up every couple of weeks was for one of us to de-camp to the pig farm along the way. A good sized pig enterprise for those days and this produced a lot of muck. Mostly a thick slurry. This one of us used to have to go and load up using a front end loader and, the first one I ever saw, a muck spreader specifically designed for this kind of job. I think it was an arrangement where Jack supplied the labour as long as the muck went on to his land. All the other field work was no more mechanically aided than I had been used to before. Almost everything was still done by hand. This was no problem except for the time when the kale had been planted beneath the approach fly path to Elmdon Airport. No problem until it was raining and then, when the planes came in low, they created a blanket of water from the wing edges to the ground. If you got caught in this it was a case of instant saturation usually in cold water. Kale harvesting time was still done by hand with a large knife or something similar. This was in the back end of the year and early winter. As I mentioned earlier the other worker was a lad called Bob. He was two or three years older than me and a tractor fanatic. All of Jack's tractors were the big old "Nuffields" made by B.M.C. and always orange in colour. Bob was always "fiddling" with these things and he'd somehow managed to get one of them to go a little faster than any of the others especially on the road. This became a cause for a little joviality and "boys games" every now and then. This one tractor he'd "souped up" was the one that had the front end loader permanently attached. This was fine until, maybe, at least one of the other tractors alongside the "Bob Special" was needed at the other farm at the same time. Then, if Bob got on the road first, he'd wait for you to overtake him and when he was behind you (because his machine was quicker) he'd get close enough behind you and get the front end loader under your back axle and pick your rear end up off the road. Basically it was two tractors going up the road on two sets of front wheels and one rear set. He would "wheelbarrow" you up the road. Jack never did find out about that one but he did have to find out about the results of the next game we played. We had been up to George's farm to load two four wheel trailers with bales to go back to the home farm. We stacked these loads seven bales high. This was a fair old height on top of the trailer bed which was at least three feet off the ground. Anyway, boys will be boys and Bob bet me that I couldn't turn off the road and up the farm drive (these were at right angles to each other) without slowing down. Well I gave it a whirl but just ended up with the trailer on its side and its load shot all the way up the grass verge. Obviously the boss had to know about this and I thought that I'd be up for the sack, or at least a sever dressing down, but the only words that came out of Jack's mouth were "It ain't a fuckin' racing car y' know" . . . that was a close one!! Tractors were quite a dangerous novelty, I suppose,in those days. None of all this anti-roll bar and big wide tyres shit like today. In fact in those days agricultural tractors were generally regarded as one of the most dangerous vehicles ever manufactured. Extremely prone to falling over sideways or turning completely upside down by means of the front end completing a complete semi-circle "arse over tip" but vice versa. This became apparent one morning when the boss sent me and his eldest lad, John, up to the other farm on a tractor. John wasn't old enough to drive on the road so he sat himself on the right side mudguard. Now, the turn up to George's place was also at right angles to the main road. A left handed turn with a phone box on the corner. Again the "no slowing down" idea reared its ugly head. Now these old Nuffield tractors were generally known as the fastest of all the tractors on the road. They'd do about 18 m.p.h. on a good day. This is a fair rate of knots for a vehicle that by its design is extremely unstable. Anyway we got to the corner and its phone box . . . flat out. John and I had agreed beforehand that we'd try the old flat out, round a 90 degree bend, trick again. I said to John to lean back as soon as we started. He did so and a good job too because the two right hand wheels came about two or three feet off the ground and we came to rest on two left hand wheels against the phone box with John hanging out over the right side mudguard like a motor bike and sidecar rider. Luckily we were both able to get down and rock this unruly machine back on to "all fours" and carry on as if nothing had ever happened. So far as I know Jack never did know about that trifling mishap. It was all part of the growing up back then I suppose.

I now had a dog of my own. My first ever dog who was just mine. He was one of our Lady's pups but we'd come to the conclusion that she'd shared her womanly favours, not only with Bill, her usual spouse (the one that always came and waited for her on the river bridge to take her for walk and whisper sweet nothings down her ear) but also, the dog from next door. This was a black and tan half bred terrier type job. My dog, I called him Bruno, bore more of a resemblance to this terrier than the rest of the litter did. Billy was also allowed to keep one of the litter. He called his Buster and he was of the usual appearance for any pups fathered by Bill. Bruno went everywhere with me. Well almost everywhere, just not dancing or to the cinema obviously but, otherwise he was never far away. He would run alongside my bike or just walk alongside me with never the need for any kind of lead. Some mornings if I was a bit late for work, to get there on time, I'd leave him tied up at his kennel and then Mrs Woodcock would let him go a while later and he'd turn up at work and lie by my bike if I wasn't around. On one such occasion he'd turned up and was lying in wait in his usual place. I was up at George's farm I should think. Anyway on my return Jack came out and told me it looked like Bruno had been shot on the side of his face by a pellet gun and was feeling a bit sorry for himself so Jack had took him in the house. Sure enough, on inspection, he'd been shot in the mouth and the pellet was still in his gum but it was easy enough to dig it out. Luckily it had hit him in the gum/upper jaw area which meant it hadn't gone in too far. He was back to normal within an hour. It was a puzzle as to how or when he'd got shot until later than evening Bobby Daniel and I were discussing it all and he recalled that days earlier we'd been arguing with two brothers who lived on Bruno's (and mine) route to work. We looked into this situation and found another one of our mates who had seen Bruno at the top of the town and he'd stopped and given him some fuss. He said he was perfect at that time. So we deduced that, since the only dwelling between where he was encountered at the top of the town and the farm was where the James' boys lived. Everyone in the area knew whose dog it was so we just put two and two together and came to the conclusion that retribution was on the agenda. It was duly metreed out. End of that little episode. No more hassle from the James lads.

Other mates and acquaintances were beginning to ask me where they could get a dog for themselves. I had a "light bulb moment". I knew that the local police station housed stray dogs and if they hadn't been claimed within a certain amount of time then they could be "re-homed". So I "re-homed" a few. It cost six shillings (30p) to liberate them from their confinement and that usually included a collar and lead. It was no trouble at all to sell them for a £1 or 30 shillings (£1.50) and their new homes were always in the area so I bumped into them from time to time. It was a way for me to make a few extra shillings and it helped the dogs at the same time. At least they weren't put to sleep so it worked two ways. I've often thought back over the years that this little project was the seed for all the years that have followed where I've always bred, bought and sold various forms of domestic animals and birds . . . but more of that to come.

So far as my love life with Jenny was concerned it was getting a bit bumpy. I think she realised that she needed to get a boyfriend who would be more "acceptable" in some way. She needed someone who was more secure between the ears than I was so she called it a day. I was heartbroken for a while until I realised there were loads of pretty girls out there and I had little trouble in attracting them. The situation needed to be explored. There would never be another Jenny Smith but I was never going to become a monk. Time to spread my wings a bit more I thought. Now Bobby and I had met a couple of girls from Water Orton who had been riding their horses in the area. Anyway we picked up with them for a while. They'd come over on their horses and Bobby and I just doubled up with them. Bob's girl was a short pretty little thing and the lady I was more taken with had long blonde hair. Always been a sucker for a girl with long hair, me!! This was all very well when I was sat behind her, with my arms round her waist, on her horse but when she turned around she wasn't the prettiest thing that was ever born. That's putting it kindly. It all made a change for a while. Trouble was I ended up getting "saddle sore" and as we hadn't got any soothing cream or similar at home I thought I'd use some of Frank's Brylcream that he used on his hair. That was a big mistake. Bloody hell it stung!! Our little excursions with these two girls and their horses came to an end when they invited us to a party but we decided it would be more fun to go dancing instead. I don't think the girls took too kindly to that so end of long haired girl, and her horse, and no more sore arse for me. For at least three or four evenings a week we'd go dancing in Coleshill, either at the good old Jazz Club above the Co-op, the R.A.F. Club or the British Legion Club. These were the places to find the girls and I've always been one to appreciate a fine example of the female form. Neither of us had a regular girlfriend for now . . . why bother!!

Another friend of ours was a lad called Brian Rowley (now sadly passed away). He also worked on a farm about ten miles away so he got himself a small motorbike somehow as a means of getting to and from his work. His father had a One Man Bakery, also in Water Orton, and some Sunday afternoons he'd ask Brian to go and light the ovens for him ready for a very early start the following morning. Bobby and I persuaded Brian to give us both a lift to the bakery, obviously one at a time, when he was called upon. The sole reason for our visits was to get hold of some of the cream cakes that his father hadn't sold on the Saturday. I don't think Bobby and I had ever ate so many cakes, either before or since. Brian's mom was also a very handy lady to have about because she was a seamstress. If we ever needed any jeans altering she'd do them for us for a small remuneration. Very handy . . . thank you Mrs Rowley!! One Saturday evening Brian turned up at the Jazz Club with a young lady none of us had ever seen before. It turned out her parents were friends of Brian's Mom and Dad. This particular young lady really took my eye so I said to Bobby "You watch me take her off him and take her home tonight" . . . Job done!! Her name was Margaret . . . Margaret Smith. I was at work that week-end so we arranged to meet on the Sunday morning until it was time for me to go to work at about 1 p.m. She went home that same afternoon but we wrote to each other for a while and I've never forgotten her address. It was 25, Elmers End Avenue, Annerley, London SE 20. Funny how some things stick in your mind isn't it. At the top end of Coleshill was situated Father Hudson's Homes, a home for orphaned and disabled kids. This meant there was a lot of nurses and some of them started to come dancing with us. A wide variety of young ladies from all over the country. Amongst them was a quite pretty, shortish, fine built girl called Paula who, it turned out, was from Norwich. She wasn't particularly pretty and had shortish hair. Not my usual type at all. Anyway we got together for a while on and off. In a way I found her quite attractive but there were other objects of my desire at the same time so it was all a bit on and off. One of the other young ladies I'd been taken by was a girl called Susan. Bloody hell she was pretty!! Eventually I managed to take her to the bus stop and "say goodnight" – for want of a better phrase. We agreed to meet at the Cinema the following weekend but by then another young lady had taken my eye so I thought I couldn't be arsed to get on the bus and meet Susan at the Cinema. I managed to persuade Brian to get on his motorbike and go and meet her outside the Cinema with some "cocked up" excuse as to why I couldn't meet her. Anyway Brian got back only to reveal that she hadn't turned up either. She'd only bloody well stood me up hadn't she? Bobby had got himself a regular girlfriend called Jill or as I used to call her "Precious Pup". She was lovely and she could really dance. They were besotted with each other, at the time, but I learned years later that Bobby had decided otherwise but, on speaking to him these days, I think she was to him what Jenny Smith was to me . . . Sad really. Sometimes when we were on the High Street of an evening these two or three school girls (about 14 years old) used to be walking about as well and one of them was quite tall, hair down to her bum and legs up to her neck. Bloody hell what a looker!! We always used to tease them by saying it was past their bedtime. In the end I even used to call the tall one "My little bedtime friend". She turned out to be a young lady called Linda Dutton. Frank had sold her one of our puppies in the past. This girl was to become my wife some years later and still is today. Now she's 69 years old and I'm 73.

At work everything was well. Nothing unusual happening of any note but two things have stayed in my memory. The first being the time when Jack decided that the cowshed walls could do with a coat of two of fresh whitewash. In those days it was a wash that included a lot of lime. This not only served the purpose of brightening the walls up but also acted as a kind of anti-bacterial agent. All done . . . and the sheds looked lovely. Just one problem though. Firstly it looked so bright and, of course, it smelled of lime. Most of the cows weren't so keen on it. The few older beasts that had seen and smelled it all before weren't so bad but the others wanted nothing at all to do with it. In those days the doors on the older farm buildings were basically only about twice the width of a modern domestic door. Not the easiest thing to get the girls through when they didn't want to go. Basically it was a case of head in, a quick look around and a sniff of the air, and it was straight into reverse gear for a quick trot round the yard. Even when we got them in it wasn't the usual stroll into their regular stall but more of an intense inspection of our decorating efforts. To get them all in, tied up and given a bit of "cake" just to settle them down, took a long frustrating time. Once they'd done it one time all was well from then on. The second thing that remains in my memory is the night the bull was involved in a road accident. I'll explain. Most farms kept their own bull back then. It was well before A.I was well established. Our man was no problem. He was an old Hereford boy who'd seen it all but at odd times he'd manage to liberate himself and this was always during the night. To get over this problem a good bowl of corn was always left on the meal house floor and he'd go and eat this and then just settle down for the night. This was a regular occurrence and it was just taken for granted that this is what he'd do, until one night, the meal house door must have blown shut somehow. So his usual "midnight snack" had become unavailable. He must have decided to have a wander around the yard. Unfortunately he went up the drive, along the lane and onto the main road. This proved fatal. He was hit, literally head on, and I mean head on by a coach. He was, of course, killed outright and the offending vehicle was basically a write off and the driver seriously injured.

Bobby's boss was a man who dealt in milking cows. He kept what was called "a flying herd". He would buy cows that had just calved, milk them for a while, and then sell them on and replace them with a new one. At the time I'm speaking of a cow that was known to be "a kicker" would often end up in the market and sold as soon as she'd calved. By the law of averages one or two or three or four of these liabilities would end up at Bobby's farm. Then it was frowned upon to sell a known kicker but not banned as it is nowadays. Bob came home from work one evening to reveal that Neal (his boss) had turned up from the sale one evening with, amongst others, an old longhorn cow that had only ever been milked by hand. Naturally they presumed that because she was an old girl and set in her ways she wasn't going to take kindly to being milked by a machine. She'd never seen or heard one so sparks were expected to fly but, no, she stood there good as gold. She never blinked or twitched. She was tied up in an L shaped shed and, when the person who was milking her walked away, and went into the stalls around the corner they noticed when they came back her machine was off. This happened time and time again so they decided to watch her to see what she was doing. She watched as the cowman went around the corner, out of sight, then put her head down, looked under her belly, manoeuvred her back foot into the middle of the cluster (teat cups) and then just gently put downward pressure on until she'd got the cups off. Who said animals are "daft". Sometimes they'd tease this old dear. They would go around the corner, wait for her to start her removal process and then shout at her, and she'd put her foot back on the floor. Bobby said that one milking they had her going at it for two or three minutes. In the end the problem was resolved by just milking her last and just standing with her. She never as much flinched in anger.... Bless her!!

At my work Jack came from market one evening. He'd taken some fat cattle in to be sold for slaughter and in the 60's all fat cattle were graded and marked as either a Grade one, Grade two or Reject before they were sold. Apparently Jack had had a beast rejected and marked with a cross. Just the kind of cattle Frank's boss used to buy. This meant they weren't fat enough to be sold for beef only for knacker. Obviously Jack returned home with this animal and he wasn't happy but the classic quote was yet to be spoken. Let me explain. The man who did the grading was Reg Wright (the owner of the kennels where Jenny had worked and the man who, along with Frank, had tried to catch me and sheep shear my hair in days gone by). Jack's surname was also Wright. It turned out that when Jack had seen that Reg had "rejected" his animal he went up to him and said: "Two Wrights don't make one wrong you know" . . . Brilliant!!!

Life was going along swimmingly. I'd got all a young man should want and need – a job, a dog, a pushbike, a safe home, a family to help care for, a good job and best of all girls and more girls. I had only one regret and that was the fact that I'd always been interested in veterinary work. Indeed at school it was suggested that this would be a perfect profession for me. I'd never got less than 90% in a biology exam. In fact one year I managed to achieve 98%. The reason for this loss of the 2% was because I'd spelled Chlorophyll wrong. My teacher later gave an explanation to me. He said that, in his eyes, it was a 100% mark but that was never awarded so he'd knocked the two marks off for my spelling mistake. My ambitions in this field were totally unrealisable. When I left school I had to go straight to work to help look after my new family and that was that. It's just the way the path through life meanders and I have no reason to mourn the fact at all.

Bruno was still my constant companion and Frank and I were out looking for firewood one weekend and Bruno was tagging along as always. We jumped over a brook and climbed over a barbed wire fence. This fence had been put up specifically to keep lambs in. There were two strands of wire less than a foot apart and reasonably close to the ground. Anyway the dog was "loitering behind". We were now the other side of the fence to him so Frank called him. He came tearing up, leapt over the brook on his usual projectory to go under the bottom strand wire, as he thought. Anyway in mid-air he must have seen that his normal route had now been restricted by this new strand of barbed wire and, while in mid- air, he literally screwed his face up and stuck all four of his legs out in front of him as if putting on air brakes. Of course this didn't work and he ended up with two ripped ear flaps and these flaps know how to bleed. Frank never ever forgot this and he'd laugh about it until the day he passed away some sixty odd years later.

Before I moved to The Cuttle, I had moved away from my natural family, more or less completely but I still visited Nan and Grandad and Nan and Auntie Barbara from time to time. I'd carried on drawing and painting from time to time mostly animals and birds. I'd done two horses' heads in pencil and a picture of a Friesian cow copied from The Farmers Weekly. I'd given the cow and one horse's head to Frank and Mrs Woodcock. "Ma" (Mrs Woodcock) still has them today sixty odd years later. I gave Jenny one of the horse portraits as a present. She loved her horses. I can now recall that I also gave some kind of picture to one of Bobby Daniel's neighbours, a Mrs Grimes, and I saw her two or three years ago. She said she'd still got it. I did it when I was fourteen and told her she still hadn't paid me for it . . . just a joke!!

Life couldn't have been better but, unbeknown to me, a major upheaval was lurking just over the horizon. For some time now Frank had been having trouble with his back, mostly, at the base of his spine. This was probably caused by, or certainly not helped by, the fact the tractor that he drove for most of the time had had a broken seat. This had to be removed and because of this fact he had to resort to sitting on a pile of hessian sack bags and straw placed on top of the back axle and seat mount. This reduced any shock absorption capabilities these old tractor seats ever possessed. It was thought that the best thing to be done was for the family to put their names down for a Council house. This duly materialised. They were offered a house in Meriden which was handy because this village was where Frank had grown up and his parents and two sisters still resided there. This move for me was a bit of a blow because I was just (as far as the Council were concerned) a lodger and Council house tenants weren't allowed to have lodgers so I was in a bit of shit basically. I needed to find somewhere else to live and pretty quick. There was no room at Bobby's place. They'd already got eleven children. I resorted to basically knocking on a few doors to ask if I could be a lodger but to no avail. In the end I decided to stay with the couple who were to move into the cottage as soon as it was empty. This couple were a man in his mid-thirties, I suppose, from Tamworth and his heavily pregnant wife Rosie, an Irish lady, not very tall with black hair. They agreed that I could stay with them on a more or less temporary basis but this had to be temporary due to their impending addition to the family. I thought this was kind of them indeed. Things trundled along in a sort of nondescript way at The Cuttle since the upheaval but something wasn't quite right. Probably just me, I thought, so I decided the best thing to do was to give Tom and Rosie their space and try harder to find a new place for me and Bruno to live. Hey-ho and off we go.

Eventually I found somewhere to live with somebody I knew in Birmingham but the less said about them the better as far as I'm concerned. I got a job in the wholesale fruit and veg market in the centre of town. I began work for a firm called William Glover & Sons. Just a small set up being the boss, Mr Bob as he was known as, a little fellow in his sixties who wore a suit, a trilby hat and glasses. There was an office boy, also a very small chap, in his early 20's who also wore glasses. I can recall a driver and me and another lad who did all the order picking and packing. The driver, a lad a couple of years older than me, was called John . . . John Taverner who, it turned out, had also gone to the same school as me. Now John was a lad full of himself. A proper cheeky chappie but to coin a famous Kenny Everett phrase :- "All done in the best possible taste!" Sometimes his nature would get him into trouble and one day, in this vein, the office phone rang and it was one of our customers, the owner of a Chinese Restaurant in town called Ying Wa. He'd rung to advise Mr Bob not to send "that driver" again because if he did then they would, in their words "Put him out through the Restaurant and he'd never be seen again." Mr Bob said that this threat should not be taken lightly because if it wasn't issued in all seriousness there would have been no warning. It turned out that John had been going in there and just being himself, a bit gobby, but they had taken it the wrong way. Anyway their warning was heeded. No more Ying Wa for Johnny boy!

After a while I got a new job as a proper barrow boy for a company called Williamson & sons. This was run by the "old man" and his son, a lad called Rodney who, like me, had a bad stammer but worse than mine. So much so that when he heard THE WHO singing My Generation his immediate reaction was to tell us that he was going to "Sue the bastards because they're taking the piss out of me". I thought that was funny. This job was really enjoyable. It was a laugh. The money was far more than I'd ever been used to and there were tips from the customers as well. Basically all it entailed was ferrying customer's orders either to their premise or, to their transport, on the barrow. Now loading the aforementioned barrow was a skill I had to get to master because it only had two big wheels in the middle and a pair of shafts or handles. If you put too much weight in front of the wheels it made it hard work on your arms to pick up and run with. On the other hand if you put too much weight behind the wheels then, as soon as you got in the shafts, and even slightly lifted them off the ground then the whole lot would, including yourself, go "arse over tip" backwards. If you got it dead right then you could arrange things so that the back was just slightly heavier than the front. In this case your feet would hardly touch the ground. Uphill it wasn't so good but downhill you could just float. A really enjoyable job, and handling fruit and veg was as close as I was going to get to being back on the farm whilst I was living above a pub in a run down area of central Brum. Williamsons had three salesmen, Rodney, an older chap, and a young mouthy little "piss taker" for want of a better phrase. Now this little idiot must have decided that every morning when a well dressed office gent came by he would gob off at him for a while. This chap wore the complete "turn out" . . . shiny shoes, three piece suit, collar and tie, briefcase, rolled up umbrella and a bowler hat – the works. The office gent took no notice at all until one morning he must have had enough when the "mouth on legs" started his usual offensive verbal diarrhoea. The gentleman went up to the older salesman and said to him "Excuse me Sir, would you mind holding my brolly, briefcase and hat for a moment please?" Once he'd unavailed himself of his accessories he proceeded to give the mouthy little chap, who'd giving him abuse, the biggest hiding of his life. The youth didn't know what was hitting him and once he'd been rendered unconscious the gentleman laid him out in the gutter and said to all present "I think that's where he belongs don't you?" On retrieving his hat, brolly and briefcase, he tugged his forelock and wished us all a good day . . . there's a lesson in life here . . . Never judge a book by its cover.

During the time I was stranded in the big city I'd regularly go and visit my adoptive family in their new house. They were much better off. Frank had got a job in the Triumph motorcycle factory, just a couple of miles up the road, and he was earning as much in a week as he would have done in a month or six weeks back on the land. Mrs Woodcock had got a job as a cook at The Bulls Head Tavern just a ½ mile away. The girls were in school and Billy was, well, Bill, a mad headed little bugger. He was always doing things before he'd really thought about them but he was an "ace" on his roller skates. Something I could never get the hang of I must admit. He was almost at a professional standard on his wheels. He got the name "Billy Whizz". He'd quite often get himself into minor brushes with the law but that's just the way he was and it was an accepted fact . . . Let's just say no more. He was still my "brother" and he remains as such as I write this. Coleshill, the dancing and the girls were still a big pull for me and I'd get over there to resume my old social life as often as I could. I now started "going out" with Paula, the previously mentioned nurse from Norfolk but I'm afraid I was still kissing other young ladies at the same time. Not a good trait really, I suppose, thinking back on it. The young lady Linda Dutton was still a part of the scenery but out of bounds due to her tender years but still very attractive. Today people go on about "The swinging 60's" all free love and drugs etc. but all that didn't really kick off in any way until the really late 60's early 70's. In the early to mid 60's if a lad could get his hands up a girls blouse – never mind anywhere between the knee and the waist he was doing o.k. Believe me, I tried and to actually get a bra off a young lady was an acquired skill. This I managed to master very well but that's as far as things ever went unless you managed to get hold of "a bike" as a girl with loose knicker elastic was known in those days. Wenches like that were never of interest to me . . . no fun, no sense of achievement. In Coleshill, Father Hudson's Homes, where Paula was a nurse, was in a gradual wind down so the nursery nurses were first to go. She went into temporary private nannying, which usually involved working for "people of substance and means". Indeed she had spells with Lloyd Grossman and the actor Anthony Booth who played Alf Garnett's son in law in the T.V. Series Till Death Us Do Part. A big change from her life in Coleshill!!

Back in Coleshill Bobby had left the farm and was working with his eldest brother Clifford in the building trade. His twin Ronnie was still butchering and Karl and Warren had both gone down the mechanic/

lorry driving route. Warren, or Wagger, as he was always known, took up the mechanics and Karl got into lorry driving – livestock transport mostly. The two eldest twins Karl and Wagger had a good friend called Bob Bagley, a friend who they sometimes fell out with in no insignificant way. Indeed I was just going up their path to the back door one evening, where, lo and behold, one of the twins was beating his mate Bobby with a kitchen chair whilst the other one stood in the doorway with another chair ready for "refuelling". It all passed over and they made up and shook hands and it was all forgotten about. On the subject of the eldest twins and their mate it came to be that before Paula left Coleshill she needed to get to Welshpool to meet her parents. Now the lads had an Atlas Pick-up Truck so we decided we'd take her there and come back all in the same night. Now, because it was Karl and Wagger's truck they decided who rode in the cab in the warm. They decided that, because it was their vehicle and, because Bob Bagley was their mate and, because Paula was a girl then those four would be in the cab and Bobby and I were relegated to sitting on the floor in the back. Bloody hell it was cold!! We duly delivered Paula to her destination and because there wasn't room for all five of us in the cab on the return journey Bobby and I had to endure the trip home, still in the back, in the cold.   On the return journey we could see and hear that Karl and Wagger were having a bit of a "disagreement" and by the time we'd got into Birmingham it must have been getting a bit over the top in there so they pulled up, both got out, had a fight, got back in again, shook hands, and we went back on our way. That's just the way they were. They loved each other to pieces but they were so alike in appearance and in their ways that it was always going to end in a fight from time to time.

For me life trundled on in Birmingham and down the fruit and veg market but I was beginning to get a bit homesick for the farms and the countryside. The domestic situation above the pub left a lot to be desired so time for me and Bruno to upsticks and move on again. I'd always bought The Farmers Weekly magazine and in those days there was always two or three pages of jobs advertised. Through this magazine I got a job as a cowman (my first "big responsible job") on a farm near Cockfosters in Hertfordshire. This came complete with a cottage and as Paula wasn't really over the moon with her own situation we decided we'd both move to Hertfordshire and live together …. Time to try and grow up then.

My new boss was a man called Phil Harman. He had a decent sized milking herd and his brother had the same about five miles up the road. This was at the time when cowsheds or such were being replaced by a milking parlour and a loose yard to house the cows in during winter. Our parlour was an abreast parlour as they were known. It was just a place where eight cows at a time would come and be milked and then let out through individual gates in front of each stall. My helpmate, during milking, was a chap called Howard who lived in the next door cottage to ours. A bit of a non-descript sort of fellow who liked a drink or two. I recall in our parlour you could milk eight cows at a time. This was considered, and rightly so, too many for one man to manage. Eight units all at once was, and still is a lot for one person to manage in this kind of set up. The milk was no longer put into churns but into refrigerated bulk tank. The first one I'd ever seen at the time. At the farm nothing of note happened really except this is where I experienced the nastiest cow I'd ever seen, before or since, and I've seen a few. Let me explain. She'd calved up the field which was all O.K. until we tried to get her and her calf into the yard. She went absolutely ballistic. Eyes out on stalks, tongue out and frothing and digging the ground up with her feet and head. I was frightened I must say. We were all frightened. She'd flipped her lid basically. The maternal instinct was strong enough in her to make her want to do anything to protect her baby. In the end it was decided to basically "pin" her between three tractors and front end loaders and "pick her up and carry her" off the ground and into the yard. This was a one off in all my experience since. I've never seen such an extreme case again. Apparently she'd never done it before and she never did it again. This was due, mainly, to the fact that the best place for her, Phil decided, was out of it so she was shot in the yard before she killed somebody. She was never going to come down to reality again. She really lost her senses and it's sad that it had to end in such a way but that's the way it goes. As I said earlier, in my experience, up until the time of writing this, it's the most over the top reaction I've ever seen from a dairy cow. Fair enough, a bit of bullying and barging and kicking is acceptable and expected at times but she'd just gone over the top. This time spent in Hertfordshire was a bit of a drag really. Not much occurred of any note except Paula and I used to go every couple of weeks to Hertfordshire Livestock Market on the bus (as I hadn't as yet got a driving licence) armed with four or five carrying baskets and buy, mostly ducks. We would take them back home (our baggage on the return journey did turn a few heads) kill and dress them and sell them on. The only Christmas we were there we'd bought a fair few Khaki Campbell ducks, really known for their prolific egg laying but not as table birds. Anyway we had a few about so in "my wisdom" I decided we'd kill a few and dress them. Hopefully they'd make a bit as it was coming up to the festive season. Anyway, said ducks were duly despatched and plucked but, horror of horrors when it came to dressing them they were absolutely full of embryonic eggs and duck eggs were a good seller. I've never more wished that I could put something back together and breathe life into it again than I did on that evening… but you learn from your mistakes as they say. I used to either walk across the fields or cycle to work every morning and because it was for milking, of course, this always occurred between 5 and 6 a.m. No problem except that Phil Harman had a big old Alsatian cross yard dog that he'd let loose every night to keep an eye on the place. All very well but this bloody dog had the habit of meeting me half way down the drive and he would insist on trying to nibble or nip my wrists when riding my pushbike. I eventually got a bit pissed off with his habit so I thought "I'll have you, you bastard". One morning I pushed a reasonably heavy hammer up the sleeve of my coat and, when he got within range, and was about to start his usual ritual {of trying to chomp away at my wrists and hand) I just let the hammer go and it clouted him on the end of his nose. That resulted in the old tail between his legs, a quick retreat and problem solved!!

One of the weirdest natural occurrences I've ever experienced took place, in the dark, one early morning. I was cycling up the drive to work. It was a pitch black sky and a skylark was singing. I couldn't believe my ears but the skylark was actually singing out of a coal black sky – how weird was that? A bit "spooky" actually. That's the only time in all my life, most of it spent in similar environs, that I've ever heard a skylark singing in the dark.

Things between Paula and I, and our domestic arrangements, were beginning to get a bit strained and awkward by now so we called it a day. She went back home to Norfolk and me and my old dog Bruno went back home to Warwickshire. By now, Frank and family had been living in Meriden for a fair while and had settled in well. Because Frank was a local boy he was well respected and liked. Everyone knew of my existence and attachment to the family. It was considered, and agreed by all, that a move back home with them until such time as I could get myself sorted, and as long as the Council stayed off our back, then there was no rush for me to move out again anytime soon.

Whilst I'd been off on my excursion into the Southern Counties with Paula things had been moving on up at home. Billy had got himself on to the wrong side of the law and had got "locked up" for a while. I already knew this because when he'd got himself arrested and put into Court Mrs Woodcock got in touch with me and told me the story. On the day of his judgement I travelled up to Coventry from Hertfordshire so I could go with her to Court as a bit of moral support. He was put away for a while. Other developments and changes involved the Daniel boys. The eldest twin Wagger had got married to a red headed young lady called Sandra who he absolutely idolised. Indeed she was really the only person in the world who could handle him because he had gone a bit wild. A sort of "hit them first and argue with them later" attitude. Usually if Wagger hit anybody once they didn't get up for a while. Indeed it got to the point, eventually, that his twin Karl wouldn't go out with him. After Wagger got married to Sandra I asked Karl, years later, what it was like for him when Wagger got married because they had always been inseparable. You never ever saw either one of them without the other. He said that to him it was like Wagger had divorced him to marry Sandra and he missed him. We all have to grow up in the end though . . . or at least try to.

Mrs Daniel had obviously got fed up with having eldest son Clifford still at home. He just went to work, came home, and went out drinking every day. Anyway he'd apparently come home one night from the pub, a bit worse for wear as they say, to find the back door locked and his clothes in bags on the step with his mother leaning out of the upstairs window shouting at him and telling him to "Fuck off out of it". Now Clifford was a big man. He'd taken after his mom's side, big heavy built people. His dad "Danny", as he was always known, was over six feet tall but carried about as much meat as a butcher's pencil. Now it turned out that one Saturday afternoon I was sitting in the Danny's living room waiting for Bobby. Old man Dan was sat in his chair, hand over his eyes and his feet up on the mantelpiece when big Clifford wobbled in, obviously in drink, and was being a bit "talkative". As the old man was obviously trying his hardest to have a nap this didn't go down that well. He told his eldest son to "Shut the fuck up Clifford". Clifford answered him back – not advisable – and before you knew it the old man had taken his feet off the mantelpiece, stood up and given Clifford such a clout in the head that it knocked him down. Old Danny then resumed his "resting position" and no more was said. When the old man decided to show all his boys (9 of them) who was boss it was literally a mad dash for the back door until he'd calmed down. Bobby, meantime, had met a man through Karl driving livestock lorries. A man called Don Upton. Don was a one man band livestock transport owner/driver and he will feature heavily in the forthcoming pages of this story because we did get into a fair few "scrapes" together. Some scrapes were funny and some a bit "iffy".

On my return to the Midlands I couldn't find a job on a farm so Frank suggested that I went to a place where he had worked many years before. The company was a timber firm that had diversified into commercial fence erection. The boss, a Mr Butler, remembered Frank from the days gone by when he was employed as a "crane rider". A job that entailed riding on the hook of a crane, directing the driver, and attaching the timber to the hook and riding it back to wherever it was needed to be placed. I was employed in the fence erecting branch and my mentor was a brilliant chap called Charlie Cowley who looked more like Eric Sykes than anyone I'd seen before or since. He lived in a big semi- detached house with a massive garden in a place called Bentley Heath. A bit of an upmarket area near Knowle. About five or six miles from Meriden. He told me he had bought the house in 1946 for £850.00. and the only reason the woman sold it to him was because, when he revealed that he'd been bought up on a farm, she thought he'd utilise the large garden in the best way possible. Charlie lived there with his wife, a German Lady, and two sons. This job suited me well. Charlie and I became really good mates (sadly he died a few years ago). He was a laugh and I was getting a bit more "up for anything" now. All the work was "piece work" and the first job I went on with Charles was the Alcester Road by-pass that was being put in around an area of West Birmingham. I call recall that we got paid £1. per bay. A bay consisted digging a post hole, putting in the post (no concrete) fitting four rails and driving in two stakes within the bay. Each rail being nailed to each stake with two nails per rail. Charlie had been at this job for years and years and he'd got it down "to a tee" and if the ground was good we could do O.K at it. Charlie taught me to dig the hole in basically exactly the right place and only dig it just a little bigger than the post itself. He always said "You don't put ground back as firm as Mother Nature did it in the first place". No brick ends etc. in our pot holes!! His spades had handles over four feet long and the blades were not much bigger than double that of a garden hand trowel. He had all his spades made up for him by a local blacksmith the very same fellow that sharpened our crow bars at least every two weeks. Charlie was like me, he loved his axe and could use it as deftly as if it were no more than a large penknife. We travelled all over the Midlands in the company's Morris 1,000 van. Charlie would pick me up and drop me off every day. As I said earlier, Old Charlie knew "all the wrinkles" as he used to say. On one job we were sent to Charlie's experience came in handy. We'd been sent near Coventry to fence the front of a new telephone exchange situated right on a main road. On arrival at the site we went to the site office because Charlie wanted to know if there were any services under our fence line. We had now been given a hand held, petrol powered, post hole auger and he wanted to check if there was anything important or dangerous down there. The foreman assured us, after consulting his plans, that all would be fine but thankfully Charlie decided we'd dig the first hole by hand just in case. Good job he did because we dropped on a mains electric cable which, it turned out, ran directly under our line. The problem was sorted in a few hours. Irish builders were sent from another site to dig another trench and move the offending cable. Bloody good job old Charles checked it out before we used the post hole borer!!

A further job we were allocated to was fencing the gardens in some old pre-war council houses in Birmingham. As was the norm these old council houses had huge gardens. This, apparently, was a matter of policy by the Councils in those days to give all their tenants as large a garden as was possible because it was thought it would enable the householders to grow as much of their own food as possible. One of the tenants was an old lady who, she told us, lived on her own and was in her mid- 90's. She prided herself on the fact that she dug, maintained and cared for her garden with no help from anyone. Now this dear old lady insisted on supplying us with absolutely copious quantities of tea. Now both Charles and I liked a cup of tea but she beat us. So much so that hidden in the undergrowth we found an old Belfast ceramic kitchen sink complete with plug. One day we thought we'd put all the tea she presented us with, and couldn't consume, into this sink just to see how much we'd been presented with. Believe it or not we basically filled the sink a very good half full. Bless the old girl's heart!!

Now, Dick, was an old man who'd worked at our firm almost all his working life and he was well in his 60's by now. Dick refused to do "piece work" and would only work for "day pay". I think, because he was basically part of the furniture in this set up, allowances were made for him. He'd been there that long that over all those years, whenever he finished a job, he took all the nails, screws, gate furniture etc. home with him. So much so that it was a company joke that Dick had more stock in his shed at home than was in the stores back at the yard. Indeed on several occasions people had been sent to Dick's house, if whatever they needed to do the job wasn't in the aforementioned yard store, just to see if he'd got whatever they needed stashed away at his place. Now Dick didn't use a firm's van. He used his own vehicle, a camper van, one of the ones that you could wind the roof up at bed-time. Quite often, just after dinner break, he would "go and put the roof up for an hour". In other words just go and have a sleep for a while. Apparently he did this most days where he was working, either on his own or with another gang. He'd been doing it for years and he wasn't going to stop now. Good old Dick. He was a funny old bugger.

Charlie and I were driving back from Northampton, or somewhere, one afternoon when he noticed a farm worker across the fields putting a barbed wire fence up and on seeing this he stopped the van, turned to me, pointed at the fellow across the field and said "Look at him over there". On saying this he got out of the motor, stood on the bonnet and shouted across to the man with the question "Are you in the Fence Erectors Union mate?" The object of his query must have said that he was because Charlie just shouted back "Good man, carry on". Then got back in the van and off we went on our way again . . . Silly sod!!

Wyckham Blackwell, the firm we worked for, were now taking on really big jobs and because of this the "brains" in the office seemed to struggle at times. On occasions they'd bring us a lorry load of materials out that were sometimes the wrong size. Maybe too big, too small, anything in that vein. This began to happen too often for Charles liking because we were expected to "make things fit". Now making "things fit" took time and as we were on piece work time was money. On the way back home one evening Charlie was not a happy man so we stopped off at the yard, went into the office – a den of overqualified dick heads who'd never dug a hole or knocked a nail in in their life. Old Charles didn't appreciate them, to say the least, so he starts ranting on about their cock ups and just ended up by shouting at them. "You lot will be sending us a fucking tree out next". He wasn't happy and he was tired as well. It was easy to tell when Charlie was tired and wanted to call it a day because, when he reached this stage, his one eye would wander about in its orbit like it had got a life of its own. After being employed here for a few

76

months I was allotted "a company vehicle" not a van (I did not have a driving licence yet). I was given a Triumph Tigress 4 stroke engine motor scooter which was capable of reaching 75 m.p.h. on a good day. I was allowed to use it not only to go to and from work and to Charlie's house, if the job was too far away, but also for my own recreational use. This opened up a new door to new opportunities.

While living back at home in Meriden Bruno couldn't come to work with me so at times he'd go to work with Mrs Woodcock. She worked at The Bulls Head Inn and Bruno must have found where they stacked the empty beer barrels and crates and he got a taste for the stuff. So much so that sometimes he'd get a bit tipsy to say the least. Sometimes he would take himself off of an evening, wobble back home, lift the knocker on the front door to be let in, and then just collapse in front of the fire. Sometimes he would collapse wherever he could stay long enough on his feet to get to. Frank was looking out of the window at one time when he started laughing "Come and look at your dog Nicky". There was my canine friend staggering and wobbling about, bumping into things etc., trying to work out where his home was – pissed as a fart.

Whilst living in Meriden I'd started to get friendly with Don Upton and in lots of our spare time Bobby and I would go with him on his journeys in his cattle lorry. This was at this time and continued to be for many years to come. Although Bobby began to spend more of his time with other mates and he'd started to drink. I never have to this day taken a drop of alcohol.

Back on the fencing scene, we'd been sent on a job between Banbury and Oxford. Now the ground in this area is basically made up of Cotswold stone which seems to lie one strata above another. All the holes had to be hand dug because our post hole borer would get stuck fast in between the layers. Now when it did this, if the throttle wasn't released, it would just take both its operators around and around. In other words the engine and handles went around the auger rather than vice versa. When this happened whoever was on the fuel trigger end of the controls got his knuckles knocked up and, the one on the handles (that he had to stand in between to guide the machine) got his thighs and legs beaten. Some days after a bit of rough ground Charles knuckles would be bleeding and my legs would end up bruised enough to look as if they had been massaged with plum jam. We were really struggling on this job to make it pay. Although Charlie had been pestering the office to give us "hard digging money" all his requests seemed to be falling on deaf ears. Charlie therefore invited a number one office wanker to come out to the job and have a go himself. This he agreed to do. This young man's name was Allan Jacques, a chap in his late 20's early 30's. A slender sort and worst of all an ex-copper with an ex-copper's attitude to all those he thought were below him. It seems, in his eyes, Charlie and I fell into that category. A date was arranged for his visit so Charles came up with a plan to put this "little shit" in his place. He would be invited to get on the handle end of the post hole borer, whilst Charlie operated the triggers, so that when the auger got caught Charlie would take the strain of the machine trying to release itself on the clutch. He would wedge the throttle trigger shut with a piece of stone and then let go. This resulted in "Jakey" as he was known, amid other derogatory titles among the fencing crews, being basically trying to hold on whilst "or biting" this vicious piece of machining until it flung him to the ground in a heap of embarrassment. Off he skulked back to his office hide away and we got our "hard digging" money. "Hard digging money" would at times work the other way for us. We were sent to put up crash barriers somewhere on the A.5. trunk road. Because this stretch was on a hill then it was presumed by the boffins in the office that this ground would be hard going and they included the hard digging allowance in the price they gave us to start with. A crash barrier in those days involved bolting the barrier on to posts 24 inches square and these posts dug, at least 36 inches, into the ground. Pretty big holes really and no concrete was allowed to be used to hold them firm. The belief was that the natural ground would more easily absorb any impact. We weren't particularly overjoyed at the prospect of this job. The weather was hot and the ground would be hard. We dug the first couple of holes in the ground that were no more than sand. It became like digging on the beach. It was a run of fence about 200 yards long and the last post was on a cut through between the carriageways. Now this was hard ground. With the original carriageway, Charlie decided in his wisdom, we weren't going to struggle digging 3 feet down into this. His idea was to cut the post off and just scratch out up to a foot into this old carriageway and concrete this last post in. Nobody will ever be any the wiser. So that is what we did. So along with the "assumed" hard ground that had turned out to be no more than sand this job paid us really well. So much so that we had to "spread it out a bit!". A "one off" kind of job never to be repeated in my time at Wyckham Blackwell.

Honiley Aerodrome near Warwick was another project for us to contribute to along with another gang. It was to erect a security fence. This involved erecting those tall concrete posts with hangovers at the top of which barbed wire was attached. These posts were heavy, probably an old fashioned cwt or so (about 60 kilos), and as it was still hot weather I never wore a shirt except a folded up one on my shoulder to ease the pain when carrying these concrete beasties. Charlie just wore a vest and carried these posts, not so much on his shoulder, more on the muscle above where your arm joins your shoulder. He was a tough old boot. Full and muscle and skin like leather. He would carry any amount of these things and end up, at the end of the day, with not more than a dusting of concrete dust on his arm and shoulder. What a tough old bugger!! Honiley aerodrome was the place where Girlings tested the brakes for vehicles. They did this on the old runways and taxi-ways. Sometimes this would involve pushing a vehicle to as fast as it was capable of and then suddenly stamp on the brakes. This they would do until the brakes eventually failed. A different method of pushing the brake system to fail was to repeatedly drive the vehicle a few hundred yards and then stop. This procedure would be repeated until the braking system failed. Jesus!! This must have driven the poor old drivers bloody mad!! I could see that old Chas was taking a bit of an interest in this procedure. What was he plotting I wondered? All was soon to become clear. He told me to go round and collect a decent quantity of small pebbles and he demonstrated they must be around a certain size. This done I returned with a nice collection of what I thought would suit his intentions. On the job we'd been given a compressor and pneumatic drill. Fair enough you may think, and it was fair enough, but Charles had the notion that said machine could be used for a bit of fun. The grass between and surrounding the runways was, because of the time of year, two or three feet tall. The perfect camouflage it was soon to be revealed. We manoeuvred the compressor and the drill as close to the runway so as not to cause suspicion . . . then all would be revealed. Charlie lay down in the grass with the drill on the end of it's pipe lying on the ground in front of him pointing towards the runways. He told me to start the machine and fetch the pebbles that I'd previously been sent on a mission to collect. These were soon to become "ammo" because he'd put a selection of them (as tightly as possible) in the exhaust vents of the drill and when the drivers, who were participating in the mind-numbing stop-start experiment, came within range he'd let rip on the throttle of the drill and pepper (or at least try to pepper) the unsuspecting driver with a hail of small projectiles. It must have relieved his boredom. This little exercise was only successful in any reasonable way before suspicions were aroused. So time to stop his bit of fun . . . who says boys never grow up? Charlie still hadn't grown up really. I don't think the bloody old clown ever did but what a really lovely old clown he was.

The motor scooter that had been lent to me as "a company vehicle" was by now starting to come in handy. Firstly it enabled me to get to Coleshill and the old haunts and friends. Before I'd acquired the scooter it was very difficult to get there from my new home in Meriden although it was only 6 or 7 miles away unless, of course, I could get a lift. It was a case of having to go into Birmingham and out again to Coleshill on public transport but the scooter put an end to these inconveniences I'm glad to say. Whilst back in circulation in Coleshill, at this time, I'd "picked up" with an Irish nurse from Father Hudson's home for disabled children because although the nursery and baby section of the homes had been closed down the actual hospital had been kept open. The nurse's name was Rosie. She was short, blonde and wore her fair share of make-up. She told me that until she came to England to work she'd never seen a coloured person in the flesh in her life. Sometimes she'd ride pillion on my scooter and when she did she always sat side saddle. This she said preserved her modesty because, let's just say, she did like a short skirt. The trouble with this little lady was that she kept trying to get me to go to Ireland with her and meet her parents!! Oops!! I didn't think it was a good idea so that little excursion was kept on the back burner. The other

Donald Charles Upton Esq. - love him.

advantage that the "company vehicle" laid on me was that I could get about more and do a bit of dealing on the side. My dealing both then, and for the rest of my life up to now, has only ever involved pets and livestock. At least I understand more about them than anything else. In those days it consisted of buying and selling chickens basically. I managed to get hold of two wooden chicken crates which I strapped on the pillion seat and off I'd go. I managed to agree with the butcher (where Bobby's twin Ronnie worked) a price per pound for plucked chicken and I'd go round different places buying hens by me guessing their weight. That didn't always turn out well but most of the time my judgement wasn't too far out. I'd put the live hens in the crates and take them off to Mr Walters (the man with the smallholding where I'd worked when I first left school) and he'd pluck them on his machine for me and I'd just tidy them up after he'd done. Bless him he did this at no cost to me but I still did go and help him out from time to time so it was considered a "fair swap". Anyway, once plucked I'd pack the chickens back into their crates with their head threaded out through the slats. It was easier to keep them clean that way and off I'd go to Marston Green and the butchers where he'd weight them all and pay me out. A handy little deal that went on for a while. At one time I'd bought 98 bloody big hens. Now, as I was only able to move about a dozen or fifteen at a time, this amount of birds was going to take six or seven trips to move and sell. I had a deal with the butcher for him to take them live at a reduced price per pound. I'd seen these hens on the farm – they were wandering round the yard and I'd caught one or two just to see how heavy they were - when I'd gone there one day whilst helping Don Upton in his cattle wagon. Anyway he agreed that if I got them caught up beforehand then he'd come in his lorry, we could chuck them in the back, and we could drop them off and weigh them up at the butchers. It turned out to be a good deal. I made two shillings (10p) profit on every hen. That was basically a week's wages earned in a couple of hours.

Don had a field in Meriden where he had erected a "Heath Robinson" structure using telegraph poles, oil drums and two sets of block and tackle. He used these to take off and put back again the livestock container from the bed of the lorry. He also kept a few sows up there. He told me that that's how he'd got his livestock transport enterprise started because he'd always loved his pigs and when he was a younger man he used to rent out boars to farmers whose sows needed serving. He used to take these boars around from farm to farm in an old van. When other people had asked him to move similar sized livestock for them in his van that's when he decided to try and make a go of livestock transporting. When he was away from his pigs, from time to time, then I'd look after them for him. I also fetched the sacks (84 lbs about 40 kilo in today's money) of food from the mill for him. I could get three sacks on the scooter. Two strapped on the pillion seat and one between my legs on the footplate. Imagine trying to get away with that these days . . . I don't think you'd get away with it. I got home one evening after one of my chicken trips on the scooter when Frank came home laughing at me. I queried as to what was funny and he told me that he'd been behind me in his motor, earlier that evening, whilst I was on my way from the plucking machine to the butcher. In those days my hair reached my shoulders and, then, it wasn't law to wear a crash helmet. He said all he could see "was a mass of black hair and a load of chicken necks and heads blowing around in the wind". Well, it made him laugh and it had made me a few extra shillings.

As I said Donald had a field, about four or five acres, and I'd started looking at cheap unbroken ponies that were coming into our area from the Welsh mountains. He said that I could put a couple in his field along with his daughter's pony. I bought and sold one or two and made a couple of quid out of them but horses weren't, and never have been, an animal I feel at any real ease with. Cattle and dogs were my kind of animals. In those days they were, and still are, my favourites along with my birds to this day. In fact in the past I have been known to say that the best place for a non-working horse was inside a good dog!!

Donald was to feature a lot in my life in the years to come, so much so, that I intend to dedicate a portion of this book to the things we got up to. To be quite honest I can't remember now when each incident happened with any kind of real accuracy. Donald Upton or Donald Charles Upton or Donald or Don or Up-to-no-good were his titles. He lived with his wife Julie, son Philip and daughter Jill about 300 or 400 yards away from our place. The family had a cottage on the village green and he parked his lorry on the other side of the road on a piece of vacant ground that was, fortunately for Donald, on a slope. Fortunate because many mornings, especially during the winter, rolling his lorry down the slope and ensuing hill was the only way he could get it started. The lorry was a Commer 2 stroke. 2 stroke referring to the way the pistons were configured and fired. This made the Commer 2 stroke a very noisy vehicle at the best of times. In Donald's case even more so because usually the exhaust system was in need of a little T.L.C. to put it mildly. The livestock container was made of wood and the cab was a bright red colour hence its nick-name "The Red Rig". Because the container was not permanently fixed to the chassis and bed then it could, legally, be roped on as it was considered to be part of the load. It wasn't designed in that way but because of a certain amount of lack of any maintenance (unless it was absolutely necessary) it often turned out that way. On the subject of maintenance of the vehicle, or lack of it, he got pulled in by the police and ministry on one occasion. They found 64 offences wrong with the lorry. A classic one was the bicycle lights that were tied to the back of the truck. These had to be switched on by hand whenever it got dark enough for them to be needed. At the other end of the vehicle the only way the cab doors could be kept shut from the inside was to have two leather belts that when joined together and could be attached to each door and pulled tight. This was with Don and two or three of us youngsters all squeezed in at the same time. This was all in the days before H.G.V. testing. Indeed when that came in, years later, the old Red Rig was confined to retirement. Bobby and I spent a lot of our spare time with Don and his lorry. We'd help him and in exchange he'd buy us a full English breakfast from time to time. Any maintenance that was absolutely a necessity to keep the motor on the road was done overnight at the Rootes Group main workshops in Hay Mills, Birmingham. The reason it was done overnight was the foreman on the nightshift was a good friend of Dons ... a man known as Dr. Tom. Any work was all done "for a drink" and kept off the books. We ended up there one Tuesday night after Don had broken down in Stratford on Avon cattle market. It was some form of engine or drive mechanism hiccup so the only way it could be moved was to be towed. Now, Donald was never "flushed" with money so a way around this problem was to borrow a tractor from a farm in Meriden. In actual fact, the very farm that I'd bought those 98 big hens from previously. Don had managed to get a lift home from Stratford and arranged for us to pick up the tractor then we'd both drive it to Stratford about 20 miles away. In those days very few tractors had cabs so it was easy enough for one of us to sit on the mudguard whilst the other drove. This was a bit of a mission, I suppose, driving the tractor to Stratford, hitching up the lorry and towing it to Doctor Tom in Birmingham about 30 miles and then driving the tractor back to Meriden. Luckily this event came about at the time of year that enabled us to drop the Red Rig off at the "hospital" as Don called Rootes Maintenance Facility. We did this in the early evening and got the tractor back to Meriden before it got dark. Bloody hell that was a long, cold expedition!! Imagine trying to get away with that these days. We towed it on a rope, not a solid bar. Because the lorry engine wasn't running then the air brakes didn't work. Donald had to use just the handbrake to save any embarrassment that would have occurred if he hadn't been able to stop quick enough and had run up my arse on somebody elses tractor!!

Sometimes, on a Bank Holiday, we'd take Philip and Jill with us. On one such occasion we'd taken Jill to Rugby Cattle Market on Easter Monday. I think she was about 3 or 4 years old at the time. A plump little thing with a chubby red face and fair curly hair. She'd sit on my lap and I'd persuaded her that, whenever we stopped, I'd put her at the open cab window and get her to shout "Shut up you lot". She thought it was hilarious. So did I really. I really got her wound up so much so that by the time we got back the poor little bugger was so hoarse she could hardly talk. Julie was not a happy woman when Don and I presented her daughter back to her in such a state of vocal distress. Jill and I still laugh about this, even today, when we see each other, which is not often. Don could have had a really good business. He'd got the job sewn up in our area but his trouble was he did like to stop at farms for a drink tea and chat. Indeed I was with him one evening and we were dropping pigs off at their destination at 11.30 pm purely because he'd wasted hours chatting and tea drinking with the previous clients. After years and years of this kind of thing, bad time keeping, a lot of his clients were finding it all a bit inconvenient and one thing Donald wasn't was a good book-keeper or manager of his finances and in the years to come he decided it was easier to drive for bigger companies. Don got a job moving some farm machinery and a 40 foot long "H" girder from a farm near Coventry to another farm in Cornwall. The machinery was not a problem but the "H" girder was a bit of a head scratcher. The only way we could get it on the lorry along with the other stuff (obviously the container was taken off) was to put the girder on, down the middle of the bed, rope it on independently and then put the tractor, the trailer, and a muck spreader on top and across it. We then roped these three on independently and wedged the girder in tight with railway sleepers basically. Now the bed of the lorry was 22 feet long and the girder was 40 foot long. This meant an overhang of 18 feet. Bloody hell that was a bit "iffy". We trundled along O.K, no real problems as such, until we got to Exeter. Exeter on a Saturday afternoon in the middle of the tourist season was O.K but a "bit tight" at times and then, lo and behold, a policeman in the middle of a crossways directing traffic. We needed to turn sharp left at this junction so to get it round the sharp corner Don had to drive up the kerb, across the paving and down the kerb. Up the kerb and across the paving was no problem but down the kerb wasn't quite so good as the back wheels dropped down. The jolt caused by this action seemed to vibrate the girder so much that it seemed like it was acting like a tuning fork... so I thought at the time. Now I was looking in the side rear view mirror at the time and I witnessed the traffic cop back on his heels and his hat on the road "Bloody hell we've hit that fuckin' copper" I shouted to Don but on further viewing through both wing mirrors we decided we'd just "put the shits up him". Now Donald was basically bald headed and he'd got the habit of picking a certain spot on his head whenever he was a bit concerned about anything. That spot saw some action that day I can tell you. Load safely delivered and unloaded and time to go home. The homeward journey took us across Bodmin Moor and it was now that a Zephyr Six car overtook us in an un-gentlemanly manner so D.C. and the Red Rig got up his arse and we chased him all across the moor but he couldn't get away. This old lorry could get a shift on when she felt like it. Indeed on that day we got from Perranporth to Meriden in just over 6 hours. She absolutely flew. Probably glad to get that bloody girder off her back and get back to the cattle job again.

Another "head scratching" time occurred when we were on our way back from somewhere in the South West and in those days you went downhill into Bath and uphill out of Bath. The downhill approach was where the problem occurred. Don put his foot on the brake and all that happened was . . . NOTHING . . . except the sound of the air tank, for the brakes, emptying . . . Oops . . . No brakes. It was a case of hanging on to the hand brake for your life. So the journey all the way back from Bath was on just the handbrake. Another job for Dr. Tom and a lot more head picking for Donald. That spot on his scalp got some stick that day again.

When things got a bit slack for him and his own lorry he'd do a bit of driving for a company called Kingsbury Mill using their lorry and for a wage. One night he turned up between 11 p.m. and midnight "Fancy a trip to Manchester to pick up some cattle grub?" he asked me. "Why not" was my response. Now it turned out that he'd been out with his own lorry all day so he was a bit worse for wear. We'd only gone 2 or 3 miles when he pulled up and said he was tired and it was better if I drove. Now, although I'd driven the Red Rig for a few miles, at odd times, I hadn't even passed a car test and this was somebody else's lorry. Now the M.6 was completed at the time so it was all main road stuff. Before he left me in control he showed me on the map where to go and went to sleep. So much so that when we got to the outskirts of Manchester I had to wake him up to show me where to go. It was to the B.O.C.M. Mill to pick up a load of cattle food, all in bags to be manhandled – no bulk feed and bulker lorries back then. As I mentioned earlier the livestock container was removable from the bed of the lorry and one Sunday we'd got to go and load up with manure to be dropped off at some allotments. The way he contrived to take the container off and on was to reverse between two telegraph poles he'd sunk into the ground. He drove below the third pole that spanned the two upright ones and this pole held two sets of block and tackle. The general way was to position the motor so that the front of the main body of the container was directly below these two block and tackles. The oil drums and various pieces of wood were put under each back corner. The hooks and chains were attached and the front of the container lifted up enough so as to clear the bed. The lorry was then driven from underneath it so that it was basically supported at the back by the oil drum and wood arrangement and the front held up by the chains from the blocks and tackle. Now this wasn't the ideal day for this job. Firstly because it was windy and secondly Don had removed the container floor in order to renew it at some time. Any animals that were loaded up were basically standing on the actual bed of the lorry so now the container was open to the elements from below when it was not in situ. We'd got the container off, drawn the lorry from under it, and were in the process of attaching a back board to it. Now as I've mentioned before I always wore a meat porter's white cap in those days and it was a windy day. As a consequence this hat blew off and I bent down to pick it up. I sensed out of the corner of my eye that the container was on the move. I shouted to Donald to get out of it quick. That's when the container landed inches away and luckily the canopy, the piece that goes over the cab, just about caught the backboard that we'd been fitting. Luckily this glance had slowed it down a bit but it had bent it up at more or less at 90 angle. What had happened was the wind must have got inside the container, lifted it up, which lifted the top telegraph pole and the blocks and tackle off the two uprights and thrown the whole lot a few feet until it came to rest too close for comfort to Don and I. We have always said that if I hadn't been wearing my hat and if it hadn't blown off then we would both have been seriously injured if not killed. That aside, the main problem now was to somehow get the container back on board the lorry and the canopy straightened out so that it would run livestock in and out of Rugby Market the following day. The allotments would have to wait for their muck. From somewhere, I know not where, Donald managed to get a mobile crane out somehow on a Sunday. He got the container and the lorry re-united and drove the lorry complete with it's canopy (at basically 90° angle to the rest of it) uphill and we set off to Marston Green to one of his customers, a Mr Harry Musson. This gentleman was a dab hand with an oxyacetylene cutter and a welder. Job done . . . all fixed and ready for work the next day. That was a close one for both of us and Donald's poor old head had been through a severe bout of picking and scratching. I always said he dug a hole in that day!!

The F.Y.M. (farm yard manure) that Don used to deliver to various different allotments came mostly from a smallholding in Balsall Common. It was owned by a chap called Harvey Skinner who, I may say, had a beautiful wife. She always made me think that she'd been plucked from a Pre-Raphaelite painting and had had life breathed into her. Harvey wasn't the most hardworking chap in the world but he was very skilful in the woodcarving department. He showed us the gun stock he had carved and I was really impressed. In the middle of his drive was a planted "rockery" that Don said suddenly "appeared" one day. The easiest way to get the lorry into Harvey's yard was to reverse it in. The first occasion Don had met with this horticultural obstruction he had to get very close – too close, it turned out – to it to get the lorry in. Whilst manoeuvring round it he heard a breaking sound to his rear. Couldn't be much he thought it's only dirt and a few rocks but on getting out to inspect the source of this sound he found that one of his bespoke rear lights, good bicycle lights they were, in pieces. It had turned out that Harvey had had a load of tarmac delivered but before he got around to doing anything with the tarmac it had gone off and gone hard. So in his wisdom he thought rather than making the effort to try and break it up and move the stuff it would be easier to cover it in earth and make a rockery out of it. Anything for an easy life was Harvey. To load the muck up on to the lorry we used Harvey's tractor and front end loader. This was an old grey Ferguson T20 tractor and the front end loader had only one hydraulic ram on the right hand side. Nobody I've ever spoken to since has ever seen such a contraption, it was lethal, especially in Harvey's yard. This was on a bit of a gradient. If you lifted the front end loader up too high when the bucket was loaded and then tried to turn too sharp then the whole of the tractor came to a serious list, usually with the two wheels on one side parting company with the ground. We called it "The One Armed Bandit". Bloody thing!!

A regular job every year for Don and The Red Rig was take the ponies from the local pony club to one of their annual big competitions. It turned out, one year, that this event was to be held at Butlins Holiday Camp in Skegness. Now I'd heard about these camps and the girls that got there, either with, or without any parental control. This was a chance that couldn't really be ignored so I thought I'd tag along. Unfortunately, the sticking point, as far as my intentions were concerned, was that Donald had only been able to get his son Phillip and Phillips's mate Griff in as passengers in the lorry. We worked out that if I put all the riding tack in the back of my van (I'd passed my driving test by then) then I could wangle my way in as an essential accessory because I'd got all the vital equipment in the back of my motor. The rumours I'd heard about Butlins camps weren't wrong. As soon as we'd got the ponies unloaded I went for a walk round and on doing so I noticed a very attractive young lady in one of the chalets. I waved, we had a little chat through the window, jjj and I'd got myself a date for the evening. Very Nice ... Thank you very much. During hay and straw carting time Donald used to transport a fair bit of hay and straw bales. These jobs all went with not a lot of hassle or mishaps except for two occasions. The first time things got a bit "off par" was when we set a load of bales on fire while they were still on the lorry in transit. Let me explain. Donald would, at times, really thrash the engine when it was under a good load. He explained that a good thrashing helped to de-coke the engine, which was a good thing for it, and he didn't feel he'd given it enough stick until he could see sparks coming out of the exhaust. That was all very well but we hadn't noticed that a couple of stray sparks must have managed to lodge themselves in our load of nice dry hay. The outcome of this was inevitable. FIRE!! The load was basically on fire and we were still going up the road at the time. As luck would have it we were made aware of what was going on so we pulled off the road and managed to solve our little hiccup. We struggled to get the now quite seriously smouldering bales out and off the load and extinguished on the roadside. Catastrophe averted . . . again!!

On the second occasion things didn't really go as planned with a load of bales was one day when we were approaching Warwick with a full load. Well more than the usual full load because we'd decided to put on an extra course of bales on the top to help bind and tie the load together. This was the usual way of helping to secure the bales together and helped to prevent any serious slippage especially on farms where the loads were hardly ever roped on. Then it was law to use the ropes when on a public highway. Nothing out of the ordinary really until we tried to squeeze under the bridge. We knew it would be a tight fit, height wise, so I got out to "watch him under" very slowly, very slowly indeed and then I could hear the strings on the top course going "ping, ping". They were catching on the roof of the bridge and snapping thus releasing a shower of hay on to the road but we squeezed through anyway. We cleaned up the road, got on top of the load, rearranged things, re-roped it all and went off on our way again. As luck would have it this little mishap occurred on a Sunday so we were able to clear up without too much hassle of any traffic and attracting the attention of "Mr Plod" as we called them . . . The Police.

An unusual accessory for having a bit of fun in the lorry was an extendable car radio aerial. This was used when we were, maybe, at a standstill for any reason in a town and there were plenty of pedestrians within striking distance. I would lean out of the window, aerial in hand, and "tickle" anybody who looked like they could take a joke especially any young lady who strayed into range. It was all done with no malice or anything like that. Just a bit of fun. You could get away with things like that back then but I very much doubt you could these days . . . politically incorrect I suppose it would be deemed as.

Whilst delving into my almost long lost memory to write this story two other "occurrences" have re-surfaced concerning myself and a certain Mr Donald Charles Upton Esq. The first occurred when he was asked to transport an amount of artefacts connected to a Country Fair to the Royal Artillery Barracks at Bistey. I think that was in Surrey or somewhere down that way. So lorry loaded and off we go. It was a Saturday evening and we had to get back home by Sunday morning. The thinking was that if we got there late evening/early morning then we could get unloaded and drive back straight away. No problem. Well, it was no problem until we got there. It was late on by now and not a soul in sight. After having a mooch around to try to find somebody, anybody, to get us unloaded, it was to no avail. In the end we decided to bed down in the cab and wait. 6 a.m. came round and still no-one appeared but after much wandering about and searching and shouting our efforts were finally rewarded when some "army bodd" came to see what was going on. How's that for security? We had sat all night in a beaten up old cattle lorry in the middle of Bistey Army Barracks completely unnoticed!! For all anyone knew we could have had a wagon full of explosives, - terrorists, anything!!

The other situation was a really "odd one". Donald had been contacted one Saturday morning and asked if he could go to some out of the way horse racing stables. This was somewhere in Warwickshire I think and load up "this blood horse" and take it to an out of the way old P.O.W camp on the edge of a little village where it would be collected on arrival. Nothing strange in that really except it was strictly specified that it had to be done overnight and as late as possible. This didn't "smell right" but I suppose Don needed the money so off we go and the horse was duly loaded and moved. We arrived at the destination some time after midnight, backed in the yard, where the recipients of the said cargo were waiting . . . Job done . . . wrong!! On dropping the ramp to unload this very highly strung and, by now, very agitated equine beast it launched itself through the internal gates and straight through us and was off into the darkness somewhere. To this day I don't know if and when it was ever caught but we were off!! We'd delivered the bloody creature to the prescribed destination and as far as Mr Upton was concerned we'd done our job. All a bit "cloak and dagger" really. We heard no more of it ever since but I doubt if poor old Donald ever got paid for his troubles. He couldn't really pursue the matter could he?

Donald Charles Upton and I were good mates right up until his death a couple of years ago. We got into a few "iffy" situations together but we had a lot of fun and a lot of laughs. We pushed things to the limit and managed to wriggle out of them. Wherever you are now Mr Upton, then rest in peace, my old mate and try and behave yourself you old bugger.

Donald's presence in my life will become evident again later on in my story but now let's get back to telling this tale in some sort of chronological order. All was going swimmingly at home in Meriden and with work and this included my excursions, for various reasons, aboard my motor scooter. But that was to change. On getting home from work one evening Mrs Woodcock handed me a letter addressed to me that had arrived via the post that morning with the postmark Norwich. It was from Paula. She was writing to let me know that she was pregnant . . . OOOOPS! . . . to say the least. What to do now then young man? Mrs Woodcock solved that little quandary. She insisted that Paula and I should get married – quote – "You're bringing shame on the family" - unquote was her way of looking at things. This, back in those days, was par for the course. Children should not be born out of wedlock and that's that. I was to consider myself to have been told and, I may say, that is the only time over the last 60 or so years that either Ma (Mrs Woodcock as I still called her then) or Frank had ever told me what to do. She did say, once the kids got married, she would stay away but would always be there if and when needed. She said that once married you had to stand up for yourself if at all possible. If you were old enough to get yourself into a situation then you were old enough to cope with the consequences. Better go and talk to Paula then. I visited her in Norwich several times before the baby entered the world. I'd go on the scooter, a journey of 152 miles each way. It took between 4 and 5 hours there and the same back. I found the best way was to leave at 2 or 3 o'clock in the morning of a Saturday. Stay in B & B Saturday night in Norwich and then travel back of a Sunday afternoon ready for work on the Monday. I recall that one early morning, it was still dark, I was approaching Kings Lyn and because the road ran close to the tidal river it had got very foggy and damp. I was kind of crouched down a bit, behind the windshield, peering as best as I could through the aperture that was built into said windscreen. This was designed to aid vision in such meteorlogical conditions. Now I knew this road pretty well. I knew that at the end of a reasonable long straight there was a traffic island. By my timing I reckoned I was getting close to this island so I decided to pop my head up over the windshield for a better view and what a view it was. I was right up the arse end of a lorry. On realising this I sort of yanked myself and my motorised steed to the right of this obstruction only to be met with another lorry coming the other way and only a few feet off. All I can remember is consciously saying to myself "This was it . . . the end." Miraculously, somehow, I came out the other side absolutely unscathed if not a bit shook up. I can remember being able to feel my coat sleeves on both sides being sucked in by each of these lorries. That was a bloody close one . . . AGAIN!! Probably as close as I'd been before, or have been since, to leaving this world in an untimely manner. Before Paula had the baby Frank came home one evening to tell me that a farm a couple of miles up the road was looking for a cowman and the job came with a cottage. So off I went to introduce myself and apply for this job. The position and occupancy of the cottage were granted to me and my forthcoming family. The farm was called Moat House Farm, right opposite the church, at the top of Meriden hill. It was run by the Wood family, along with another farm about four miles away, near Fillongley. The boss was a man called Tony Woods who lived with his wife Monica, their three sons, Clive, Richard and Peter and daughter Carol (the youngest if I remember correctly). This farm at Meriden was where the milking herd and calves were kept.

Tony's mother and his sister Jean, along with her husband John Harrison and two children occupied the other farm, Hayes Hall, at Fillongley. The Fillongley Farm was where the beef cattle were reared and finished along with a good size flock of sheep that were Jean's main concern. Corn and potatoes were also grown there. All the potatoes being riddled and bagged then sold at the door over each winter. I agreed to start work there a week before I got married then go to Norwich on that Saturday and return the next day with wife and child to start work properly on the Monday. Paula had given birth to a little girl that we named Joanne Avril and when I went to Norfolk to see her I couldn't get over, of all things, her little fingernails. I even came back from this visit telling Mrs Woodcock about her little fingernails as if she hadn't seen a baby before. I've never forgotten those little fingernails.

The day of the wedding came, Bobby Daniel was best man, and Donald drove all three of us to Norwich and back again, the same day. I can remember that for a lot of the journey on the way there, I came really close, on more than one occasion, to telling him to turn around and go back but that wouldn't have been the right thing to do.

Everybody was installed at Moat House Farm and off we go. The milking herd was about 100 milkers, plus the dry cows - a pedigree herd. The Janwood Herd that had been built up by Tony, his sister Jean, and their parents. We milked them in an old metal "bail" which was basically a little parlour that stood six cows at a time. It had originally been designed to take to the cows in the field as a semi-permanent fixture rather than taking the cows to it as a permanent structure. They were common in those days and all the milk cooled and then sent away in 12 gallon churns. Not the normal 10 galloners. All these churns were, of course, man-handled on to the lorry at collection time. Now, although I was now a married man I still appreciated a fine example of the female form so I stuck pin-up pictures on the one blank wall of the parlour. Tony and his wife "raised an eyebrow" at this but nothing was said. This "feature" gradually became a bit of a joke and a talking point. Tony was a good boss and a friend really. I visited him and his kids (Monica, his wife, died of cancer at a young age) once or twice a year or whenever I was in the area right up until he sadly passed about ten years ago. The Janwood Herd was a good herd of cattle but my job was to try and make it better which, with Tony's help, we managed to do to a fair extent. The herd's yield was all individually recorded weekly by us and every month by an official recorder from The Milk Marketing Board. This was when milk samples were taken from each individual beast and taken away for analysis. This was all logged, printed out, and a copy sent to the farm for reference. Hence the lifetime's yield of each cow was officially recorded forever. Above a certain yield in a lactation (305 days) and of acceptable quality would be rewarded by the cow being registered on the Register of Merit (R.M) and these initials would be added to her name and registration card. This card was postcard size with blank outlines on each side and head and tail of the beast which had to be filled in with her individual markings, birth date and Dams and Sires names. This stopped any falsification of things in the case of any future sales etc. We managed to clock up a few new R.M's in my time there. This was rewarded by a bonus in my wages. This back then was £40.00 for a 48 hour week, plus, of course, the rent free tied cottage. Couldn't be bad. Especially with Tony because he basically didn't mind what animals I bought, sold or bred at home. This was to me a Godsend because I had, by now, advanced from buying and selling a few chickens with the aid of a motor scooter to larger animals. Goats, sheep, etc. – all manner of things really. Basically if it had hair or feathers it was worth looking at. By now I'd bought us an old car. A "Ford Pop" the old sit up and beg type. It cost me £10.00. taxed and M.O.T.'d. It was a handy old thing because I could take the back seats out and I'd made a frame out of chicken wire and wood which wedged in behind the front seats. I could then open the boot and just put any livestock into the vehicle via this route. When finished as a livestock transporter it was just a case of swilling the back out (there was a rubber bung in the floor) with the hose, putting the rear seats back in again and off you go . . . no problem. All I needed to do now was to pass my driving test which I managed to do on the second attempt. The first attempt I took the test in an old Ford Pop but failed on the hill start. The examiner pulled us up to a standstill on a hill and said "From now on I want you to use hand signals". Problem, how could I release the handbrake, put the motor in gear, steer it and have my right hand out of the window all at the same time? This I found out from my instructor was the oldest trick in the book once the examiner knew you had never had an official lesson. He also told me it was a just a case of holding the motor "on the clutch" to get underway. I took 6 lessons after my initial failure to pass on my first attempt. Second test time now and I passed O.K. In fact I was more concerned with my stammering when it came to answering the Highway Code questions than I was about the actual driving. The examiner was an understanding kind of chap. He suggested that instead of trying to actually "say" things that I should, in a way, try to sing them. Good advice. Thank you Mr Examiner.

Everything going well at work and things at home were O.K. you could say. Paula and I were never "a match made in heaven" but let's try and get on with it and make the best of things. I'd met a chap called Jack Pittaway (through my dealing). He and his family lived in a tied cottage a couple of miles away. He was also known as "Jack Rabbit. A man of smallish proportions and very scruffy. He usually wore an old coat, wellingtons and a flat cap and what seemed to be permanent facial stubble and was not to be judged by appearances. It turned out that he was a National and sometimes International Judge of fancy rabbits and guinea pigs, so he must have smartened himself up at some time or other!! As I said Jack and his crew lived in a tied cottage. A detached place with loads of ground around it. He didn't have a proper shed to house his collection of rabbits and guinea pigs. These were all top of the range exhibition animals don't forget. Instead he'd made four walls with an entrance out of straw bales and put a corrugated tin roof on top held on by lengths of tree wood. No artificial lighting, nothing. You'd wonder how any animal could survive in there never mind thrive. Because thrive is what they did because when he bought any specimen out into the daylight they looked as if he'd been up all night polishing them. Their coats were like glass. I'll never forget seeing them for the first time. I was gobsmacked. When he handled them it was just as if they were almost a part of his body. This is the best way I can think of describing his "One-ness" with his furry little friends. I learned a lot off old Jack. Just little tips he'd learned and tried out over the years. You cannot read experience from a book. Now Jack had two little side lines. The first was selling oats to his fellow fanciers. These oats weren't the normal oats but black oats. An old fashioned cereal that his boss used to grow. Rabbits and guinea pigs thrived on them. You never see them these days. In fact I think the last ones I ever saw were in Jack's hands. He used to "borrow" a few bags full at weekends and sell them to fellow fanciers. His other side line, which I also got into, was selling buck rabbits and guinea pigs to a Mr Barber who, along with his son, supplied the Birmingham Hospital Board with animals for research. The buck rabbits were used for research into Venereal Disease. As long as they'd got big enough bollocks they were acceptable. The guinea pigs were a bit more of a problem because Mr Barber used to breed vast quantities of them and his stock was more or less of a known blood type to the laboratories.

Hence he was only supposed to supply them with his own stock. On occasions when he hadn't been able to keep up with the demand he'd buy "pigs", as they were known, from outside and on one occasion he must have run a bit short of supplies so he got in touch with Jack to find him some more. Most of Jack's stock was too good for this job so we'd buy them from Henley-in-Arden Auctions or where ever else we could find them. We would then sell them on to the Barbers along with any buck rabbits we'd been able to obtain from similar sources. It all earned us a few shillings. Neither Jack, nor his wife or his kids could drive so if the Barbers didn't come out to collect the mainly buck rabbits then I used to take them to Sheldon. This was a couple of miles away from my old secondary school, actually, in old Ford Pop. The first time I went to the Barber establishment was a shock. "Come through to the shed" the old Mr Barber said. SHED!! Some bloody shed!! He'd got an asbestos agricultural type barn in his garden. I say garden, cautiously, and it was full with rows of tiered cages full of guinea pigs. I was gobsmacked to say the least. We had the deal and we stood there chatting but it sounded like rain landing on the roof. I mentioned the fact that it was raining outside and the reply that came from Mr Barber was that it wasn't rain but just the sound of the guinea pigs eating!! I've never seen so many guinea pigs in one place since. Sometimes when I'd come home with whatever animals I'd managed to buy we'd have a look through whatever pretty rabbits or guinea pigs I'd got and keep the few "best" ones for ourselves or the pet shop run by a friend of mine. This was also in Sheldon. On returning home one evening I noticed I'd got a Peruvian Guinea pig. Now this species has extremely long hair that parts down the spine and when being shown is combed out each side of it. This was a stunning little fellow. A creamy fawn in colour and I said to Paula that we'd keep it. He was a weird little chap. Where ever you placed him then it would just sit there, perfectly still. Indeed we put him on the mantelpiece and he just sat there like an ornament!! Stranger still was when you spoke to him. He would look at you sometimes by just moving only his eyes. We didn't keep him. I sold him to my friend with the pet shop and it spent the rest of its life wandering around the premises at liberty entertaining the customers with his quirky ways. Back at the cottage we bred a fair few rabbits, either for pets, or to grow on for meat. We were beginning to run out of decent hutches for them so we placed an advert in the Coventry Evening Telegraph for unwanted rabbit hutches. Collection free. The response was amazing. We were being offered them from all over the place. Tony agreed that he and I would go, one evening, and pick up any that might be of use either to me or him and Monica. She kept and bred poultry and quail so she was always on the lookout for a decent pen or two for any chicks she bred. That all worked out well and we divided what ended up as a lorry full between us. I had my eye on a double tier run of three hutches on top of each other. A really strong weatherproof construction which I put into immediate use for breeding does. Now, because rabbits are a bit averse to jumping down off any decent height then the run of cages on the top tier hardly ever had the fronts closed in warm weather. On this subject Paula and I were in the kitchen and we heard one of the does chattering away very loudly and leaning out of the front of her hutch obviously in some form of stress and anxiety. On inspection it became clear that the youngsters had decided to "shut their eyes and walkabout". They must have run out of floor space until they'd ended upon the ground below the hutch and mother was leaning out, looking at them, and giving them a serious amount of verbal. As I put the youngsters back to her one at a time she smacked each one of them with her front paws and really did give them a good old fashioned scolding. I've never seen anything like that since in a so called "simple animal" but the more time I've spent over the years working with birds and animals the more this kind of behaviour seems to have cropped up.

Bruno, my old dog, was of course still part of the family and by now we'd started to re-home a few unwanted dogs. These, when they had been in residence for a day or two, we'd let them out of their run or off their chain to wander about at will. I've always said a dog will never stray far from a warm bed, a full belly and a bit of love. We never lost any of them. This was no thanks to Bruno because once he could see that any new dog was at liberty he used to stand on top of a piece of raised ground in the field behind the cottage and entice them off "for a walk". They would always go off with him but he always returned on his own wagging his tail and full of himself as if to say "That's got rid of that one (or two or three) but when his new found "friends" eventually returned to the fold he would skulk off and sink into some form of a sulk. He thought he should be the only dog, especially male, that should be in residence obviously . . . Bless his cotton socks!!

The old boy loved his ladies. He'd mate anything that was warm with a hole in it. I used to say that "if you rolled a bottle of warm water down the yard then he'd get it in pup". As usual he'd mated a little collie bitch we had and she decided one night that she'd have her pups in an

96

old chicken ark we had lying about. Now on the night of parturition it snowed, really snowed, and it hung around for weeks. By the time the heavens had dumped their first offering of "the white stuff" a good drift had built up over the ark but the little bitch had just dug an opening big enough for her to get in and out and go to the loo and have a drink. She seemed perfectly happy and settled and we fed her though her "front door". Why bother to move her and her family? It was snug and warm in there. The snow was insulating it really well so we just left her to her own devices – nature's way – I always think. After three or four weeks she emerged with her little family and introduced them to the big world. They were as fat as butter and as sleek as baby seals. Motor Nature knows best!! At times we'd buy the odd dog or two just to sell on again. One evening we came across an advert in the newspaper for some crossbred pups for sale so off we went to have a look with the usual yarn that we wanted a pup and a couple of relatives wanted one as well. By the time we came away we'd bought all of them, about four, if I remember rightly. Anyway we kept them around hoping to sell them locally but without much luck so we decided to advertise them in a different paper. A gentleman arranged to come and have a look. He wanted one for his daughter. No problem, until he turned up. It was the very same man that we'd bought the pups off a few weeks earlier. It turned out that his daughter was so upset when he sold us the pups that he'd decided to find her a replacement. That situation took a bit of wriggling out of may I say. What a small world. He went off happy in the end and everyone ended up happy. I may say that was the only time in all the years before or since that such a situation presented itself.

Paula had a friend who lived a few miles away. They had been nurses together at Father Hudson's Homes and they both came from Norfolk. The friend had met a boy in Coleshill. They had got married and were renting a cottage, as I said, a few miles away. They kept a few chickens and goats and a couple of dogs. Let's just say looking after animals wasn't their strongest point and I noticed that they'd got a black and white collie type bitch tied up down the yard. This bitch was in pup, and thin, very, very, very thin. I'd tried to buy her but to no avail and I was beginning to really worry about her. I told Paula that I was going to go and steal her away from such misery. The dastardly deed accomplished I got her away quietly into the Old Ford Pop. On the way home I popped into old "Brens Cottage". (The older farmer in Coleshill who I've mentioned earlier in this story). He was horrified at the sight of her. He offered her a piece of dry bread about the size of a good tea-cup and it went down whole. You could actually see it going down her neck just like a snake. Now old Bren was an old man, and had spent all his life with cattle, so he'd seen a few things but the sight of this bitch gulping this lump of bread down in such a manner made even him heave his guts. All this happened on a Saturday evening and not long after I'd got her home and fed and settled she started to nest and have her pups. I cannot recall how many there were, but no problem, I'd been thinking about all this so I told Paula that I was going to get the R.S.P.C.A. out in case anyone ever saw her in such a state and thought she was one of ours. Sunday morning and out comes the R.S.P.C.A. "Operative". I've never called them "Inspectors" because I believe that to be an "Inspector" you need to know what you're looking at. Most of them didn't and don't possess such knowledge. I told him that I'd stolen the bitch the previous evening and where I'd stolen her from and that in my opinion he should go and "have a word" if nothing more. This he refused to do because he said that Paula's friend and husband could just plead that they didn't realise she was in pup!! Whatever next!!!. She'd looked like a pot-bellied famine victim when I stole her because that's exactly what she was. He even suggested that

Colette, Joanne, Sam and Naomi - children from my first marriage.

Me with the bull that liked treacle sandwiches:- circa 1967.

if anything like this should happen again that I give the dog a morsel of food, wrapped up in tin foil, because then any food that was in the stomach would be made obvious by the fact that the tin foil would create a reflection off it under an X-ray. That was bad enough but, to cap it all, this very same "Operative" had had a go at me the previous Wednesday in Henley Auctions for carrying chickens by one leg. What a wanker!! By the state of this bitch it was plainly obvious that, no matter what you did for her, she was never going to be able to rear all her pups so I insisted that he took all the pups but one and put them to sleep. This he agreed to do after a lot of persuasion and presentation of the facts before his very eyes. The poor old bitch settled down perfectly well with her baby. She got fat, the pup got fat, the pup was happy, she was happy and they both went on to pastures new. All's well that ends well. I don't think Paula's friend ever knew that happened to that dear old dog.

At work all was going well. Tony and I got on really well. As long as I did my job properly and well then he didn't mind what I did after work. He'd let me use any vacant boxes if I needed anywhere to put any of my own animals. He told a friend of mine, in later years, that he never knew what to expect to find at any given time.   He didn't mind because I eventually turned out to be the best cowman he'd ever had and the only bloke he'd ever seen that the cows went to even in the fields.   So that was a nice thing to hear. Tony used to come out every morning to feed the calves on the bucket and one morning, for some unexplained reason, he'd gone to a loose box that was tucked away in the corner of an old yard. We only used this to store muck in until we could get it out onto the ground. Because this pen was hardly ever used the top half of the stable doors were always left open. Now I'd been out and bought a few Muscovy ducks, drake birds. Now Muscovy ducks can fly and fly really well especially the old drakes. Especially if they'd never had their wing flights clipped and anyway I'd got nowhere ready to put them at the cottage.   We had come back late in the evening with them so I thought I'd just chuck them in this loose box overnight until I could get a place sorted out for them. Anyway, be that as it may, Tony must have noticed that the top half of the loose box was now closed and it was never closed so his curiosity must have got the better of him. He decided to go and have a look. It seems that as soon as he'd got the top door open enough, to have a look over, then these old drakes had got up in the air and were gone… over and around his head. "What the fuckin' hell have you put in there?!" he asked me. "They nearly took my bloody head off" but the offending birds were up and gone never to be seen again. I never put another Muscovy down again before I'd clipped its wings.

Back to my proper job, the cows. As I've said all was going well. They were milking better etc, etc and I loved the cows. Still do to this day, actually, and I can recall that because were a "self- contained herd" and no females were ever bought in we had a family of cows called "MARGARET". Now at this time we had three generations, at least, in the herd. The oldest one, the matriarch of the family, would never leave the yard gate when the rest of the herd went out to graze if one of her daughters or grand-daughters was, for any reason, having to be kept in for any time.   The youngest member of this family was a really big, strong heifer who was so laid back she just seemed to plod through life without exerting any more energy than was absolutely vital. In fact I watched her one hot, sunny, day after she'd come into the main herd to calve and start milking. The field they were grazing in had a single great big old oak tree in it. This cast a shadow on such a day and I noticed that this heifer was following the shadow around so that she could lay down in the shade all day long and just graze near to where her nest place was. One afternoon she was getting near to her time to have her first calf and she didn't come home at milking time with the rest of the herd so I went to look for her. There she was, under her tree in the shade, along with her new baby and, believe it or not, lying there with her was her grandma, the old matriarch Margaret . . . Blood is thicker than water after all. This youngest of the "Margarets" never kicked or showed any kind of malice even the first time she was milked. She never so much as twitched. Anything for a quiet life was her mantra . . . I think. She did milk. In fact on her first lactation she got The Register of Merit. It wasn't often that a heifer did that. According to Tony in later years her female calves were exactly the same as her in temperament and milking ability. She was never surpassed in the herd as a heifer and she was sired by a very special bull through artificial insemination. A bull called Rurick Charon who was held at stud near Stratford-on-Avon by Avoncroft Cattle Breeders. He'd sired good stock before and since. We only used A.I for the few very best of cows because, in those days, most dairy farms kept their own bull on the premises. We were no exception, the only problem with our bull was, although he could throw some good sorts, he was a bit short in the leg department. To serve the cows we'd walk them down a sloped path, let him go behind them and he'd serve them in this way. He was basically on higher ground when it mattered. This all worked well. He knew what was happening. The cows knew what was happening. Then one evening, after milking, he was asked to "perform his manly duties" but for some reason things went wrong. We decided the cow would probably still be "standing" next morning so Tony and I decided to put the bull back in his pen overnight. This didn't go down too well with the fellow to put it mildly. He lived in an old fashioned brick built pen, with a really thick plank door, that was situated between two solid brick pillars at least two feet square. It was held shut by a steel bar that was slotted into two iron fasteners that went right through each pillar and were bolted on the inside. Well, he must have decided that, on this occasion, being penned up so soon after his failed attempt at doing his job wasn't where he wanted to be. He walked to the back of his box, put his head down and walked straight through the front wall, door, pillars and all and stood in the yard letting his opinion be known. Now this was not so much at this time, but definitely in the future, a problem and probably a potentially dangerous problem because he'd learned that he could walk through walls any time he wanted. His future was secured … he was shot in the yard that evening. Unfortunately for him a sad end to his story. In those days, because A.I was on the rise it was considered a bit silly to keep a bull that knew he could be the boss if ever push came to shove. He was replaced by a hand reared bull a photo of him and I together is on display in my living room today. He was a Friesian Bull. Black with white legs and a white splash down his shoulder. He had been "trained" with treacle sandwiches. He would go anywhere for a treacle sandwich and he was as safe as any bull was ever going to be.

After this event had blown over Tony and I were discussing it one day when he told me a story of an event that had happened, in earlier years, on his parent's farm. They apparently ran a Hereford bull with their cows. This was common back then and was no problem until the cows and the bull were at the yard gate waiting to come in for milking. At this time the bull had got into the habit of misbehaving unless there were two people there to let the cows in to be tied up and milked. He'd be shut up for the night in his own pen. If there was only one man in attendance he would have a go at them. Tony relayed to me the story of a certain Sunday afternoon. His family were entertaining visitors in their kitchen when the cowman came to the door to let them know he was at the gate and that he needed company, as usual, to get them in and tied up. Apparently this had become a bit of an unwritten law on the farm. There must always be two people when it came time to let the cows and the bull into the yard. No question about it. Now, apparently, because the family had got visitors, they took a little time before one of them went out to be the ever needed presence at such a time. It soon became apparent that the cowman had got tired of hanging around waiting and decided to do the unthinkable. He let them in on his own. The sight that met the person who had gone out to help him was not nice. Apparently there was a sort of trench that had been "ploughed" by the bull down the earth drive and yard and straight through the cowshed walls with bits and pieces (for want of a better description . . . sorry) of the cowman deposited along its route. It seemed the bull had got him down and just kept pushing him into extinction. The bull had to be put down on site. The silly habit he'd got into, and been allowed to get into, had led to his end. I suppose to read such things in this modern age must seem unexplainable and totally inexcusable but back then things on the land were different. A good many men got seriously injured by cattle, pigs, and horses. It's just how it was back then. Men got injured or killed regularly on farms.

At the front of our cottage we had a fair old piece of land which we fenced off into three different little paddocks. These we used to put mainly goats in or, at one time, a Jacobs sheep. The reason for having this Jacobs ewe was that I had seen, somewhere in the press or on T.V, that in Australia they used to let a billy goat run with the ewes to supposedly keep the dingos etc. away from the flock. Now according to the press, on odd occasions, it seemed that the goat and the sheep had cross-bred. The offspring of which they called either Geeps or Shoats. So in my wisdom I thought we'd try and replicate this wonder of nature. We decided that as Jacobs sheep tended to be a bit more "on the wild side" we'd try and get a couple of them to go with a little English billy goat we'd got. He was a mad headed little sod, with a really nice big pair of back swept horns, and so much curly hair on his forehead that he looked a bit like a burst sofa. Anyway, we found some Jacobs sheep somewhere in Leicestershire so off we go in the old Ford Pop to have a deal with a man. We paid £6.00. each for two Jacob ewes and when talking to the vendor I mentioned that we were going to cross them with a goat. This statement caused much amusement as far as the man was concerned. So much so that he offered us £100.00 for every lamb, or kid, we bred. Couldn't be bad, I thought! We chucked the two ewes in the back of the motor and headed home. On the way we stopped off to show Tony's sister who was well into her sheep and shepherding. She fell in love with one of the ewes so I sold it to her for a few quid more than we'd paid for it. We ended up with just the one ewe to try and breed from. We let the ewe and the billy goat run together and as it was the back end of the year she was soon in season and standing for him. He mated her at least the once but, alas, no pregnancy. I decided to do a bit of research into it all and it turned out that the presumed Geeps or Shoats were probably a "con" as nature had decreed there was a difference in the chromosome content between the two species. Apparently one of them has tear glands or ducts and the other one doesn't. Therefore it was extremely unlikely that any successful breeding between the two would occur. So that was that then! I wasn't going to keep this ewe for another 10 or 12 months to try again so she went off to join her mate with Jean's (Tony's sisters) flock. The Billy goat went on his way. It was worth a try especially for £100 a lamb.

The goat job was a good thing back then because a lot of dog breeders used to like to keep a milking nanny. Goat's milk was good food for rearing any sickly pups. We had a woman pestering us to try and get her a milking nanny for this very reason. We were having trouble finding one but in the past I'd bought one or two goats off a family who had a bit of a smallholding between Balsall Common and Berkswell. I thought

I'd go and give them a try. They were a real old world family. Father, mother and two sons who all looked as if they'd been plucked out of the 1920's or 30's. A proper old fashioned lot but lovely people all the same. Anyway, as luck would have it, they had got a milking nanny with three kids. Off we go to have a look and see if she could be bought at the right money. Now, in the yard they'd got one of those old railway box carriages that seemed to me, on first sight, to contain no more than muck. This muck was four or five feet deep. "She's up there" the lad said "I'll go up and get her". He put a small ladder up, climbed up, and passed me down a big old tri-coloured nanny and her three kids. What a sight she was, to say the least, she'd got feet that were so overgrown, and curled up, Aladdin would have been proud of them as shoes. She was blinking her eyes in the sunlight. She'd obviously been living in her twilight world for quite some time but she wasn't overly thin and had a bag of milk on her that many a Jersey heifer would have been proud of. I bought the old girl but left the three kids where they were. I didn't want the hassle of bottle feeding them if and when I sold their mother. The old nanny loaded in the back of the trusty Ford Pop and off we go home. Home for a good manicure, some fresh air, and fresh grass. The biggest problem we had with this lady was milking her. Her bag was so big that Paula had to lift her back end up off the ground so that we could get a saucepan or similar under her. The first time we milked her she gave almost 9 pints of milk!! That is a hell of a lot of milk for one nanny especially considering that she'd been feeding three kids and where she had been living. She soon got used to her new life and new "footwear" and she bloomed. I passed her on to her new owner, a lady called Jessie Kimbrell, who will feature again in the forthcoming pages of this story. Goats came and goats went, along with rabbits and guinea pig, and a few bits and bobs of poultry and, as always, a few dogs. One late winter or early spring we seemed to have "collected" a few too many goats and it was a stretch to accommodate them all during the day. Night time was a bit easier because we'd just bring them in and feed and house them inside. Directly opposite the farm was Meriden church and graveyard. This graveyard looked to me to be very unkempt if not overgrown in places . . . great stuff! Plenty of food and grazing for the goats in there. We proceeded to stake out and tether maybe up to 4 or 6 goats at any one time in there. This caused Tony to "raise an eyebrow" shall we say. All seemed to go without much problem until the weather got a bit sunnier and people started to attend and tidy up any grave relevant to them. Now "the shit hit the fan". The sight of a few goats tied up in hallowed ground, and goat kids jumping on and off gravestones, didn't go down too well with those concerned even though my ruminant charges had tidied the place up. No more overgrown areas to say the least. Next thing you know a visit from the vicar. Now I am a total atheist so no amount of "God bothering" troubled me. The church's heavy brigade was also wheeled in - some Deacon or somebody? I didn't really know who he was but I knew he lived in his "tied cottage!" No better than ours and further down the lane. He started to come the old high and mighty with me so I just asked him if it was his land to which he replied that it was. I then asked him if he owned it to which he replied that yes he did. So I then asked him if he'd actually bought it and, if so, then could I see the deeds to which he said that he hadn't so I just told him to piss off until he had. This didn't go down too well. He went to see Tony about it all and asked him if he realised that his cowman was a "non-Christian" to which Tony replied that he didn't really care as long as I did my job properly. Anyway, when push came to shove it was decided that I could tether the goats up in the churchyard as long as they didn't trespass on any graves. All's well that ends well!

Paula was now pregnant again. I blamed the Catholic Church. She was a Catholic so contraception was a big "No, No", and so the baby was due. The time came for the birth and she was admitted to Marston Green Maternity Hospital. As we were going in for the confinement who was coming out? No other person than Lin! (She of the long legs and long hair). It seems like she'd got herself pregnant and married – Snap – and she'd just given birth to a little girl - one week earlier. Our new baby arrived, another little girl, and she was little, very little, weighing in at just under 3 lbs. She thrived and we named her Colette but her nickname was "inch" because she was so small but what a bundle of spirit she was. Frank and I used to toss her to each other (in safe surroundings) and we'd do it in such a way that she'd do a somersault in mid-air. She thought all this was great fun but, the little bugger had got a mind of her own. She still has actually. Most nights she'd start to cry and wouldn't stop until she was picked up. She hadn't got wind, she wasn't hungry, she just wanted attention, I suppose. Once she'd been picked up the crying stopped and a big grin would appear on her little face as if to say "I've won". This habit of hers was beginning to get a bit out of hand. Every night the same. I was getting up every morning for work well before 5 a.m. so this play acting was beginning to wear a bit thin after a while. I said to Paula that enough was enough. Colette wasn't ill or hungry or anything so she's going to have to get on with it. I took her downstairs in her carrycot. At times she'd have a bit of a tantrum if she didn't get her own way so I made her secure enough, so that she couldn't come to any harm, and I let her cry herself to sleep. We only had to do this once and the problem was solved. She leant that she couldn't always get her own way and sleepless nights were no more than a memory. Bless her little heart.

In those days farm workers were expected to take any annual holiday in the slack time. This was usually the few weeks between haymaking and combining. When the time arrived we decided to put ourselves and the two girls in the old Ford Pop and go to Barmouth, just on a whim, nothing booked or anything like that. Just get in and go. Tony and his wife had agreed to keep an eye on our livestock. I used to do the same for them when they went on holiday because Monica's hobby was keeping chickens and quail. To move on we got to Barmouth, had a good look round at the places that Grand-dad had taken me to as a child, and stayed a couple of days. All of us sleeping in the car. When I just said "Sod it, we'll go and see your Mom and Dad for a couple of days" We drove from the Welsh coast to the Norfolk coast, in one go, in the old Ford Pop. The maximum speed was a mind boggling 40 m.p.h. While in Norfolk the old motor had begun to get a bit temperamental engine wise. It seemed that as soon as you took your foot right off the throttle the revs went down and then it would stall. It was a nightmare to get it started again. A case of me winding it over with the starting handle while Paula sat with her foot on the throttle. Basically it was a case of working both the clutch and the brake with the left foot so that the right foot could permanently keep enough revs to avoid the engine stalling. Now that's all very well, not a real problem, until the A47. The main road between the Midlands and Norfolk had to go through Leicester where it became the Inner Ring Road. Now the Inner Ring Road seemed to have traffic lights every couple of hundred yards. In fact it was known for it at the time. This fact became a bit of a problem, in our mechanical circumstances, but we did manage to negotiate our way through. In the past this could sometimes take up to an hour, even on a good day, and with a reliable vehicle. On this day we eventually arrived back home all safe and sound but with the thoughts of replacing the old, long suffering, Ford Pop with a more reliable and roomy vehicle. As we had now got the two girls the rear of the vehicle was really needed for more family orientated tasks. In other words . . . livestock out and kids in!! The old "Pop" was replaced by a Ford 7 cwt van. It was bigger but that's about all. It wasn't one of the most favourite vehicles

I've ever owned but it did its job. More room in the back. Room for the kids and any animal passengers all at the same time. This was good because on the odd evening in Spring and Summer we'd have a ride around local farms and smallholdings looking to buy and sometimes sell anything that was covered in fur or feathers and wasn't too big to get in the motor. On one such occasion it had come to our attention that some chap, somewhere, I can't remember who or where, had got two Billy Goats for sale so off we trot. All four of us to go and try and have a deal with this man. On arrival the man greets us and asks that if we buy the two goats off him then how were we going to get them home. He said that our van wasn't big enough. I poo-poo-ed this suggestion saying that I'd had plenty of goats in there but on seeing them he was right. I've never, before or since, seen such tall goats but it was agreed that we could get them in by kneeling them down. The deal was done. They were now ours, like it or not. So it was a case of going back a couple of days later with an empty vehicle and picking them up. They really were big old goats. The one wasn't looking too happy with himself at the time. Sadly a few days later he popped his clogs. He was a really dark mahogany colour. Not quite black so I decided to have him skinned. Bobby's twin brother Ronnie, being a butcher, came out to skin him. He could be guaranteed to make a good job of it because I wanted to get the hide cured and made into a rug. When Ron came to skin him he asked me if I had got a bike pump ... of all things. I had got one and I queried why he needed it so he showed me. He made a small nick in the goat's navel, inserted the pump, and blew it up. This separated the skin from the flesh and could be removed easily and best of all with little risk of damaging it. Job done! I'd soon have a goatskin rug and the dogs dined on goat meat for a while. That was, and is, the only goat I ever had die on me. During our travels, in any spare time we had available, we called on a farm near Tamworth. A place called Ashlands Farm on the Ashby Road. This place was run by a man called Eric Ball. A really small man. Probably no more than 5' 3" tall who always wore a flat cap, hobnail boots and leather gaiters. His wife was Dorothy, who had a bit of a hunchback and cackled like an old witch, but had a nice kind way about her. There was also her father, an old man called Mr Simpson, and their son John, a youngster in his late teens who had his fingers into everything. A bit like me really. They had dogs, chickens, ducks, goats and a few pigs as well as the dairy herd which was the mainstay of the whole enterprise. After a while they realised, as far as dairy cows went, that I was pretty good at the job. They were always trying to get me to go and work for them but they had no accommodation available. They'd rented out their tied cottage. Because I had a wife and two children, and one of them only a baby, and I was very happy working for Tony, I always declined their offer.   The buildings on their farm included two runs of brick built pig pens and runs. About a dozen of them. Six each side of a central aisle and all contained within a building of their own. They'd obviously given up on the pig job because they only had four pork sized animals left. These I bought off them and sold to the same butcher who had bought my plucked chickens from me.   Young John Ball had converted all the pig pens to house dogs but he couldn't really get on with dog breeding. Over the years I bought them all off him in ones and twos. I recall buying a pair of fawn coloured Pugs. The only pugs I've ever owned. I remember paying £7.00. each for them - a dog and a bitch. I put them in the motor and they immediately shit all over the place. Talk about snort!! They sounded like two pigs in a deep slumber snoring their heads off continuously the first night. With them at home was more than enough. We kept them in the house due to the lack of anywhere suitable for them outside. One night of them was enough. I said to Paula that they'd got to go - so off they went. I sold them to Jessie Kimbell for £40. So that was O.K. She had good kennels outside so, to her, their incessant snorting was no problem. Indeed she did well with them I recall. Previous to the Pugs I'd sold Jessie a little "Jack Russell" pup that I'd bought from a man called Bert Southall who was well known in the area for his terriers. Always small bold little dogs. I'd bought this pup, along with the rest of the litter, and had rehomed them all except this little chap. He was extremely small but a strong little chap all the same. Now Jessie's husband, also called Bert, was a big hunting man and he liked his terriers but he didn't like this one. So far as I was concerned I'd had a deal with his wife and not him. He used to have a go at me about it every time I went there. It eventually became a bit boring. I arrived at their place one day and off he went again, as I thought, but he didn't moan. He just asked me where I'd got the dog. I told him that I couldn't remember. Of course I could but I didn't want him sniffing around Bert Southall. I asked him why he wanted to know. His reply was "Best little terrier I've ever had". Just goes to show! Don't judge a book by its cover! I'd already sold this little dog's sister to a friend of mine. The friend was one of our group in the teenage years. This little bitch was also very small but, as was not uncommon in small terriers back then, was black and tan. He called her "inch war" partly after our Colette and I think partly after a T.V. advert that was running about this time. He had her all her life and loved her to pieces.

Back at Ashlands Farm I was in the house paying for whatever I'd bought. I'd had all the dogs over time, except one, an old Lassie Collie dog called Tibby. He lived permanently tied up on the corner of a Dutch barn where they'd left a space in the bales as a kennel for him. He'd been there all the time that I'd ever visited and I'd never seen him loose. I asked if I could buy him as well as he was the last one. After a bit of "umming and aarhing" he was mine. I paid £2.00 for him. Probably the best £2.00 I'd ever spent up until then. He was a lovely dog. A proper "Old fashioned" Lassie Collie and well bred. He came with his pedigree but unfortunately he was blind but once he knew his surroundings this never bothered him at all. His main problem was that he was a bad feeder "a picker" of his food. This, in the years to come, I discovered was a bit of a trait in the breed. In fact years after I'd had him, and I kept him all his life, I mentioned to a vet who was on the farm one day about this "picking at his food" habit and I asked the old Vet to run his hands over him "Nothing wrong with him Nick. Put it like this if he was a rabbit he'd be a fat rabbit". End of story and worries. As I said we kept old "Tibby" all of his life. We used him as a stud at odd times with both Border Collies and Old English Sheepdogs. Sometimes he'd come with me to get the cows in and although he couldn't see them, he could hear them. He'd stand still, listen, and when he could hear that there were none behind him he'd walk up and down barking. Then he'd stop, listen again, wait until he could hear that all the cows were in front of him and repeat the process. Funnily enough I'd mentioned to the vet that he was blind and he said better to be totally blind than half-blind because when they're only half blind they tend to see a shadow on the ground, try to walk around it, and in doing so very often walk into whatever was casting the shadow in the first place. Old Tibby was a wonderful old dog and he did us proud over the years.

Back at work Tony had decided to have a new parlour put in. To go off the churns and onto a bulk-tank with all "mod cons". Before all this could be put into operation the whole set up had to be approved and inspected on health and hygiene grounds. This approval was all down to the opinion and acceptance of an inspector. The inspector for our area was an old spinster in her 60's a Miss Smith (she who must be obeyed). A dumpy old maid who wore a tweed skirt and jacket. A Miss Marple type of character. She'd been doing this job for years and had got a terrible reputation for being a stickler for the rules. If she was upset she could be an awkward old bugger. Not long before her visit was due she'd been called to a farm near Hampton-in-Arden to approve a new set up there. This farm was run by two bachelors, Styles and Healy. They lived together on the premises and apparently these two lads had been giving Miss Smith a bit of grief in the past before she'd finally approved the place. That wasn't the end of it. She turned up for the first morning milking and pulled the boys up for wearing dirty clothes and told them that they couldn't start before they'd been and changed at least their milking gowns. Now being bachelors, laundry was not on the top of their list of priorities. They were unable to conform to her standards. She did no more than sit in her vehicle in the yard until such time that the shops had opened and the boys could themselves acquire some clean attire. The old cow had the last word!! I'd been working for Tony for long enough by now for him to realise that officialdom and I didn't make the best of bedfellows to say the least. He decided that when the time came for the dreaded yay or nay inspection from Miss Smith then it might be better if I stayed in the background just in case the "old bird" duly arrived and went round the place with a magnifying glass and fine tooth comb. Well that's what it seemed like anyway. She agreed to sign all the relevant paperwork on the agreement that wire mesh screens be fitted over all opening windows and drains. Tony breathed a sigh of relief. He was in the yard chatting with "Miss Marple" during which time a cow had started to calve in one of the loose boxes so I went in to give her a hand. Calf safely delivered. Miss Smith, who was by now watching over the door with Tony, said that she'd never seen a calf born before and remarked how well developed they were at birth. I couldn't resist it. She'd signed all the papers now. So I just replied "Yes, eyes open, all its teeth in place and more brains than you'll have if you live to be 200!!" Tony turned a nice shade of beetroot red and diplomatically called it a done deal. Time to get the new set-up off and up and running.

The new parlour was a metal portable milking bail but fixed permanently in one place. Standings were put in which meant that the cows now stood about 18" off the floor at milking time. This made them more accessible if the need arose. This milking bail was constructed of a galvanized box frame covered in thin galvanized steel sheet. No problem with that. The problem was that the exit door, from each standing, was only held in place by small hinges that were pop-riveted in place. A handle that ran the full length of the stall was used to open and shut the doors. Problem was with this set up was when an individual beast decided she'd been in there long enough. The odd one would have eaten all her food and she would butt the bottom of the door and slightly bend it outwards. This was as far as it ever went except for one beast, a heifer, a bit of a nutter who didn't want anything to do with anything when she first came in. She didn't stop at butting the door. She just forced herself through it and off she'd go. The damage to the door was bad enough. In addition, as she pushed it open, the handle used for operating it would fly up and smash the glass tubing that the milk ran through into the dairy. In the end it came to the point that we'd leave a standing empty for her but before we let her in we'd back a tractor up against the exit door and that stopped her antics. As soon as she learnt that she was wasting her time and energy trying to liberate herself then she came to her senses. She behaved herself thereafter but she'd done some damage in the process of getting there. Bulk milk tanks were not common at this time and their biggest let downs were three fold. Number one, you could do the milking and then discover that you'd left the pipe from the parlour to the tank out of the tank. Any milk, up until this fact was discovered, just went down the drain. Even today, all these years later, I still have nightmares about "leaving the pipe out". It did happen once, just once and this was at Tony's place. I'd finished milking one afternoon, went from the parlour to the dairy to start washing up, to be greeted by a white floor. Tony wasn't happy. His remark was that "We'll have some fat rats now, just be careful". Enough said. It was easily done which Tony would find out for himself, at a later date, because the second let down was doing the washing up and leaving the pipe in the tank. This meant that all the water that was circulating the system ended up in the tank with the milk. We had gone onto a hot acid method of circulation cleaning. This was all the rage at the time. This involved, the system being rinsed through with cold water, then boiling hot water, that had been infused automatically with acid, would be circulated as a cleaning agent for a set amount of time. This was then automatically released through the milk discharge pipe and then be rinsed out again with fresh water. Tony managed (on my day off) to complete this sequence with the discharge pipe still in the tank. A total loss again but this time the other way round. "Easily done Tony" was my response to this event . . . time to call it quits!! The third let down with this system was that if you were not careful and you let the milk into the tank from a cow that, for one reason or another, was receiving any anti-biotic then there was trouble. Once it was in the tank you couldn't get it out again. This wasn't a massive problem as long as you realised what you'd done and as long as the tanker driver wasn't on his day for sampling. Each farmer's milk was individually taken back to the labs for analysis. If you were unlucky enough for your mistake to coincide with sample day then the usual way out of the situation was to make the drivers time worthwhile. He would accidently "drop" your sample bottle rather than you be fined and the worth of 24 hours milk production subtracted from the monthly milk cheque.

Teething troubles with the new parlour and set up were over. Everything was going well. It was quicker and easier, until the first winter when a "one off" problem reared its ugly head. Not so much with the set up, but more with the collecting yard. This is where the cows waited to come into the parlour. What seemed to have been overlooked was the fact that in the fence on one side of the yard, a small narrow, almost garden gate, had been put in to allow easy access into the yard from the back of the parlour. It literally was an old wooden garden gate, held up by string, a few nails, and a lot of will power. Anyway, one really wet Sunday afternoon I was milking away as normal but when I opened the door of the parlour to let some cows in nothing happened. Seemed like nobody wanted to play this afternoon. I looked out of the door… not a beast in sight anywhere. There was the remains of the aforementioned little wooden gate, just wide enough for the cows to get through in single file. It seemed the girls had got fed up standing around in the rain and decided amongst themselves to go walkabout. Not such a big problem in itself. The problem arose when, after liberating themselves, they'd decided to go and "do a bit of gardening" in the garden of a lady called Mrs Poutney who lived on the other side of the lane. The "gardening" idea was bad enough in itself but Mrs Poutney's back lawn was made up of Westmoreland Turf. The most expensive turf available at the time. It was actually more commonly used for bowling greens apparently. Well after 30 or 40 cows, full of the joys of spring, had taken a somewhat over the top excursion around her grounds her Westmoreland Turf landscape, complete with its flower borders and small orchard, looked more like a crazy golf course after a whirlwind. It had been raining permanently for the previous few days and because of the sheer joy and exuberance being demonstrated by our bovine charges the "footprints" they left behind more than resembled small grenade craters. Mrs P. was not a happy lady to say the least.

The big foot and mouth outbreak was doing the rounds at this time so obviously a very keen and wary eye was kept on the ladies because they were still out during the day grazing on kale. When it was time for them to come in for milking in the afternoon we arranged things so that they could only enter the yard in single file. This was because it was easier to look at each beast individually. All was O.K. for while but one afternoon I noticed that one of the ladies was walking as if her feet were a bit tender and drooling from the mouth . . . shit and double shit . . . I immediately found Tony and told him what I'd seen. On receiving this news every drop of colour drained from his face. He stood there as white as a sheet. Don't forget this herd had been built up by his family over at least two generations. By him, Jean, their parents and I think their grandparents. He phoned Jean and the vet. Jean arrived in the same state as Tony and the vet not long afterwards. On studying the cow in question the vet diagnosed kale poisoning and not the dreaded foot and mouth. He informed us that the symptoms of both these problems were basically the same except that in one of them (I cannot recall which now) the beast grinds its teeth and in the other it slaps its tongue and cheek. "Slaps its clops" were his exact words . . . disaster avoided. The kale poisoning problem was soon rectified. She obviously loved the stuff and had gorged herself on it. No more kale for her then. She'd have to stay in during the day now.

The vets Tony used were a firm of two really old fashioned farm vets. None of this poncing about in a white coat crowing about how many degrees they'd got and all that crap. Not like today. They were just two good old fashioned country vets who'd seen it all and didn't mind "bending the rules" from time to time. This fact became clear after we had a cow that needed a caesarean. Not a common thing back then. As we were a bit short of loose boxes at the time it was decided that the best place for her was to go back to the surgery for this procedure. The surgery was situated on a farm with plenty of empty accommodation and both vets lived on site. The operation went well. A good strong calf entered the world who, after a couple of days with its mother, was brought back home to be reared on the bucket along with all the others. Ned (one of the vets) thought it best that the cow should stay where she was for a couple of days just to make sure her wound didn't open up again. They would milk her there. That was all O.K. except that no message came from the vets to say that all was O.K. and she could come home. This situation prevailed for about a week so Tony rang up to enquire about the situation. He was told that she'd ripped her wound open and they'd had to put that right. In their opinion it was best she stayed where she was for another few days. This scenario was repeated a couple more times, with different reasons, for it being best if she stayed where she was for a bit longer. By now Tony's curiosity about what was going on got the better of him so he decided to go and have a look for himself. On arriving at the premises he was greeted by a red faced Irish Veterinarian and duly led off to have a look at his cow. There she was, as right as nine pence, no sign of the scar but had two calves suckling off her. It turned out that the vets, who kept their own cattle, had got a couple of calves about and they thought it would be easier to stick them both on our cow instead of trying to get them on the bucket. It was all done in the best possible taste and no harsh words were exchanged. I presumed that the bill for the operation was deemed null and void and it was all forgotten about.

The other "iron in the fire" of the management team of Woods Farms was Jean's husband. A man called John Harrison. Not my favourite person in the world. Before he married Jean he was an agricultural mechanic and apparently a very good one. I watched him at one time dismantling a tractor and it seemed he could do it with his eyes shut almost, but, as far as I was concerned that's all he could do. However, he did like to throw his weight about at times. An example of this came to pass one really cold, snowy, winter's morning. At their farm they employed two people. An old single man from Cheshire called Ted and a young lad called Colin. Now Colin wore the really old type "bottle bottom" glasses and, without these, he was basically as blind as a bat. He was only a young a lad in his early teens who lived 3 or 4 miles away and cycled to and from work every day. However on this particular morning it seemed he'd fallen off his bike on the snow and ice and damaged his optical accessories. He had to get off his bike and push it the rest of the way to work. It must have been a good couple of miles at least. Anyway, on arrival at the farm his hands had frozen, through his gloves, onto the handlebars. We had to pour warm water on them to free him from his predicament. John Harrison never said a word to him until such time as we were all in the barn potato riddling. Then he started to try and show the poor lad up in front of everyone else. Colin did no more than turn around look John straight in the eye and say "Excuse me Mr Harrison but I was at work before you this morning and you've only got to walk across the yard". That shut him up. Well done young Colin!!

John and I rarely saw a lot of each other but it came to pass that I was up at his place one morning, after breakfast, for what was supposed to be for a couple of hours until dinnertime. At the time we'd got a sick calf back at home and it was time for me to go off early and see to it.

114

This didn't go well with Harrison. He started blabbing off at me saying there was no need for me to go early to tend to the calf. That didn't go down too well with me. I told him that he didn't know what he was on about. That he'd never reared a calf in his life and to concentrate on what he could do . . . his mechanics and furthermore "That I could be King if I was shagging The Queen" and off I drove. He must have gone directly to the phone and reported to Tony, the big boss, that I had been insubordinate to him because when I got back home Tony came rushing out to enquire what I'd said to John. I explained to him the whys and wherefores and told him exactly what I'd said to John that "I could be King if I was shagging the Queen". The matter was never mentioned again but Harrison and I never talked to each other again . . . The jumped up Twerp! Get back to your tractors and go and play".

The only people employed at Woods Farms (Meriden) Ltd were myself at Moat House Farm with Tony and young Colin and an old boy called Ted at Hayes Hall Farm with Jean and John. Old Ted was a "died in the wool" bachelor in his mid 50's. He originated from Cheshire. He lived in his tied cottage which was basically a one up one down dwelling in a stand alone, round tower, type of a building. Hence its name "The Round House". Now old Ted had two or three side lines dealing in eggs, wood shavings and baler string. He collected all the sisal string off the bales but only if the knots were at one end and nowhere in between. This he sold for linoleum backing. He had two main habits. The first was taking snuff in copious quantities and the second was taking his own teeth out. He did this by constantly waggling at any of his teeth he targeted. He said that in the end the constant waggling loosened the tooth enough for him to pull it out. You'd often see him with a finger and thumb stuck into his mouth. I can recall one time when he and I were mucking out some loose box or other his fingers were covered in muck. In they went for a quick waggle on and off all day long. I asked him why he took snuff rather than smoking. He said that when he was a lad in Cheshire the first thing any employer asked was if you smoked or not and if you did then you didn't get the job because of the fire risk. Hence the snuff . . . Sensible!!

During busy times, bale carting, potato harvesting and riddling, we were joined by a chap called Alfie Bourne, another bachelor man, whose main love in life was fox-hunting. He was employed by a local hunt to control the foxes in such a way as for there to be just the right amount of them on this particular hunt. If they were in short supply any year then his job was to go onto the adjoining hunt, dig up cubs and put them down on this hunt's ground. After he'd been doing this for 25 years he was presented with a brand new chromium plated spade. That was his pride and joy!! He and I often worked as a pair at bale carting time. Just using pitchforks. John Harrison, in his usual "up himself" manner bet us two that he could get a load on quicker than us, on his own, using a mechanical loader. No chance mate!! We beat him hands down. He hadn't come to terms with the fact that as soon as he'd loaded the stacks (6 or 8 bales) on to the trailer, he'd got to get off the loader, get on to the trailer to re-stack everything, get off the trailer and move it, and then walk back to the loader and so on. Of course, the higher the load got the longer each round of manoeuvres took. Whereas Alfie and I, even though we were only loading the bales one at a time, because one of us was permanently on the ground pitching the bales up and moving the trailer, and the other one of us stayed on the load at all times, it was a piece of piss to put Mr Harrison back in his box.

Sometimes on a day off Paula and I and the girls would nip over to Coleshill and visit the Daniels family. Indeed the youngest girl Karen would babysit for us from time to time. Every now and then we'd bump into Lin and her daughter who she'd called Mandy. She'd still got those long legs and long hair. I was chatting to Bobby whilst there one day and he asked me if I could get him a Lurcher. Two or three of the brothers had got into hunting with dogs by this time. To cut a long story short I'd heard of a bloke somewhere in Oxfordshire who had got some nice whippet crosses for sale. One evening after work we got in the motor (by now a Morris Shooting Brake with a split windscreen – very desirable) It was easier to move the goats in this vehicle. I'd screwed hooks into the wooden body framework thus enabling me to tie the goats up. At a push I could get six of them in head to tail. Off we went to look at these pups. Arriving at the place I saw a face I recognised. Seems I and this chap had met in the past. Anyway, I bought a little fawn coloured bitch pup and duly delivered it to the Daniel household. Bobby was over the moon with her. He called her Jill. I always said he named her after his first lady love. He kept her all her life and bred one or two nice litters from her. He always reckons, to this day, that she was a dog in a million but then again he was biased in his opinion I suppose.

As I've mentioned already we quite often went to Henley-in-Arden livestock sales on a Wednesday and sometimes to the monthly horse

116

sale at the same place. Now on our journey there we used to pass The Trumpet House Donkey Farm at Claverdon. Over time I'd noticed that these premises were gradually undergoing a process of being "tarted and tidied up" and in the end donkeys started to appear there again. It had, in the past, been allowed to run down ...."Mmmm" I thought why? Is the donkey job picking up again? Seemed like it was so on seeing two donkeys for sale in the Coventry evening paper I went to have a look. They were only about 5 miles away at a place called Corley. It was a Saturday evening. The lady wanted £30.00. each for them. She had two. One Jenny and one really big Jack donkey. I bought the Jenny. Donald took it home for me in his lorry. All was well until about 11 o'clock that evening. The phone went and on answering it the lady on the other end was in a bit of a panic. It was the very lady I had bought the Jenny off earlier that evening. It seems that since being separated from his lady the Jack donkey was a bit upset braying his head off constantly and her neighbours were not amused. By now it was revealed that they'd lived together for years and he was not happy about his wife being taken away. So, although I didn't really want the Jack donkey, I could see that civil war was about to erupt in Corley if nothing was done. I agreed to give the lady £15.00. for him and come and get him immediately. That meant getting Donald out of bed and into his lorry. Off we went and the deal was done. I was now the proud owner of a very peaceful pair of donkeys. We decided to sell them straight away. After placing an advert in a different newspaper I had a call from a farmer's wife in Maxstoke called Mrs Gould. I'd bitten my lip and told her a "little white lie" that as far as I knew the Jenny was in foal. Was she or wasn't she? How should I know? The deal was done and, on her approval at seeing them, they'd be hers for 95 guineas. Now I'd only paid £45.00. for them. So it turned out I'd earned over a week's wages in one deal but for years I steered clear of the Gould farm just in case the Jenny hadn't been in foal.

Tony's sister Jean kept a donkey which she used as a pack animal in the winter to help her with feeding her sheep. Now this donkey was a proper nasty piece of work. It hated everyone and everything with a vengeance but he really loved Jean. Now her son Derek was a boy scout and one year it was decided that a sort of scout jamboree would be held at their place. To help attract visitors a Donkey Derby was booked for the event. This involved a chap turning up with half a dozen donkeys and some jockey's silks and all the tack. The only problem was that Jean's donkey was more than aggravated by all of this and was letting his feelings and his temper be known to all of those present. He really was "on one" On seeing this the owner of the Donkey Derby was almost begging Jean to sell him her beloved pack animal which she refused to do a point blank. It seems that an animal with such a temperament was well sought after in the Donkey Derby world as an extra attraction. The idea was that one of their staff, an accomplished jockey, would ride this beast and, of course, it would play up at such a time and this apparently was a good crowd pleaser. Jean's donkey never left the place until he went to the big Donkey Sanctuary in the sky.

When we could get a babysitter, and if we had time, we'd go back to Coleshill of an evening when any dance was on. This wasn't really a very good idea . . . too many pretty girls about . . . say no more!! Pretty girls were at that time still a bit of a problem for me. I liked them too much really and they seemed to be attracted to me. Such a scenario arose one afternoon at work. Mrs Poutney (she whose garden had been "re-designed" by a few of our cows that past wet Sunday afternoon) had a daughter. Her name was Susan. She was a pretty young lady about 18 or 19 years old and she'd often come and hang around in the parlour when I was milking. It wasn't my fault. This habit of hers hadn't come to Paula's attention at all, but one afternoon I was doing something down the fields on a tractor. This young lady must have noticed where I was and was sitting on the mudguard of the tractor while I was doing whatever I was doing. No problem until Paula came down to give me a message or something only to be greeted by the sight of this very attractive young lady sitting on the mudguard of the tractor less than a foot away from her husband. This didn't go down well needless to say . . . Women eh!!!

Back with the cows. I seemed to have found my forte and word was apparently getting around that I was becoming pretty good at the job. So much so that one afternoon I was milking and a neighbouring dairy farmer called Dick Beatty came into the parlour and basically offered me a similar position to that I had at Tonys but with more money. I said I'd think about it and as Mr Beatty was going out through the door Tony was coming in . . . Oops! Obviously Tony asked what he'd come to see me for so I told him. He'd come to offer me a job but with more money. On hearing this Tony went off and phoned Jean. He came back and matched Beatty's wage offer. He said to me "I can't stop you going but take it from me you two won't get on. You're both temperamental fiery sods. You'll probably end up killing each other but it's your decision". I decided to stay where I was for now. "For now" being the operative phrase. With everything else that I was managing to cram into my life (today I think back and wonder how it all fitted in, family, work, buying and selling etc). I would still stay up some nights to draw and paint. I recall painting pictures for Tony's kids. Indeed on visiting the family some 40 years later his daughter Carol told me she'd still got the picture I'd done for her. Indeed she showed it to me. It was a bit the worse for wear but still in one piece and recognisable. I thought that was nice. On one such evening I was sat up doing a bit of artwork when a film came on T.V. called "Cathy Come Home" and it frightened me to death. To those who haven't seen it then it's basically the story of a young married couple who started off with everything and through no fault of their own ended up losing everything, their home and their children. They ended up living on the street and the children put into care. Now I'd got two young children asleep upstairs and I didn't want to end up like the couple in the film so I just calmed down by telling myself that as long as I kept working as hard, and as long as I could, then I'd be able to overcome any problems that may arise in the future. I can remember that, at the time, this film caused a national and governmental awakening to the "unseen" homelessness of the time. I know it made me sit up and think and I've never forgotten it or the effect it had on me at the time.

Things were going well at Moat House Farm but my restless nature began to rear its head. Time to look for new horizons and new challenges. On these grounds we managed to get the tenancy of an empty tied cottage at Bickenhill near to what is now the N.E.C. It had a massive garden, plus a small paddock, that just needed fencing in. It had acres and acres of unused barren land that had been set aside to accommodate certain sections of the yet to be built N.E.C. That meant plenty of free grazing for the goats. The agreement, as far as the cottage was concerned, was that we could live there rent free as long as I did the milking every weekend (a very small herd still milked in cowsheds with bucket units). The landlord was a man called Bill Wardle who just seemed to plod on in his own little way. A nice enough chap all the same. Across the lane from us was a pig farm that belonged to the family of one of our group of lads from years earlier, Vince McCrilly, his father (also Vince) and his brother. They fattened pigs for bacon. All "swill fed" pigs which meant that they had a massive steel tank filled with swill that would be bubbling away 24 hours a day. Then at the top of the lane there was a big black and white farmhouse and buildings which belonged to a man called Bob Hadley, his wife Susan and kids Robert and Archie. They had a pet shop near my old school at Sheldon and Sue also groomed dogs. Bob, being an ex-police dog trainer also ran dog-training classes. I can recall the first time I went into their house I saw they had a tame, well tame-ish, monkey known as Lawrence and a cat that lived up the chimney of all places . . . hence its name Sweep! More of Bob later. After getting settled in our new abode I began "relief milking" which entailed going on to a farm and doing the cows for anyone without a permanent man for any reason. This worked out well because it allowed me time to carry on doing a bit of buying and selling as in the past. I was milking for a family that I'd known for a while, an old Welsh woman called Maggie Jones, who could, and did, swear worse than anyone I'd ever met before or have met since. I mean I can swear but she made me look like an amateur. She never swore in a "bad or offensive" way. It was just part of her normal vocabulary and everyone knew it so it just went unnoticed really. Her daughter, a middle aged women, called Jenny Harris who farmed a couple of miles away, was definitely a "chip off the old block" as far as questionable expletives were concerned. She wasn't quite as bad as her mom. Everything was working well and running smoothly with this arrangement. I'd milk there twice a day and in between times carry on with our goats, dogs and poultry etc. I'd got home one evening, sat down, having food, when a knock came on the door. It was Tony's wife Monica from Moat House Farm. Apparently there had been a fatal accident with the potato harvester up at Hayes Hall and a young lad had been killed. He had fallen off the tractor and gone through the harvester. Naturally Tony and all the family were beside themselves with grief but it hit Tony really badly and he was in no fit state to carry on his normal work. Now since I'd left he'd been doing the milking but obviously at such a time this was out of the question, for a while, until he could get himself together a bit. Monica asked if I could go and do the milking, just the milking, the rest could be done by others. I explained to Monica that she'd come at a bad time because I was already working for old Maggie Jones but if it was O.K. then I would go and milk Tony's cows at about 3 or 4 o'clock in the morning, then go on to Maggie's, then go back to Tony's about 2 o'clock in the afternoon do his cows and then go back to Maggie's and milk hers. A bit hectic for a few weeks but it was necessary. It seemed odd to me that Tony paid me more per week for just doing the milking than he did for working there full-time. I was leaving there one afternoon when who should come into the yard but Jean's husband, John Harrison. He'd never spoken to me since I'd put him in his place months before. He didn't speak to me on this occasion either, not even a thank

120

you for giving the farm a hand when they were in trouble. But there you go I suppose he always was up himself, but he couldn't milk cows could he? . . . the wally!!

While I was milking for Maggie Jones young Colin from Hayes Hall Farm got in touch with me to say that his mom had gone out and bought a black Cocker Spaniel bitch puppy. A very rare colour in Cockers at the time. It was turning nasty and she wanted to re-home her. Would I go and have a look. This I did. He'd told me his mom only wanted £10. for her, which wasn't expensive, so nothing to lose really. I arrived at Colin's home, was let in by his mom, and shown the young lady. She was busy laying claim to the settee on which she'd planted herself. She showed every sign of being well on the way to ending up a nasty little piece of work. All growls snarls and lip curling. She'd obviously been allowed to do what she wanted, if and when she wanted, no good to anybody or herself. I gave the lady her £10.00, grabbed this young delinquent of a dog by the scruff of her neck, gave her a good shake, looked her straight in the eye and just shouted "No!!" This was a new experience for her. She'd either like it or have to lump it. After a few days of learning her place she agreed to the former. She finally realised that she wasn't the boss and was never going to be in my eyes. She was just being her own worst enemy. The good sharp shock to her ambitions proved successful and she ended up a really nice, if not a trifle independent, little bitch. I re-homed her and, as far as I know, she lived happily ever after as they say.

At about this time a friend of Bobbie's had asked me if I could get him a small Jack Russell puppy but he continually emphasized the word "small". "It MUST be small" he'd say. I knew a man who bred very small Jack Russells. I'd had a few off him in the past namely "Inch War" and the pup that I'd sold to Jessie Kimbnell - the one that her husband had given me so much earache over. So off I popped to enquire if a similar pup was, or may be in the future, available. In those days you could buy a Jack Russell pup for as little as a pound if you knew where to look and especially off this man. I was in luck he'd got one really tiny little bitch puppy ready to go. Nobody else had wanted her because of her tiny size. I immediately paid him a couple of quid for the dear little pup, stuffed her up in my jumper, and went off to find Phil (my prospective customer). It turned out that he was in the pub with Bobby so (although I didn't then and still don't like entering pubs) in I go. I located Phil and Bob and told Phil that I'd got him a pup. "It'd better be small" he barked. On this I retrieved the little girl from inside my clothing and sat her in Phil's half full pint glass. "Is that small enough for you?" I asked him. Job done!! I think I charged him a fiver for the pup. Not bad for an hour's work I thought. Right up until the time I am writing this Phil has bought 2 or 3 more dogs from me and they've all lived with him and his family all their lives. That is a span of getting on for 50 years. This is nice I think!

By the time Tony had got himself back together after the upset of the tragic loss of the lad in the potato harvester then Maggie Jones was also back up to full strength, worker wise, so my time relief milking came to an end. I'd never really enjoyed it anyway. I've always said that anybody can learn to milk cows but the hard part is being able to manage the herd well enough to get enough milk in the right place at the right time. That's what I really loved to do. I got my old job back on the fencing but this time with either old Charlie or his son Peter. We also seemed to be buying and selling, or breeding, a few more dogs and goats as well as one or two ponies and calves and a pig or two from time to time. We found, what today would be classed as a "puppy farm", in Wales selling pups of varying breeds for £10. each and they would send them to you via British rail. You couldn't order any specific breed. You just sent your money and they sent your pups. Any breed could turn up. We got Sealyham Terriers, Cairns, Scotties, Westies, Jack Russells and on one occasion a Dalmatian of all things. That was the only Dalmatian I'd ever bought and the only one I've ever owned. We re-homed it to an Irishman who came knocking one Sunday afternoon looking for a Jack Russell pup. No problem we'd probably got 5 or 6 of them running about. It would be good to thin them out a bit. No chance. He went off with the Dalmatian and our Jack Russell club remained as it was. So far as the goats were concerned we were lucky. We not only had the free grazing on the ground where the N.E.C. now stands but also the little paddock adjoining the cottage. We usually had at least 4 or 5 knocking about. When they'd got used to going down the lane to graze, and then back home again at night, it was just a case of clipping on their chains and following them up or down the lane. One old Nanny in particular stays in my mind. We'd had her for a while and her night time pen had a slatted door that opened outwards. She'd run up home and wait to be let in for her food but to my curiosity she had learned to let herself in. This was puzzling. So one evening I asked Paula to go and let them off and I'd hide and see how she was doing it. All was revealed. She put her head on one side and this enabled it to fit between the slats on the door. She'd then turn her head so that it wouldn't come out the same way it went in, walk backwards, thus opening the door. Then she'd look down, put her front foot behind the door to stop it closing again, and then remove her head and open the door fully with her leg and foot, go in the pen and the door closed behind her!! Clever old bugger!!

A couple of miles away Mr Wardle had a little triangular piece of ground, about 2 acres, that was bordered by a dual carriageway on two sides and a river on the third side. It was just a piece left over from when the main roads had been upgraded in the past. He told me that as long as I looked after it then we could rent it from him. This we did. Mainly we used it for popping in a pony or two from time to time. We used to buy "wild" ponies straight off the Welsh hill and get them reasonably quiet and stable. There's nothing worse than having a horse you cannot catch. We never kept them long just enough time to get them halter broken and "quiet in traffic". The latter state we achieved by making sure we had them as secure as possible. We sometimes using two separate head collars and if the worst came to the worst a neck collar as well. We would then attach good strong lead ropes and walk them up and down the central reservation. It could get a "bit hairy" at times to start with but they soon got used to it. Hence our term "halter broken and quiet in traffic".

We used to buy a few calves and re-sell them. While at Stratford-on-Avon market one Tuesday, trying to buy calves at the right price, I noticed an extremely thin, if not emaciated, Channel Isle heifer. She looked like some kind of crossbred and she was obviously in calf. After chasing it up it was obvious nobody wanted her. I found the owner and bought her off him. We put her in the little triangular paddock down by the river and fed her well. She began to improve and looked a lot happier and was beginning to gain a bit of weight. That was all good except one day I made the classic "amateurish" mistake of putting two ponies in with her. Now the unspoken rule in those days was that to be on the safe side just assume that horses are best kept with only other horses. This was soon to become obvious when Frank turned up to say that he'd been driving past the paddock and that the ponies had harassed the little heifer and got her in the river and wouldn't let her get out. So off me and "the old man" went with a halter and some rope and after a bit of a struggle, a very wet struggle, we got her on to dry land and I walked her back home into a nice dry shed and the little paddock next to the cottages. She eventually had her calf. It looked like a little Aberdeen Angus cross. She and her baby thrived and after a time both went off to a new home.

I was milking at Mr Wardles, as was my duty, one Sunday when he came over to me and asked if I wanted to buy his Hereford bull. He was in the loose box near the cowshed. I said "At the right price . . . then yes". A price of, if I recall correctly, £90 was agreed. It was arranged that I'd get Donald to come and pick him up on the Thursday and take him straight into Banbury Market. A good place to sell cull cattle. Don and I had agreed that if he transported the bull then we'd halve any profits. He'd had a look at the animal and thought that I'd "bought him right". Job settled. Donald came round on the Thursday evening with hardly a look of glee about him to utter the immortal words "That fuckin' bull must have been made of cork". It wasn't as heavy as we'd both thought it would be. We'd both, me in particular, made the mistake of pricing the bull while he was still in his pen. He just looked bigger than he was in the "real world" outside. I think the whole transaction yielded a miserly profit of a couple of quid each but that's the way it goes sometimes I suppose. Over time I'd cultivated a good relationship with a farmer called John Minshull at Packington Hall. He used to buy calves and run them on to either stores (half grown) or fat cattle. He used to pay well for good Hereford or Hereford X calves. I always remembered what old Mr Walters had told me years earlier. I had asked him why he only ever bought such calves and only the ones with colour around their eyes. He told me to go and look at any bunch of beef cattle and the best beasts were usually always the ones with such facial markings. So I did go and look and 9 times out of 10 he was right. Hence my habit of only buying beef calves for Mr Minshull that had these markings. We'd come to an agreement of, I think it was, £50 per good calf. He was happy and I was happy at that. Now at this time there was a chap called Mr Roach, an Irishman who also bought and sold a few calves like me. Apparently Mr Minshull told me one day that the Irishman had been there trying to sell his calves and he'd said that he could get calves such as mine for £10. each!! The cheeky twat. So I did no more go to his place. I confronted him with the fact that he reckoned he could get such animals for £10 each to which he agreed that he could. I therefore offered to give him £500 cash and asked him to get me 50 such calves next week. He slammed the door in my face and our paths never crossed again. I did manage to buy a very pretty fine boned roan coloured pony off his next door neighbour at the same time. Killed two birds with one stone . . . nice!!

One of the biggest chicken dealers in the area at that time was a chap called Terry Goodfellow who had two brothers Martin and Graham. Now Terry was obviously the odd one out of those three. He was black haired, brown eyed and had an Asian looking skin but the other two brothers were fair haired, fair skinned and had blue eyes. "The talk it was" that Terry was the cuckold son of an Italian biscuit manufacturer from Birmingham. Hence the fact that he always seemed to be better off, financially, than either Graham or Martin. Somehow he had managed to get the contract to be the sole supplier of live chickens to The Fleur-de-Lys Meat Pie Company. Very often you'd see him at Henley sales of a Wednesday when he'd park his cattle wagon right next to the doorway of the poultry sales shed. Invariably the lorry would be full of chicken crates which he would do his utmost to fill on every occasion that he was present. This was much to the annoyance of basically every other chicken buyer that was in attendance. Between him and a man called David Southall (the brother of the Mr Southall I used to buy Jack Russell pups from) the chicken and rabbit job was more or less sewn up. David Southall – No 1 - as he was known had a meat stall in Coventry Market. Hence his love of meat rabbits. Nobody could really compete with either of them, at the time, so far as the chicken and rabbit job was concerned. All they left for others were all the "fancy" varieties and waterfowl and small animals. This suited me anyway so I wasn't over bothered by either of them. In fact on one occasion I saw a pair of Egyptian Geese in the sale not big birds but rare. I'd never seen any before but I knew what they were and fortunately nobody else seemed to possess my knowledge. The birds' apparent value was being assessed purely by weight by everyone else who showed any kind of interest in them. They are not very big birds so I managed to buy them for just 3 or 4 pounds. I later sold them to a young John Ball at Tamworth for £15. He subsequently sold them on to Twycross Zoo for £40. So everyone was happy.

David Southall, like his brother, bred dogs. Not terriers but Bassett Hounds so when I had a customer for one of this breed I went to his house, one evening, on the off chance that he may have a pup available. I knocked on his door and it was opened only to reveal this "vision of female loveliness". His daughter. She was stunning, bloody stunning. "Sod, the dogs, let's talk to her instead." was my immediate reaction. It turned out he hadn't got a puppy available at the time and unfortunately I was a married man with two little girls at home . . . Ah well . . . You can't win them all!!

Back to the Goodfellow brothers. Graham used to buy and sell a few pigs and from time to time he'd drop one or two off with us for a couple of weeks, either to put a bit more weight on them, or just as a drop off point before he sold them. Now in this vein he turned up one day with three extremely stunted specimens. These three had thick bristles at least 2 or 3 inches long all over them. A certain sign of an unthrifty pig. Not big pigs but they looked old. As soon as I saw them I recognised them. I'd seen them months before at Harvey Skinners place running round in a big metal barn open to the elements on all sides with not a lot of bedding. Now pigs don't like to be cold. Hence their appearance. As soon as Graham turned up with them I said to him "I know where they've come from." We stood there looking at the poor buggers and I asked him how old he thought they were. He said he hadn't got a clue but he had posed the very same question to Harvey himself and the answer was "Put it like this . . . they've had a birthday". We kept them for a few weeks but to no avail. They just wouldn't respond in anyway, shape or form, but they were happy enough. Just not saleable really so Graham and I decided to call it a day with them and cut our losses. He took them off again to meet their end I suppose. On the other hand big brother Terry was doing really well with the chicken job. He'd go anywhere and buy any amount. He'd buy all by weight. He had a set price per pound that he'd pay and that was it, take it or leave it. He knew what he was doing. He'd got the job sewn up in our area and he was doing really well but then he got greedy and decided to go into buying and selling calves. A big mistake. There were two or three big calf buyers doing the rounds of all the local markets and beyond so him sticking his oar in wasn't well received. He was a chicken man, he knew the trade inside and out, so he should stick with his chickens. He knew nothing about calves or cattle and in the end, messing about with something he knew nothing about, bought him down to the level of his two brothers Graham and Martin. He ended up "scratching about" like the rest of us. He lost his big farmhouse, his lorry, his contract with Fleur-de-Lys, all of it and the last I saw of him was years later when he turned up at the Coleshill Hotel where I was working at the time. He was doing no more than peddling bacon and cold meats to the catering trade. He'd learned the hard way.

One of the lads that used to knock around with us a bit when we were in our early teens was a kid called Johnny Devlin. He was the only one of us that didn't or hadn't worked on the farm, although him and his Dad – absolutely "Staunch God Bothering" Catholics had managed to get hold of a few acres of ground and a run of really good brick built loose boxes behind the Father Hudsons' Homes – run by Catholic nuns – at the top end of Coleshill. They kept mainly pigs and the odd beast or two. Then they started to buy and rear calves . . . not really a good idea. They were a bit like the aforementioned Terry Goodfellow – didn't really know what they were doing with them. Quite often young John would turn up and ask if I could come and have a look at the calves. This was O.K. by me I could get anti-biotics etc. off the farms if I asked nicely. It was usually just a case of bad feeding and bad husbandry that had bought on these small problems. I enjoyed it – the frustrated vet in me I suppose! Now back in those days before the right medication was easily available a common scourge of cattle, that were kept outside, was Warble Fly Strike. The fly would lay its eggs under the skin along the beasts back. Here they would grow and eventually emerge as grubs about half the size of a man's little finger. This, of course, caused a lot of discomfort and if not remedied before the bugs emerged then the cycle would just repeat itself, and so on and so on. The other thing was that they basically de-valued the hide in the end because it would be riddled with holes. John came round one day and asked if I could go and help him squeeze the bugs out of the cattle's backs. He had a few half grown beasts around … no problem. I'd never seen cattle so badly infected. You could actually watch the grubs moving under the skin. I mean back then Warble Fly Strike was common. Indeed as young lads we used to enjoy popping the grubs out and treading on them. When you did so you could hear them "pop" under your feet but these cattle of Johns seemed to be alive with them. Indeed I can remember we got a jam jar full of grubs out of one of the poor sods. Why do people mess with animals they don't understand? I've always wondered that. It shouldn't be allowed. These are, and were living things, that you are exposing to the results of your ignorance!! Enough of that. Young John seemed to lead a "charmed life". He seemed to come out of everything "smelling of roses". In fact we all used to say "If Johnny Devlin fell of the roof of Rackhams then he'd land in a gold lame suit." His father, also called John, was a bit of a know it all. He knew his pigs but that's as far as it went really. He had the habit of, when in public, especially at livestock markets of pulling a roll of notes out of his pocket trying to make out he was the "big man". We always said that that was all the money he had and if he wasn't careful then he wouldn't have even that for long. If he carried on in that way there was a fair chance he'd get the money robbed off him as a result of his show off ways. I don't know if he ever did. He wasn't a man I had a lot of time for on a good day!!

By now I'd got friendly with Bob Hadley at the top of the lane. A bloke I suppose 10 or 15 years older than me. He had this pet shop in Sheldon as I mentioned earlier. He was a "Broad Brummie". He said it as it was, either black or white. So much so that I recall I was in his shop at one time, and this old lady had been in and spent a significant amount of money on dog food. As she was leaving the shop Bob said to her "Thank you darling – Fuck the rent, feed the dogs." or words to that effect. At least if trade got a bit slack at any time he'd ask me to take a goat to his shop and we'd tie it up outside. That drew the crowds . . . no mistake. He said to me one day that a new pet shop had just opened near his premises When I asked him if he was worried about having to share the trade he said it would be no problem because he'd let a few mice go free through their letterbox. "By the time they realise they're there then there'll be hundreds of them chewing everything up and shitting in the bird seed. That'll slow em up". No messing with Bob!! He came to the house in a panic late one night. He used to import tropical fish and his consignment had been held up for hours somewhere en-route from the Far East but they were due to arrive at Birmingham airport anytime soon. He was worried that they'd get cold and die so could I go with him to pick them up and take them to the shop, unpack them, and get them into some warm water as soon as possible. This we did. I didn't then, and still don't, know one tropical fish from another but I do recall a couple of boxes contained individual clear plastic bags. Each one wrapped up in Chinese newspaper. I enquired about this and Bob told me that they were Siamese Fighters. If they could see each other through the bags then they'd try and fight and more than likely die of exhaustion. You live and learn. I've often thought about that. Bob used to hold dog training classes of a Sunday afternoon. It turned out that in a previous life he'd trained dogs for Yorkshire Police. He showed me his old leather sleeve one day. It looked as if a crocodile had been clawing at it. So although he kept a few Alsatians and Great Danes he wasn't what you could, in all honesty, call the best kennel man in the world to put it mildly. He could train a dog no doubt about it. I was watching him one Sunday afternoon. He had 2 or 3 clients in his yard when a car pulled up outside and out popped a three quarter grown St. Bernard with its owner. A little middle- aged lady about 5' 4" or so tall in tow. Where ever the dog wanted to go he dragged the poor woman with him. Bob introduced himself to the lady and her "pet" then bent down to be at eye level with the young fellow. He grabbed him by the flews (the skin around the corners of his mouth) looked him straight in the eyes at very close quarters and uttered the immortal phrase "From now on you are going to do what I fucking well tell you to do Sonny." On this he stood up, kept the dog on an extremely short leash, with his head tight against Bob's leg and they both vanished off down the lane. They returned 10 minutes or so later.

The dog off the lead, still well "at heel". They walked up to the end of the yard. He told the dog sit down "and fucking well stay there". The dog obliged. On this Bob walked to the end of the yard, maybe 20 or 30 yards away. The dog still obediently remaining in his allotted place and Bob did no more than to stand there, telling the dog to stay. He proceeded to throw stones at it and Mr. young St. Bernard didn't move. He wasn't totally at ease but he didn't move. Hence he was rewarded. I'll never forget seeing that. I often wondered if he was as well behaved with his owner as he had been that afternoon. He might have been well behaved for Bob but who could say he would be for anybody else. I doubt it. It was more a lesson and a demonstration than life long cure I think. Bob "had the way" but would little Mrs. St. Bernard? Who knows? Things turned out well for Bob, Sue and the boys because his property was on a corner of the main A45 duel carriageway and our lane. The N.E.C. was about to be built right on the doorstep. He'd been offered vast amounts of money from developers – mainly hotels, for his property. He refused to sell. Instead he rented out his ground for a ready mix concrete plant and storage area for construction vehicles etc. He made a fortune. Indeed the last time I visited him he showed me his bath with gold plated taps. He was really proud of them. He still had Lawrence his monkey and the cat still lived up the chimney!!

Of course Donald and I still saw a lot of each other and he turned up one evening with a Chihuahua pup he'd bought for his daughter, Jill's, birthday. He wanted us to keep it for him until the appropriate day…. a few weeks away. It turned out that this little pup was probably one of the "dirtiest" dogs I'd ever owned. Piss and shit everywhere. It wouldn't learn. If you put it in a confined space it would be dirty and then lie in it even. I don't think it ever got really "clean". It turned out he'd bought this puppy off one of his customers. A man called Trevor Howard who worked at the Massey Ferguson factory in Coventry. He had a side line of obtaining old packing cases and the like and re-selling them. When he'd got enough put to one side at work to make up a load then Donald and The Big Red Rig would be employed to move them back to his place. His place was a bungalow situated on the top of a hill with a field that dropped down to buildings below. This is where he stored all his etc. Massey Ferguson merchandise but he also had an extensive set up of kennels where, with his wife and daughter, he bred a lot of dogs mainly Beagles. (Talk was, at the time, they were bred for research but that fact was never fully established). Bloodhounds, Bassett Hounds, Chihuahuas and I think, if

I remember rightly, Scotties and Westies. This was a full time job for his wife and daughter really. Donald had been and picked a load of packing cases up from "The Fergie" as it was known and I'd gone with him to have a "sniff about". After unloading the lorry back at the Howard ranch we were sat in his house having tea. I always remember Trevor was sat in his chair nursing and stroking a little Beagle pup that was obviously having a bit of a hard time but was receiving the full amount of love, care and fuss that was available. We were all sat there chatting when the subject of Chihuahuas came up and I let it be known that I'd be in the market for a bitch puppy if not a young, and I stressed the word young, bitch. Had he got anything available. On this he had a few words with his daughter, Susan, and off she went down the field to the kennels and returned with, according to Trevor, a young bitch. Well, I opened her mouth to have a look at her teeth. A good sign of age. Never buy any animal before looking at its teeth I'd always been told. In this case it was more a case of "lack of teeth". She'd hardly got a tooth in her head and those she had got were no more than little brown stubs. According to Mr Howard she was only 2 years old!! He was taking me for a prat. This wouldn't be forgotten! I politely refused the deal and put this experience "on the back burner". My time would come.

Work back on the fencing at Wykham Blackwell carried on where Charlie had left off in days gone past. It was typical Charlie. We'd been sent to a site in the middle of a wood near Warwick to fence around a newly built crematorium. All oak timber, oak posts rough cut, oak rails and oak pails. No problem but the "spec" was that no nails should be used to secure the rails. That meant they had to be made safe by the use of wooden dowels. The size of this dowel was specified but the snag came when it arrived on site. It was too big and the powers that be in the office insisted that we shaved it all down to the correct diametre. This didn't go down well with old Charlie. This was piece work after all. In his wisdom he decided it would pay us to go out and purchase our own dowel. Unfortunately it turned out that the pre-drilled holes on the posts were bigger than anything we could buy off the shelf so it was a case of "sod it". The old boy decided that we would try and get away with it by using the "shop stuff" and trying to hide the fact by smudging dirt, old moss, etc. over the ends. This was O.K. until the Clerk of the Works came around to check the work. He noticed what we'd tried to do straight away. He walked up to the first post he came to and just pushed the offending dowels out with his finger. Back to square one. In the end it was agreed with the office that they'd pay us more per bay as long as we drilled everything to accommodate the original material. Good old Charles . . . bless him. The fence line on this job ran through the trees but the main contractors had cleared our way by cutting down all the trees, evergreens, that would have blocked our way. They'd not only felled the trees, but they'd also trimmed them and cut them into 8-10 foot lengths. Handy I thought! I came to an agreement with the main man that enabled me to take as many of these poles as I liked as long as no mess was made retrieving them. After work I'd stay behind. I was using my own transport by now. I'd carry them out and stack them near the road by hand. I then got a friend who drove an open backed sand and gravel lorry to go over with me and chuck them all on his wagon and take them home for me. Once home I stacked them all up on end outside the cottage with a "For Sale" sign on them and eventually managed to sell them all from there. Most of them went for horse jumps and fence rails I recall. Who cared, it was easy money at the time.

One Friday night we'd gone to the yard and offices to pick up our money. Who should appear but no other than the aforementioned Mr Harvey Skinner. Apparently he'd come on a bit of a hard time and needed to earn some money. He'd heard that Blackwells had got a big job on. It was either Chelmsley Wood or Woodrow Redditch. Both new big housing projects. Trouble was Harvey had basically only put up barbed wire or pig netting. He must have blagged his way in somehow. He told me that when he went for his interview he flowered up his experience and was accepted with open arms by the newly installed manager. A proper jumped up ex-army officer who talked like he'd got a mouth full of plums . . . for want of a better phrase. Never knocked a nail in or dug a hole in his life. A man called Mr Currell. A property dick-head universally hated by all. Anyway when Harvey had finished giving him the banter he apparently uttered the words "By Jove Mr Skinner you're truly God sent." to which Harvey replied with the immortal phrase "No I'm not sir . . . I came on my bike, its leaning on the wall outside!!" When he found out the job was a bit more complicated than knocking a few posts in and stringing up a bit of wire (this was really all he'd ever done in the past as far as fencing went) Harvey was a chap who didn't mind bending the rules a bit. So because it was all piece work he was struggling to make it pay. In his desperation, after learning there was a "hard digging" price that could be paid if the ground warranted it, he decided to bring his own "hard digging" to work every morning from home. Old brick-ends and bits of hardcore etc, and sprinkle them around the posts to make it appear that he'd had to dig them all out … the crafty sod!! This lasted for a while but his little game was eventually rumbled and that was the end of his career at Blackwells, sad to say. My own career at the firm came to an abrupt end also. Charlie was now basically retired. We'd been working on one of these big sites and it was a job to make a lot of money at it. Charlie had asked the office to move us to other jobs but they'd refused. We thought they were running late on their contract and needed every pair of hands on these big sites that they could get. Old Charles was having none of this. He said he'd get us shifted off the job one way or another. It came when we were putting up an open pail fence. This meant that all the pails had to be an equal distant space apart and, of course, be 100% on the vertical. By now Charles had come to the end of his tether. He was the oldest and longest serving member of all of the fence erectors. He'd been with the firm for donkeys years and he'd got it into his head that the aforementioned Mr Currall (the high and mighty Mr Currall) was "taking the piss" in Charlie's words. So, back to the open pail fence. He said to me that he'd mark the rails and I'd nail up the pails. No problem. He'd gone on ahead marking and I'd begun to do the nailing. I'd put a few up and it did seem, to me at least, that they were gradually drifting off the vertical. I mentioned this fact to the old boy but he just told me to stick to his marks which I did. Now if your first pail is off the vertical then the further you proceed then the more this fact becomes exaggerated. It was soon obvious that everything was on the slant to say the least but he insisted that things be left as they were. We were thrown off the job once he refused to alter anything and not long after that he decided he'd had enough. He was old enough to retire. So that is what he did. When this time came I was put to work with his son Peter, who was a nice enough lad, who'd worked at Blackwells since leaving school and had had a good teacher in his Dad but he wasn't his Dad. We got on well enough… no problem but me and the old boy were both a "bit nutty" and we'd got on like a house on fire. We both sang off the same hymn sheet really and I missed working with old Charles. Time went on and eventually Pete and I were sent to one of these two big house construction sites. I can't remember which one, either Redditch or Chelmsley Wood. Whichever one it was the job was coming to an end. These contracts had lasted for years but all that was left by now were the really awkward bits. A couple of bays here and there, on top of walls and things like that. Overtime the other gangs had done all the easy stuff, packed up, and left. The office insisted that Pete and I had to do these bits at the old piece work rate. Now there's a difference between putting a fence up with your feet on the ground and trying to do the same job in a really tight, cramped, gap between walls or stand on ladders or steps to erect a fence on top of a retaining wall so we decided to "fiddle a bit". We got away with it for a while but in the end we were rumbled. We were summoned into the office to be chastised by "he who must be obeyed", Mr Currall. We went in. He was sat behind his desk in all his pompous glory as usual. He started to question us and then informed us that we couldn't fiddle him "Chaps" because he knew where every nail on the job was. I did no more than took a couple out of my pocket and said to him "Where the fucking hell did they come from then?" That was it, my time at Blackwells was terminated on the spot and I can truly say that was the only time in my life that I'd been given the sack but it was worth it just to put the slimy pompous wannabe in his place. Pete stayed on and Charles moved to Germany with his wife (who was German) and I think he "quit this mortal coil" over there. R.I.P. Charlie my old mate . . . and thank you!!

Paula was now pregnant again. I always said that if the Catholic Church could decree that contraception was a big no go area then they should pay family allowances for any children born as a result of this policy that they, basically, invented. It was my view that it was a sure way of keeping the world well supplied with "God Botherers" but that's the way it goes I suppose. Financially things were a bit tight after my "entrance stage left" from the employ of Wyckham Blackwell so it was time to get a full time job with the dairy cows again. Time to move on again especially as a new baby was on the horizon. The Farmers weekly magazine always contained an array of "situations vacant" at the time so we had a good look through and decided to apply for a single handed herdsman's position at a farm in Pailton near Rugby. The interview must have gone well, and Tony Woods had given me a glowing reference, hence I was offered the job. I accepted it after the "terms and conditions" had been adjusted. The original offer was the wage plus one weekend off in every three. No bonus was mentioned but after a little discussion this was extended to one day off per week plus the same bonus that I had received at Tony's (i.e. 1% margin over concentrates which meant I received 1% of the difference between the cost of the concentrated feed fed in the parlour and the value of the milk sold). All was well and we moved into the tied cottage within a couple of weeks. The business went under the title of Gray and Harrison, Warwickshire Pheasantries, Pailton. It seemed that at some time in the recent past the place had been under the ownership of the Harrison family, Jim Harrison, the livestock auctioneers at Rugby Livestock Auctions, and his brother Josh Harrison who was in control of the farm. This was mainly a free range producer of pheasants for the hunting, shooting and fishing brigade. Hence most of the fields were surrounded by 7' high wire mesh fences etc. Miles and miles of it, as it seemed to me anyway, containing thousands of breeding pheasants. These were spread over three farms all adjoining each other at some point or other. Obviously the Harrisons had encountered some form of financial difficulties and sold the place and the existing dairy herd to John Gray and his father. They were beef, sheep and arable farmers originally from nearer to Coventry and had never had anything to do with milking cows or a dairy herd. John admitted that it was all new to him and that my job was to run the herd on a day to day basis with no interference from him unless things should ever start to go wrong. I'd get help if and when anything needed to be done that warranted the use of more than one pair of hands. He'd make sure all the feed that would be needed would be available on site at all times. When it came to mucking out the over wintering yard then the tractor drivers would come in and see to that. Otherwise it was a case of "There's the cows, there's the set up, get on with it" really. After I'd settled in then some weeks I'd only see John when he bought my wages. This was the job I'd always wanted. The herd was made up of between 100 and 120 milking cows plus all their calves that were reared on the place until weaning time and then taken to one of the other farms where they were either fed up for beef or the heifers grown on as replacements for the dairy herd. The only bull that was on the place was an Aberdeen Angus that ran with the heifers when they were old enough to be put in calf for the first time. This resulted in nice small calves that were easy for the young girls to give birth to without too much wear and tear or stress. After that all the cows were inseminated by good quality bulls. It was, after all, a 100% pedigree herd of British Friesians. Apart from the normal black and white form the herd also contained a few of the old fashioned red (brown) and white strain. These were becoming increasingly rare by now. The whole set up especially the cows themselves were in need of a bit of love and attention. The Vet was there basically 2 or 3 times a week for one thing or another but mainly to treat cases of chronic mastitis. It seems that the herdsman John had inherited left a lot to be desired. In fact I can remember one beast. She was No 10 and her short name was Julie. She only walked on three legs because apparently one day the bloke was fetching the cows out of the field on a tractor. A big No, No in my book. You don't look at, hear or "sense" your cattle unless you are close to them and on foot. He'd run into her on the tractor and smashed her shoulder in the process. He was "let go" anyway. Hence the position that I had just filled became vacant. After time things with the general health and wellbeing of the cows started to improve. The Vet was called in less regularly and a bit of good old fashioned animal husbandry was starting to show a few positive results. The Vet or Vets were a partnership of the old man, Sandy Lyons, and his young partner, Sandy Bell. Now Sandy Lyons was an ex-Air Force chap in his mid sixties. An upper middle class gentleman with a very pretty young wife about 20 years his junior who would often accompany him on his visits. Sandy Lyons was a lovely, really helpful chap who liked to impart his extensive veterinary knowledge to anyone who'd listen. I definitely listened and learned and then learned more. I'd just bring up a subject I was keen on and interested in and off he'd go just like switching on a light. He could see I was interested in the "Vet Job" and so encouraged me so much so that a couple of years later, we were T.T. testing the cattle and John was helping, when Sandy said that anytime I wanted to I could go and work with him as a sort of unqualified apprentice. He said that "I doubt if John would agree to that." and John's answer verified his assumption but it was a nice offer. Anyway I had a family to keep and house. When we arrived a Pailton the herd was being milked in an old 6 abreast parlour which had seen better days. After about a year or so John said he'd decided to have a complete brand new set up installed which included a new 5/10 Herringbone parlour, new cubicle housing (this meant the old deep litter over wintering yard was to go) This I wasn't so keen on. I wasn't convinced about cubicles. In my eyes they weren't so good "cattle comfort" wise. Also there was to be new collecting yard, a bulk cake (concentrated feed) bin that automatically augered the feed into the parlour. No more carrying bags of cake in and out and up steps by hand and another bulk tank as the present one was slowly becoming too small and on some occasions over filled. This resulted in some of the milk being transferred into the old churns which meant less money was paid for it so we would have two tanks in the new dairy. While all the rebuilding etc. was going on an old Somerset milking bail was bought in as a temporary measure. Everything would be new except for the old calf rearing pen and the loose boxes. Now the old calf rearing pen defied all the modern thinking of how calves should be housed. It was in an old cowshed below a big high wooden granary that hadn't been used since "Adam was a lad" to quote a local saying. Hence it was dark. The only lighting was a string of light bulbs all the way down the full length of the building. It had a partial earth floor and the individual pens were made from wooden pallets tied together with baler string. Everything "modern science" said it shouldn't be but the calves absolutely thrived in there. Nobody, not even Sandy Senior (the vet) could see why. They just did. One calf in particular. This little chap had been born with a "hair lip" which meant he couldn't suck a teat. Indeed he could only drink by tipping his head on one side and sucking his milk up through one side of his mouth. To start with I fed him through a tube but he eventually, after much coaxing, learned how to drink and eat just using half of his mouth. He'd been born out of season so therefore was one on his own so he got "spoilt" by me. He basically became a pet. A scenario that was basically frowned upon but John let me carry on with it. This calf just "bloomed". He became too big for his pen so eventually had to be moved to one of the other farms with the rest of the beef cattle. I can remember that when he got into natural daylight he shone as if he'd been polished. A lovely young fellow. All the calves were reared on the bucket on artificial milk. This was done by teaching them to drink, as opposed to suck, with their heads down. Not a natural position. This was achieved, hopefully, by getting them to suck your fingers then gradually lower their heads into the milk. They'd gradually, or in some cases, instantly, learnt to drink. This was a hit and miss sort of thing. Some took to it, no problem, but calves, usually those that had come from a beef bull crossed with a Friesian heifer, could be stubborn. I always said that because of what they were then beef x calves they hadn't got the get up and go of a dairy calf. The odd one had to be fed via a tube for longer than was really desirable and in that case they'd be put on an old "nurse cow" that was kept for such occasions. Getting calves to drink out of the bucket usually meant getting cut fingers from their teeth as a result of them learning to let go of your digits and drink. It was a task that would, in common opinion, test the patience of a saint. The usual remedy for a stubborn drinker was to get a woman to train them. For some reason, in nine cases out of ten, this worked. In fact I was chatting to a chap one day who used to buy Charolais, beef breed calves, and rear them up. He'd bought this one calf that absolutely refused to co-operate so he fetched his Mom out of the house. He asked her to have a go and within 5 minutes the bloody stubborn little calf was drinking independently, perfectly well, as if he'd been doing it for weeks. On this subject John was telling me one day that he'd been to visit a friend of his who also reared beef calves in this way but on arrival at his place he couldn't find his friend so he had a wander around the yard. He heard cursing and swearing coming out of one of his loose boxes so he stuck his head over the door to be greeted by the sight of a calf covered in milk and his friend ranting "there you bastard if you won't drink it, then let it fuckin' soak in!!" We all knew just how he felt. Some of them would indeed test the patience of a saint.

At home Paula had given birth to our third daughter who we called Naomi. It was now a house of one man and four women. I recall that after Naomi was born they wouldn't let her out of the hospital because they couldn't get her temperature down for any length of time. We went to visit her every day and we noticed that her cot was pushed up against a radiator that came on at varying intervals. We suggested this might be the problem and asked if she could be moved to a cooler spot. This they did and the problem of her fluctuating temperature soon resolved itself and she joined the brood.

At work the new buildings and parlour and dairy were now up and running smoothly and after a few early teething problems the cows had got used to their new surroundings and milking routine. As well as getting them used to all this I decided to milk them every 12 hours. This was a much debated point amongst dairymen and some believed that milking three times a day was better but I didn't prescribe to this opinion so decided to give 12 hourly milking a go to see if it would improve, not only yields, but also general herd health. This whole process involved starting to milk at 3 a.m. and 3 p.m. daily, 365 days a year. Early mornings had never been a problem for me as long as I could grab 2 or 3 hours sleep in the day whenever circumstances allowed which was usually most days anyway. This regime soon started to show improvements and indeed after the first year our herd had crept up to being the second best herd in Warwickshire. This was all calculated by official records of milk production and quality and calving intervals (the time between each calving) and food conversion. Things were looking good and although my father had told me, as a child, that I'd never be any good for anything, I was now proving him wrong at least and I was a proud young man at last. The best herd in Warwickshire at that time was owned by a man from Hampton-in-Arden called Charlie Hughes and he and his herd seemed to be out of reach of everybody. I was talking to John about this one day and questioning why. He told me he believed that it was generally recognised that Mr Hughes had the ability to grow good grass (the best food of any kind for dairy cows). Indeed he said that if Charlie Hughes walked down the yard then grass grew in his footmarks. That was a gift apparently. No one could understand how he did it.

Calving between 120 and 150 cows and heifers a year by the law of averages, presented difficulties from time to time but nothing that couldn't be overcome by a bit more manpower. If such an occasion occurred during the day then any of the other workers that were near enough at the time would give me a hand but if it happened at night then it was a case of getting John out of his bed. That was an understanding we had so no problem. I can only recall having to get the Vet out for a calving on just two occasions. The first time young Sandy Bell came out and ended up performing a caesarean but it was a bloody big calf. When old Sandy found out that his young partner had resorted to the knife he wasn't best pleased. His quote was "You don't need a knife. All you need is plenty of Fairy Liquid and patience". He told me he'd only ever done a caesarean on one big animal in all his years as a Vet and that was on a mare. The second time we had to call one of them out was when it looked. and felt, like we'd got a big dead calf to try and liberate from its mother. This time Old Sandy came out and decided that, although it would take longer than opening her up to get the calf out, then as it was dead, then the best way forward was to perform an embryotomy. This involved cutting up the calf inside the cow and getting it away in pieces. This was achieved by using a wire cutting string threaded down and through two separate stainless steel tubes. These were inserted into the cow and a loop of wire put over whatever needed to be removed and though using a sawing action the limb or whatever it was could be sawn off and removed. This took a long time. Indeed, Sandy had to go back to the surgery to fetch more wire. Eventually everything except one leg had been extracted but this last leg was posing a problem. Apparently it had splintered and left a jagged shard of bone still attached. Sandy was frightened that if he tried to take it out as it was then there was a fair chance it would rip the inside of the cow. He decided to wrap the splinter in cotton wool or lint, keep it in place by wrapping suturing thread around it and then carefully remove it. This he did and all was well. The cow had been lightly sedated but she stood up through all of this. The whole procedure lasted more than 6 hours. So well done old girl and very well done old Sandy. What a job he did that day. It was well known that he was a very well recognised and respected canine vet, especially with the large and giant breeds. People from all over the country with problems in this area would be referred to him. Apparently he revealed one day that his main speciality was with horses!! I learned a lot off this man over the years. He never spoke down to anybody. Never came out with the "high and mighty vet" trip. At the time, although we'd had our old Lassie Collie dog for a couple of years, he was still a "bad feeder" and wouldn't put weight on. This was a bit of a worry so when Sandy was at our cottage one day I asked him to have a look over Tibby. He ran his hands down his back and over his ribs "Don't worry, if he was a rabbit he'd be a fat rabbit". He said. The old dog lived on for years and never did feed any better or get any fatter.

When John had taken over the farm he inherited the staff of the time. These were three middle aged chaps, Bill, Bert and Alex. The latter being a Polish ex-prisoner of war whose wife and daughter were still left stranded in the Russian section of their homeland without any chance of obtaining an exit visa. Likewise poor old Alex was stranded over here with no chance of getting an entry visa to his homeland. His case was fought in British Courts, mainly financed by Josh Harrison and John but all to no avail and he sadly died without ever seeing his family again. He, like John, was a typical "gentle giant". Bill was a little old fella with a big swollen red nose and gout. He only did what he had to do. This was demonstrated most mornings when he and Alex would come into the yard to meet John and be given their allotted tasks for the day. Now at this time Alex would find something, anything to do, but not old Bill. He'd get out of his car, pick up an empty watering can and walk about pretending to check the tractors for water until John turned up. Bert spent most of his time on the other two farms along with Mick, a young lad John had taken on since his arrival. The Pheasantries were still in operation, although apparently in a pared down way. They employed 5 or 6 people, including an old bachelor man with the name of Ted. He lived on his own in a beaten up old caravan just up the track from our cottage. His only job was vermin control. Foxes being his speciality. They reckon he could smell a fox a mile away and, on some evenings and night times, he'd be up listening for his prey. I was talking to him on one such occasion and he heard foxes calling somewhere off in the distance "I'll have them bastards before long". he said. I expect he kept true to his word. Before the new dairy set up and bulk cake bin was installed all the cows concentrate feed came in paper sacks. A lot of paper sacks and so did all the feed that was used on the Pheasantries. I'd collect , bundle up and keep all these empty bags until I'd got enough to make up a van load and then sell them for one penny each to a re-cycling firm in Rugby. Over a year this all added up to a nice little bit of "pocket money" but of course the new bulk bin cut this little perk down by almost half.

139

Josh Harrison still lived in "the big house" at our farm and John and his family lived at Little Walton, one of the other farms. Josh was a man I didn't really like typical "hunting, shooting, fishing" lazy country gentleman. I use the word "gentleman" under pressure may I add!! He strolled about as if he owned the world but in fact he was a failed farmer and spoke in a very clipped upper class way. We hardly ever spoke. He obviously disliked me as much as I disliked him. This all came to a bit of a head one morning when I noticed he'd let one of the fresh calved cows, that was in the process of being weaned away from her offspring, back in the loose box with her calf. He'd done this several times before apparently. He didn't want to listen to the concerned bellowing of mother all night. Too bad mate. No wonder you were a failure if that's how you went on. Anyway this particular morning I wasn't in the best of humours and ironically this mood coincided with the old "jumped up snob" walking across the yard. I went off like a box of fireworks and he started to come the high and mighty in his posh accent This cut no ice with me and in the end I asked him why he spoke like he'd got a pound of plums in his gob because he was just like me really …… as common as shit. This couldn't have gone down too well. He must have reported the incident to John because not long after the boss arrived and asked me what had gone on. I told him and said it wasn't the first time Harrison had done it. John just said "Well if he does it again then tell me and I'll sort it out". End of story. It never did happen again. Josh eventually closed down the Pheasantries, had a sale, and moved out of the big house and John and his family moved in. The fact that Josh Harrison and I didn't really like each other came to a head one day when one of the cows kicked me in the face and split my bottom lip wide open. There was nobody about to take me to hospital except Josh. He put me in the back of his Hillman Humber Snipe Estate car and on the way to the hospital the only words that were exchanged between the two of us was when he said "I hope you appreciate and realise that I should be on my way to Huntingdon now"… thank you very much Mr Harrison. He dropped me off at casualty and left it to me to get back home somehow. John had been told what happened and he came and fetched me and my stitched up lip back home.

At home the cottage next to ours was rented out to a woman in her 50's and her partner and three of her lads. She was called Dora, her partner was called Tom, and the kids were Nobby Julie, and Rose. She was a local woman who also had three older children, Bernard, Fred and

Pamela. Pamela also had four children. All three of her boys worked on farms and Tom, her partner, was a lorry driver who, along with young Nobby, raced "Banger" cars at every opportunity. Pamela had recently split up with her husband so she and her kids rented an empty old house that also belonged to the farm at the end of our track. Dora had got all of her brood, apart from Bernard and Fred, all within a couple of hundred yards of each other. A lovely wholesome friendly clan they were as well. Really good neighbours and friends. Paula and I had an Old Commer Cob Van at the time. This I'd managed to prang and basically "written off" the one front wing. Tom said that if I could get him some empty 5 gallon cans then he would fix it. This I did and one Sunday afternoon he and Nobby removed the old wing. Manufactured a new one out of the available cans and pop riveted it back on to the vehicle. The only thing they hadn't done was to put the lights back in place but I did this by wedging them in with bits of wood. Image trying to get away with that these days. I painted the whole thing bright red and decorated it with some nice paintings of Disney characters. The vehicle ran on to its next M.O.T. which, of course, would have been a waste of time so I donated it to Tom and Nobby for their Banger car collection. They did well with it apparently because they took the radiator out and installed a domestic hot water tank in the back instead. This proved to be a magical move, so they said, because every time it got hit during a race it basically wrote off whatever vehicle had tried to "bully" it due to this mass of water concealed in the back . . . nice one!!

Before he closed down the Pleasantries and retired and moved out Josh Harrison or his "Secretary" used to come over to the dairy and collect their cans of milk for the house. Every time they'd leave drips of milk on the tank lid. This really used to piss me off so in the end I put up a sign saying "Please leave this place as you find it . . . Bloody Clean!! I prided myself on keeping the new set up clean after every milking. I'd scrub all the walls in the parlour with a hose pipe and brush. I also cleaned the feed troughs and any of the ironwork that had been shit upon. Every two weeks I'd strip all the milking points and units down to their bare bones and then scrub them all piece by piece in the wash up sinks and then re-assemble it all. I liked things as clean as possible and I also liked recording everything to do with the herd. I made each cow an individual card on which I entered all veterinary treatment etc. The milk yields I recorded every week so as to work out how much cake each of the girls should be given at each milking. I used to carry a little diary and pen at

141

all times where I could jot down any relevant detail I'd observed at the time and then transfer the information onto each cow's card. This all helped to the general day to day management of the herd. This was the job I really enjoyed and had been aiming at since I was about 14 years old. I loved every minute of it. John had started to drop hints that he had been looking at the possibility of maybe constructing a whole complete self-contained dairy unit, including new loose boxes, and everything on the other side of the lane and increasing the number of cows and then converting the current buildings, which were still new, to the beef job. I wasn't so keen on the idea really because it meant, if we had more cows, then I would have to have a full time helper and I didn't really fancy that. I liked to do things my way and, as things stood, I could just about manage what we'd already got on my own but we'd see anyway. Things were improving all the time and you can only push things so far in my eyes. This seemed to be illustrated perfectly well when one of the older girls in the herd "Kimton Val Dixie" short name Dixie gave the equivalent of 45 kg of milk in one day during the height of one of her lactations. She'd been slowly building up to this over the last couple of years but she never exceeded it. She'd reached her limit and that was it. When she eventually became barren I tried to convince John to let her retire and let her live her days out at home but, of course, this was business and there was no room for my sentimentality. I refused to load her on the lorry when her time came to leave. Of course every herd of cows has its "Star" but Dixie and another girl called Lorna were our two "big hitters". Lorna was almost as good, sometimes better, than Dixie, but her quirk was that at some time or other in the past she must have swallowed a piece of wire that had apparently got itself wedged in one of her stomachs. Normally it was no problem but every time she had a calf then the resulting temporary trifling re-adjustment of her inner organs brought up the threat of this wire interfering with her diaphragm hence causing very big problems. To overcome this threat, Sandy suggested that for a couple or so weeks after she'd calved then we should keep her tied up in a stall with her front feet higher than her back feet. This would help to keep the wire further down her gut until everything had settled back down again. It worked every year . . . good old Sandy!!

At home things could have been better, as they say, between Paula and I but, as I said earlier, it was hardly a marriage made in heaven but the girls seemed happy enough. Joanne was settled in school. Colette was "Daddie's best mate". She used to wait on the verge and watch for me to come out of the yard after work and then run up to meet me. Lovely . . . some little thing I'll never forget. She was a tiny little girl, with a big cheeky grin across her face. We still kept a few goats and she enjoyed spending time around them. We had them tied up on a bit of rough ground opposite the cottage. Only a couple of them now and only a couple or three dogs as well. Just no time for any more these days. Joanne had got into the habit of going to get on the school bus and then turning back up again 5 minutes later saying that the bus hadn't come so I watched her one morning. She went out and hid behind the shed until the school bus went past and then came back with the excuse that it hadn't come. I told her I'd just watched her hide behind the shed so she would spend the rest of her day in the bedroom with nothing to read or anything like that and no visits off Colette . . . That cured her!! She never missed the bus again . . . Bless her.

I'd begun to go out with Mick, the youngest member of staff at work, and a lad called Stuart, who was employed initially at the Pheasantries. We used to go to a dance once a week at a teacher's training college at Newbold a few miles up the road. Oops… that was a bit of a bad decision on my part. There were too many pretty girls there and although married I still had a soft spot for a pretty young lady anywhere, anytime. A girl with long red wavy hair, green eyes and freckles kept catching my eye … trouble on the way …. Turned out her name was Cathy. We got on well, very well, and the original flirting took a step or two onwards but I was never completely adulterous and things just fizzled out between us after a little while. I stopped going to the dances with the lads. I just couldn't resist a pretty face, best to be safe than sorry I thought. Time went on and things at work were now working as I wanted them to. Everything was as much under control as anything can be with being in sole charge of so many animals. I was thriving on it anyway. Eventually Paula got pregnant again but this time the birth of our next child was to prove a bit more complicated than the three girls. In the end Paula had to be taken to Leicester Hospital and after a difficult time the baby was born, a boy at last. We named him SAMUEL (a family name over the years on my side) FRANCIS (after Frank) and ARTHUR (after Paula's dad). During Paula's confinement Beryl, the eldest of my foster sisters, came and stayed for a few days to look after the three girls. She then had to go back home ready for school. Because it was difficult for me to get much time off work a friend of Paula's (from her days as a nurse at Coleshill) said the children could go and stay with her and her husband and kids until such time as Paula and Sam could come home. This was only for two or three days and I went to fetch them back the evening before Paula was due to bring Sam home. When I got there they looked dirty and unkempt and said they were a bit hungry. I asked them what they wanted to eat. They just wanted Corn Flakes. Something they had every day at home so on the way home Corn Flakes were purchased along with a jar of honey. We got home. I put the girls in the bath and gave them a good scrub. I washed, dried and brushed their hair. The beloved Corn Flakes were served up with a good glob of honey on top. I put them all to bed in our "big bed" along with me and we all cuddled up and slept. They woke up and waited for their Mom and their new brother to get home.

The first Christmas with four children was only a couple of months away and I was getting a bit worried about having enough money for everything so I asked John if I could work all of my days off for the next 9 weeks. He said that if I thought I could do it then it was no problem for him but if I did get too tired I was to let him know. This really was the busiest time of the year in the dairy job because the working days were at their longest . . . maybe 10 hours a day on a good day. I didn't get too tired and Christmas came and went with everything I thought we, and the kids, needed.

At work and at home things trundled on. Work was challenging at times but very rewarding. The herd was doing well apart from the usual, expected, hiccups and small emergencies. This only made life more interesting. Things were going swimmingly but unfortunately the same couldn't be said about life at home. Things between Paula and I had really become a grind. We were just winding each other up constantly, arguing and rowing at almost every conceivable opportunity. Joanne and Collette, and I expect, maybe Naomi were beginning to notice. Sam was too young to realise what was happening so I decided it was time to call it a day and Paula didn't object. I didn't want the kids to grow up in the same atmosphere that I had before I upped sticks and went to live at The Cuttle. In hindsight both Paula and I agree, to this day, that we should never have got married in the first place as neither of us were ready for it at the time. It was time to call it a day for everyone's sake but, even to this very day, I still feel a certain amount of guilt about the whole situation as far as the children are concerned. Both Sam and Collette agree that it was the right thing to do for us to separate. As far as Naomi is concerned then, unfortunately, she blames everything for her

144

own failings and I'm afraid to say, is under the impression that she was, and still is, hard done by and that the world owes her a living in some way or another. That's up to her. That's just the way she is. It's not really her fault I suppose. Joanne became the real problem. What I was in fear of, i.e. her being mentally scarred by the whole affair, came to be. She was the eldest and could remember more because she was old enough to have absorbed more of the tension in the air during her early life. After a few "explosions of temperament" she decided to isolate herself from all of her family once she got old enough to get married and have children of her own. It's sad but I can understand why. Time went on. I was still working and all that but things were beginning to get a bit messed up "between my ears" so one day I decided that it would probably be the best all round if I "knocked it all on the head". I swallowed 75 aspirin and went to bed and tried to go to sleep, probably, and hopefully, never to wake up again. After 3 or 4 hours I still wasn't asleep. I was drowsy but fully conscious. I thought this wasn't going to work like this so best get it sorted one way or another. I phoned Frank and he came over and took me into hospital. At least they'd know the score. Anyway my stomach was duly pumped. I thought at the time it's like trying to swallow a drain rod. After a few days of treatment and copious amounts of Vitamin K being administered I made a recovery. I was allowed home but only after being told, in no uncertain terms, by the nurses that I was extremely lucky to have come out of it. As far as they were concerned the lethal dose of straight, stop bought, Aspirin was 9 tablets in one go . . . I had swallowed 75!! Apparently this drug doesn't put you to sleep it just burns its way through your stomach and you die of internal bleeding. Hence the Vitamin K treatment. It's known as the best aid to blood clotting. John was completely understanding and patient. In fact he came to visit me in hospital at least once and on returning home I eventually got back on my feet and back to my beloved dairy cows . . . ready to go again.

Since Paula and I had separated I'd begun to take Beryl, and sometimes Jackie, out dancing with me. I'd drive over, pick them up and then take them back home again before getting back home myself. I'd have a snooze for a few hours before starting work at between 2 and 3 in the morning. Not a problem. I was young and strong at the time. Beryl had a friend called Valerie. Not a lot to look at, but, bloody hell could she dance. Quite often I'd pick her up and we'd just go out dancing just for the love of it. Nothing more than that ever happened. Not even a peck on the cheek but we had good fun. We were never any more than dance partners.

The time had come round for the yearly Coleshill Carnival Dance so off I went. I picked Valerie up and proceeded to Coleshill Town Hall for a good night "strutting our stuff" as they say. I bought our tickets and in we went. Surprise, surprise who was in there, sitting on the stage with her brother and one of his friends? Only Linda Dutton. She of the long hair and even longer legs. She looked stunning, and sexy, as usual. She joined Valerie and I for the rest of the evening and when it was time to get my partner home I duly did so. After dropping Valerie off I raced back to Coleshill before the dance ended. I hooked back up with Lin and her brother and a few of his mates. We all went back to The Dutton dwelling and spent a few hours telling jokes, drinking (only tea in my case … a lifelong Tea Totaller … that's me) until it was time for me to leave. I went back to Pailton, ready for work, but not before Lin and I had agreed to see each other again the following evening. This was to be the start of a courtship, a relationship, and eventually a marriage that lasts until this day. I'm grateful for it because the road ahead would turn out to be very rocky at times. Emotional, exhilarating, worrying, but best of all bloody good fun for the best part anyway. THANK YOU LIN!!

There are new horizons ahead so let's turn our back to the wind, hold hands and see where it blows us!!

From now on Lin and I spent most evenings together. I'd drive over from Pailton to her Mom's place where she was living with Mandy and pick her up. We'd either go out somewhere or back to my place and then I'd take her back home at about 1 a.m. so that I could get back in time to start work as usual. At the time I had an old Austin Cambridge car which wasn't over keen to start in the mornings but if you more or less just waved the starting handle at it then it would fire up straight away. In those days I'd never buy any car that didn't come complete with a starting handle. I was no mechanic back then and still aren't today. Best to be on the safe side I always thought. Early one morning we were on the trip back to Coleshill, in the middle of the night basically, and were driving through Bedworth when there they were blue lights, sirens, the works . . . Mr Plod. They pulled us in, obviously convinced they were going to fill their little book up but, for some reason, they couldn't find anything wrong with the motor. This really seemed to infuriate them and I can remember them skulking round like blue arsed flies, underneath the car, checking everything they could lay their hands on but to no avail. They were muttering to each other that "There must be something wrong

146

with this motor somewhere". In the end they admitted defeat and let us go . . . the pair of plonkers!!!

Previous to this I had befriended a lad called Stuart Scull (during the time that he had been working at the Pheasantries) but he had moved on to become a gamekeeper on an estate in Wales. He invited us down to go and stay with him for a weekend in his cottage. A really old Welsh mountain cottage. The thing about this cottage that struck both Lin and I was the walls were made of stone and seemed to be at least 2 or 3 feet thick. We travelled there after work on the Friday evening. All three of us went out dancing at some club or other in Wrexham which wasn't really my scene as the night went on . . . too many pissheads about. We left earlyish and went for fish and chips and on the way home we drove past this club and it was surrounded by police. It seems we'd left at the right time. An enjoyable time was had by all three of us and early evening on the Sunday it was time to go home. Both Lin and I had to be back for work next morning. A nice peaceful drive back was on the menu but a spanner was about to be thrown into the works. I never drove anywhere at a sedate pace, to say the least. It came as a bit of a shock, when, on the descent of a decently steep Welsh road I put the brakes on to slow down a bit but nothing happened . . . OOPS!! The handbrake would have to hold the old car. The Austin Cambridge was a proper old fashioned, well built, heavy motor, so it was just a case of hold on tight and hope for the best. We went, basically in free fall, straight over a dual carriageway and a live level crossing before eventually gliding to a halt with the handbrake ratcheted up to its full extent. That was a bit of a close one again. Anyway, no real problem after that. We managed to nurse the old motor home using just the handbrake but it was time for the old motor to go to the "big garage in the sky". Shame really. I liked that old car.

The travelling to and fro from Pailton to Coleshill almost every evening lasted for a few months but in the end Lin and Mandy moved in with me. The cottage next door where Dora, Tom and the three kids were was eventually needed by John for another worker so they all moved out to an old farmhouse that had become empty on one of the other farms. A lad called David and his wife Rita moved in next door. He was a general farm worker/tractor driver but I had to teach him to milk so that he could do the jobs on my days off thus freeing John up to do other things. At times John got invited to various "off the farm" seminars and

147

demonstrations which up until now he'd managed to get to from time to time.   Now that David was able to milk then, if any invitation arrived that had got anything to do with the cows, he'd send me in his place. I only ever went to two. The first was at a big "experimental" dairy set up at Knaptoft in Leicestershire. This was a project run by the animal feed manufactures B.O.C.M. (British Oil and Cake Mills) where they would experiment with new feeds that they'd developed. They had five separate herds all managed and milked under separate regimes. It was an interesting day out. The second place I visited, on one of its open days, was at The Royal Showground in Kenilworth. This was where the M.M.B (Milk Marketing Board) "layed off" all the bulls they were using for A.1 (Artificial Inseminating) while the capabilities of the stock they had sired could be assessed. This was known as "Progeny Testing". These bulls were kept altogether in a big yard, with catwalks over the top, so that the stockmen could keep an eye on them while still remaining safe and out of harm's way. I always remember we were all on the catwalk being shown around by a member of the staff when the question was raised whether these bulls ever fought in any serious way.   It was revealed that they'd generally squabble between themselves and test each other out without any serious harm ever being done but, at the time we were there, it seemed that the "Numero uno" bull was a, not very big, Ayrshire. He was the smallest animal in the yard and when questioned as to how he'd managed to obtain and keep the number one spot in the pecking order our guide told us that this, almost little, bull would wait until his adversary got into such a position near the feed racks. He would then get this head and neck underneath his target and quickly lift and flip him up and drop him into the feed rack out of the way. Apparently this had happened several times and it had always ended up with the men having to go in and cut the unfortunate victim free with oxyacetylene torches. He may not have been the biggest bull in the yard but he was definitely the cleverest!!

Most of the big animal feed producers had their own farms in those days where they could experiment with different recipes and forms of livestock feed on their own stock but the most popular, because it was local, in our area at the time was a company called Midlandshire Farmers. Now, this firm didn't have their own farms or animals which, during my time with Tony Woods, came back to bite them in a big way, it seemed, in the end. A batch of bad feed oil had been used in their cattle feed operation. None of the cattle or calves would eat this food on any of the farms this product had been sold to. This ended up in the company having to re-call and collect all the offending feeds. This was O.K. for them when it was only bagged feed that they'd got to collect and replace but when it came to bulk feed it wasn't so easy. Our new parlour at Tony's had overhead bulk cake storage which fed the individual feeders below. When they had to come and remove everything (several tons) out of the cake loft it meant they had to send two or three men with sacks and manually remove it all by crawling on hands and knees for hours on end. Serves them right!! I'd never had a lot of time for M.S.F. or their feed. I didn't like the way they sort of experimented with their customers, stock, and livelihoods. Years and years later this fact came back into my life. I was a bit bored with life, as it was at the time, and at a bit of a loose end when I noticed in The Farmers Weekly Magazine the Midlandshire Farmers were advertising a job for a cattle feed salesman. Although I knew I'd have no chance of getting the job I applied anyway. An interview was arranged at their main mill at Stratford-on-Avon so off I trot. At the end of the "grilling" I was asked if there was anything I'd like to ask the assembled forum before I left. I just said "Yes there is really. What do I say to people when they ask why your cake is basically shit?" Needless to say I didn't get the job but it stuck one up em!!

Back at Pailton all was going well. Mandy was in school. The job was becoming more interesting and challenging and we still had a couple of goats and a few dogs knocking about. Old Tibby (the aged Lassie Collie dog I'd bought from John Ball years earlier) was still going strong and throwing some nice pups. Most of these we sold to Jessie Kembrell who we'd dealt with for a long time. She bred a lot of Afghan Hounds in those days. We'd bought a young bitch off her, called Kinky, because at some time in her past she'd managed to break her tail and it had mended with a kink in it. Jessie had a fair few Afghans all of which she called Karla. Every one of them. I asked her why they all had the same name and she said "Well if they get out then they will all respond to the same name won't they?" Good thinking because they were pretty good at liberating themselves from time to time. Up to the point that if they got too far across the fields she used to have to go and retrieve them on horseback. The exception to "The Karla Rule" was the stud dog. A nice big silver coloured boy that she'd named "Beautiful Boy" but his temperament defied his name. He could be a nasty piece of work if the mood took him and for some reason one day he decided that he didn't like Jessie anymore and got his front paws on her shoulders and bit her in the head.

Ever since that day she couldn't go to him unless she was wearing a crash helmet. A shame really because he did throw some nice pups. We used him in the years to come on a couple of our own bitches. Jessie would buy the pups back off us at £40 each. (I wish you could get them at that price now). She sent most of them off to Holland I think.

At home Tibby had been doing his stuff and we'd got four nice little half bred pups from him. They looked pure but they weren't. Three sable pups and one tri-colour. Jessie said she was interested in them but not the tri-colour. We took them down to her. "Lovely pups, but I don't want the Tri, you can't sell 'em. Everybody wants a sable. I don't want it" was her first remark. We didn't really want to be stuck with just one pup back home so I had to get the "old charm offensive" out but it had never really worked before. She was a hard bitten old bugger. "Come and look at my horses while you are here" she said. Begrudgingly I agreed. I wasn't the world's number one horse lover at the best of times. Off we trot up the field to view her beloved equine creatures. All going well. Everything she was telling me about them was going in one ear and out of the other but it kept her quiet. No problem. I thought, maybe if I keep going I can sell her the tri-coloured pup before we left. Then, as the horses were nuzzling around us both, one of the bastards trod on my foot and I was only wearing flip-flops. Should I chastise the beast or grin and bear it? The latter option prevailed. Back in the yard it seemed that my presumed interest in her horses had softened the old bird a bit. We got back on to the subject of the aforementioned tri-coloured pup. She eventually, reluctantly, agreed to buy it but we parted with her remark of "I bet it'll still be here next time you come!!" "Don't worry" I said "It will sell itself". We had no reason to return to the Kimbrell premises for a few weeks but when we did go back I asked her where the tri-coloured pup was. "Well" she said "I had someone here looking at them and they weren't at all interested in it, as I told you, but where ever they went it followed them and when they stood still it sat on their feet so they bought it and took it home in the end." "There you go" I said "Told you it'd sell itself" . . . Touché!!

Back at home, Dora's eldest daughter, Pam had moved into an old white cottage at the top of the lane. It was known as "The White House" . . . Mitchell it was good for Mandy as it gave her someone to play with. Pam decided that she preferred our cottage to The White House. More room for her brood, and a bit more modern, so we swapped homes. Lin, Mandy and I moved down the lane. The old cottage suited us O.K. and it was a fresh start really. We started to keep a few birds again and I'd scrounged a few of the redundant pheasant pens which we kept in the garden. I also converted one of the outside sheds into an aviary. Foreign birds were a lot cheaper back then and more easily available. We still kept the goats and the "doggy family" had grown. We'd bought a little Yorkie pup . . . and she was little. She could stand full length on one of my shoulders. She might have been small in size but she was a feisty little cow. She absolutely hated Kinky the Afghan. She'd get on the arm of a chair, wait until Kinky got close enough then launch herself at her and grab hold of her mouth flews. The poor old Afghan would be running about yelping her head off and trying everything she could to get rid of this hairy little parasite that was clinging on to her lips for all she was worth. "Spanky the Yorkie never ever grew out of this habit and she'd fight anything all her life. Yorkies back then seemed to grow their second set of teeth well behind their first set for some bizarre reason. This could cause a problem. Spanky adhered to this trait so Sandy advised us to let him take her baby teeth out because her second set weren't "pushing" them out. Off she went to the surgery and returned with less teeth than she'd gone in with. No problem. Now if Sandy ever came to the farm and I was home he'd just come up to the cottage, knock the door, shout "Its only me", take his boots off and just come in. This scenario occurred one lunch time. He knocked the door. Shouted out his presence to which Spanky pricked up her ears and started to growl. She must have recognized his voice and related it to her visit to his surgery. This she obviously hadn't enjoyed. She stood behind the door and as soon as an unbooted foot appeared she stuck her teeth in and latched on much as she would do with Kinky. No hard feelings!! Sandy thought it was laughable.

Kinky had inherited the habits of her "Karla family" and was not averse to taking herself off across the fields, whenever the chance arose, but she'd always come back but one day she didn't come back. I took two or three more dogs off with me to seek her out. In the past they had always found her before me. We eventually came across her lying down nursing a broken back leg. She'd broken the thigh bone somehow. This was not good news in a youngish, long legged, dog. Sandy decided it was best to have her in and put a rod down the bone until it healed. This he did and the bitch didn't seem to be bothered by it all until, whenever in later years, you told her off she'd all of a sudden start limping. "You can't tell me off – I've got a bad leg". Not so daft as silly looking!!

It was about this time that something happened that I'd never seen before or have seen since. I was fetching the cows in one afternoon, a hot afternoon. We'd had a spell of really sunny weather. I noticed that one of them was acting a bit "dippy" wandering about as if she was almost in a bit of a daze. I had a close look at her over at least a third of her body. The skin wrinkled. What was going on here then? Anyway we called Sandy out to cast his ever experienced eye over her. He concluded that she'd got sunstroke and that the wrinkly skin was the same as a human getting sun burnt. She eventually came back to reality and he made up some "Yellow Oils". A sort of very thin cream which I applied to her daily. The hard "burned" skin gradually softened enough to peel off but it was a slow job. The wise old vet reckoned that in "the old days" if ever a beast was prone to "taking the sun" then all her white parts would be painted with ink. You live and learn!!

Milking, one Sunday morning, one of the girls came into the parlour only to reveal that she'd badly damaged one of her back teats. It wasn't in a good way at all. Now, usually in cases such as this we inserted a teat syphon up through her teat and into her bag. This served two purposes. Firstly, once in place, the little plug at the end of the syphon could be removed and the milk in the quarter would drain out. Well that was the theory anyway. It usually worked for a while but most times after a couple of days the quarter would become infected and if antibiotics didn't work then she'd probably end "firing on only three" which, if she was a good, well bred, animal wasn't too bad because she would always have the chance of breeding some nice daughters. The second purpose of the plug was that it stopped the end of the teat from healing over completely which would have not been good news. This type of injury was not overly uncommon. I always made sure that we had a tub of plugs at hand. They were called "Columbus Teat Plugs" and came immersed in something similar to Vaseline in a little dark blue tub. One of these I noticed we would get in the Veterinary Medicine Box but on fetching it out, and opening it, I saw that it was just an empty tub. I'd overlooked that one. Now this beast really needed to have her teat plugged in some way, at least until the next day, when the empty tub could be replaced. I decided to make something similar using a very thin piece of wire covered in a couple of layers of thin bandage. This would at least stop any premature healing taking place. This was just a stop gap. As luck would have it Alec, the Polish fellow worker, was in the yard that morning . I asked him to give me a hand please. No problem. We put the patient in the crush (a large steel crate with a head yoke and a rear bar to hold the beast still . . . supposedly). The problem with this lady was that her teats pointed forward. A bad thing because to insert a plug the offending appendage needed to be as straight and true as possible to avoid any unnecessary further damage. I thought if I get in the crush with her then I'd be able to do the job without actually having to bend her teat from its natural position. We put a rope around her back leg, on the offending side, and hooked it over the top bar of the crush. This enabled Alec to lift her leg off the ground and keep her as still as possible. That was the theory anyway. It worked until I actually inserted the home made plug. This was thicker than the ones "off the shelf" which could usually be put in place no problem at all and pretty painlessly. This one was different. Bigger. Hence it hurt a bit on insertion and it was at this moment that she started to object. She began to throw herself about a bit and although she was reasonably well secured at both ends she somehow managed to knock me down on the floor. I basically ended up partially sandwiched between the cow and the ground. Luckily Alec was on hand and he let her back leg down and she stood up on all fours and I could get out of it. A bit battered and bruised but, as I thought at the time, no real harm done. It would have been worse without Alec because I'd have tried to do it on my own. Just lifting her potentially dangerous leg up and tied it off with rope to the side of the crush. If this scenario had evolved then I would have been up "shit street" but anyway for her all turned out well. After a bit of treatment and antibiotics she went on as normal but I was beginning to get a few twinges below the waist and in the base of my spine. This was to be expected I suppose. It didn't really make a lot of difference until a few days later we'd got a cow that had "slipped her calf". This meant it was born way too early and dead. This, in those days, was a worry because it was a recognised symptom of Brucellosis, contagious abortion. So until blood tests had been taken, and proven negative, then any animal in this situation had to be totally isolated from the herd and her milk thrown away. This meant back to the old hand milking for her for a day or two. This was when my back started to suggest that maybe I'd done more damage in the previous accident than I'd thought, or dared to assume. I was squatting down milking this lady by hand. No problem until I tried to stand up. It seemed all the power in my legs was having "time off". I just couldn't seem to have the strength in them to get myself upright. I just grabbed hold of the cow's tail, gave her a prod and this spurred her into action and more or less enabling me to hoist myself back up to the vertical. It was decided it would be best if I went and had the injury looked at. The X-rays revealed that I'd damaged 2 or 3 vertebrae in the bottom of my spine. Not enough to warrant surgery so the prescription was pain killers and rest. I was O.K. with the painkillers but you could stick "the rest" up your arse. I didn't do "resting" if I could help it. This injury would keep coming back to let itself be known for years and years to come. No treatment ever worked only Morphine in the end but that was probably 20 years on.

Time went on, no problems, until one day a "spanner was thrown into the works" . . . Paula. Although she was living with the kids in Norfolk she had managed to get a council house in Pailton just a mile down the road from us. This was trouble and upset all around on the horizon. I've never blamed her for doing that, for herself and the kids, of course. It just seemed strange that she must have been able to pull a lot of strings or something to get a Council House over 150 miles away from where she was living. I could see what was going to happen. Time to up sticks and move on for everyone's sake. I went to speak to John and his wife about it all. Although he was sad that a parting of the ways was inevitable he agreed it was the best thing for all concerned. I was sad. This was the best and most satisfying job I'd ever had. I'd worked and tried hard since I was a kid to get where I was.   Not only the job but also John. He was the best boss I'd ever had or would have. (Sadly he died 15 years ago). I often wonder, up to this day, what would have happened if we'd stayed there for any length of time. Would I have got bored? Would my restlessness have come back? Who knows? I think eventually I would have somehow taken up Sandy Lyons' offer and gone and worked at the vets and then I would have studied Bovine Veterinary Medicine. Just specialising in cattle disease and ailments. Although I like and enjoy keeping most animals I love my dogs. I also love my birds but if I had to choose one animal to work with full time then it would be dairy cattle in some way or another, especially the veterinary side of the job. As it turned out in years to come Mandy would probably have taken over from me on the farm with the cows because during the years to come we'd still be "messing about with dairy cows". Mandy liked to come and help me whenever she could. She was keen, interested and was willing to learn off "the old man". I thought I'd teach her all I knew. Most of that was to be seen as old fashioned ways but that's the way I learned and it did me good. It set me on a good grounded path because no matter how much mechanisation and computer based technology you have none of it will ever replace the herdsman's eye, touch and feel or "third sense" and good honest down to earth old school stockmanship. No college or form of technology can ever teach that. It's like an old farmer once said "The best fertilizer in the world is His Masters Foot". I've always had and still do, to this day, the belief that a good stockman uses all his senses and you only acquire those by a compilation of starting at the bottom and learning the hard way. That never goes away and these days I often wonder how many college educated young cowmen can actually milk by hand nowadays. It's all beyond me and when I see so called modern practices on T.V. it makes me bloody mad. I really get on my "high horse" about it. Enough said.

All the above is "ifs and buts" . Life didn't turn out that way and, if it had, my story from now on would have been completely different to how it turned out. The restless spirit and the hunt for "something out there" was about to take over our lives. Sometimes for the good and sometimes for the not so good. Time to go and chase something that I couldn't see . . . and still cannot, even after all these years of looking for it!!

Well time to start reading the situations vacant section of The Farmers Weekly again and try and find a job that was somewhere near to the one that I was about to leave. Basically it was more or less a case of taking the first one I was offered that might suit me. This turned up in the shape of David Fletcher who farmed at East Leake near Loughborough in Leicestershire. The job seemed O.K. (I say this reservedly) but the thing that actually helped us decide to give it a go was the house etc. that came along with it. A big old farmhouse and all the outbuildings that we wanted to use . . . within reason of course. Ideal for the dogs we thought. Bags of room and it would help on the financial side of things. Lin got a little cleaning job a couple of miles down the road to see us over until we could get up and running and Mandy started school and settled in o.k. The actual job was basically shit. The kind of work I was doing 10 years earlier. A step down the ladder, basically, rather than a step up. It should have at least been on a par to that with John Gray at Pailton. Anyway we carried on. We managed to get a few more dogs together, basically from people we already knew. An Afghan bitch from Jessie Kimbrell called Karla of course. A couple of Shetland Sheepdogs and we'd got to know three ladies who bred dogs out towards Worcester. Lin had always wanted a Great Dane so we contacted a woman named Mrs Seager who kept, bred, and showed this breed. She let us have a youngish bitch that had come to her as a rescue dog. We called her Mandy and she stayed with us and bred some nice pups for years to come. We also managed to get another Afghan bitch from a woman who moved in the same "doggy circle" as Mrs Seager. This bitch had just got through a very severe case of fox mange. One of the troubles with keeping dogs out in the sticks. She'd been successfully treated and had by now grown the most beautiful silky coat I'd ever seen. She was a bit of an aristocratic, for want of a better word, character. She didn't like getting wet or getting her feet dirty in anyway shape or form but she settled in well. Basically by keeping herself to herself. Indeed she went missing one day. We couldn't find her anywhere but Lin said she'd go and have a look in the house and on entering our bedroom lo and behold there was "Lady Portia" in our bed, covers pulled up over herself and her head on the pillow fast asleep. A sight to be seen indeed. The other woman in this trio of dog breeding friends, from that little area near Worcester, was a lady called June Nevette. She was almost another Jessie Kimbrell. Dogs everywhere. Cocker Spaniels, Poodles, Old English Sheepdogs to name just a few of the breeds housed at her establishment. Things were "a bit rough" at her place. We took a couple of Cocker Spaniel bitches off her, a black and white one called Megan and a golden roan one called Sheba. Two nice little ladies. In fact Meg turned out to be one of the best brood bitches we ever had. Then there was Tess. Now Tess was an Old English Sheepdog bitch with "problems between her ears" is one way of putting it. For no reason at all, anytime of the day or night, she'd just decide that something, anything, was "hers" and guard it with her life. Indeed, on one occasion, Mandy had gone to get on her bike, which was propped up in a corner in the yard, but Tess had decided, in her wisdom, that this was now her bike and no one was having it. A quick smack up the ear soon resolved that problem. There was no rhyme or reason to her behaviour. Sometimes she would go for weeks without it happening and then all of a sudden this mood would overcome her again and she'd decide that something, anything, it could be a bucket, a shovel a dish anything was hers. She'd keep it up for a few hours or maybe a day or two. Then she'd get fed up with it and come back to the real world for a while.

We decided we'd like a Bassett Hound. We had all the room in the world at home now. I knew someone who kept and bred, Bassetts, Beagles and Bloodhounds. A certain Mr Trevor Howard, the very man who, years earlier, had tried to take me for a fool with the so called "young" Chihuahua bitch. I hadn't forgotten. Let's go and see what we could do. Off we went. By this time his daughter, Susan, had basically taken over most of the dogs and she'd got some young Bassetts. We bought and paid her for a lemon and white bitch. We called her Bimbo. She used to make us laugh because when they are puppies their ears are still extremely long, and because they are vertically lacking in the leg department they do, at times, stand on their own ears. This is funny. Poor little Bimbo would break into a bit of a trot and her ears would take on a mind of their own. From time to time she'd go "arse over tip" because she had trodden on her own ear. She soon grew out of it when her legs started to grow. Anyway back to Trevor Howard. We'd had a deal with Susan when the man himself turned up and revealed that he'd got two Bloodhounds he wanted to re-home. A bitch called Eva and a dog called Jonny. We couldn't afford to buy them so he said that we could take them away and when they bred we would have to give him two pups as payment. Agreed, so off we go back to East Leake with a pair of adult Bloodhounds and a Bassett pup. The three new dogs settled in well but Jonny was a bit of a pain in the arse really. We decided to sell him out of the way. He went off to be a pet at a big old house/come small estate. He settled in well there and from correspondence we had from his new owners he basically took over the place and was the life and soul of the party. Apparently he had almost a free run of the place. His only problem was that when his new owners had a dinner party or something posh like that he'd just run up to everybody and slobber all over their fine party clothes but he was well loved.

Spanky (our tiny little Yorkie bitch) was still pursuing her career of hassling Kinky at every possible chance. She never, ever, stopped this habit but it was revealed one day that Kinky had hatched "a cunning plan" to deal with this little parasite of hers. We looked out into the yard one evening and she was busy burying something at the time. I said to Lin "What the hell has Kinky got now". She was a bit of a delinquent at times. We crept upon her to see that she'd dug a hole. She must have then gone and caught Spanky, put her in the hole, and was holding her in there with one of her front feet and was proceeding at a frantic pace to try and bury her!! I asked Lin to go and get the camera quick but it was too late the little sod, Spanky, had managed to escape, run off and lived to hassle poor young Kinky another day. That really was a once in a lifetime sight.

Everything going O.K. with life now except for two things really. First of all the effects of my accident at Johns, where I had damaged the base of my spine, were now beginning to make themselves a bit more apparent. The pain, due to an aggravated sciatic nerve, was now getting to be a bit of a problem. At odd times I couldn't stand up. I was more or less in constant pain of varying degrees and was popping pain killers like they were going out of fashion. As it turned out, this problem was to be something that would stay around for many years to come. The second thing was, my job, so boring, so frustrating. All that I was doing or less in the years earlier. My "career" in the dairy industry was slowly grinding to a halt. Time to bail out and try and find something better. For years John Ball and his family, at Tamworth, had been trying to persuade me to go and work for them. The trouble was there was no cottage with the job. However it was agreed that they'd supply us with a caravan in the yard and we could use two runs of brick built pig sties that had been roofed over etc. to form one complete building to keep our dogs in. I'd bought many a dog out of this building in years gone by. We agreed to give it a go and Lin, Mandy and myself moved into our new place. The trailer (caravan) was about 20-22 feet long but we'd see how it went for a while. It wasn't the best situation in the world because at the time we had no vehicle and the public transport only went past the farm every couple of hours. This was O.K. for shopping but not so good for getting Mandy to school. It meant that Lin had to walk her to school, about 2 miles away, and then walk back again. The same again at home-time. This wasn't a leisurely walk up and down some pretty country lane. Most of the journey entailed walking on the grass verges at the side of the main "A" road between Tamworth and Ashby. This wasn't good. The job was O.K. Somewhere in between what we'd just left at Loughborough (which was a bit of a step in the right direction) and the position I'd created for myself with John. I was beginning to despair that anything like that would come around again but, as I know now, a similar opportunity would present itself in the future but, of course, I didn't know that at the time. Early one morning, it was still basically dark, I was in the cattle sheds when a Barn Owl flew right past my head. I didn't hear it coming at all, just a ghost like experience, and I thought to myself, I've just heard silence. An amazing bird.

The dog part of our life began to expand. We had now acquired a little Pekinese bitch called Mae Ling. A Standard Poodle bitch (Polly) and a Red Setter (Patsie) that at some time must have had distemper because she had chorea, a permanent shake, in one of her front legs. Therefore she was unwanted so we gave her a home. She had come from June Nevette who we'd had deals with in days gone by. We also got from this very same lady, an Old English Sheepdog called Danny, who, June had said could be a handful and could be a bit Up himself at times". She said that if we took him she'd give us two miniature poodle bitches, sisters, a chocolate young lady called Flotsum and her sister, a black bitch called Jetsum. She said they were no good to her "Because she couldn't get them in pup". We agreed to take these three along with the Irish Setter. She bought them over to us but made it very clear that Danny could be a bit nasty at times. She bought him into the trailer where he was confronted by the little Peke bitch who wasn't impressed by his presence and she made this fact be known in no uncertain terms!! He just stood there and piddled himself. He turned out to be no more than a great big kid. A bit thick between the ears but totally harmless. I said his brain feel out at the same time his tail was taken off. He lost them both at the same time in my eyes but he was a laugh, a proper clown. We had no transport so we arranged with a reasonably local slaughterhouse to have "X amount" of dog meat. Mainly tripe and sheep's heads to be delivered to us every Saturday morning. The dry food was delivered whenever we needed it. This worked out O.K. until, one Friday, the slaughterhouse phoned to say that they couldn't deliver this week because their motor had broken down and wouldn't be on the road for a few days because of the Bank Holiday. What a time for all this to happen!! We had got enough dry food for a day but that was it. This meant that the dogs had gone two days with nothing to eat so as a last resort we bought some rolled barley and cow cake off the boss. We emptied our cupboards leaving just enough for us until the shops re-opened on the Tuesday after the long weekend. Everything went into a big mix, the rolled barley, jelly cubes (I always remember those) sugar, milk gravy granules, potatoes, all the tinned food we could spare. They would have to eat this and eat it they did with a passion. In fact, they literally "Polished" ... in the true sense of the word...."Off". I use the word "polished" in this case because the kennels they lived in were old brick built pig pens. The troughs were made out of glazed ceramic and built in the pen. After that fed they really shone squeaky clean. Anyway, things righted themselves the next day and all was well. Over the years we would always fed dead calves or lambs to the dogs if and when they came along but, typically sods law, nothing like that was available at this time of need.

Because we had no vehicle then taking the bitches off to be mated had to be done by using public transport. This was not too bad. We had found a woman in Lichfield that bred miniature poodles and had a stud dog which was good because within a few weeks of us having Flotsum and Jetsum they both came into season. We got them both mated with the stud dog owned by this lady. Eva, the Bloodhound, was a bit more of a problem. She was a big old lump at the best of times. The nearest dog we could find was a breeder called Mrs White whose family ran a coach business in Nottingham. We contacted her and she agreed to let us use one of her dogs but, first of all she wanted to see Eva to check she was good enough to use one of her dogs on, before she agreed to anything. So off we trot, via public transport, with Eva to Nottingham. Luckily Mrs White and her daughter liked her and agreed that a mating could be arranged when the time was right. She said she'd got two males. Her prize stud called "Deburn Ulysses" and a younger boy that had never been used. He was about 5 years old and she thought that we should try him on Eva. All agreed. Time went on, Eva came in season, so time for another trip to Nottingham. She was well ready to be mated so her suitor was introduced. He was like a mad bull at a small gate and our girl was having none of it. She'd never been mated before and if this is what it was like then she'd decided she'd rather remain virginal . . . thank you very much. It was decided that between us we'd try for a mating anyway. The dog was put on a lead and so was Eva. I stood with her head between my legs, Lin held her body still, and Mrs White's daughter bought the dog up on his lead but he was still rampant and as soon as he mounted our bitch she was having none of it. She'd bend her head as far round my leg as she could and snapped at him. This only resulted in him getting aggravated and then start snapping at her. My leg and Lin's arms were between the two of them. Someone was going to get bitten here at this rate. It was decided to call it a waste of time and effort. He would be put back in his kennel and the "Old boy Ulysses" was introduced. He greeted her with all courtesy and good manners, washed her face, nuzzled her ears, a perfect gentleman. All that was missing was a bunch of flowers so far as Eva was concerned. This was much better so we let her off her lead and they played together. He was whispering "sweet nothings" into her big pendulous ears. They eventually took themselves off up the yard, hand in hand, so we just left them to it for a while. They went out of our sight amongst the parked up coaches. They hadn't reappeared for a while so I went and had a look. He'd mated her no problem. It seemed she preferred being "wined and dined" to being basically raped. Job done at last. Now it was just a waiting game. Time to go home and see what happens. As the weeks went by it was obvious she was in pup. Whether it was a change in her hormones or what I don't know but she began to get a bit "Broody and Moody". This came to a head one day. She got out of her kennel and managed, somehow, to get hold of Polly (the standard poodle). They fought. Polly came off the worst, of course, and we lost her. Lin was extremely upset to say the least. It turned out, in years to come, that Eva had acquired the art of being able to climb most things but it was a sad day especially for poor Lin. Both the poodles were now in pup so they moved into the trailer with us and just wandered about outside with the Peke. Exercising all the others meant taking them all out twice a day for a good run and play across the fields and down to the river. This was a job my good lady took on along with Mandy when she wasn't at school because I was at work. It was no problem. Well it was no problem until it came to the Afghans. It is a brave man that will let Afghans run free in an unrestricted environment. They just don't know when to stop. Jessie had demonstrated this years earlier when her Afghans got out. It was a case of catching them up on horseback. We managed to partially overcome this problem by tying 2 or 3 washing lines together, attaching this to their collars, wrapping them around a long stick, holding this in the crooks of our elbows across our belly, and then just them run until the line ran out. They could then run about as much as they liked but we could still get them back with no problem. A bit time consuming but it was the best we could come up with and it worked well. Flotsum and Jetsum both had got their pups by now. Thirteen between them. Not bad for two bitches that supposedly couldn't get in pup . (No wonder, it turned out that June Nevette had been keeping them in a coal house!!) Flo (Flotsum) had seven lovely pups. Jet (Jetsum) had five lovely pups and one "dyer" that spent most of its time trying to depart this world but Lin managed to keep it going. Jet didn't want anything to do with it. She would push it away to the edge of her nest. She knew it wasn't right. I always say Mother Nature knows best but Lin insisted on perservering with it. I'd give it to her when I got up early in the morning and she would feed and have it in bed with her. I told her she was wasting her time. The pup wasn't thriving at all. It was just being kept alive but she insisted and carried on. It eventually got to the point that as soon as Jet heard me get up in the morning she'd bring this dear little pup and put it on the bed for Lin to sort out….. cheeky little sod. One morning I put my foot down. The pup was just surviving but it wasn't happy or thriving. I put it straight back in the nest with its siblings. Jet looked at it, sniffed it, turned around and promptly and deliberately sat on it and killed it. She knew it was never going to be any good, and she was right, a mother's instinct. Flotsum and Jetsum reared the twelve remaining pups, no problem, and we sold them all to the lady in Lichfield whose dog we used. We already owed her two of them as a stud fee anyway. She also bought the two sisters and kept them for herself. It all worked out well in the end. We had found Flo and Jet a good home and sold the ten pups all in one go. Not bad for two little ladies that had been subjected to a life in a coal house and rendered unbreedable from. Tess and Daniel (the Old English Sheepdogs) had "got married" but managed to produce only one puppy. As I said earlier Tess was in the habit of suddenly deciding that something, anything was "hers" and getting really possessive over it. This habit got to the extreme with her pup. When she wasn't feeding the pup she'd bury it sometimes, along with a bone or a piece of meat, in her nest and gently lie on top of it guarding it with her life. She meant it, no messing. Strange bitch with a strange habit but there you go. It takes all sorts.

Everything was O.K. at work. It was a zero grazed herd. This meant that the cows stayed in all year round and the grass was harvested and taken to them to feed on in the yards. This was supposedly done to "save the land". It was a system I'd never had anything to do with before this but, before we moved to Loughborough after leaving Pailton, I had applied for a job with a 300 plus strong herd of Ayrshire cows that were milked three times a day and were kept on this system. It was a huge set up for those days. They were basically milking up to 24 hours a day on a shift system. They had been doing this for years apparently so they really understood the job. When I went for the job I commented on how many silage harvesters they had got on the place and the boss said it was a necessity in case of breakdowns with over 300 cows dependant on all their grass being taken to them. There was no time for mishaps. I asked him what was the most important thing about managing so many highly productive beasts on this system and on this scale. He said that what he'd found over the years was to get the vet in once a week to walk through the herd and observe the herd on catwalks. A fresh pair of eyes because things could go unnoticed by the herdsmen when they were always in such close contact with so many cattle. Basically, almost a case of "familiarity breeds contempt". This wasn't a system I thought I could get on with. By the time we ended up at Tamworth and was confronted with the same scenario, although on a much smaller scale, I still couldn't get my head round it to any form of satisfaction but needs must.

The back problem of mine was slowly but surely getting worse. Basically the pain in my left leg was more or less constant to varying degrees and I was now walking with a limp on that side. Most days it was just a case of "shut your eyes and keep going". But sometimes it got a bit much and I was referred to the hospital in Lichfield to see if anything could be done to ease things. After the usual X-rays etc. etc. I was given an appointment to see the specialist in such matters. He said that he thought he could see what the problem was but not really clear enough to risk an operation especially at my relative youth. He told me that they did not really like to perform such a risky procedure on anyone under 50 years old because if it did not go to plan it was not so good. He said to me that I'd walked into the hospital that day but if he operated I would leave in any one of three ways :- Either walk out, go out in a wheelchair or be carried out in a box . He advised me to keep going on as I was and that there was a slight chance that things might put themselves right sometime in the future especially if I tried to take things easier and find a job that was less physically stressful. That that might be a problem in my life. I'd never known any "less physically stressful" way of life. Time for us to sit and think about what to do next. We came to the conclusion that perhaps find a job in kennels somewhere. That work would be a lot lighter and would suit us all because by now the doctors had referred me to The Medical Board to have my condition assessed by a panel of doctors and they decided that I should temporarily be registered as disabled. So time to try and slow down a bit at least for a while anyway. After trawling through the Canine Press we found a position in Wiltshire for a couple to manage a boarding kennel and cattery with chalet accommodation on site available and "own dogs welcome". We arranged to go for an interview. We travelled by train to Trowbridge and were met by a lady called Marion Wells and from there went on to see the kennels and talk about the job and things. Our destination was Elmsgate Kennels on the outskirts of a little village called Steeple Ashton, some five or six miles out of Trowbridge, on the way to Warminster. A lovely "old fashioned" kennels were revealed. Four rows of good sized grass runs with their own individual wooden kennels all surrounding a grass paddock that must have been at least an acre in area. The site also included a block of indoor kennels. A big outside cattery and a big inside cattery. A two or three acre paddock and a chalet for us to live in contained in its own compound. All terms and conditions were agreed between Marion, Lin and myself and we agreed to move in, along with most of our own dogs, within the next month. On getting back home we talked things over with the Ball family and they agreed it was the best thing for us to do. It was better than staying there, struggling on trying to do the best I was now capable of, and risking making the spinal condition worse. They wished us well for the future and we departed on good terms which was nice at least. We had no car so we hired a van and Lin's uncle drove us. Along with her Dad we loaded our very few belongings and most of our dogs. We had to rehome a few because we couldn't take all of them with us. By now Karla (one of the Afghans) had got a litter of pups. We'd managed to get her across to Jessie Kimbrells (where she had come from) and get her mated there. So off we went on to a new chapter and not too much of a lifestyle change really. Just no cows anymore but a physically less demanding way of going on. When we'd originally gone for our interview with Marion another woman was also there. An older woman called Rae Norris. It turned out she'd got kennels further up the road and she was there to offer us a similar position if we couldn't come to an agreement at Elmsgate Kennels but that was by the by now. It was a nice offer anyway. Within the first week of arriving in Wiltshire Marion bought her husband, Barry, to meet us. It seems their marriage had broken down and at the time they were trying to sort things out between themselves. Barry had moved back to London and Marion and their daughter, a little girl called Denise, the same age as our Mandy, had moved into a rented cottage in Trowbridge. This left the day to day running of the kennels up in the air. Hence our introduction into the business. The wage wasn't that good but it was free housing, electric and water etc. and it was a lovely place. Just outside the village. Within easy walking distance to the shop and school for Mandy and we could keep as many of our own dogs there as long as they didn't impinge on the overall business of the place. There was a couple of aviaries on site which were also at our disposal. Although the paddock was rented out to a girl who owned a pony we could also share that by mutual agreement. Marion used this space for part of her dog training classes that she held weekly. Young Denise and Mandy got on really well. Both the same age and with the same interests. She had been sent off to boarding school but when she came back home she spent most of her time living with us in the chalet. It seems like she wasn't her Mom's number one love in life but it was no problem her staying with us anyway. It was a shame for the little girl really, being passed between her Mom in Trowbridge and her Dad in London. This situation was eased for her once she started to stay with us. It was obvious that her and her Mom were not on the best of terms but she loved her Dad, Barry, and he'd come and visit her whenever he could. She was always a bit tearful when he went away again although most of the time she was "parked" at boarding school. She and Mandy seemed to be almost like little sisters. The poor little bugger must have been lonely and bewildered. She told us that she hated going back to the school but at least she was happy when she was staying with us. There were two other people that were more or less "attached" to Elmsgate Kennels. A young lad by the name of Steve who dossed in the indoor cattery and was a bit of an odd job man. Cash in hand to supplement his dole but he was just a dosser really. This didn't go down too well with me so he eventually "moved on" out of the way. The other lad was a lad in his late 20's a bit of a "hippy" chap for want of a better word who did Marion's dog meat round for her. Delivering door to door around the area. Seems he was divorced and homeless so he did this job for her and slept in the delivery van overnight parked up on the car park at the kennels. He was a lovely bloke, really funny and at least he was trying to help himself not like the "ex cattery dweller". He became a good friend (more of that to come) and he was good with Mandy and Denise. It turned out he'd got two daughters of his own about the same age. He would come over to our chalet from time to time and we'd feed and water him whenever he needed it. Somebody had recently contacted Marion to say that she had got a Doberman bitch that was in pup but she didn't think that she had the capabilities or room to let her have and rear her pups at home. She was wondering if she could leave her with us during the time of her confinement. If we agreed we could keep all of the pups except one which she wanted for herself. She would take that away with her when she collected the bitch…. Deal done. Rusty, as the bitch was known, turned out to be a bit of a strange one. She'd be perfect for days on end then, all of a sudden, she'd just turn on you and she meant it at the time. A bit of a psycho really. Anyway she whelped and reared her pups fine, no problem, so after a couple of months she, along with one of her pups, were collected by her owner never to be seen again. The rest of the litter Marion sold to a dog dealer and Great Dane breeder near Heathrow Airport that she'd worked for in the past. More about him later. Eva the Bloodhound had also become a mother by now but it turned out that although she was lovable she was a proper wimp. At the merest suggestion of any sort of pain she'd start to howl and cry and at the time of her parturition the first pup was well forward and impatient to be introduced to the world outside. As soon as it got to anywhere near being born the pain seemed to be "More than I can possibly bear" in Eva's words. She got up, sat down on her arse as hard as she could and basically crossed her back legs, shut her eyes and howled. We could feel it wasn't a big pup. She could have had it easily if she'd grow up. This scenario continued for a while so we decided to get her up to the vets for an injection of Oxytocin. If the pups were capable of being born naturally then she'd have to have them now and sure enough, before she knew what was happening, she was a mother and she was a good mother. She had three pups. One dog and two bitches. We kept the two girls, a black and tan called Gretel and a liver and tan called Sloopy. The boy went off to a man who owned a pub in Somerset. He also wanted Eva. He absolutely fell for her but we said no. In the world of "well wrinkled dogs" a common problem was a condition known as Ectropion eye lids. This basically means that due to the weight of skin on the head then, sometimes, the upper eye lids get pulled down out of their normal position. Hence causing the eyelashes to aggravate the actual eye. Gretel was a text book example of this although Sloopy and the dog pup didn't suffer this affliction. We decided to have this rectified at the vets so off she went for the procedure but once everything was healed it turned out that she was cross eyed!! It didn't bother her in the slightest and it was humorous to look at her . . . bless her!!

The love of Marion's life was Bulldogs. She had four or five of them. Not our favourite breed (bad luck carriers). She would "park" one or two of them with us for a few days from time to time and the one that sticks out in my mind was a white bitch (an ugly little sod) called Sadie. She was no problem but Spanky (the professional Afghan Hound plague) took an instant and utter dislike to her. She hated her with a vengeance. She'd get on the "bunk" (bunkette) in the trailer and every time poor old Sadie came anywhere near her then she'd totally "loose her rag". She never actually bit her but the verbal abuse and intended carnage absolutely flooded out of the little dog but Sadie was never impressed. She'd just put her head right close up to her and snort in her face as if to say "Shut up you silly little twat, I ain't going anywhere" This attitude totally wound poor old Spanky up even more and she'd get into such a state every hair on her body would stand upright. Her eyes would bulge and her teeth would be on constant view below snarled lips. I said that one day she'd explode with hatred and frustration. It was almost as if she was actually standing up on her toe nails but Sadie just took no notice at all and more or less snorted "Whatever!!" Poor little Spanky. She went through life convinced she was the biggest and most dangerous dog in the world . . . bless her. She only stood two or three inches high.

Time went on and either Kinky or Karla (the Afghans) had given birth to a litter of pups. We had her in the trailer with us for a week or two until she'd settled. She loved her pups. The trouble was so did one of the Peke bitches (Mae Ling) and every time mother left her brood to go outside then the Peke would jump in and "take over". This habit we had to keep an eye on because she did mean it. So much so that the mother more or less had to ask permission to have her pups back. The situation needed to be kept an eye on because sooner or later the maternal hormones would have taken over and we'd have ended up with a mess. Fortunately that scenario was averted and mother and babies went off outside into a kennel and run of their own.

On the subject of Afghan hounds we used to have a male of the breed come in for boarding. A real handsome boy called "Groovy". A black dog with tan featherings. He stood probably getting on towards 30 inches (75 cms) at the shoulder and sporting a coat to die for. The silkiest most flowing hair I've ever seen on a dog. He was groomed every day by his owners and they paid us £6.00. a week to do the same. It was a joy to look at this dog. So much so that we'd let him out in the compound and he would just sort of float around in front of all the surrounding kennels and runs letting all the other residents "gaze upon his very presence". I always said he was like some hippy bloke…. "Yo girls, ain't I the coolest dude you've ever seen". At times he'd get excited and show off even more by tearing round the compound in "full flight" just a mass of black silky hair and head held high. He really loved himself. If ever a dog suited his name then it was this fella …. Groovy by name and Groovy by nature!!.

We had still got Mandy, the Great Dane, but by now our Dane collection had grown by two. Firstly a black dog called Nero. Now in those days it was a general rule of thumb that there was no such thing as a "good" black Great Dane. In fact it was even being considered by the "powers that be" that if shown in the ring then they should be in a class of their own because they were generally such bad examples of the breed. Nero was not an exception to this rule. A skinny thing with the most "dished nose" you could imagine. Lin had gone off somewhere and bought him and when she arrived home with him I wasn't a "happy chappie". I Just said "What have you bought him for ? His nose is that dished that it could hold enough water to keep bloody goldfish in". To which she replied "Well at least he was cheap. I gave 20 quid for him". Welcome to the fold Nero. The other addition came about when somebody from somewhere miles away in Surrey had contacted Marion to say that she'd got three dogs she wanted to re-home and that if we fetched them then they'd be for free. No payment involved. It turned out that they were three bitches, a fawn Great Dane (Sarah)and two Bullmastiffs. A cream bitch called Hannah and a red bitch called Samantha. Marion agreed that we'd go and get them that evening. Now at this time she'd hooked up with some bloke called Howard. A proper prat to say the least. One of those blokes in his early 20's who reckoned he'd done everything, knew everything and been everywhere. In reality he was no more than a useless "gobshite". Anyway he and I were despatched off to Surrey, one early evening, to collect these three canine ladies in Marion's motor. A very old Saab estate in need of a bit of care and attention but it really did motor on. The two front doors were held shut by a piece of rope across the front seats. We duly arrived at our destination, picked the dogs up, and began the return journey. By now it was the early hours the next day. I was tired and hungry and this dick head Howard was really "getting on my tits" by this time so we pulled into some overnight café for a cup of tea and a sandwich. Howard was by now really winding me up with his "I am the greatest thing since sliced bread" attitude when two or three loud mouthed, seemed like London, blokes came in "giving it large". This was, to me, adding insult to injury. I had not only been listening to this idiot for the last God knows how many hours and now I had got to put up with a group of "all mouth and trousers" dick heads. I had had enough so I turned to my travelling companion and said to him in a voice that could have been heard through the whole establishment "Do you know Howard if there is one thing I can't stand then its fuckin' Cockneys." I've never seen a bloke move so fast in all my life. Howard was up through the door and into the motor, had it started up and was shouting to me "Quick get in". What a proper wanker but at least he was quiet the rest of the way home.

Lin loved her Great Danes but they did nothing for me and never have done. As far as I was concerned they were just great big lumps full of nothing. No real life in them as far as I could see but Sarah wasn't typical. She was full of spirit and would stand her own ground up to a point. I liked her but Spanky had diverted her hate away from the Afghans and Bulldogs and had now got her sights on the big, new, leggy, woman who had dared to try and introduce herself into HER space. She constantly hassled poor young Sarah at every opportunity. Basically she was, in Sarah's eyes, no more than a bloody nuisance until one day she must have had enough. The kennelmaid came rushing in shouting and screaming

168

that Sarah had got hold of Spanky and was running around with her almost completely entombed in her mouth. Anyway, we went to find the Great Dane trotting about, as pleased as punch, with her head held high and a couple of the Yorkie's legs just visible poking out between her jaws. When she saw us coming, and after being shouted at, she dropped the pesky little shit. We kept Spanky all her life. She was always a little dog with a big attitude but this was the closest she ever came to being killed. At the time of her release, from the jaws of doom, she just lay on the ground sporting one, two, three or four puncture holes in her torso and head each of which was spurting blood in various degrees. We washed her off, stopped her bleeding, treated her wounds and put her in a nice warm, dark, bed next to the fire and after a couple of days she started to recover. It was a slow recovery but eventually she returned to her old self. We used to have a break mid-morning most days and go in the trailer for toast and a drink. The seat where we usually sat, at these times, had an opening window directly behind it at head/shoulder height and it was the time of year to have this window ajar. I used to throw my toast crusts out through it and the dogs would pick them up. Sarah got this worked out. She realised that if she stood up on her back legs she could rest her front paws on the sill and stick her head through the window and get the crusts all to herself. Spanky was now back to her old self and she'd noticed this habit of her potential bearer of doom, gloom, and serious injury and was starting to have a go at her again but from the safety of our laps. One morning she got on the back of the bunk and hid behind the curtain out of sight. Sarah duly stuck her head through the window and POW!! Little Spanky pounced like a cat and let rip at the Dane's lips and snout. It was so fast I don't think Sarah ever knew what had hit her. She never so much as put the end of her nose inside the window again. The little shit Spanky had got her own back, just as she had with Sandy the vet years earlier at Pailton, after she realised he was the one who had taken her teeth out years earlier.

Most of the dogs either we, or Marion, owned lived with us in our trailer and in the compound in which it was situated. This was no problem. All the big dogs, Blood Hounds, Mastiffs and Danes had their own kennels outside where all of them spent the nights. The trouble was the trailer door did not close very well. Many mornings we would be woken by a selection of said specimens jumping up and down on top of us in bed. They were evacuated in a no uncertain way amidst choice expletives originating from myself. All the dogs came in at some time or

169

another except for the young Bloodhound, Gretel. I couldn't understand this really. She never came in but by nature she was not one to hang about in the background. I got up early, and very quietly, one morning and watched. It was revealed that Gretel had learned to open the door, let all the others in, and then just sit outside watching through her cross eyes. As they all went out, one at a time, a damn sight faster than they had gone in, you could almost see her sort of sniggering under her breath. Time to get the door fixed I suppose!!

We had still got the two Cocker Spaniel bitches and we had managed to get Megan, the black and white one, in pup. As her time got close she had started to nest in her bed under the table. I said to Lin we had best keep an eye on her in between doing the jobs outside. We left her for an hour or two before checking on her. When we did check we found she had presented five or six lovely pups to the world and there was no sign, apart from a bit of dirty bedding, that she had ever had pups. None of the usual blood and green slime. She stayed with them for a while, made sure they were all fed, washed, toileted and fast asleep. She then got up and went outside, as usual, as if nothing had ever happened. She then came back an hour or so later, repeated the process, and off she went again. The only time she ever actually lay with her brood was overnight. This was a habit she would repeat every time she had a litter. Her female mate Sheba never had pups. In fact I don't think she ever came into season. That is probably why she was given to us in the first place. They were good dogs and when they were not out and about snuffling around they would spend a lot of time in the car. We would leave a window open for them to come and go as they pleased. I went out one day to get in the car to be greeted by the sight of Megan standing up on the driver's seat with her front paws on the steering wheel. Sheba was fidgeting about on the front passenger seat having a bit of a "verbal nag" at her mate as if she was saying "Come on you're the driver let's go". They were two lovely little bitches. One productive and the other no more than ornamental. The two Bullmastiffs we had got from Surrey (Hannah and Samantha) were typical Mastiffs. Basically the only place they wanted to be was partially parked on your lap at every possible chance. This could be a bit of a problem when only one lap was available at any one time. This usually ended up with them grumbling at each other under their breath but nothing more. It is a trait most Mastiffs seem to possess…. this partially sitting on your lap business. They achieved this by reversing up on to your lap and sitting down with their back legs stuck out in front of them with their front feet on the ground. Every Mastiff we have ever had, of any sort, had this habit. Samantha was no trouble at all but Hannah had revealed her vice. She was a chicken killer. Any chicken, anywhere, anytime. This did not go down too well with Marion because apart from her bloody Bulldogs she loved and took pride in her rare breed Araucana chickens. One of the few breeds of fowl that lay a blue or greenish blue egg. Unfortunately once Hannah had clapped her eyes on them they had become even rarer by the time she had had her way. She killed a fair number of chickens of various breeds, shapes and sizes and it was a habit she could not be steered away from. No matter what we tried. She seemed to have the attitude of either the fowl died or she did. It was something we had to learn to live with.

As I mentioned earlier Eva, the old Bloodhound bitch was 100% a big baby. Even the slightest hint of, or even a suggestion of, pain she would sit down, throw her head up in the air and start howling. Now we kept all our syringes and doggy first aid equipment in a high up cupboard in the kitchen. She had learnt where they were so, to wind her up, at times I would get her attention, go to the cupboard, open the door, make out I was taking something out and say to her "What's in here Evey?" She would immediately plonk herself down on her arse and let rip with the howling, in no uncertain terms, until I shut the hated cupboard again and walked away. We only ever had the three pups out of her and Trevor Howard never did get his one. That would teach him to try and pull the wool over my eyes, as he had done, with the Chihuahua years earlier. Eva gave us a lot of pleasure and amusement … a proper "one off" character. A great big sloppy sod!!

Tibby (the now getting on in years Lassie Collie dog I had bought from John Ball at Tamworth years earlier) was still in residence but he was now too old to mate any bitches of which we had got two. We decided to get a new dog. We bought a blue merle youngster. I had always been interested in the blue merle colour in any breed. On reading up on the subject it was accepted that to breed a good, well marked, specimen it was advised to put a tri-colour with a white. To get a tri-colour was no problem but the white would be more difficult. Very few, of any worth, were known to have been bred because to breed one meant putting two blue merles together. This colour is a "recessive gene" so if a white could be bred then it was 90% certain that it would either be born deaf or blind but I was interested in this kind of thing and we decided to give it a go.

We did this by purchasing our dog's full sister because looking through their pedigrees they carried a lot of merle blood well back through their forebears. We called the bitch Ellie and the dog went under his pedigree name of Arro. Just a case of waiting for them to be old enough now. Eventually we got them mated and Ellie produced five puppies, three tri-colour, one blue merle and one white pup that had a tiny little merle patch over one eye. However as time went on it became clear that this little white puppy (a male) was blind. His eyes never opened and on gentle examination it was clear that his eyes had not fully formed in the first place. We did manage to rehome him to a lady who was willing to take him on as he was. If he turned out to be anything like Old Tibby (the now very old original Lassie Collie dog) then being blind would not have been so much of a problem for him. We never repeated the mating mainly because of Arro's untimely demise. This event occurred one early evening. The kennels were closed for the day and at this time we had let Kronus out of his run and he had just wandered about at will in the interior exercise compound. It had never been a problem until this particular evening. We were in the chalet when all of a sudden the sounds of a dog fight came from the kennels. Lin and I rushed down and found Kronus (a Neapolitan Mastiff male that had, by now, joined our kennel along with his wife). More of that later. The Mastiff was lying on the ground with Arro's two front legs locked in his jaws. The Collie must have got out of his run somehow. Kronus was just lying there holding him but, of course, the Collie was struggling to escape. This action only made things worse. On command Kronus let him got but Arro was in a mess. I always remember that his two front legs felt like a pair of tights filled up with gravel. He had to be put down straight away. No hope for him unfortunately.

The kennels had a lot of "regulars" and we were one of the few establishments that would board bitches in season and Alsatians. The latter were usually a bad breed to board because if given good outside accommodation, with good runs, then they would pace up and down constantly thus losing weight. This we explained to any owners that if they accepted this fact then we could take their animals into our care. The bitches in season were less trouble, most of the time anyway, but very few other kennels would take them. We had therefore basically "cornered the market" in that respect. "Kes" was a little Lakeland Terrier dog and one of our "regulars". His only foible was that he was an escape artist. The runs were fenced in with six foot (2 metre) high chain link fencing concreted into the ground. No problem for Kes because if he could not dig his way out then he would keep on working at one place in the wire with his snout. He did this until he had stretched it enough to squeeze through. When he had liberated himself he never went anywhere. He would just sit outside his run wagging his tail … the little bugger!! Because of this habit the insurance companies would not accept him as a risk. His owners fully understood this. In fact when they bought him in for his holiday they used to joke that he had bought his wire cutters, spade and rope ladder. He was no problem once the fact had been accepted that he was not going to stay on his side of the wire.

"Boris" was a Pyrenean Mountain dog who came in for a couple of weekends every month. He was owned by an elderly woman who stood less than 5 ft (1¾ metres) tall. She did not take Boris anywhere when he was on his lead. He took her. She had just one rule, for us to obey, when he was with us and that was that at feeding time he must be made to sit and not touch his food until you had clapped your hands not once but twice. This rule we obediently adhered to. Other "holidaymakers" included four Boxers that all came in at once and two Samoyeds who came in together. The Boxers "party trick" was to tip their water bowls up in the grass run until they had made enough mud to paddle in. No matter how often you gave them fresh water it always ended up in the same way. We mentioned this to their owner and she said that they did exactly the same thing at home. She had even concreted their dishes into the ground but they just dug them up in the end. The Samoyeds were show dogs. They had come in as white as the driven snow but, if we had rain, then they could make enough mud to roll around in and usually ended up like two hairy chocolate bars. The first time this happened, after we had a lot of wet weather, we thought their owners would be less than pleased but it turned out that they took the attitude that as long as they had had a good time then that's all that mattered. A long haired Dachsund turned up one Friday to be left for a week. It was made clear to us that she could be a nasty piece of work if she felt like it and she would bite if given the chance. I went to take her lead off and at this point she sunk her teeth into my hand and escaped. She shot off underneath a block of wooden kennels and no amount of kind words or coaxing could get her out. We ended up putting her food and water just inside her "lair" during all of her stay. We explained to her owners what had happened. They were not at all surprised by her actions and proceeded to go down the kennels and just call her out. She emerged, tail wagging and off they went but we

173

never saw them again. It turned out, after talking to other kennels in the area, that she had been around them all at one time or another.

Nail clipping was another little add on at Elmsgate Kennels and, on this subject, a male Lassie Collie turned up for a manicure one Saturday afternoon ready for a show the following day. No problem but there was a small problem. He had one black toe nail. These were notoriously risky to trim because you could not see the blood vessel. So we nipped it back bit by bit but eventually went too far and it bled and bled and bled. We managed to stop it by sealing it off with a hot poker being careful not to singe any hair or pads. His owners came to pick him up and we explained what had happened and refused to take any payment for the little job. They all went off quite happy. I thought we had heard the end of it until the following Monday they congratulated us on doing a good job. It seemed that up until this time the dog had always dragged the foot with the black nail while in the show ring and this, of course, went against him. On the previous day he had actually gone in the ring and moved freely. More than luck than judgement, but all's well that ends well as they say.

It was at about this time that three new dogs "joined the club". An English Mastiff bitch called Delilah and a male and female Neapolitan Mastiff. The only two of this breed in Great Britain at the time. Delilah was offered to Marion free of charge as long as we went and collected her ..... from Cumbria?? This involved Marion, that twat of a boyfriend of hers Howard doing the driving and me going along to sit with the bitch on the way home. It was a long journey from Wiltshire to Cumbria and back in one go but in for a penny in for a pound. We arrived at our destination and, on arrival, we were informed that only that morning the bitch had cut her front leg badly . . . Yes sure!! Her owner took us down his garden to a ramshackled old kennel and run to meet the reason for our journey. She had "papers" but I was not convinced they were straight. She was a nice big young lady but in my eyes her coat was too long but it wasn't my decision. She was taken into Marion's ownership complete with a badly cut leg and questionable papers to say the least. Marion had quite often mentioned her time spent working for a Mr Trevor Lewis. He was a well known dog dealer and part time Great Dane breeder based near Heathrow Airport and how he'd imported two Neapolitan Mastiff pups from Italy a few years earlier. These were the first specimens of this breed ever to come into this country and they were still the only two over

Lin, 1975, Wiltshire.

here at that time. A male called Kronus-del-Prese and a female called Ursula. The first time I ever saw these two was at the time when we took Rusty's (the Doberman) pups down to him. He had bought them all. Trevor Lewis was a big man but spoke, dressed and moved in a very effeminate way and looked half Italian. He had got a son, a lad called Ashley who lived with his dad and Grandma (Trevor's mom). I asked him if he had still got the Mastiffs and if he had then could I have a look at them please. No problem. They were housed in an extremely secure and very heavy duty kennel and run around the back of the kennels out of the way. They were big lumps. Kronus stood about 27"-28" (70-75 cms) at the shoulder. He weighted a good 13-14 stone (about 80 kilos). It turned out he had got a 42" (about 90-95 cm) chest and a 27" (70 cm) neck. He was now spending his time threatening me by throwing himself at the chain link run and bouncing off again. Ursula was a bit smaller but seemed to be a bit more sparky and mean. Because they were imports they had both had their ears docked. Kronus was a mahogany colour and looked and moved more like a bear than a dog. Ursula was jet coal black with orange-ish eyes and looked more like a panther and moved like one. They looked like a bit of a handful. They had been born in Italy at the same kennel and had never been separated since. I asked if they had ever bred them? To which he replied "It is impossible to breed them". This struck a chord with me. I liked a challenge so I immediately replied "I'll breed them". He thought about this and agreed that we would take them back to Wiltshire, keep and feed them and, if they ever bred, then we could keep half of the proceeds from the sale of any pups. Hands were shaken and a deal was done. They were so big we only had room for them in the motor one at a time so we took Kronus back with us that day and Barry would pick up Ursula and bring her up in the next couple of days. It had turned out during our chat with Trevor that whenever Ursula had come into season Kronus would try to mate her for a while but was never successful. He just kept lumbering about unsuccessfully until she became non-receptive. I thought he was just saying to himself "Sod it!. She'll be her tomorrow". Little did he know but I got a shock in store for this young man! Safely installed in his run with his kennel then the usual kennel practice was put in place. All dogs shut inside their kennels at night. Well he was having none of this. He had never been shut in a kennel in his life and he wasn't about to start now…. thank you very much!! He just walked through the side of his wooden bedroom, no chewing, no scratching, no barking, just put his head down and kept walking. That was his answer and we had them for years to come and neither of them would ever put up with such indignity. I decided the best thing to do with them was to separate them (for the first time in their lives) in an effort to "keep him keen" when she came into season. They each had a kennel and run within sight of our chalet but out of sight of each other. We gave them both a car tyre to play with. Kronus did not even look at it but Ursula would sometimes get hold of hers and run round with it in her mouth. We managed to "smuggle" her in without them seeing each other. This was O.K. for now but he realised she was there when he heard her barking. I was looking out of the chalet at him that day and he was just charging at his fence like a bull. I said to Lin "Fuck me if he ever learns he can walk through his chain link run as well as his wooden kennel then we would never do a thing with him" Time for a confrontation. I ran down to him, gave him a liberal dose of verbal abuse. Went into his run to look him in the face and show him who the boss was. He stood there, a leg on every corner, feet planted firmly on the ground, tail in the air and looked me straight back in my face. I thought "Well sonny boy it's either you or me now. There's only one boss here and it's not going to be you". So we stood there, a metre (3 or 4 ft) apart glaring at each other. My immediate response was "Get in your fucking bed you". To which he immediately did by putting his tail and head down and lumbering off into his kennel. That could have been a lot worse but in the years we had him he never did a thing wrong towards either me, Lin, or Mandy. That incident had got him sorted. Ursula could be a nasty piece of work when she felt like it but never towards any of us. Anybody else would be a different thing but she learned respect in her own way . . . Slowly. This was the beginning of new experiences and new journeys with this pair. I will tell the full story of our journey with these dogs somewhere in the forthcoming pages of this "tome".

Let us get away from the dogs for a while. Since Marion and Barry had separated he had apparently picked up with a kennelmaid in London called Joan. She had now ended up working for Rae Norrie (the woman who was present at our originally meeting with Marion and offered us a job working for her if needs be). She rented an old farmhouse and buildings and yard similar to the place we had in Leicestershire previous to going to Tamworth. She kept Alsatians – bloody rubbish things in my opinion. I have never liked them. The whole place, especially the house was a complete shit hole, except for Joan's room. Rae was no cleaner. She must have spruced herself up for our first meeting at Elmsgate Kennels. Apparently she never washed. She wore long skirts and when one got dirty she would just put another one on top. Whenever she ventured into the shop in the village they would spray the place out with air freshener!! She showed us some old photographs of herself from years before. She had been a starlet in the West End of London. She was a beautiful girl back then but she had certainly let things slip now. The whole house she lived in, with Joan and anyone else who could suffer it at least for a while, was absolutely filthy. Not dusty or a few muddy footprints, just grime from floor to ceiling. So much so that when she was confined to hospital for a few days then Barry and Joan hired an industrial pressure (steam washer) and blasted the whole house out, top to bottom, floor to ceiling!! Barry and Joan had obviously split up because she came to visit us one day with her new boyfriend, Mick. Otherwise known as Mad Mick. He really was off his trolley most of the time. This became obvious on two occasions. The first one I heard of was when he was in the local pub. He was stabbing the curtains because he was convinced someone was trying to get him and that they were hiding behind the curtains. The second time was one Saturday at Elmsgate. Joan and he were in the chalet with us having tea when the phone rang. Mick picked it up. It was apparently a lady ringing up to ask how her dog had settled in for his holiday to which Mick replied "We have shot the fucking thing" and proceeded to open the window next to the phone and scream out "Stop them fuckin' dogs barking or I'll shoot the fucking lot". . . OOPS. That did not go down well obviously. Mad Mick was never allowed near the phone again needless to say. A few months into their relationship Mick and Joan decided that it would be healthier to move out of Rae's house and into a tent in the field. This was O.K. until the weather started to deteriorate. Joan was insisting that they find somewhere warmer to live so Mick put the following advert in the local paper:- "FOR SALE. 2 man tent or would exchange for council house in good condition". We all laughed at that one. Not long after that they both just moved on somewhere never to be seen again.

The weather was now getting colder, not only for Mick and Joan in their tent, but also for Brian sleeping in the back of his pet food van. One evening he quietly knocked on our door and sheepishly asked if he could come in and get warm. No problem. He could sleep on the bunk in the lounge. He was no problem. A really nice young man. He could sleep there. Mandy had her own room that she shared with young Denise when she was staying with us. Lin and I had the designated double bedroom. As I mentioned earlier the paddock at the kennels was rented out to a girl who kept her pony there. Brian had taken a shine to this young lady and although he was a really good looking lad, and loved the company of women, he proved to be extremely shy with this young lady. We didn't know what her name was, at the time, but we knew her pony was called Henry. Brian's initial approach towards courtship was to write her poems. He put them in an envelope, addressed to "Henry's girl" and attached them to the fence of her pony paddock. It worked because she eventually moved in with us as well.

The time came for one of the Great Danes to have her pups so we had her in the chalet with us. Because we had to stop up with her we suggested that Brian and Bridget move out of the lounge and into our bed in our room ..... that was the last we ever saw of our room or the bed again . . . Hey ho. After a while Bridget's parents were beginning to get a bit concerned about their girl's relationship with this seemingly waif and stray. They only lived in the village and Brian was summoned, along with

Bridget, to be "Inspected and either approved or disapproved of" by the concerned parents. It turned out that during this session the question of "Brian do you love Bridget?" was addressed to him and his answer was "Well yes, at the moment I do but if she wakes up in the morning with an acute case of the shits then I'm not so sure" At least he was honest and all was well for them. Life went on as before and he was accepted by Bridget's parents.

Christmas was on the horizon so Brian and I decided we would take ourselves off to Chippenham Livestock Sales and buy a live bird ready to kill when the time came. Unfortunately we arrived a little late and there were only a few birds left to sell. All of them too small for four adults and a child but there was one big, really big, stag amongst them. He would do. It seemed nobody wanted him. He was too big for your average oven. If he weighed an ounce he must have weighed well over 20 lb (8-9 kilo). The time came to despatch him. Bloody hell he took some killing. I did him the old fashioned way. Mr Walton had shown me how to kill a big bird using a broom handle and brute force when I was a kid. The bloody thing was huge. To get him cooked we had to cut the carcass up into four pieces and cook them in the oven two at a time. We lived off turkey for what seemed like a lifetime after that. Brian and Bridget had now settled in well with us. Bridget working in a shop in Trowbridge and Brian with his dog food delivery. His most valued possession in life was a hand written letter he had received from John Lennon (no less!!). Apparently he had invited Mr Lennon to his wedding years earlier and had received a letter back to say that due to other, already arranged, commitments he would not be able to attend but wished Brian and his future wife all the best for the future. That letter would be worth some money now no doubt.

As I have mentioned earlier the kennels were just on the edge of Steeple Ashton, a small village with just a few houses, a shop and a pub, The Long Arms, named after Lord Long who still resided in a "small mansion" just off the High Street. He was a typical over educated upper class twit. No use to anybody. Apparently he was so strapped for cash that he would quite often have to borrow the money for his train fare down to London so that he could get to the House of Lords, sign in, get his "attendance fee", and the come straight back again . . . easy money. He had come to some arrangement or another with the village's oldest resident, Reg, that allowed the old boy access to the Manor and its grounds. Now Reg was a total kleptomaniac. He would rob anything, at any time, but this lifelong habit of his was generally accepted by everyone in the village. It was just the way he was. In fact people used to plant enough stuff in their gardens to allow for what the old boy would inevitably pinch. In fact a lady was telling us one day that she looked out of her window and lo and behold there was Reg in her garden going round all her cabbages feeling them one at a time. She rattled the window, the old man looked up, shook his head and muttered that "They're not ready yet!!" Cheeky but lovable. Another of his "Sticky fingered" habits was to go into the pub (he had his own chair in there anyway) and wait until the barman had gone out of sight (it had an "L" shaped bar). Then he would be behind the bar helping himself, filling his pocket, for all he was worth. On almost every occasion he had been caught in the act the barman would just shout "Reg put it back" and shake his finger at him to which the old man would return to his throne. As I have said he seemed to have free range of Lord Long's estate and gardens. So much so that he'd got into the stables, pinched some horse tack and a saddle and then gone round to the front door and sold his Lordship his own stuff back. I was talking to a chap in the shop one day and he said he looked out of his window (which overlooked the High Street) very early, one morning, to be greeted by the sight of, in his words, a "small haystack on the move". It turned out to be that Reg had been out and "liberated" three bales of hay that he had somehow managed to wedge/hang on his bike and was taking them off to their "new home" but the classic of all his wheezes

came to light on the occasion when the local butcher knocked on his cottage door to ask his wife if she could square up the bill for all the meat she had had. Apparently there was an arrangement that had been made between the two that "Mrs Reg" would pay the butcher weekly at the time he delivered that week's meat by leaving what she owed him under a stone by her door. It now became clear that she thought this was all going as planned because every week when she went outside to pick up her meat the butcher had apparently taken the money and left the change so in her eyes all was well. But no the butcher hadn't been taking the cash and leaving the change but Reg had the crafty old bugger!! The village was still covered by some really old historical law that if anybody did anything trifling illegal then the residents could form a "court" and try the offender. If found guilty then they could impose a maximum of 24 hours detention in a small stone built jail located on the village green. It was all perfectly within the law of the land to do so apparently. I bet old Reg had spent a few days constrained in such a way in his past. Sadly they don't make people like old Reg anymore.

During our time in Wiltshire we befriended three very individual ladies all connected to the dog job in one way or another. The first and most insignificant one was Susanna De Forest Keys. A middle aged American woman who, along with her American husband, an ex lawyer, lived in an "upside down" house near Marlborough where they had set up a canine security service and were constantly at war and loggerheads with a commune of Moonies that were squatting in an old building on the other side of the lane from their place. This did not go down well with the De Forest Keys and they were in constant conflict. When visiting them it was blatantly obvious that they were almost constantly battling with each other as well as with their Moonie neighbours. So much so that one afternoon Suzanna turned up at our place with a Golden Retriever bitch on a lead. She immediately conveyed to me that she wanted me to shoot this dog. When I asked why she answered in a broad American drawl "Well I can't shoot my fuckin' husband so I want you to shoot his fuckin' dog" This, of course, I did not do but we did take the bitch off her and eventually she went to live with my foster brother Billy. Strangely enough she shared her name with our Ma . . . CLAIR. Suzanna had expressed an interest in taking one of our two young Bloodhound bitches, either Gretel or Sloopy, on breeding terms, which meant she would not pay money for the dog but would agree to give us two or three pups from her in exchange sometime in the future. We agreed to this idea but she wanted to discuss it with her husband first. No problem. She reappeared a few days later with a dossier of terms and conditions compiled by her lawyer, other half, that we were expected to sign. There were two or three pages of "ifs and buts and maybes" contained in this proposed agreement. You could tell it had been compiled by a lawyer. No way were we even going to think about signing such a thing so the young bitch stayed with us, at least for a while. We did eventually sell Sloopy to a man and his family in Somerset but she would come back to us in years to come to have her puppies.

The second lady I would like to mention was a typically upper crust outcast of about 50 years old. She lived at a stables in Farleigh Hungerford where she taught disabled children to ride. She was a lovely lady. A typical penniless aristocrat. She lived on her own in a flat converted out of an old hay loft above the stables. She invited Lin, Mandy and myself over for tea one evening We arrived and were led into her dwelling which was a bit topsy turvy and disorganised to say the least. The main attraction and centre of interest was a Bull Mastiff bitch she called Teddy.

She was lying on a settee which she had already chewed one arm off and was slowly working her way along the rest of it. Miss Young noticed us looking at her and just said "Don't worry when she has finished that one I'll just get her another". The other dog that lived with her in the flat was a half bred Foxhound that stayed in the adjoining room, the kitchen, with just her head protruding. If looks could have killed then all three of us would have been dead. I mentioned this to our host and she warned us to take no notice of her but do not go anywhere near her. We obliged. This bitch meant it and was just waiting for a chance to have a go at the first opportunity. Because of her heritage Miss Young was well into her fox-hunting. Now Lin and I were on the opposite side of this debate so the good lady suggested we agreed to disagree and the subject was never discussed again. Both Lin and I had a lot of time for Miss Young (We never found out her first name) and the feeling was mutual. We were friends for years and it was to come to pass that in time she would turn out to be a big help to us with the Bloodhounds.

The third and final lady I would like to introduce you to is a lady in her mid-sixties at the time. Meet Dorothy Norman. A really short skinny little being that scurried around like a mouse on speed. This woman was a proper little nugget. She had been in the dog job all her life. If you had have cut her in half, like a stick of rock, then she would have had an A-Z of show dogs running right through her. She used to tell us stories of her past. Her purpose in life was to select a breed, any breed that she liked the look of, and keep and breed them until she had managed to breed and show a champion of her own. Then she would get rid of all her stock and start all over again with another breed of her choice and go on again. She revealed that she had managed to do this with about ten different breeds. Afghans, Bloodhounds, Bullmastiffs, and Pekes. When we knew her the objects of her attention were her Manchester Terriers. Although she still kept a Bullmastiff dog as a pet/guard. Her place consisted of a beaten up old wooden bungalow, no electric, just bottled gas and well water. Attached to the kennels were her "boarding" kennels and cattery. She had a licence to board about 10 or 12 dogs and half a dozen cats. Their kennels and pens were about as beaten up as her bungalow. I always said the only thing that kept the runs from falling down was their covering of Russian Vine and Honeysuckle. She had her regular customers that used to go back time and time again so the dogs really did not want to get out anyway. In her little yard a few yards away from her front door was an old dark green caravan in which dwelt Arthur. Arthur it turned out was actually Mr

Norman, her husband. She told us they had separated years earlier but he had been taken ill. As they had got no children she had agreed to "keep an eye on him" in her words. He was not really allowed in her bungalow unless it could not be helped. He was basically exiled to his "kennel". Indeed we were visiting one day, sitting in with Mrs Norman having a chat, when Arthur dared to intervene in our conversation. This did not go down well with his wife who immediately snapped at him "I am talking to Nick and Lin so just keep your nose out. Go and make tea and then get back to your caravan." Mrs Norman said what she wanted to, whenever she wanted, wherever she wanted. She was a force of human nature. She said she had refused to clean Arthurs "Kennel" because he just "Sat in there all day smoking and the floor is thick with fag ash". Lin and I used to visit her whenever we could. All three of us got on really well. I loved going there. Here was this tot of an old woman, old fashioned, set in her ways, cantankerous, outspoken who did not suffer fools gladly. Just like I am now really. You could learn more off this old dear by listening to her, and watching, than you ever would some jumped up over educated, book learned, twat with more decrees than a thermometre. She had been there, seen and done it. I loved the old bugger!!. On one occasion we were visiting her place and she had prepared one of her Manchester Terriers for a show. We were in the middle of a really sunny spell of weather which, according to Mrs Norman, was detrimental to the black short coat of any dog marked in that way. So to avoid any minor fading of the coat colour she used to keep any dog she was intending to show inside for a few days prior to the event. They were not just kept inside her bungalow, no! She had converted two of her cupboards in the living room into two small "kennels" by removing the panels from the doors and replacing them with a wire grid. She demonstrated to us how to stand a dog on the show table by taking one of the dogs she was going to show in a couple of days, out of its temporary abode, and its coat just shone. As if someone had spent hours polishing it. It reminded me of the days when, years earlier, I had watched old Jack Pittaway take his show guinea pigs out of the little orange boxes etc. He used to keep them in at times. They were the healthiest looking specimens I had ever seen. It is known in the livestock world as "having the touch" and no amount of book reading could ever teach that. Back to Mrs Norman. She had been telling us about this little bitch that she used to show quite often because she thought it was "A good un' " Apparently every time she took her to a show a young couple were always there watching on and they would go and have a chat with her about this bitch. Anyway it eventually turned out that this scenario

183

reoccurred one weekend at some big championship show somewhere. Mrs Norman's little lady had won her best in class and on the way out of the ring this young couple were standing near the exit and came over to chat to Mrs Norman. "You two really like this little bitch don't' you?" she said to them. They agreed that they did. At this point the old lady handed them the lead and said "Take her and look after her". She had given her away. She had done all she could with her so it was time for her to go off and live the rest of her life .... What a woman the old bird was!! As I mentioned earlier, in days gone by, one of the breeds she had concentrated on was the Bloodhounds. I asked her if we could take our young Gretel over for her to caste her eye over the dog. I thought that our young bitch was a nice thing. She was the image of her father (apart from her cross eyes) and he was generally regarded as one of the best about at the time. We arrived, took our bitch out of the motor, and let Mrs Norman give her the once over. When she had assessed the dog in front of her I asked her what she thought of her (making allowances for her optical foible). " Nice bitch that! Trouble is, these days any judge of that breed would not know a good dog if you slapped him around the head with it!!." A woman after my own heart. She advised us to take her away and breed with her and see what happens. This we did eventually. Time went on. We kept up our contact and friendship. We were visiting one day with one of our Bullmastiff bitches (Samantha) to see if we could get her mated to Mrs Norman's old Mastiff dog. He was getting a bit long in the tooth now and, with help, he tried his best, but it was a half hearted attempt and did not produce anything. We put Samantha back in the motor and were "taking tea" when it was disclosed that Mrs Norman had decided that she wanted to move in with her sister up north and retire but she was worried about what would happen to her kennels. She just said to us "Look, this is an offer for you two only. I'd like you to have the place and you can have it for £2,000!! If you can see your way clear to do that". What an offer but we had not got that kind of money. What people of our age, living the life we were, in our predicament during those days, could come up with that kind of money. Sadly we had to turn her down. What a chance missed. Lin and I still talk about that even today but life had not got that settled sort of life in store for us obviously. It was probably the best offer we have ever been made but we just were not "tooled up" enough to take it on. She eventually sold her place for £6000. And moved into retirement with her sister. I don't know if she took Arthur and his "kennel" with her or if she ever did add the Manchester Terrier to her long list of breed champions.

Meanwhile back at Elmsgate Marion had been approached by a woman and asked if we could clip her Old English Sheepdog bitch who, in her words, "Was a bit of a mess" because she did not like being brushed. No problem. A chance to earn a few easy quid we thought until the aforementioned "beast"... I use the word "beast" advisedly arrived. What a bloody mess stood before our eyes. This bitch's coat was like a solid mass of matted hair rooted in concrete. It looked like she had never seen a comb or a brush in her life and she had a temperament to match. You could hardly get near the bloody thing. First job was to get her mouth tied up then at least we could have a look and give it a go. She was throwing herself everywhere. Eventually we managed to get her on the floor and strap her to a fence. Time to have a go with the clippers but you might just as well have thrown them over the fence. They would not touch the mess in front of them so we (me, Lin, Marion and her gobby boyfriend Howard) decided the only way to relieve her of her hairy carapace was by hand. We used scissors, little, very little, bit at a time. I recall it was on a boiling hot Sunday and it took over four, very hot, sweaty, ill tempered hours, to complete the job. We had agreed to do it before we had even clapped eyes on the dog. We had got a few well needed quid for it but it could not be said it was easy money in any way shape or form.

On the subject of bad tempered, temperamental, animals we had seen a three year old male donkey for sale in the local paper. It was at a place on the top of Clevedon Gorge near Bristol so we agreed to take transport and go and have a look at it. It was cheap anyway. We arrived at the place and were shown the donkey in question. The trouble was it was a three year old Jack, still with his manhood intact, and worst of all had never been handled or away from its mother since the day of its birth. He was not prepared for any other way of life. Too bad mate you are in for a shock!! With the aid of its owner and mother we managed to get him loaded up and home. Bloody hell! He was a right bastard. He could kick the eye out of needle at 200 metres. He had a mouthful of teeth and a temper. Like an explosion in a firework factory. If ever this lad had got loose he would never have stopped going. We put three halters on him and a good thick leather collar and then decided to see what could be done with the fella. He bucked, he kicked, he tried to bite. He threw it all at us. Eventually he decided he had had enough and that it did not look like he was going to win and he quietened down enough for us to be able to tie him up. The worst was now over and there was a small improvement in his outlook on life. We had managed to get him to agree to walk on a halter and lead but he still was not at ease with things. We made allowances for him anyway. This was all happening during one of the spells that little Denise was staying with us. She and our Mandy would go off and play round the kennels and paddock. One day they seemed to have been gone for a while. I asked Lin if she had seen them and she said she hadn't. Best go and check on them then. We could hear them chatting away in the donkey's stable. We crept up quietly to see what they were up to and were greeted with the sight of Denise standing there holding the donkey's head collar. Mandy was sat down on the floor, with one of its back legs up in the air, and its hoof less than a foot away from her face. Time for a quiet retreat on our behalf. The power of innocent children eh? We eventually rehomed this equine wannabee Al Capone to a pub called, ironically, The Kicking Donkey. The last we saw of him he was settling into his new paddock and stable in front of the premises.

Elmsgate Kennels was attached to the very large garden of Elmsgate House where lived a Mr and Mrs Larkin. It turned out that they had built the kennels and business in years gone by and had now leased it out to Marion and Barry. Here lies our next hurdle in life... which I will illuminate later on in this text. Mr Larkin was telling me that the main "claim to fame" that the business had during his time of running it was that they had, at one point in the past, boarded the first ever Lhasa Apso dog ever to come into the U.K. It had been introduced into this country by Sherpa Tensing, the man who accompanied Edmund Hillary on the first ascent of Mount Everest.

An incident happened, one evening, at the Kennels. Lin and I were sat in the chalet having a bit of a rest. Brian and Bridget had gone out and Mandy was in her room. All of a sudden a car came into the forecourt with two or three loud mouthed gobshites in it shouting their mouths off and generally remonstrating. I went out to see what was going on. On the way out I picked up a good strong dog lead just in case. It seemed like these twats were looking for drugs. Although they were about, in the area, we never allowed any on the place nor did we allow alcohol. The bloke in the passenger seat seemed to be "in charge" so I asked him to wind his window down a bit so I could hear what he was prattling on about. As he did so I looped the dog lead round his neck and over the top of the partially open window and sat down pulling on it. By now Lin must have seen what was going on. She came screaming out "Let him go Nick, let him go, you'll kill him!!" This I did and as soon as he was free, although struggling to get enough air into his lungs, the three of them cleared off in no uncertain haste never to be seen again . . . plonkers!!

Autumn had arrived one year and the kennels were basically closed for the season. Hence money was a bit short so time to look for some extra work. Barry and I would spend the odd night chicken catching. Just a "Cash in hand" thing that popped up every now and then but I had seen an advert for a relief milker. Only a few cows about 20 or 30 ...... something like that. I gave the man a ring and he arranged to come out to the kennels to interview me as a starting point. it was hardly a big deal. That is the way he wanted it so let's go with it. He duly arrived and on chatting it was revealed that he was a lay preacher. A part time vicar. At this time in my life my hair was still jet black and hung in ringlets that almost reached my shoulders. He made a questionable remark about my long hair to which I replied that as far as I understood things it is what was INSIDE my head that mattered and not what was on the OUTSIDE. I mentioned an assumed fact that, as he was a lay preacher, then he had probably heard of a gentleman called Ludwig Van Beethoven to which he replied that he most certainly had. At this point I retorted "Well he had long hair and a lot of people said he was a genius!! . . . end of interview . . . No job for me but I probably would not have got on with him anyway.

Let's return to Marion and Barry and the lease they held on the kennels. We had noticed that in the past there had been numerous "private" meetings between Marion and Barry and the odd trip to see a Solicitor. In the end it turned out that they were well in arrears with their rent on the place and that Mr and Mrs Larkin were in the process of trying to evict them. This had been the situation when we had originally gone there. They had kept that one quiet!! As soon as we found out about it all we went to see Mr and Mrs Larkin to see where we stood in the great scheme of things. By then we had received an order to vacate the premises so that Marion and Denise could move back in thus making it more difficult for the Larkins to reclaim their own property. i.e. the kennels. They were a lovely couple, probably in their late 60's I should think. They actually manufactured dog food on their premises. The very food that Brian used to sell and deliver out of the back of his van. They explained to us what had been going on over the years. Apparently the rental payments were well in the debit column. That was also the reason why the electric had not been on since we arrived because the same financial situation applied to that as well. Basically it had been cut off but we never bothered about that anyway. If we really needed it then Brian, who in the past life had been an S.E.B. linesman, knew how to get around the problem by fiddling around with something at the top of the pole. He did this a couple of times and it was never detected so that was O.K. It was put to us, by the Larkins, that if they could evict Marion and Barry before they could evict us then we could stay and run the place "as was" so it was all up in the air again now.

Before I put the Larkin's story to "one side" I can remember Brian coming round from their place on day with a message for us from the lady in "The Big House". That message was "Please tell Nick and Lin that I do think Eva (our old Bloodhound bitch) is a real daring but I am getting a little tired of going upstairs in the morning to find her fast asleep on the bed". As I said earlier Eva was good climber and we had watched her go up and over the 2 metre (6' 6") chain link fence around our compound. She would go scuffling off for a while but she always reappeared. We had no idea where she was taking herself off to but we knew now!! Off for a bit of peace and quiet and a comfortable snooze on the Larkins bed!!

So it was time to make plans in case we got chucked out before Marion and Barry did. Time to find somewhere else to live, possibly for me, Lin, Mandy, Brian, Bridget and, as it turned out Barry, plus whatever dogs we could accommodate. I knew lots of farmers back up around home . Maybe one of them had, or knew of, an empty cottage they would rent out. Brian and I went for a day out around my "old haunts" but sadly to no avail. The next house hunt took us down to a very remote farm in the middle of Dartmoor. When I say remote, it WAS remote. It was down a long old track, 6 miles away from the nearest shop. No electric (no problem) but well water and bottled gas. The property to rent was an old stone built place next to the main farm yard. When Brian and I eventually found the property it was like stepping back into Victorian times. Two kids appeared wearing proper Victorian clothes. The girl had a ¾ length dress on and high laced up leather boots. The boy had long short trousers, a flat cap and similar footwear. Their father looked as if he had just stepped out of a Charles Dickens novel. We never saw the Mother. Now we had arrived in a beaten up old Mini Van. Not known for their ground clearance at the best of times. On seeing our transport the boss queried how we had managed to get down there in the thing. He revealed that in the winter it was quite possible to be snowed in for days, if not weeks on end. A Land Rover would be advisable, or at least something with a four wheel drive, but he did offer to rent us the place anyway. He said we would have to go and speak to the woman first although we already knew that this was a step too far. My immediate reaction on the way home was "What happens if we go to the shop and forget the sugar" It was bloody 6 miles away. No problem in the summer but certainly a problem in the winter. That was the last we ever saw of the place.

The next option came in the shape of a farmhouse and buildings somewhere in Wales. It was owned by Trevor Lewis, the man who owned Kronus and Ursula, the Neapolitan Mastiffs. He said that although he was trying to sell the place we could all move in there dogs and all. This would be in his interest as well because by now we had managed to breed his "Impossible to breed dogs"... his words. So off we went, one Sunday, me Lin, Barry and Mandy and a bale of straw in the old Mini Van to have a look at the place before we shifted. It was big enough for all of us and all the dogs. Job done. If we were forced out of the kennels then at least we had got somewhere to go now. Staying at Elmsgate would have been preferable but as weeks went on Court Orders arrived from time to time but we were going to hang on and hope for the best. Then Trevor wrote us a letter to say that he had sold his place in Wales by now so it was back to square one. The only quick option at the time was an old empty house on the edge of the village. The farmer who owned it had actually sealed up all the doors and windows and used it as a grain store. He used to auger the corn in through the bedroom window out of a tractor and trailer parked on the side of the road but it was worth asking anyway. So Lin and I went off to see him and I can remember him saying "I've got nothing against you but if I let you in there then I'll never be able to get you out again. The answer is No I'm afraid." So that was the end of that idea. Time to look elsewhere. We had all decided that it was time to go our separate ways. Barry would have to sort things out with Marion. Brian and Bridget would look for somewhere of their own. Likewise, me, Lin, Mandy. We resorted to gleaning through the area newspapers and came across a place near Lymington on the edge of the New Forest so off Lin, Mandy and I went to have a look at the place. A nice little farmhouse in a working yard, only a very small farm, about 20-30 cows and that was it. It was worked by the owner David Perkins who lived in a house across the field with his Auntie. There was no cash rent to be paid. I just had to work for him for 20 hours a week unpaid and that was it. We could take all our dogs etc. So it was a case of a handshake on the deal and all was settled…. Hampshire here we come!! A shame really because we had all enjoyed our time in Wiltshire but sadly Marion had won the eviction race with the Larkins. Barry used to come and visit us from time to time and vice versa until he and his new lady moved to Australia but we never saw Marion or little Denise ever again, nor Brian and Bridget. A sad day when we left Elmsgate Kennels but a new journey was about to commence. In a new part of the country for us. Lets go!!

The cottage on the edge of The New Forest was a quaint old farmhouse with a fair bit of ground at the back of it. Most of this was fenced in enough to stop the dogs getting out but our biggest problem now was to split the ground up into individual runs with their own kennels. The actual kennels themselves were no problem because we had found a firm up in Wolverhampton that manufactured kit form sheds from tongue and groove off cuts etc. They came complete with floor, door, window and felted roof. It was just a case of bolting them together really. The runs were a bit more of a problem but when taking the dogs out for a run across the fields I had noticed an evergreen plantation about ½ a mile away. In times gone by the trees had been thinned out, trimmed, and cut up into lengths of about 2-2 ½ metres (about 7 foot). It was just a case of carrying enough of these home, one at a time, on my shoulder until I had got enough to erect the individual runs. We also bought a couple of lorry loads of off cuts and slabbing from a local timber yard. With all that and the wire netting (we only ever used 5 ft (1 ¾ metre) high chicken netting we had our runs. We had taught the dogs that this was a fence and that they belonged on their side of it. The Mastiffs and Great Danes were quite capable of traversing or just walking through the obstacle they never did.

All this construction work took time. I did it in the afternoons because money was now short. Lin had got a job as a receptionist at a Solicitors office in Lymington. I had got a job as an evening "pot wash" at a hotel in Sway, a couple of miles away, plus I was still receiving a small disability pension (thanks to the injury to my back sustained at Rugby). I had found that coming off the farm and into the kennels at Steeple Ashton, the pain was now a lot less frequent or severe, so all was going in the right direction. The dogs all settled in well now. We started to keep, buy, and sell cage and aviary birds again and also, now, fancy poultry. Most of the poultry we used to buy at about 10 weeks old from a company in Stoke on Trent called Birchalls. They were well known breeders of fancy poultry back then. We would just buy them in. They would come down by train and we would sell them on again. One of our really good customers was a chap who owned a building firm in Luton in Bedfordshire. He bought most of his fowl from us. It turned out that he had wanted to emulate a fellow "builder" Sir Alfred McAlpine who, at that time, owned probably the largest collection of fancy and rare fowl in the country. Apart from buying chicken from Birchalls we would also buy from, and sell to, local people. Through advertising we had managed to get our feet in the door of a couple of big "park collections" and a zoo but more of all this later.

Things were now beginning to get a bit hectic really. I had got the bit between my teeth. There were not enough hours in the day and the world was not big enough. Lin now had got a full time job at a tomato and chrysanthemum nursery a couple of fields away. Once all the "hard work" i.e. building the dogs accommodation had been done, I had worked out that if I could get all the animals and birds sorted out and fed (along with Lin's help of course) before it was time to do my work for David then there was about 3 hours spare in the afternoon between 1.30 pm. and 4.30 p.m. I therefore got a part time job at Arnewood Turkey Farm a couple of miles away. That left me an hour or so to go home, get a bite to eat, and do a few jobs before starting an evenings work at the hotel in Sway. Everything was at full bore now. 16 or 17 hour days, mostly 7 days a week. As the birds, poultry, dogs and by now anything with fur or feathers gradually became more intensive I was able to give up the "pot wash" job.

As well as our own dogs we were now taking in Trevor Lewis's Great Danes. Mostly Harlequins to whelp and rear their pups as well as keeping a couple of Shit Tzu bitches alongside a couple of Yorkies and Bulldogs for him. Basically if ever he had any dogs he, or his staff, could not manage he would send them down to us. He did, of course, pay us in a fashion for all this. The trouble was you never knew what was going to turn up until it got there. However he did allow us to use his Great Dane stud free of charge on our bitches when needed. This operation entailed Lin taking our bitch on the train all the way to his place near Heathrow which was a bit of a pain I suppose. Just before Christmas one year his driver turned up with a Great Dane bitch. We did not even know she was coming until she turned up at the gate – supposedly in whelp and "due any day now". You could not see that she was in pup but if you "felt" her it was pretty obvious that there was something in there at least. She duly presented us with one pup on the evening of Christmas Eve but she would not settle. She was up, down, up down, and at times you could feel something still in there. What she really needed was a dose of Oxytocin but Trevor would not sanction it. He just said "leave her for a day or so and see what happens". So that meant we spent all of Christmas Day running her up and down the lane, on a lead, trying to move what we hoped was this other pup. Eventually the exercise worked and she presented us with her second pup on Boxing Day morning. I think that was the end of her breeding career because we never saw her again. Mandy was now of an age to be a big help with the dogs, especially at whelping time. We used to have a room that we kept basically as a "maternity ward" and if needed then Mandy would have a day off school, take herself off into this room, with some food, drinks and a couple of books (she had always got her head stuck in a book – bless her) and she would just get on with the job. She knew what to do and how to do it by now and she managed as well as either Lin or I could have . . . Good girl!!

Gretel the good looking young Bloodhound bitch we had bred in Wiltshire was now old enough to get mated when the time came. It was now time to find her a husband as close by as possible. We found a breeder near us. A man called Barry so we arranged to go and visit him. It turned out that he was a man of not insignificant wealth who had decided to go into breeding Bloodhounds as a hobby. Nothing wrong with that at all. Anyway on looking around his place and talking to him it soon became apparent that most of his best stock had been either bred by, or at least was descendant of, The Barsheen Kennels. Now at the time this kennel was generally recognised to have, or have bred, some of the best Bloodhounds in Europe. It was owned by a lady called Yvonne Oldham. We knew this but Barry obviously did not know that we knew this because after chatting to him it was clear that he was a proper "up his own arse" sort of fellow. Been in the job for 5 minutes and thought he knew it all. During our chats I bought up the names of Yvonne Oldham and Reg Wright (my old friend from Coleshill that I've mentioned in pages gone by). We discussed Reg breeding and keeping working Bloodhounds for as long as I could ever remember, and even before that. His response to the name of Yvonne Oldham was words to the effect of "That silly cow. The kind of woman that sits down to a Christmas dinner of toast while at the same time giving her dogs the turkey". His response to the name of Reg Wright was similarly dismissive. I had heard enough by now so I let rip at this jumped up dick head by saying " If Yvonne

Oldham was such a silly cow then how come all his best dogs were, if not actually bred by her, then at least came from The Barsheen bloodline" and as far as Reg Wright was concerned I said "I know for a fact that Reg had been in Bloodhounds for probably as long as anyone else in the country. He had more than likely forgotten more about the job that you will ever know". This did not go down well and we were asked to leave. This at the time was no problem but it turned out that Barry held a lot of "sway" within the Bloodhound Club. I do not know why. Maybe it was his money and that he was an "easy target" but it seems he had been on the phone or whatever and got us "blacklisted". We could not get near a stud dog anywhere and by now Mrs White (whose dog was Gretel's father) had now retired but all was not lost. We were talking to Miss Young our friend from Wiltshire. She had been blacklisted, the same as us, by the Bloodhound fraternity for similarly speaking her mind. We were discussing it one day and it seemed that she had still got a male Bloodhound but he did not live with her. In fact he lived with an M.P. from Reading. She said that when it was time she would go and fetch this dog, drop him off with us, and take him back when he had done his job. He was not an easy dog to handle but I can recall getting them mated about 2 a.m. one morning in the kitchen of our cottage. Gretel went on to have a big litter. I cannot remember now exactly how many but it was in the teens. That kept our Mandy busy for a while. It was lucky because, at the time, we had got one of Trevor's Danes with us who had got only a few pups so she was eventually persuaded to take on a few of Gretel's brood. So all was well. We eventually re-homed her along with her mother Eva to a man in Somerset who had bought Sloopy (Gretel's sister) off us in days gone by.

By now Lin had taken our oldest Great Dane bitch, Mandy, down to Trevors to get her mated. She had a good litter, two of which we kept. Our Pekinese tribe had grown. We had bought ourselves a nice, good looking, male called Kwong and he had fathered a litter from Mae-Ling. I must say that after all these years, and all the dogs we have ever had, then the Peke pups have got to be the prettiest little things we have ever had. Just like a big ball of fluff blowing across the floor because if they have got a good coat and hold their tail over their backs then you cannot see their legs, feet or tail. They are just one big fluff ball with a massive pair of black eyes and nose at one end. Lovely little things.

Lin had always wanted a Clumber Spaniel. We managed to find

a bitch pup in Bournemouth and she, Bella, joined the household and would later present us with a fine litter of pups. Although her name was Bella I always called her Selwyn Froggitt because where ever she went accidents would happen. I used to say that if she walked past a shelf it would fall off the wall. You could basically "track" her movements by the amount of disorder she seemed to leave behind. Although she lived in the house with us, along with all of the other smaller dogs, they all had access to a big paddock outside. We kept a pet pig in this paddock that just used to wander in and out as it pleased. This pig was Bella's best mate. They would play for hours. In fact one Saturday afternoon we were sitting in the living room when all of a sudden this rumpus could be hard coming from the next room. On investigation it became clear that these two had got a new game. Bella would chase the pig in from outside. They would do two or three circuits of the room and then the pig would chase Bella back outside again. So on and so on until they got bored with it all.

It is clear that the dogs kept us busy but the bird enterprise was also blossoming a bit by now. At this time we had bought most of our birds from private breeders. Sometimes whole collections. In those days most private collections consisted of commonly kept birds at the time including Zebra Finches…. the ever present Zebra Finch. Not a bird I liked, too inquisitive, too bossy, and could never mind their own business especially in a mixed flight. They had just got to interfere with everybody's plans. I recall that when we were at Pailton we had a flight of small birds that I had built into one of the outbuildings. Just a few common foreign finches. We also had a pair of Silverbills that had actually gone down to nest and were sitting on eggs. That was until the Zebra Finches decided to "show them how to do it" by evicting them and making their own nest on top of that of the poor Silverbills and proceeded to rear a brood of their own. I have never really forgiven this breed of a bird for doing that. If we ever went to buy a collection that included any of these little sods then we always made it clear that we would take them away for nothing. If this was not agreed then the owner could keep them. Invariably they stayed where they were. An old woman who lived in the forest had heard we were buying birds and she contacted us to see if we could come to some agreement to buy her birds from her whenever she had a surplus. We went to her place to discuss things. It turned out that she kept a free flying flock of Budgerigars, in excess of 200 birds, that were at total liberty around her place. They nested in the trees around her place in boxes she had provided. The only time they ever came inside was for food. She fed them in a big wooden summerhouse which they used to enter and leave through open windows. She wanted a customer for all the young birds that she had bred outside. We agreed a deal. We would give her £1.00 per bird and take all that were available at any one time. The only condition was that as soon as she rang us and told us that she had got chicks ready to go then we had to go and collect them immediately. This was because she did not like them to be in the summerhouse for longer than needs be. She would catch them by not feeding them for a day or two so that they were hungry. She did this by closing the windows thus stopping the flock from entering. She would then open the windows to let the birds see that she was feeding them now. Word would soon get around. Within minutes most of them were inside. It was then that she would close the windows from the outside thereby blocking off any escape route. We would then go in the shed. She would catch up any young birds she wanted to sell. We would pay her for them and the job was done. We had to take ALL the birds she wanted to sell no matter what colour or sex. ALL of them at £1.00. per bird. She called us one day to say she had got some ready to go…. so off we went. There was a fair few of them. The trouble was they were all green and nobody really wanted green budgies in those days but a deal was a deal. We had got to take them. The only saving grace was there was one white bird in amongst them. At least that was something. I had built small aviaries outside within the dog runs plus the kitchen had a row of cages on a shelf high up on one wall. There were cages in all the downstairs rooms. We decided to put the one white budgie in one of the outside flights with a few of the green birds but unnoticed by us there was a small hole in the wire and the one bird found it and escaped …. the white one!!!

Word had got around the area we were buying and selling birds, a few rabbits and guinea pigs etc. so the local council came to call one day to inspect the premises and amenities to check all was up to regulatory standards. It was so they issued us with a Pet Shop License on the premises there and then. We had got a few regular customers by now, mostly pet shops but also private people. Most Saturday mornings we would be busy. As I had to work on a Saturday morning it was all left to Lin and Mandy to see to it. A lot of the budgies we used to buy from the lady in the forest we sold to an aviary at Christchurch. This man would buy any amount of these birds, from anywhere, at any time at a fixed price. He would wait until he had got enough together and then export them all to Brazil. Brazil was then, and I think still is, a country with more budgerigar fanciers than any other country in the world... believe it or not.

One of our regular customers was a lady who had a pet shop in Bournemouth. She used to buy budgies, finches and the odd rabbit and guinea pig. She had arranged to come over one evening to pick up some birds from us but at this time we had found a bird importer and wholesaler we had started to deal with. He used to sell us baby Greater Hill Mynahs. Mostly "gapes". This meant they were still being hand fed which was good because they were all really tame. We used to sell them for £75.00. each or £100.00 if they had started to talk. The lady arrived from Bournemouth to pick up her birds and at the time we had one baby Mynah for sale. She paid us our £75.00. for it and off she went with a new stock for her shop. No problem. She was a regular customer. We thought no more about it until a couple of days later she rang to ask "How long has this Mynah bird been talking?" So far as we were aware it wasn't talking and I told her so. I asked her what it was saying. She told me it was saying "What you doing Nick?" It must have picked it up from Lin I suppose. I said to the woman next time it asks what I am doing tell it that I'm coming over to ring its neck .... It owes me £25.00!! That scenario has been a source of amusement between us ever since.

Lin and I had been living together for a few years by now so we decided to get married. This we did at the registry office in Lymington, just a small affair, no big reception. Just a gathering of all those present, with a few bites and drinks in our cottage. It was a bit like holding a small wedding reception in a pet shop I suppose. Lin's Mom and Ma and Frank travelled down. John Gray and his wife Barbara and daughter Katherine came, along with Dora and Tom (our old neighbours at Rugby). One of Dora's sons Nobby joined us along with his now wife. Barry Wells also came with his new lady. They were now living in Cirencester. Mandy was our "bridesmaid". It was a lovely day, nice and sunny. It was a long way for everyone to come so all except Lin's mom left for home that evening. I always remember Nobby checked he had got enough money in his pocket. "Just in case we have to buy a new motor on the way home" he said. We had hired a car for the weekend but when I took it back on the Monday the rental company insisted I had scratched it. We lost the deposit we had paid when we picked it up. This was a bit of a blow because we had very little other money until the next pay day. For three or four days we existed on egg sandwiches, cake and left over bites from our wedding day.

The following weekend it was back to work again for both of us plus, of course, we had our menagerie at home. This seemed to be evolving and expanding at a fair rate of knots. Looking back on it later it was all, slowly, getting too big for just the two of us and Mandy to manage as well as doing our outside jobs. The early signs of this were when my back started to become a problem again. More pain, more often, but I wasn't about to give in. Then, one afternoon, at the Turkey Farm I was forced to. I noticed I was having problems moving my legs. I was bundled into the back of a motor and taken home. Lin was called home from her work and by now my legs were unresponsive. When the ambulance arrived it had got to the point that I could not feel anything when pins were pushed into them.   It was off to Southampton Hospital that evening. I will always remember the consultant who, apparently needed to assess my state of affairs, was out at a dinner. When he arrived he was still dressed in his "best bib and tucker" complete with a white silk scarf and dicky bow.   He examined me and came out with the never to be forgotten quote "Do you know Mr Homfray I hate bad backs. Give me a good old fashioned broken leg or arm any day but I fuckin' hate bad backs".   Obviously not a happy man to say the least.   The following morning things were improving. I could now feel my legs again and by the afternoon I was able to shuffle/walk again so I was allowed home. It had all been a strange experience. It went almost as fast as it came. Looking back on things I think it was Mother Nature advising me to slow down a bit but I wasn't listening. Things to do and all that!! This would all come back and get me in the end but, of course, I was having none of it. I was a driven man. Always had been since a teenager but this was becoming a bit of a problem. Easy to say in hindsight but not so easy to recognise at the time unfortunately.

The "pet shop" side of life was growing and by now we had seven adult Neapolitan mastiffs at home. Trevor Lewis had imported two more bitches, Regina and Asta, so after doing their quarantine they came to us. All these seven plus the others, Pekes, Spaniels, Danes, Shi Tzu's and Afghans. That is without what might turn up for whelping from Trevor. As long as all was going well then it was manageable ....Just about. Apart from the dogs, the chickens, birds and a few small animals kept coming and going. We had been buying from and selling a few fowl to a woman

Wedding Day, 1976.

called Mrs Simm. She had a smallholding come riding school a couple of miles away where, apart from the poultry and horses, she also had Vietnamese Pot Bellied Pigs. Quite a rare thing to come across back in those days. She had two sows, one of which had two youngsters. At some time these two sows must have had a fight because the one had a wound on one of her hams (thighs) which was partially healed. The trouble was these two girls were not the most sociable creatures on earth to say the least. They knew they had got teeth and they knew how to use them. To treat the wounded sow's leg it was a case of heating up the Stockholm Tar, a good old fashioned all round treatment for open wounds, putting it in a tin on the end of a stick and waiting until the sow was asleep. We then got within the stick's length of her and poured the tar over her wound. After a couple of weeks it had completely healed over so it was time to sell these four on. The sow that had been attacked went to a lady we knew who had had one of our Neapolitan Mastiff pups off us. The other sow and her two young we sold to a zoo in Bognor Regis in the late 70's.

A lot of zoos were being sold by councils into private ownership so there were deals to be done. We hired a small horse box and driver to take the Pot Bellies down to their new home. After unloading them I asked the man in charge if he had got anything he wanted to sell while we were there with the transport. He said he had a male Llama. This perked my interest because Mrs Simm had told us on several occasions that she would like a Llama but it must be good with children and quiet with horses and ponies. I was keen to have a look at it anyway. There is was, the biggest Llama I have ever seen and, best of all,it was living in the Childrens' Zoo along with a Shetland Pony!! Perfect. I asked the man how much he wanted for it (male Llamas were worth about £100.00 each in those days). We knew this because we had previously tried to buy one from Longleat Safari Park) and he said "Oh give us a tenner and take him away". I was ready to load him up but then I was struck by a flash of common sense. What would I do with it if Mrs Simm decided she did not want it. Best to talk to her first. I told the man to give me a couple of days and I would get back to him. He agreed this offer. On getting back home I went round to see Mrs Simm and told her exactly what I could get for her on "the Llama front". She wanted to know where it was so that she could go and see it first!! The cheeky cow". I said to her that as far as he was concerned then I had got it. We had a fair few deals with the poultry in the past with no problems either way. If she could not trust me not to offer her anything that was not right then she had best forget about it. I was not going to tell her where it was and have her go off and buy it behind my back … one for "the back burner". My day would come. The lady never did get that Llama through me. I had never knowingly sold anyone any animal that I did not think it was as I said it was (except maybe the two donkeys years earlier and they were sold on a presumption). I have always said over the years, and still do so even today, that I would rather give someone good stock than sell them bad stock. I had my pride and a bad reputation can never be shaken off anyway.

We had been in touch with a small zoo in Winchester that had offered us some Jungle Fowl chicks. Little stripey buggers that seemed to spend most of their time fighting each other. Nasty little pieces of work. At about the same time we had also got some Oxford Ginger Game birds that were also known to be "fighters". These birds were of interest to certain sections of society especially travellers. Anyway, word must have got around and it was circulating that we had got these Oxfords and the Jungle Fowl because a travelling man turned up one evening. He did not say that he wanted anything in particular and that was the problem. He was a huge bloke. If he weighted an ounce then he must have been nearly 20 stone (120 + kilos). He could see we had got a few dogs about

Mandy, Lymington.

but only the small ones were visible to him. He started crowing about this Staffy he had got and how it would kill or fight anything. By now we had invited him in for a cup of tea mainly because we did not want him to see what we had got out the back. He was now sat in the armchair and still prattling on about this "man eating Staffordshire Bull Terrier" he had got. According to him it would kill anything. He was beginning to piss me off now so I just said to him. "Wait there a minute and I will be back". I went outside and got Kronus and Ursula. Now they weighed more than he did between them, around 25 stone (well over 300 kilos). I took them inside to meet him. At this point he picked his feet up off the floor onto the chair and was pressing himself as far back as he could. He had basically "welded" himself in there. He was shitting himself now. I just said to him to stop crowing about his "Man Eater Staffy" because these were the first two real fighting dogs he had ever seen. He asked how many we had got and where did we keep them. I told him that we had got seven of them and that they were all out the back looking after the chickens he had come to "suss out". He left a bit meeker than he had arrived.

There must have been a few travellers about at the time because we had acquired an old B.M.C. van that was basically a heap of scrap.

Me and Mandy one Christmas.

The most worrying thing was that I thought it needed a new alternator because the ignition light never went off and it was drinking oil like there was no tomorrow. We decided to get rid of it and sell it "as seen". I took the bulb out of the ignition light and filled it up with good heavy thick old tractor engine oil. We advertised it and a couple of travelling lads turned up to have a look at it. The lad who wanted it fired it up then drove up and down the drive in it. The other lad stayed in the yard with us along with a little girl about our Mandy's age. The chap came back in the motor and we had a deal and that was that. However the next day he turned up again and I said to Lin "Here's trouble now" but no, not at all. Apparently he had seen one of Mandy's bikes leaning against the wall and he had come to see if we would sell it to him for his daughter. The little girl must have seen it when they had come and bought the motor . . . phew!!

We now used to place an advert in The Exchange and Mart magazine stating that we could find and supply "Anything from a mouse to a donkey". This threw up a few "interesting" situations. One in particular was a man with an expanding private zoo somewhere in Somerset. He had got in touch with us to ask if we had got a Cockatoo. We always tried

201

to keep at least one of these birds at all time. On being told that we had got one he arranged to come and visit us. He wanted the bird plus, maybe, one or two others at the same time. He arrived and bought the Cockatoo and a few more birds. We were standing around chatting and he made it clear that he was just beginning his collection with the aim of eventually opening a small bird garden/zoo sometime in the future. He asked us if we knew of any available stock to suit that role. Well we had just heard through the grapevine that a Council owned zoo up in the Midlands was in the process of closing down at this time and that they were looking to rehome some porcupines and two adult giraffes. He was not keen on the porcupines but he was extremely keen on obtaining the giraffes. He needed a week or two to go home, and sort things out first, but he said if we could come to some sort of a deal then could we get them for him? Me, like the hot-head I was back then just said "Yes, sure, no problem". We parted on those terms. I was now absolutely shitting myself. What happens if he came back and said he wanted them? How were we going to move two adult giraffes from the Midlands to Somerset? We had never had giraffes before. So far as I could see the actual transport could be overcome. We just wanted someone with a lorry and a high sided open topped trailer of some kind. We could blindfold the animals to help keep them quiet. Sedation of any major form was out of the question … too risky. Our biggest head ache, in my mind anyway, was low bridges…. believe it or not. I had many sleepless nights pouring over O/S maps trying to plan a route that would hopefully avoid such obstacles. In for a penny in for a pound!! The time had come to give the man a ring to see what he had decided. He picked up the phone and told me he really wanted the giraffes. (I thought "Oh my God here we go. We are right up shit Street now). BUT he had priced up the cost of actually fencing and housing these pair and had come to the conclusion that it would be all too expensive for him. I must say, at this point, I quietly heaved a sigh of relief. A shame really. I liked a challenge and if he had said that he did want them then a deal was a deal. On reflection that was a close one but we continued to supply this gentleman with birds when we had any that he wanted. It would have been something to tell the grandchildren I suppose.

Through our advert in The Exchange and Mart a lady with one or two pet shops in the area asked us if we could get her some mice. Not ordinary mice, but piebald and champagne/tan mice. We said we would look into it for her and let her know if we could find what she wanted.

We did find what she wanted in the shape of a little old man who lived in Hampshire who had bred fancy mice. He could supply us with what we were looking for but we had to take them all. About 200 of the little creatures. This we agreed to do. A price was agreed and we arranged for him to deliver them. At the time we had no housing for so many so we went out and bought a selection of plastic fish tanks and lids. These we placed on the table in the parlour. This was basically, by now, a pet shop really. Our vendor duly arrived on a bloody moped of all things. His cargo all housed in wooden mouse boxes that he had somehow managed to secure to his two wheeled mode of transport with bungee ropes, string, and straps. He had already separated all the males and females so it was just a case of transferring them all into their waiting temporary accommodation. He apparently included a "special pair" of champagne/tans that he suggested we keep separate from the rest so he left them with us still in their mouse transport box. This would suffice until next morning when we could get them something better. Deal done. No problem, as we thought. It had become obvious over the past few months that a cat had been coming into the kitchen overnight. There were dirty footprints on the surfaces. We always kept the back door open from outside into the kitchen and also the door between the kitchen and the parlour. It was never really a problem because Ursula always had a bed downstairs that she always slept in. Now she hated nothing more in the world than she hated cats. The feline nocturnal visitations were never a problem. As soon as the old bitch realised there was a cat in the kitchen she was up and at 'em. With this in mind we returned to bed but on coming downstairs next morning we were greeted by the sight of a "killing" field. Dead mice, most of them headless, everywhere. The tanks on the floor. Total mayhem!! In our rush to get these little creatures rehoused, fed, and watered we had overlooked the fact that Ursula was no longer on guard because she was in the whelping room with a new litter of pups. Talk about an oversight!! We managed to catch up any survivors and there were not many of them. Sods law all those that had survived were of the piebald variety and these were a lot more common thus less valuable than the champagne/tans. All the latter had succumbed to the night's feline holocaust except the "special pair" that were still safe and sound in their transport box. All the survivors went on to the lady who had originally ordered them so in the end we managed to recoup the initial cost of our foray into the Fancy Mice World. It now seemed a good time to replace Ursula on guard duty with one of her first litter that we had kept . . . Blossom. She was a lot more laid back than her mother and she had got used to spending time in the house over the years. She would do the job.

Through the same advert we had a man get in touch wanting two Jack Russell pups, preferably from the same litter, for his children. Now we had a strict rule never to buy and sell dogs at this time. The risk of bringing in a disease could have reeked havoc amongst our own dogs. To us they were too valuable for that. We had taken a long time to get what we had got but I knew that Trevor had just bought a litter of Russells. I arranged for him to deliver two of them to us on a certain day and we had also arranged with our man to come and pick them up later on the same day. That was that one sorted. Another satisfied customer. The trouble was during the few hours we had them Mandy had fallen in love with them and wanted one for herself. She obviously could not have one of those two so we agreed to find her one locally. She had earned it. We let it be known that we were on the look out for a Russell pup and eventually a call came from a man in The New Forest who said he had got a litter and that we could go and have a look at them that afternoon. I remember it was a very wet Sunday, torrential rain. The man had given us an address and directions so off Mandy and I went. We hunted high and low for his place, following his directions, the lot. We must have spent a couple of hours looking but in the end we both agreed that it seemed like somebody was "playing the prat" with us. We gave up and went home both soaked to the skin. Neither of us in the best of humours. However, next day I went down to the local shop and there was a card in the window advertising Corgi Pups for sale. When Mandy came home from school she said she would like to go and have a look at them anyway. This we did and came away with a little bitch pup that she called Megan. Megan soon became Mandy's best mate and "confidante". She took her to bed every night, told her all her troubles, the works, and little Megan stayed with us all her life. She lived for a good ten years. She never had any pups. She was the yappiest dog we had ever owned but she loved Mandy and vice versa . . . so all was well there.

The advert also generated an enquiry from a lady who rang up one day to ask if we could get her a "Sun Bear!! My first reaction to this was to ask her if she was taking the piss or something. I explained what had happened a few weeks earlier with the Jack Russell mystery tour but she assured me that she was 100% genuine. Her husband had a small collection of bears but he really wanted a Sun Bear. They are all out there. These people with, what seems to your "average bod", strange hobbies. Obviously we could not accommodate her needs. I wonder if she ever got one?

Finally on the most bizarre request that was generated by The Exchange and Mart advert was a lady who rang up one day looking for a fruit bat. We had seen her on T.V. weeks earlier on the That's Life Programme where she had explained that she kept her tame bat flying free around her house. She said that it roosted on the headboard of her bed. By the time she had got round to ringing to us it had sadly died. I explained that we had not got one at home but I put her in touch with a couple of chaps that might be able to help her with her search. This advert really was uncovering some interesting people but we liked that. Variety is the spice of life as they say!!

Winter was upon us again. All was going well. Blossom was due to have her pups any time soon. Everything running smoothly. We had got less small animals about outside now because of the colder weather. Everything was "tickety boo" for now. Then, I was woken very early one morning by the sound of splashing water. My immediate thought was Blossom had, somehow, managed to get into the bathroom (it was downstairs) and jumped into the bath that I had not emptied earlier that evening. Our cesspit needed time to soak away on the odd occasion. I went downstairs to investigate. On opening the door into the parlour in the dark I immediately stepped into two or three feet (1 metre) of filthy water. WHAT was happening now!!! On wading through into the kitchen (Blossom was, by now, actually floating around on her bed in the parlour) I was greeted by the sight of a torrent of water flooding in through the back door and gradually building up inside the whole of the downstairs area. I thought the only thing, or the best thing, to do was to try and open the front door at the other end of the kitchen and and let the water out. This proved to be a struggle because of the weight and pressure of the filthy soup that was busily trying to do as much damage as possible inside our dwelling. As luck would have it a police patrol car was passing the end of our drive and saw there seemed to be a small lake evolving on the main road about 200 yards (150 metres) away from our place. They had driven up the drive to investigate. Good job they did because I was having trouble opening the door but, with the two of them pushing from outside, we managed to achieve this thus relieving the pressure inside. It was like taking the plug out a bath. Luckily the front door was wider than the back door so although the water (which by now was running clean) was still cascading in luckily it was draining faster. The police contacted the Fire Service and Water Board. Both duly arrived and began to investigate the root cause of our increasingly aquatic environment. It turned out that due to a frost that night a 12" (30 cm) mains water pipe had burst in the field behind our cottage. As our open back door was the lowest escape point for the now liberated water supply then it all funnelled through out kitchen. Fresh water would not have been quite so bad but, on its way to our house, it had washed through the cattle slurry collection area. Hence the original smell and sight of this interference in our lives. The Water Board immediately isolated the supply and the Fire Brigade began to pump us out. I can always remember me and a fireman sitting on top of the cooker. He said to me that he could smell smoke!! I asked him how on earth could anything be on fire amidst so much water. He was right because we began to investigate and on entering the living room the electrical sockets on the skirting board were smoking!! Why they were able to do this would become apparent the following day. He fiddled about somewhere under the stairs and managed to isolate our supply. One problem sorted. By now another fire appliance had arrived with its pumps. It seemed they were not making the expected progress so it was decided to lift some floorboards and pump out from there. This took time. The reason it took time was that the cottage had originally been built on top of an unfinished cellar. It was just sat on top of this huge cavern. Worst of all it had been built with no foundations at all. This could have been a problem. It was explained to us later if we had not managed to open the front door, thank you Mr Policemen, then the pressure of the gradual increase of the water inside the property would have eventually pushed all the ground floor walls out. Now that would have been a mess. A proper mess!! The Fire Brigade and Water Board were brilliant I must say. They could not do enough for us. They bought in space heaters to dry the place out. The Water Board gave us a cheque to help us out straight away. We were not insured of course. The best part of it all was when Mandy rose from her bed. She came downstairs and asked what had been going on? She had slept through the whole lot of it!! The next thing to be done was to solve the problem of the smoking electrical sockets and on inspection by the power suppliers it was revealed the whole place had been wired upon the cheap i.e. "a bodge job" A bodge job that could have ended up tragically. Luckily it did not. The next problem, as I thought, was going to be the dogs and animals outside. How wet were they? As daylight revealed itself not one of them was any more than damp. The water had found the lowest route thus missing any kennels etc. The closest that a disaster got was when we could see the water had risen to a level of about an inch (2 1/2cms) of Ursula's bed complete with her pups. Luckily we had moved her and her brood into an outside pen a few days earlier. That is providence for you but, on the other hand, for poor Blossom the shock of it all must have been too much. She seemingly "took her pups back". We lost out a bit there . Once the smell had dispersed and the place was dry again it was just a case of carrying on regardless. "Britain did not build an empire by letting a drop of water get in the way!!"

We had, by now, befriended a chap called Keith. Keith had a little bungalow with a bit of land where he lived with his wife and daughter. They kept a few pigs and poultry there and they also ran ponies and cattle in The Forest. The best way I found to explain Keith was to say that he could blag his way out of a locked safe that had been concreted into the foundations of The Tower of London. He turned out to be an interesting sort of fella. We got on well. Keith and I helped each other out if needed. He would sometimes bring us poultry back from Ringwood Market and on one occasion he turned up with, what we thought, a cock bird of a species called Houdin. These are rare birds but they look remarkably like another breed called Standard Polish. He had only paid 60p for the bird and we gave him a drink on top and the bird was ours. He was an old bird at the best of times. His spurs looked more like small tree branches. Time for a manicure old man. With Spurs trimmed and camouflaged he looked years younger. Lin went and fetched our book on the Standards of Fancy Fowl. We checked all was well. It all fitted until it came to the feet. Apparently Houdins have five toes (one extra to a normal fowl). Our man only had four so he was just a Standard Polish. Not worth much more than we had paid for him but a plot was hatching in my head. I rang Mrs Simm and told her that it was her lucky day because we had just had a cock Houdin come in. She loved her fancy fowl. I said I was giving her first refusal on him. If she liked him then he could be hers for a tenner (£10.00). She said she would come round straight away. True to her word she drove into the yard five minutes later. Trouble was she was clutching the same Breed Standard book that we had checked our bird against within the last hour . . . OOPS. Out she gets and started to check the bird. Like us she agreed that everything fitted until she came to his feet. She counted his toes and said "He only has four toes. They are supposed to have five. Oh never mind what's a toe between friends?" She gave us our tenner and took the bird home. This was not the end of the story. Oh no. It turned out she was good friends with a chap called Jack Hargreaves, an old, supposedly country, man who presented a programme on the T.V. called "Out of Town". Back in those days and it was on one of his shows that our "Houdin" was next seen by us. He was there at Bournemouth Poultry Show cooing over our ex-bird saying how rare the Houdin breed was and all that rubbish. The trouble was he was not showing a Houdin in the country via the power of T.V. No, the silly sod was drooling over a common or garden "Standard Polish!! A classic!! The affair with the Llamas and Mrs Simm was still niggling away in my mind but we had got our own back now at least.

As I said Keith and I helped each other out if and when needed. Hence he came round one Saturday morning to say when he had gone to feed his pigs he had found one of his old sows dead in her bed but she was still warm. Could I go round and help him get her out, wash her, shave her and butcher her because he had already sold her pre-packed and freezer ready. His customer was due to come and collect that late afternoon or early evening so we had to get out fingers out. Within a couple of hours or so we had managed to do all that was necessary and the old sow was now butchered up in Keith's freezer. I asked him who he had sold her to and he informed me that he had got a couple of friends in London who owned a shoe wholesaling business and they were Jews! He had sold pig meat to Jews!! He could "blag" anything.

Birds were also a small interest of Keith's and he had a Cockatoo and an African Grey that roamed at liberty around his place. He would buy and sell the odd bird or two. Now, he had a friend called John O'Leary who had just moved down from London with his family. John was an old friend from back in the 60's when both he and Keith had been in "The Pop Scene" at the time. More about that later. Anyway John had decided he and his wife would like a grey cockatiel as a pet for their new home. We had usually got a couple of these birds about. They were everywhere in those days. We used to sell them for about £10.00. each at the time. Sods Law we had not got any at that particular time. Keith knew John well and he said in the past his friend would often have these strange fancies but in his experience the novel idea would soon pass. We had better "strike while the iron was hot". We had not got, and could not find a Cockatiel but we had just heard of an African Grey parrot for sale in Portsmouth. We agreed to drive over and have a look at it. If we could buy it at the right money then we would share the deal. Journey made and the bird and cage bought. Now was the time to try and find it a new home with John, or John O, as we called him. We arrived at his place took the bird inside plonking it, in its cage, on his living room table. He was not interested at all in the bird and nor was his wife. He wanted a Cockatiel not an African Grey but as luck would have it he had just redecorated his living room in shades of grey and pink. I pointed this out and said that the bird was colour co-ordinated with its surroundings and that we would leave the bird where it was until next morning by which time "We are sure you will both have fallen in love with it". Next day arrived. We went round to see John O's and sure enough our prediction that he and his wife would have fallen in love with the bird turned out to be true. We managed to get £110.00. for it and as far as I know it lived with the O'Leary's for the rest of its life.

Now let's elaborate on Keith's past life in the 60's pop world. It all came to light by accident. He was a massive record collector. Especially Blues Music. I always remember a shelf in his living room wall. It must have been 20 feet (6 metres) long and it was crammed from one end to the other with L.P's. Neither Lin or I had ever taken a lot of notice of it. Everybody of our age had a collection of vinyl records back then but Keith had got one hell of a lot. Anyway, enough of his record collection. I popped in one day to see him but he was not there. His wife was going about her business but she had a record playing that I had never heard before. I asked her who it was and she told me it was Keith playing on there. She would not expand on this fact. Fair enough but by the time I met Keith again she must have told him that she had "let slip" this fact because he immediately started to enlighten me on the subject. In his early teens he had been quite a respected base guitar player. He performed with several bands of the time including John Mayles Blues Breakers, Georgie Fame and The Blue Flames amongst others. He had even been on tour in America in a supporting band for Jimi Hendrix and by the time he had reached his mid/late teens he was earning £40.00 a week. When you consider the average wage for an adult farm worker over here was only £10.00 a week then he was doing well. Apparently it all got too much for him and he decided to pack it all in and go back to his old life in The New Forest. He said he thought no more about it until, one day, he got a phone call from his old music mates. They explained a couple of them had got together to write and record a song specially aimed at the No. 1. Spot and would he, Keith, play base guitar on it. Apparently he refused saying that he had had enough of all that stuff but his mates persisted. In the end he told them to hum the tune over the phone and if he liked it then he would agree to play on it. If he did not like it then they should never contact him again. They hummed the tune. Keith did not like it so that was that. The only regret he had afterwards was that the new band turned out to be Procol Harum and the song was "A Whiter Shade of Pale". One of the biggest records of the time!! AND he had said it "had got no chance".

Terry was another friend of Keith's that we had been introduced to. Now Terry was a big built, tall sort of bloke, with a bald head skirted by a cranial fringe of long straight hair almost down to his shoulders. His passion in life was big pigs. The bigger the better so far as he was concerned. I had never seen them but I asked his boss one day how big they really were. He told me that he had never seen bigger or fatter pigs. He said that Terry had kept three of them in a loose box, big enough for 2 adult cattle at a push, and they were crammed into the space. He said that in his opinion they must have weighed about 5 cwt (250 plus kilo) each. Now Terry lived, along with his pigs, in a mobile home on a piece of ground that was a reclaimed rubbish dump. Keith told me he was out there, visiting Terry one day, and they had gone inside for a cup of tea when the mobile home began to shudder and move. Terry revealed the reason for this was he had got a couple of sows that actually slept underneath. (They had apparently excavated themselves a "boudoir" amongst the unearthed rubbish down there). They were down there "just having a bit of a scratch". There was, in those days, a privately owned Ice Cream Manufacturer situated in Boscombe, a few miles up the road towards Bournemouth, who gave away any product that they had overproduced to anyone who would take it. The only condition to securing this deal was that whatever happened then any excess production had to be taken away immediately it became available. Terry got into this arrangement gleefully. Free food for his monster pigs!! Indeed Lin and I were having a mooch round the antique shops one day in Boscombe when the faint sound of "scraping" began to get closer. Lo and behold it turned out to be Terry driving up the High Street in a beaten up old Morris 1,000 pick-up piled high with bins full of ice-cream. It was so over loaded the tail gate was scrapping along the road. There he was, at the wheel, bald head and flowing pelmet of hair, arm resting on the open driver's window. Not a care in the world. Our man's "Ice Cream Venture" had now come to the notice of the local press and indeed the B.B.C. television had got on to it. This culminated in Terry appearing live on Nationwide one evening. Of course, we tuned in to witness this event and there he was, in all his glory, being interviewed by, I think, no lesser woman than Sue Lawley. I always remember she asked him what flavour ice cream his pigs liked best and he informed her that their favourite was Vanilla but they were not too keen on the Rum and Raisin. The ice cream deal was O.K. to start with. Production was not at its highest and Terry and his merry band of overweight pigs could keep up with the supply. However, as Summer got into full swing and, production at the factory increased, so did the supply of over production. Terry was contracted to remove this anytime, at any cost, and it all became too much in the end. Indeed Keith said he had gone up to Terry's place one day and there were containers of unusable fermenting ice cream everywhere. Terry managed to see out his yearly contract but after that he relinquished his deal. It turned out later that nearly every pig producer in Hampshire and Dorset had, at one time or another tried, "the ice cream job" but they had all failed to keep up with the supply.

We had still got our "pet" sow at home and she was now old enough and, as we thought, big enough to be bred from so we agreed with Terry to use his boar on her but he wanted to see her first. He came round one evening to view the prospective bride but he just shook his head and said "My boar would flatten her". By now she was a good strong young sow so that idea failed to bear fruit . . . or piglets.

Terry worked on a farm a few miles away and his boss had a Border Collie dog that we wanted to use on a bitch we had been given a few months earlier. This was agreed and when the bitch was ready to be mated I took her down to stay with her proposed "husband" for a few days. I pulled into the yard and there was Terry splitting logs with an axe. I dropped the bitch off with the dog and went across to have a chat with him. I asked him how big his pigs really were. I had never seen any of them. He thought for a second or two, rubbed his chin, and said "See that chopping block". This was a hefty piece of timber to say the least "Well I have got pigs with bigger ears than that". Apart from his pigs Terry's other big love in life was attending re-enacted mediaeval banquets. Apparently he had all the costume and everything. Considering his "hair style" we used to bet he really looked the part. We could just imagine him sitting there throwing the odd half eaten leg of venison other his shoulder to a waiting Irish Wolfhound behind him.

I had been working at the turkey farm, in the afternoons, for a fair while by now and I had also managed to squeeze in a few hours mowing lawns for old people from time to time. I was getting £3.00 an hour. It was cash in hand for these little jobs. I decided to give up the turkey farm and just get another one or two more lawn mowing jobs. I had four regular customers and I would spend a couple of hours with each one. At the time we did not have a vehicle so it was just a case of making sure they were all within 5 minute cycling range. It worked out well and gave me more time to spend with our animals and to be quite honest the old back problem was not getting any better. Pain killers were now forming a considerable part of my diet or so it seemed. I was beginning to lose weight and get heart palpitations etc. etc. The writing was on the wall.

By now Keith had met a man called Ernie at Ringwood Market and he bought him round to our place. He was a man who stood getting on for 6' 6" tall (2 metres). He was as thin as a rake and walked with a permanent stoop. He lived in a big detached house with about an acre of land and a row of wooden stables on the edge of The Forest a few miles away. Ernie had moved there from somewhere near London with his wife Sheila and two teenage children to, apparently, try and live "the good life". Trouble was none of them knew anything about anything as far as that was concerned. In my eyes Sheila's only claim to fame was that she could roll a cigarette using just one hand. I have never seen anyone else in my life who could or can do that. She was the opposite of her husband. He was tall and skinny. She was short and fat. A bit like Jack Spratt and his wife in the nursery rhyme. Ernie came to me one day to say that he wanted a milking goat. I told him we did not keep our goats anymore but I could find him one if he wanted. He agreed to this. I duly found him a young nanny who had just had her first kid but it had unfortunately died. She would be fine as a house goat. We purchased her and sold her on to Ernie explaining the situation that she might be a bit fractious for a day or two until she had got properly used to being hand milked. No problem . . . wrong!! A few days later the man himself (Ernie) phoned up to say that it was impossible to milk the goat we had sold him. I told him there was no such thing as a goat you couldn't milk. I said we would go round and sort it for him anyway. Keith came round and picked me, Lin and Mandy up in his car and off we went to see what was going on. When we arrived we were escorted down to the stable where this young Nannie was tied up with a bag so full of milk it looked and felt as if it had been carved out of granite. The poor thing must have been in pain by now. If not, then it was extremely uncomfortable. I told Ernie to go and get a saucepan or something and I would milk her for him. She was not happy about this at all and I do not blame her. She must have been really sore. She was tied up by her neck collar so I told Ernie to hold her back end as still as he could. Well, she kicked, she bucked, and she trod in the saucepan I was milking into. She piddled and some of that went into the milk as well. She also managed to flick a not inconsiderable amount of shit into the milk. Job done!! Goat milked so I just handed the man himself a pan full of milk complete with essence of goat urine, floating goat shit pellets, bits of straw and hay etc. I told him never to tell me that I had sold him a goat that was impossible to milk again. The best or worst was yet to come. He walked out of the stable, complete with his "stew" of goat milk, goat urine, goat shit and various pieces of dried herbage. He put this up to his mouth and was drinking it straight out of the pan. It was there and then we could not, any of us, believe our eyes. That is what he did. It turned out, Sheila, after a while and a bit of practice, managed to get the hang of hand milking their goat. I have seen some things in my time but that episode, that day, with Ernie and the goat milk rates highly on my "Bizarre scale".

We had all, especially Keith, realised what a dick head this Ernie was and Keith would really wind him up. More so than me. To me he was just becoming an irritant. Everything we did with the animals he would try and copy. He wanted to know exactly what we were up to, where, when and why. Keith told him we had bought the porcupines from the zoo up north and resold them. We hadn't really. Not only that but we had sold all the quills, they had shot out in the process of moving them, to a fishing tackle shop in Lymington. The shop had turned them into floats. Ernie took all this in. So much so that he even went into town to look at them. As I said earlier Keith could blag his way in or out of anywhere and he had really got his teeth into this bloke by now. More so than I had, but he was beginning to get up my nose a bit as well. In the end I think he came to realise we were both just winding him up and got fed up with us but not before an event happened one evening. Keith, myself, Lin and Mandy had gone round for a passing visit when all of a sudden, out of the blue, the sound of "Adder, Adder, Adder" was heard emanating from Ernie's house. We all rushed up there to investigate only to be greeted by the sight of Sheila, with a dutch hoe, beating the living daylights out of some unfortunate reptile that she had found basking on her tiled front porch. She had bludgeoned it to such an extent that, by the time we had got there, basically there not much more to see than a rather smudged outline of the poor beast. Keith always said I had put it there on purpose, just as another wind up, but I truly hadn't. I think Ernie was under the impression that at least either Keith or I had been at the root of his wife's panic attack. Hence we never heard much more from him or his family after that little episode.

As I mentioned earlier we used to sell any surplus budgerigars to a local aviary and dealer. I will call him Mr 'A'. At times we would buy a bird or two from him. Indeed we bought what, he insisted, was a Triton Cockatoo but to cut a long story short he ripped us off with the bird. On talking to several of our contacts we were not the only people Mr 'A' had "taken in". It all came to light one day when a chap came round to have a look at another cockatoo we had got for sale. He was a dealer and in the past he had also fallen prey to Mr 'A' the same man who had hoodwinked us. He told us how he repaid him. He had done it by ringing this fellow up one day and pretending not to know anything about birds. He said that his wife had got a pair of Rosette Cockatoos. These were rare birds back then, as now, and that the female had hatched these chicks but would not rear them. His wife had hand reared them and they were so tame that they were a "Bloody nuisance around the place". He wanted rid of them for whatever he could get for them. He and Mr 'A' had "a deal" over the phone for some ridiculously low price and he said he would deliver them to the aviaries in a day or two. Of course he didn't because they had never existed in the first place but, of course, Mr 'A' had already got them sold at the going rate and he had got customers queueing up for them. Those few "little white lies" put one up Mr 'A' as a starter. More was to come in the not too distant future but more of that in a while.

The chap who had initiated this wheeze had come to us to buy a cockatoo was an interesting kind of fella. Well in the bird trade he was anyway. It turned out, from time to time, he used to smuggle wild caught Macaws into the country. He said that when he received them, all in a very clandestine way, they were all absolutely wild and vicious. He said that if ever one of them got hold of you then you definitely knew about it . . . to say the least. He told us what he used to do with them was to gradually get them used to eating raisins and sultanas. He would then gradually soak these in Brandy until the birds, overtime, became tipsy and more lethargic and handleable. He would then scour the adverts in Avicultural Magazines for any dealer who had any type of tame and talking parrot or cockatoo for sale. (In those days there was a bird dealer/ aviary in almost every town). He would get in touch with them and agree to exchange two or three of his "steady" (only because they were under the influence of alcohol) birds for one tame or tame and talking specimen. In his words "By the end I had got a roomful of tame or tame and talking parrots, all sitting in armchairs, reading The Radio Times. At the same time there was, doted about the country, a collection of very angry and spiteful birds. Once they had sobered up they returned to form . . . Wild!! "You would never get away with anything, even near to that, these days but that is how things were 40 odd years ago.

Peter was another chap who had been "duped" by our Mr 'A', the budgerigar buyer come purveyor of birds, who turned out not to be as he described. Peter had an axe to grind as well. We used to deal with him from time to time and he, as we did , wanted to get one back on this fellow. As it turned out we had bought some quite rare small finches that, to keep in tip top condition, really needed to be kept warm and have access to live food. The latter not being easily available back then as it is now. To get over this we had them in cages, in the living room, with a heat lamp over them. This was next to a window that we would open at night. The heat lamp drew in moths and insects during the hours of darkness and we managed to keep these birds going like that but they were not thriving at all and they were expensive little birds. We hatched a plan. Lin would ring up the aviary offering to part exchange these birds for, basically, anything that was of comparable value. Mr 'A' agreed to do this. Because he would recognize Lin or I then Peter agreed to take the birds over and come back with whatever he could. I told him that before he showed the man our birds to make sure he rattled the cage so that they would become startled and tighten their feathers up and look healthier than they really were. All went to plan. We gave Peter a drink out of it and we had all had our own back. The dealer was none the wiser as to where these little birds had originated from and so he still kept buying budgies off us. Keith had an African Grey Parrot that used to live free, along with an old Cockatoo, that he had had for years and was part of the family. The Grey had turned spiteful. She had already bitten the cat's tail off and was beginning to target the old Cockatoo. Keith was having none of this she had to go. She had got to the point if you could find a cage strong enough she could not snip through the bars (she had a beak like a pair of bolt cutters) then she would just scream all the time she was in it. She was just wrecking the place but worst of all she just did not like cages, any cages, empty or not. She would just go up to them and snip through all the bars. It became her favourite hobby. Keith decided

215

that the best place for her would be the dealer we had been having a bit of trouble with previously. He gave him a call and agreed some sort of deal with the man. Now not only was this renegade of a parrot off Keith's premises she was soon to become a big problem for the aforementioned dealer who thought he was too clever for his own good. I can recall when Keith returned after dropping off this troublesome Grey Lady he said "I bet by now she has got out of her cage and is busy going round his place snipping through any bars she can see. I bet there is newly liberated birds everywhere over there."

Back at our place a lady who lived in one of the houses on the main road, about ½ mile (500 metres) away from us, turned up one Saturday morning with an injured fox she had found in her front garden. The poor thing was in a bit of a mess. Well a lot of a mess really. It looked as if it had been hit by a car at least. It was dragging it's back end and it had a fair array of cuts and grazes all over that area. Now I knew that a few doors away from her lived a serving R.S.P.C.A. officer so I asked her why she had not taken it to him. She replied that she already had and his response was "It's my weekend off. I can't do anything about it" . . . The bastard!! We agreed to take the poor thing in and cleaned it up. We stitched up a couple of deepish cuts it had sustained and made it a warm bed under the stairs with a heat lamp. The worrying thing was that it had got no reflex responses in its back end or back legs. It had obviously damaged its spine. We managed to keep it hydrated by tubing fluid into its stomach but it died on the Sunday evening. At least it was comfortable now.

We had also made friends with a lady only known to us as Dianna. She was a woman in her mid 40's I suppose. Her husband, who we never met, was a long haul/test pilot for British Airways. She had two main loves in her life (as far as we were concerned anyway). The first was the colour mauve. She only ever wore clothes in that colour and her little mini van followed suit. The other main love of hers was chickens. These could be of any colour, shape or size in her world. I can remember going down to her cottage at one time just as she was arriving back from collecting her bags of poultry feed. She pulled up her driveway, opened the back doors of her van and just threw the sacks of corn out on to the ground. She broke them open and then the chickens appeared from all over the place and dived in. She just walked away and revealed that was it. "When they have eaten that I will get them some more" she said.

That is how she went on. Apart from the fowl she had two other birds. The first was a Bronze Turkey stag and he was a nasty piece of work. Just inside her front gate was a big old Holly bush and this bird would hide inside it and wait for anyone to set foot on "his ground" and then he would pounce. He really meant it. He was as bad as a bloody dog. Indeed she even affixed a "Beware of the Turkey" sign on this gate to warn of the possible impending peril. Dianna loved that Turkey. The other bird she had was a pet Tawny Owl that lived free inside her cottage. She apparently used to get up in the night just to play with the bird and keep it company. This lady also had a part time job some afternoons at a really "Upmarket Boutique" on Lymington High street. When she was at work she would park her little mauve mini van right outside. Apart from the bits of straw shavings and corn that would be liberated on to the path every time she opened the door there were also as many as 6 chickens inside. These usually roosting on the back of shit covered seats. A rare sight indeed especially in such a location.

Another visitor we used to get every month or so was a little old Frenchman who used to come over in his Morris 1,000 Traveller to buy old pine furniture and if he could one or two puppies. The latter he would smuggle back into France somehow. The pine furniture was apparently a project for his wife. She would hand strip it all, wax it and then sell it on. He had bought a few pups off us in the past and each time he came I noticed he kept glancing at an old 3 drawer painted chest we had in the parlour. To us it was just some beaten up old bit of firewood really. We used to keep a few of Mandy's clothes in it. On one of his visits he asked us if we would sell it. We had never thought about it before but everything is for sale as they say. He ended up giving us £10.00. for it. He then explained that underneath all the years of paint was a really good piece of pine furniture. It even still had all its original "bun" handles. Job done. Mandy's clothes were evicted and the painted chest was strapped on to the old boy's roof rack and off it went across The Channel!!

By now it just seemed, for all three of us, there just was not enough hours in the day. It even got to the point that I was getting up at 3 or 4 o'clock in the morning during the autumn and winter just so that I could groom the Pekinese before they went outside and got too wet. I was pointing downhill in no uncertain manner but worst of all, although I could not see it at the time, I was dragging Lin and Mandy down with me. One of the worst days came when a friend of ours (who we had originally sold one of the Vietnamese Pot Bellied Pigs to) came over to pick up a Neapolitan Mastiff youngster off us. We had agreed to let it go on "breeding terms". Always a bit of an "iffy deal" that kind of thing. That was O.K. but the trouble was I agreed to let her take Lin's two young Great Dane bitches that we had kept back from our original Great Dane's (Mandy) litter. I should not have done it but all I could see in them was two big dogs that had got to be fed. It was going to be at least a year before we had any pups to sell from them plus we had by now got 6 adult Neapolitans plus a couple of youngsters and a few little dogs. The little dogs were no problem but these big dogs cost a lot of money to feed and keep and if a bitch failed to produce any pups when her time came then that meant she was "a passenger" for the next 6 months. Needless to say when Lin came back from work that day she went bloody mad. Even to this very day she says that was the closest we ever came to getting divorced . . . SORRY LIN!! Mentally I was wobbling by now but I was then, and still am, a stubborn cantankerous bastard and I was not going to give in. By now the back injury was really giving me trouble. I was shovelling pain killers down my neck like sweeties. I was losing weight and had become more and more irritable and fractious. I found that if I could keep moving I was more or less O.K. It was bearable. The trouble was, at the end of the day, when I tried to sit down the pain just got worst. I had got to the point where I had to keep going until I just basically fell asleep as soon as I stopped. It seemed to be the only way to handle it. I went to see the doctor in the end. I always remember that occasion. He was a youngish chap who looked like a bit of an ex-hippie. Hair down to his shoulders, beard, flared trousers, the lot. We had a chat and he had a look at me. He sat down at his desk and uttered the immortal words "You are blowing a fuckin' fuse man". I have never forgotten that. He explained that my body was telling me to stop but my mind was overruling it or, at least, trying to over rule it. He said that in the end Mother Nature would win because she would just render me not only immobile but probably unconscious if I did not listen to her. I went away from him with this new understanding lodged between my ears. It was O.K. for a while but then the old "I will not be beaten" attitude returned but, for the worse. We had now resorted to selling our best clothes to keep going. These Neapolitan Mastiffs were doing us in. Easy to see in hindsight but I was blinkered. In my eyes we WOULD succeed. A totally blinkered view on my behalf. I can remember the Border Collie bitch (we had been given previously and had mated at the farm where Terry of The Big Pigs worked) did not look as if she was in pup. Lin and I both agreed on that so we sold her.

We were then told that she must have been in pup because she presented her new owner with a fine litter of little ones. That was bad. We did not usually get things like that wrong but this time we did and it had cost us. Probably cost us the chance of carrying on.

Time went by. I had nipped down to the shop. I remember particularly buying sweets for Lin and Mandy but when I got back they had both gone. They had left. Looking back they had had enough. I do not blame them. They had gone back to Lin's Mom. I was absolutely devastated to say the least. I just broke down mentally and physically. I was done for . . . finished. A jibbering wreck of a man weighing only about 7 stone (approx. 50 kilos). I was getting heart palpitations most nights and the old stammer had returned in no uncertain way as well. What to do now? Had my stubbornness, my will to succeed, my determination at all costs, to succeed at something cost me my whole world as I knew it. I was right "up Shit Street" now and could not see a way out anymore. I was done for and broken all round and in every aspect. What a "Dick Head" . . . a failure. In all honesty I cannot really recall the timeline of the next few days. I just remember crying permanently, being sick, and phoning The Samaritans who came out to visit. I really had "blown a fuckin' fuse man" this time. I can just recall giving Frank and Ma a phone call and they told me to get on a train straight away and get myself up there. I remember getting on a train to Birmingham and in a taxi to Meriden. I had left the dogs and all the animals on their own. What a terrible thing to do but I was not thinking straight anymore. It turned out that Lin had found out that I had left everything and the animals on their own but I had managed to be "with it" enough to make sure that they were all fed and watered before I "abandoned ship". Lin got hold of Trevor Lewis and he and his staff went down the next day and collected all the dogs and Keith went along and picked up all the birds and small animals. I have never seen any of them since. What a fuckin' mess I had got myself, Lin and Mandy into. Would I ever learn how to do things properly. I can recall one evening Ma bought me some food. I was sitting in the armchair. I looked at the food and just started to sob and shake uncontrollably and ran up to bed. Frank came up to find me lying in the bed crying my eyes out and convulsing. He telephoned the doctor who came out and gave me an injection of something or other and I just went to sleep. I do not know how long I slept for but at least when I did wake up I had stopped crying and shaking so much but what now. I had had enough thank you very much!!

As I have mentioned earlier in this script Kronus del Prese and Ursula (at the time the only two specimens of this breed in the U.K.) came to us because their owner and importer had had them for a couple of years or so but failed to breed them. He said to me, at the time, that it was impossible to breed them so we took on the challenge and if we managed to get any pups then we would be paid a percentage of anything they sold for. This back in the 70'S never amounted to a lot because if the pups sold for £150.00. each then that was their limit. It was usually more like £100. each. Nobody over here had ever seen one unless they had stumbled across the odd dog on the continent. They were so rare. Indeed in 1946 only 8 specimens were known to exist and they all belonged to one man, an Italian who, as the story goes, had managed to get these dogs together and on doing so he had spent the whole of the Second World War living in the mountains of Italy with them just to keep them safe. On saying this there was strong talk that Zurich Zoo in Switzerland had actually got a pair that had produced pups but the father had killed them. How true that story is I do not know but it was a strongly held rumour at the time. Back to Ursula and Kronus. As soon as we had got them home we separated them out of sight of each other but still within hearing distance. We had decided to do this because Trevor had told us that, in the past, Kronus had tried to mate his wife but never managed. He had always climaxed and "tied" with himself outside of her and when she first came into season with us the reason for this malfunction became clear. He was too wide in the chest. He was the proud owner of a 42" plus (105 plus cm) chest and a 27" (68cm) neck but he was too short in the back leg to get far enough on to her to actually mate and tie "properly". We solved this problem by "helping" him. This involved Lin holding Ursula still by using her collar while I "put him in the right place" and held him there for as long as possible. This procedure we used every time he mated a bitch. He soon got used to it. Indeed after a while we had trained him to get excited by just saying to him "Coming to make some babies Kronus?" He soon learned what was expected of him!! The first mating we managed between the two proved to be successful. Ursula was in pup. The only thing that worried me at the time was the fact that our Old English Sheepdog male, Danny, was at liberty most of the time. His main obsession in life was running around the place carrying my axe in his mouth . . . the daft sod!! I was being niggled by the chance that he could have somehow got to Ursula but all was well. She whelped her

The Main Man:- Kronus

first litter on the day before Christmas Eve. Seven live pups. Four liver coloured, two blue and one black. Plus two more liver and one more black that were born dead. Seven live pups was good and plenty enough for her to look after anyway. We kept one of the blue bitches and called her Blossom. SEEKAPETRA CHRIS . . . her registered name. I think I am right in saying that three of the other pups stayed in this country. One went off to Spain and one to Norway. The latter was the first ever Neapolitan Mastiff ever to go into Scandinavia. The reason for this being that no dogs were allowed to be imported into Scandinavia from the European mainland at the time because of Rabies. We were the only place back then that dogs could be imported into Scandinavia. There was the U.S.A. but I do not think they had many, indeed, if any. I can recall receiving a phone call one evening concerning the pups. The call lasted well over half an hour but the line did not seem to be that good. I asked the man on the other end where he was phoning from because at times we were having difficulty understanding each other. "Oh" he said "I'm phoning from Oslo in Norway. My name is Fred Brekke". So Fred Brekke owned the first Neapolitan Mastiff ever to go into Scandinavia . . . and we had bred it . . . chuffed with that to say the least!!

Ursula came into season again and we mated her again. Best strike while the iron is hot we thought. She was as fit as a fiddle and a picture

KRONOS DELLE PRESE
Mirko Di Ponzano X Astra 13.02.1971

URSULA
Ursus Delle Prese X Mascia 03.05.1972

BROOM LODGE CARLOTTA 27.12.76
Kronos Delle Prese X Ursula

ROSEMAUND NINA 01.08.78
Kronos Delle Prese X Broom Lodge Carlotta

1980 Symposium – All Mastini
Sired by Kronos Delle Prese

SEEKAPETRA BEONA 23.08.78
Kronos Delle Prese X Seekapetra Chris

SEEKAPETRA BELLA TIGRATA 01.04.79
Seekapetra Trojan X Brunilde Del Conte

Apart from Kronus and Ursula we bred all these dogs back in the '70's.

of health.   We used the same mating procedure as before.   This resulted in her second litter.   This was five pups.   Two silver fawn, two liver and one blue. We kept one of the silver fawn dog pups and called him Troggy. SEEKAPETRA TROGAN.   All the other pups stayed in the U.K. except for the blue bitch that went off to Sweden . . . another first!! First one into Sweden and now two into Scandinavia.

Time moved on. Blossom and Troggy were growing well. Good and strong.   Kronus and Ursula now basically lived full time in the house with us. They used to lie in front of the fire on the mat with their front paws over each other just like they were having a cuddle. A lovely thing to see. One of the funniest things occurred one late afternoon. I had told Kronus off for something or other so he had planted himself in the corner of the room to have a good sulk. Mandy had just come in from school so she did not know he had been told off. She went to her room, got changed then came back down and sat in my armchair. Kronus was still feeling sorry for himself when Mandy just said to him "Good boy Kronus". In his mind he had been forgiven so he lumbered across to her tail "A waggin' " and jumped, all fours, on tops of her. Now he was a big old lump to land on top of an adult never mind a child. The chair tipped up backwards and they all ended up in a heap on the floor with Kronus on top of poor little Mandy licking her to death. At least he had got one friend!!

Trevor had now imported three more Mastiffs from Italy. A black brindle bitch called ASTA . . . Brunilde Delle Conti Biancanzano... registered name. Also a blue bitch called GINNY . . . Delia D'Arpierio ... registered name and a blue dog known only as MARCELLIANO. Why he was only known as this I will explain later. They were all put into quarantine at Weston- Super- Mare. I had been down to see them once. Trevor had come down to Hampshire from London, picked me up, and off we went to see how they were settling in. I thought Asta was a bit tall and that her coat was a bit on the wirey side. Her ears had been cropped basically to nothing. It appeared she had little more than a hole on each side of her head in fact. I often wondered if she was pure but she had a wonderful soft temperament. Ginny on the other hand was a bit more "stand offish". A bit more wary and had a bit of a cunning look about her but there you go. We could only work with what we had got. Marcelliano was a really big heavy lump. Bigger than Kronus probably about an inch (3 cm) taller and about 2 stone (14 kilo) heavier but he was just a big soft old thing. It was nice to see them anyway but another visit to them cropped up out of the blue one Friday evening.   Trevor rang up to say that The Daily Mirror had heard about the Mastiffs and wanted photographs ready for the following Monday's paper. Could I go down and photograph them before Sunday evening. Well, I was not a photographer in any way shape or form but Barry Wells (ex Elmsgate Kennels) was. Indeed he was a semi-professional. He and his new lady were now living in Cirencester so he agreed to come down on the Saturday, pick me up, and we would go off to Weston and he would photograph the dogs The film would be couriered to Trevor on the Sunday in time for him to pass it on to The Daily Mirror for publication.   I remember we took a big double mattress for Marcelliano to lie on. This was approved by the kennels because by their very nature quarantine kennels tend to be very stark and clinical but we put his new bed in with him and went off to photograph Asta and Ginny. When we returned back to him we found he had completely shredded this mattress. Within 5 or 10 minutes it was everywhere. Much to the disdain of the kennels. Photographs of the man himself now taken, along with his two lady friends, we returned home complete with the roll of film. The courier came and picked it up. It was now just a case of waiting to see our new dogs in the national press… or so we thought. On the Sunday evening Trevor rang up to say that they had the film developed but the images were no good because somehow there was "a light stripe" through all of them. Barry was perplexed. He had taken literally hundreds upon hundreds of photos in his time and this "light stripe" was a conundrum to him. Anyway the pictures were never published but Barry did get the film back and the prints. I do not know what happened to them. Towards the end of the quarantine Trevor had the dogs moved to a new kennel nearer to him at Heathrow. He said it would be easier when the time came for their release. Three days before the release date tragedy struck. Marcelliano had been found dead in his kennel. According to the kennel they had a local thunderstorm. He had panicked, slipped on his wet floor and ruptured his spleen. At the time I was suspicious of this scenario and urged Trevor to question it but he never did. A post mortem was performed and I can remember seeing a print out of the results which basically said that "This dog did not die of Rabies or Anthrax". That was all the Ministry were worried about. As long as there was no evidence of a "notifiable disease" they were not bothered. Quarantine completed Trevor delivered our two new girls to us. It was such a shame about Marcelliano because we really needed new male blood as well. The only males in the country were

Kronus and his sons. We would have to do our best with him and Troggy now. Blossom was, by this time, in her second season so we decided to put her back to her dad Kronus. She had five pups. One female LUCY …. Groom Lodge Carlotta. She went to live with a Mrs Bachus. She came back to us for mating. Back to her dad Kronus. One of her pups PAULA…. registered name Rosamund Nina went on to join the Kwintra Bullmastiff Kennels in The Forest of Dean. These kennels were owned by the doctors Clarke and they would eventually became stalwards of the breed in years to come. Lucy eventually ended up back with us. Mr and Mrs Bachus were finding her "a bit hard to handle". After she had thrown herself through a plate glass window to get hold of the postman they eventually gave up on her and asked if we would have her back. No problem. They arrived one Sunday with her. I put her outside in her kennel and run and went back into the house for tea and a chat with the Bachus's. Then Lucy started barking, howling and really giving it the works. No amount of verbal reprimanding was having any effect. Time for a visit to put her straight at least. A swift smack across the arse did the trick. She yelped once, very loudly, and that was it. Job done. Welcome to the club. As long as you tow the line. I must say she was never any trouble at all after that. I hate a noisy dog and the trouble is when you have got a few about then it becomes a case of "one bad apple". They all knew that there was only one boss when push comes to shove and that was me. This turned out to be a good thing one morning. I used to take all of them, seven adults by now, for a run. All together across the fields every morning. Once they were off "their own patch" there was never any friction between them but the Neapolitan Mastiff, as a breed, is a" holding and gripping" breed and quite often one of them would just walk by my side with my wrist in it's mouth. No sweat but Troggy, being the young adolescent show off that he had by now grown into, used to take this wrist holding one step further. He would run about and grab my wrist whilst on the move. He did this one morning when I was not actually feeling at my best or strongest and in doing so knocked me down to the ground. Within seconds all seven of them were around me. Tails up and the mood changed. The pack instinct had kicked in. The boss is injured time for a sort out or thoughts along those lines to say the least. Then old Kronus was there. I just shouted at him "Don't you fuckin' touch me you bastard!!" He did no more than put his tail between his legs and skulk off. Just as he had years earlier when I had to confront him at Elmsgate Kennels. On seeing that he had backed off the other six followed him. I got up, gave them all a bit of fuss, and normal service was resumed. If I had not already impressed on them that I was the boss then I probably would not be here today. There is a line between respect and fear. As long as you can keep it at the respect level then there should be no problem.

Time trundled on without anything much out of the ordinary occurring but we had got a Pekinese due to whelp anytime soon. Just before going out to work at my part time, afternoon, job I moved a few of the dogs around to accommodate the forthcoming Peke parturition. Not thinking I put Troggy in the pen with Regina next to the pen that Kronus and Ursula used on nice days. They had been in the same situation before with nothing more than a few "dirty looks" being exchanged between the two males so off I went to work thinking no more about it. That was until David, our Landlord, appeared to tell me to get back home quick because the dogs were fighting. On getting back I rushed around to the dog pens to find Troggy in Kronus and Ursula's pen bleeding badly from his one front leg. Kronus had a dribble of blood running down one side of his face and the same on one of his front legs. Ursula was pacing round, screaming like a peacock, with her head up sniffing the air. The smell of the fresh blood had really got her excited by now. She could be a nasty piece of work if the fancy took her. Next problem. How on earth had Troggy ended up in his Mom and Dad's pen. He was lying near the solid wooden gate that allowed access between the two runs. So far as I could work out he must have stood on his hind legs, front paws on top of the gate and stuck his head over. At this point I assumed Kronus must have grabbed hold of his head or front legs and pulled him over. Whatever had happened he was in a bit of a mess. Kronus did not seem to be as bad off. On examination it appeared that all he had got was a couple of tooth holes in his head near his ear. Good job his ears had been cropped as a puppy in Italy otherwise he would have been in a mess. Nothing bleeds like an ear. Hence the continental habit of cropping. Troggy on the other hand was a mess. He was covered in blood with a really badly gashed front left leg. Luckily after cleaning him up that seemed to be the only really significant injury he had sustained in his disagreement with his dad. When Lin and Mandy got back we stitched this leg up and treated the wound. It ran from his knee right down to his foot. Just a good honest clean wound. Kronus on the other hand seemed to be struggling a bit more with his front leg. He had got a tooth hole right on his elbow joint. A bad place for such a heavy dog. We treated them both ourselves. In those days veterinary medicines etc. were more easily available than they are now. Kronus was getting stiff in this elbow joint. I expect a bit of the joint fluid had leaked and it was "running a bit dry" so we decided to give him physiotherapy. We taught him to sit down and give us his paw on the bad side. This made him move his elbow joint and kept it from seizing up. We would make him do this as often as we could and eventually it worked. The trouble was that he had learnt a new habit so every time we sat down he would give us his paw on his ex- bad leg. Well it was not so much "a give" as "a swipe" because of his natural conformation. It was easy for him to use a "sideswipe" action rather than a gentle lift up and place. Many a time he would smack us one, expecially Mandy, when she was sat in the chair. She was very often low enough to catch a paw up the side of her face, poor girl. He never forgot this and the habit was with him for everk more now. Troggy was a different kettle of fish completely. His leg constantly filled with blood which we drained every couple of days but it was not healing as well as we liked. The draining process had to be administered over a few weeks. In fact he got so used to it he would actually hold his leg up on a voluntary basis ready for the procedure. As I said this went on for weeks until one day his leg had got to the state where it resembled a huge sausage with a few toe nails peeking out at the bottom. Not good on this day. I just said to Lin "Fuck it, lets open this right up again". We gave him a good dose of local anaesthetic all down the wound which was, by now, beginning to knit together quite nicely except for the now ever present drain hole. I just made a brand new cut all down his leg from his knee to his foot. Then I drained and flushed out all the blood and muck that was in there. I sewed him back up, applied a copious amount of Stockholm Tar and bandaged him back up again. If all went well he would end up with two scars instead of the original one. Luckily all did go well. It seemed the last heavy handed procedure went well and had done the trick. It took time but in the end all that was vaguely visible were the two scars and you had to look and feel really hard to find them. Indeed we were asked to show him at Windsor Championship show a year or so after and even there the judge did not pick up on it . . . a pleasing outcome!!

Kronus and Ursula were only ever happy when in each other's company except when she had got pups to look after. So much so that the only dog she would ever let near her when she was in season was "her man". We even used to "tease" Troggy with her when she was ready to be mated but she would have none of it. When it came to Kronus then that was a different matter. When she was feeling frisky she used to try and get him to play. He would go along with it for a while and then get fed up. At times she would keep on going. I watched them one day. He had got to the point of having enough of it all so she took to jumping on his back holding on with her feet and nibbling his neck. He would just shake her off but on this day she would not let things go. He did no more than grab her by the neck and throw her up in the air. She flipped over and landed on her back. At this point he just stood over the top of her, looked her straight in the face as if to say "that's enough woman". If nothing else it demonstrated the sheer power he had got. I mean Ursula weighed getting on for 12 stone (about 75 kilo). He was a wonderful dog with a wonderful "wife".

Asta had developed skin trouble for some reason. She was the only one out of all our dogs that had got this problem. We tried everything to get rid of it but to no avail. I had got hold of an antique veterinary chemists "recipe" book. There was a formula for a medicine designed to alleviate such stubborn problems so I took the book down to our local little independent chemist to ask if he could make it up for me. He looked at the recipe and uttered the immortal words "This could be a bloody bomb, no chance, but could I borrow the book?" No problem. He borrowed the book and I forgot all about it. Because we used to buy "out of date" baby food from him for the birds and pups I used to visit him quite regularly. The next time I went to see him he told me that he had shown the book to a really old chemist who had managed to make this "bomb" or medicine. I always remember it looked like Mercury and smelled horrendously sickening. We managed to get the first dose down Asta's throat but once she had learnt what it was the dosing became a real struggle. She was a big old girl but we persevered and it worked. Her skin problems vanished never to return. Asta and Ginny both came into season more or less at the same time. We mated Troggy to Ginny but decided to use Kronus on Asta. Due to his mating difficulties we decided to keep her still by securing her collar to the fence. We would go on with him in the usual way i.e. holding him in place for as long as we could and hope it worked. It always had with any of the other matings but Asta had the habit of sitting down once we had got him mounted and "in situ". That meant that I had to support her by putting my one arm underneath her with my hand, holding the fence, and supporting her that way. I put his "manly attribute" in the right place while Lin held his back end "up and in" for want of a better phrase. We did this a couple of times. Now it was just a case of waiting for her and Ginny.

Both these bitches were now in pup. Asta went on to have 6 pups. 3 blues and 3 brindles and Ginny had 4 pups (Troggy's first litter). I cannot recall what colour because I have lost the relevant registration documents but I do know that one of the pups, a bitch, went off to Canada along with one of Asta's bitch pups to be the foundations of The Thundermug Neapolitan Mastiff Kennels. They were bought by a couple called Gary and Lin Travers. Two Canadians living over here at the time who were re-locating back to their homeland to establish the country's first kennel for this breed. They wanted us to go over with them and help with this project but we declined. I recently (at the time of writing) heard from Samantha, Gary and Lin's daughter, to say that due to illness her dad's Thundermug Kennels had been forced to close. He had kept at it for well over 35 years and had bred some nice dogs in that time. Two of Asta's pups went on to Spain. The others remained in the U.K. along with the other three pups from Ginny's litter. The next time we mated Blossom we put her back to her brother Troggy. She had seven pups, three black dog pups, one blue bitch, one black bitch, one silver fawn dog and one silver fawn bitch. They all ended up staying in this country. One of the black dogs ended up at a Chinese Restaurant in Oxford called "The Opium Den". I can recall the owner turning up to buy the pup, along with an interpreter. It turned out he could not speak a word of English!! The interpreter explained to us that the restaurant owner had, somehow, got on the wrong side of "The Triad", the Chinese mafia. He was scared for the safety of his wife and child who, if not spending all their time with him, meant that they had to be left at home alone. He was scared something not very nice might happen to them. Hence his search for a good guard dog and his visit to us. He went off with his dog and we heard no more from him for months afterwards. Then one day he turned up, along with his interpreter, in search of another pup. It turned out his first pup was "doing his job really well". Let's just leave it at that. He now wanted another male puppy to do the same job but at his next Restaurant. We had not got any pups so he asked if he could buy or "rent" Kronus. I told him that the dog did not go anywhere without me. He did no more than to offer to pay for the both of us. Me and Kronus to go and stay at his restaurant for a while!! No bloody chance mate!! No amount of money was going to tempt me to get on the wrong side of those Oriental lunatics. I declined his offer and never saw him or his interpreter again. The silver fawn dog from this litter went on to a Mr Adams from London. He had heard about us months before. He asked if he could come and see the dogs with a view to buying a puppy in the future. No problem. He turned up. A huge great man, along with his father. A mousy ferret looking like kind of a chap. He was about one third the size of his son and dressed in Country and Western clothes, complete with cowboy hat, boots and string tie. They came in and we showed them the dogs. All they were interested in was Troggy. They absolutely loved everything about him and especially his colour. They wanted to buy him but he was not for sale. We needed him to carry on trying to build up a good kennel. We agreed that the next dog pup we bred of that same colour then he would have it. Hence Blossom's pup went off to him. The only worry he had was that, as he had already got a Bullmastiff male, then would his present dog be a bully to the new pup? I told him not to worry about that in the slightest. We all sat drinking tea, both the Adams men, me and Lin. I asked him what business they were in. It turned out they were "money lenders". In other words loan sharks but the deal had been done and off they went with their pup. We heard no more from them for a fair while until Mr Adams Junior rang up one day to say that his older Bullmastiff and the younger pup he had bought from us had been "squaring each other up" at the top of his stairs and that the pup had picked up the older dog by the scruff of the neck and thrown him down the stairs. I just said to him that I had told him not to worry about the pup being bullied in the first place.

Sometimes, if a chance arose, we would take Kronus and Ursula for a run on the beach. This always created a few strange looks. I do not think anyone had ever seen anything like them at the time. One Sunday we decided we would take them to The New Forest Show and enter the old boy into some little novelty class or other. Mandy wanted to take him in the ring and show him. We thought that was a nice idea. It would be good for both of them. The trouble was Kronus weighed about 15 stone+ (85 milos+) and his head was about as far off the ground as Mandy's chest was. I told her it would be alright as long as he did not see me at the ringside because if he did this he would just want to "Go back" to his Dad. This worked well. Then whoever I was standing behind must have moved and he caught sight of me. That was it . . . he was off. Mandy and all, whether she liked it or not. I can see her now, hanging on for grim death, trying to hold him back but he was having none of it. He just pulled her out of the ring and back to his Dad.

The phone rang one Saturday morning. It was Trevor Lewis in one hell of a state to say the least. Esther Rantzen and the "That's Life" programme had got their teeth into him. It seems that he had been selling a lot of "iffy" pups that were either ending up at the vets with their new owners or dying within a few weeks of being purchased. I think we had only ever been to his place a couple of times and let's just say we had seen better pups. Let's leave it at that. It had nothing to do with us what went on there as far as we were concerned. The Mastiffs and us were a totally separate thing anyway. He was going to Court that very day. That must have cost him a fortune in legal fees to try and take out an injunction to stop the programme going out on T.V. the following evening. He failed in that effort. The feature was broadcast. We watched it, of course, and to put it mildly it did not look good at all. They really laid into him. They had got him by the bollocks and rightly so. I have always said I would rather give a good thing away for free than sell a bad thing. I still think like that today. It is called "peace of mind". Trevor rang up on the Monday in a worse state than he had been on the Saturday . . . 2 days before. He said he had had death threats. There was a crowd of angry people outside his place. More than that he was worried about his mother who lived with him and his son Ashley. He was thinking of taking her to Italy just for her own safety until it all blew over. It did eventually blow over but it ruined him basically and probably rightfully so. Later that week I managed to get hold of the "That's Life" team at the B.B.C to let them know who we were and what our connection to Trevor was. We were told in these exact words . . . "Yes, we know all about you and we are not interested in you in anyway". Not long after this uproar in the press we received a visit from the local council concerning the fact that we had not got a "Dog Breeding Licence" on the premises. This was a new thing back then supposedly designed to aid the welfare and well- being of the animals but basically it was to stop puppy farming and that could only be a good thing. It was also a back door into the finances of any dog breeder. It stated that a maximum of six Breeding bitches could be kept. It did not matter how many males or doctored bitches any one establishment kept. You could shoot holes through this "Act" anywhere you liked. It was just a very badly thought out and implemented piece of petty legislation. Now we kept our dogs as "natural" as possible. We had done so for ever. We fed them raw meat. They lived in wooden kennels in natural earth and grass runs. Indeed in hot weather the Mastiffs used to dig themselves big "Dens" in the ground and lay in them. All their sleeping beds were about a foot (30 cms) deep with dry shavings, shredded paper, and straw all mixed up together. This alleviated any sores or callouses on their joints ever rearing their ugly heads. When we cleaned out their sleeping quarters then all the old bedding and all the daily fowling of the runs we put in a "muck ruck". This was fenced off, away from the dogs, in our little garden at the far end of the place. In the end I told this jumped up little council idiot that he could bring any vet of their choice to inspect all our dogs and if he could find anything more than the odd flea then we would pack up tomorrow. Furthermore we were not going to change our ways. If needs be we would welcome the chance to go to court and argue our point. If it ever came to this then we would expose the "local officialdom" as being the bunch of uneducated dimwits they really were. A vet did come out to inspect our dogs and he could not find even a flea. After this I wrote the following letter to the Council Department concerned and we never heard another word from them.

The time had now come for Ursula to retire. She had done enough and could live the rest of her life out in peace. She and Kronus now lived in the house permanently and they had their own big joint bed in the parlour. They just wandered about at will. Now Lin and Ursula did not really see eye to eye. It seemed in Ursula's eyes, at least, that Lin was "below" her. She would do what Lin asked her to do . . . eventually and, as she let it be known, by the look on her face unwillingly. She had got into the habit that if Lin tried to call her anywhere she would just squat on the floor, piddle in front of her, and then do what she was being asked to do. As if to say "There clean that up then". It was just a silly habit she had got into. She was just showing off her natural defiant nature. Just part of her make up and indeed part of the breed's psyche. On one occasion she took it too far. She was lying in the living room one evening and Lin was trying to persuade her to move elsewhere. She eventually stood up with the usual "O.K. if I really must . . . You old cow" look on her face. She immediately squatted but this time she did not piddle, she actually shit right in front of Lin. I just got into the room in time to see her do this. That was it. You have gone too far this time old girl. I gave her a severe verbal reprimanding and a good kick up the arse at which point she went and sat on her bed in the parlour. I followed her and was still letting her know, in no uncertain terms and eyeball to eyeball that she had just pushed it too far. She changed. She put what ears she had got back, flared her eyes and opened her mouth. At this point my voice raised several notches and I just screamed at her to get outside. The back door, as always, was open thankfully and so she was able to beat a hasty retreat. She eventually sloped back in, very sheepishly, a few hours later. All was forgotten and the defiant piddling episodes stopped. She never

232

really "spoke" to Lin much after that. I can safely say that, on that one occasion, I did get a bit scared of her but luckily a loud voice and an open door saved the day because if she put her mind too it she could be a nasty piece of work.

BRITAIN'S FIRST AND FOREMOST IMPORTERS AND BREEDERS
OF THE
NEAPOLITAN MASTIFF

1514

Kronos Delle Prese

Owner and Importer:

MR. T. LEWIS
BROOM LODGE
STANWELL LANE
HORTON
SLOUGH
BUCKS
Tel. COLNEBROOK 2165

Breeder and Handler:

MR. N. HOMFRAY
BOWLING GREEN FARM
SWAY ROAD
LYMINGTON
HANTS
Tel. LYMINGTON 77515

Your ref. JES/PN/S.5a.

Dear Sir,

Thank you for your letter dated 2.5.79. You invited me to comment on your proposals which I shall now do.

I entirely agree with the Fire Office r and will fully endorse his suggestions. Now to the heart of the matter. On these premises I am trying to establish a pack as opposed to a kennel of one of the six rarest breeds of dog in the world (indeed there were only eight specimens known to be in existence even as late as 1956) this fact in itself makes me wonder wether or not these premises should be classed as a dog breeding establishment or a private zoo. If the latter, then your proposals would be a complete nonsense, worth thinking about do you not agree? Anyway for the moment let us assume that the premises are a dog breeding establishment and are therefore covered by the Dog Breeders Act of 1973 which so far as I understand was introduced with the interest of canine welfare at heart. Am I correct? If so can your vet categorically state with hand on heart that my dogs are unhealthy or unhappy due to the lack of amenities he has proposed. I think not, which so far as I am concerned is the end of the matter but apparently you do not. So my main proposal to you is that there is no reason why I should not carry on as I am because so far as your first point is concerned, this establishment is on a farm, and on almost every farm in the world there is a muck ruck, cattle and poultry are kept on deep litter with no apparent environmental or animal health risk. My dogs do not sleep on top of the muck ruck as they would if subjected to deep litter confinement. So far as the storage of meat is concerned may I ask how many foxes, wolves, coyotes or any other wild canine (which are all carrion eaters) have a deep freeze in their den? Why do canines bury meat? (as indeed do I for my dogs) because it not only keeps away fly borne disease but it also tenderises, therefore making for easier digestion. So far as deep freezing meat is concerned I was recently involved with correspondence with Canine F oods Ltd., about the amount of water there is in a bag of frozen tripe after it had thawed. They told me that their Laboratory had found that freezing meat releases all the natural liquid in the meat when thawed. Surely there must be a lot of natural goodness in this liquid which would be drained off and thrown away. Now in my eyes if I did that I would be depriving my dogs of some of their food, which firstly I will not do and secondly if I did I would not be keeping them as well as I could and may be considered to be in breach of the Animal Welfare Act. In my opinion anyway.

So far as your third point is concerned. I dont really see any point. My tripe is cut up while hanging in mid air on a meat hook. The meat hook (which is the only point of contact) is clean and any meat that is cut up in very small pieces (as for puppies) is cut up on a wooden block, which is washed twice daily. So far as a wooden block being used is concerned, then may I just say that I have a friend who is a chef and believe it or not he prepares all of his meat

FREE BREED INFORMATION ON REQUEST   INSPECTION INVITED

Owner and Importer:
MR. T. LEWIS
BROOM LODGE
STANWELL LANE
HORTON
SLOUGH
BUCKS
Tel. COLNEBROOK 2165

Breeder and Handler:
MR. N. HOMFRAY
BOWLING GREEN FARM
SWAY ROAD
LYMINGTON
HANTS
Tel. LYMINGTON 77515

Kronos Delle Prese

for human consumption on a wooden block.   The bins where any meat which is
not buried is stored are washed out every time they are emptied.   In the
winter they are washed in plain water and in the summer in vinegar water,
which again helps to repel flies.
Before I close may I just add that I am not trying to be awkward or funny
in this letter but I do have strong beliefs so far as my dogs are concerned
which I will not depart from particularly so far as food is concerned, although
I could be persuaded to move the muck ruck but I can see no reason for doing
so because as I stated at the beginning of this letter.   I don't think that
your vet (or any other) could find any animal that is unhealthy or unhappy due
to the way that they are fed and kept.   Indeed, I invite you personally to
my premises and we can talk canine welfare for as long as you want.   Remember
there are thousands of human beings in this country who live in very hygenic
conditions, with waste disposal units, exhaustingly prepared food and
extremely clean floors.   Very ideal but very unnatural conditions.   I
wonder how many of them are happy at heart?   I guarantee my dogs are happy
if they were not I would not only not keep them I would not be able to.   You
see my eight dogs weigh over ½ ton, and they are happy and perfectly
controlable which is surely my main concern and I always thought was the main
concern of the D.B. Act 1973.   After all who wants half of a ton of hungry
unfit and mentally unstable Neapolitan Mastiffs roaming free certainly not I
and certainly not the people who devised that act - after all is that not
what it is meant to stop?   Think about this letter before you decide - indeed
come and see me and my dogs anytime you like.

Yours faithfully,

N. HOMFRAY (MR.)

P.S. Have you ever wondered why one naturally reared and mentally alert fox
     so often outruns and outthinks 20 or 30 hounds that are fed mainly on
     cooked meat and biscuit and housed under cramped conditions - it makes
     you think who is better off the fox who is ruled by mother nature or
     the hounds who are ruled by H.M. Government.

FREE BREED INFORMATION ON REQUEST   INSPECTION INVITED

Ursula was controllable but volatile. This was demonstrated one day.
We must have been out shopping or something because when we got
back home Barry was sitting in his car in the yard looking a bit "pale". It
seemed he had gone to our door and was knocking to be let in. Of course
we were not in but Ursula was and she was letting him know it. The door
had etched Perspex windows that began over half the way up it's length

and reached to the top. Through this Barry said he could make out the shape of the old girl going to the far end of the kitchen and throwing herself at the door. Because the walls inside were just painted brick she was actually getting hold of the corner where it joined the door frame and gnawing at the bricks. She was not having any of it at this point. She scared him at least. Once she realised that Lin, Mandy and I were out there she stood down and just let Barry in, along with us, as if nothing had really happened . . . I loved her spirit.

We decided to mate Blossom for the third time then she could retire and live her life out. She had earned her keep. She carried her pups normally and whelped normally and was rearing them on well. I went to check her before I did my jobs for David. All was well but when I went to check her 3 or 4 hours later two of the pups were dead and the rest were on their way out. Typical symptoms of what was generally known back then as Puppy Fading Syndrome. Probably the worst thing that any kennel could be afflicted with. Indeed we knew of people that, once it got into any place, then it would stay for years. Basically it would kill every pup that was born. Nobody really knew what it was or what caused it in those days. It was just a threat you had to live with. It could reduce a healthy litter of pups to a heap of dead bodies in a matter of hours. The classic symptoms were chronic (acute enteritis and worst of all loss of body temperature). It was now time to call in the vet. We could not get hold of the relevant medication without him. We knew what would be the biggest help, an Aureomycin based paste drug that was originally intended for use in pigs, but that was no longer available. We knew this drug worked because years earlier whilst living in Tamworth we had had a taste of this disease and the local vet at the time (a real old fashioned "dyed in the wool country vet") said he had used it before in similar situations, but it was only licensed for use with pigs, so if we wanted to sign a "disclaimer" he would give it a go with our pups. We did, he did, and all the pups survived. We told the current vet about this but, as I said earlier, this specific drug was no longer available. We had to try other things. He came out every day basically. More out of interest than anything else. He was learning on the job as were we. We discussed the situation at length and he was as willing to listen to us as we were to listen to him. All to no avail. Sadly over the next few days all the pups faded away. Hence the term Puppy Fading Syndrome. All except for one. A little black dog puppy. Somehow, more through extensive nursing, we managed to keep this little one going, just about. We left him in the bed he had been born in but we arranged his bedding in such a way that he could position himself and lie in any position he found most comfortable at any given time. We also hung three or four heat lamps in different places and at different heights so as to enable him to decide for himself how warm he wanted to be. The vet had left us a batch of glucose/saline which we injected, in tiny amounts, under his skin every half an hour or so . . . 24 hours a day. We also swabbed some into him through his backside. This seemed less stressful for him. We went on like this for days. A little bit but very often and he seemed not to be getting any worse at least. Slowly we were managing to get liquid into the dear little chap via his mouth because he had now stopped being sick. Very slowly and very surely we managed over a period of weeks to get him back to normal puppyhood but he was, by nature of things, very stunted and under grown. At least he was a happy, bouncy, and healthy puppy again at last. We re-homed him to the tanker driver that used to come and pick the milk up every day. He had always been interested in them but could not afford to buy one. We gave him "Samson" as we had called him for nothing. He told me that his kids absolutely loved the little fella so all our struggles to keep the little bugger turned out to be worth it in the end. Plus we had learned a lot. Apparently so had the vet. In fact he came to visit one day when he was in the area just to see how we had got on with the pup. We told him that he had survived and gone on to pastures new. He was amazed. In fact his very words were "You ought to write a paper on this really". We never did. Too busy trying to make a bloody living. As I said earlier, Puppy Fading syndrome was basically accepted as an occupational hazard in those days, but in the years following a lot of work and research has been done on the subject and the generally accepted opinion now is that it is caused by a virus/bacterial infection allied to Feline Influenza and is ingested, if present, through the pups mouth through the fluid present in the birth canal at the time of whelping. Preventative treatments are now readily available. These dogs played a big part in our lives but they also played a big part in my own personal temporary downfall but you do not know that at the time do you?

Back at Meriden with Ma and Frank. The youngest foster sister Jackie was also at home. She had got herself pregnant and given birth to a baby boy called Wayne and she had a new boyfriend Simon. A really tall, skinny chap. When they were both together they looked comical. Jackie was less than 5' 3" (1 metre 60 cms) and Simon was well over 6' (2 metres) tall but they were happy so that is the main thing. Older sister Beryl was now married to Tim and had two daughters Eve and Kelly. Brother Billy had been married and divorced and was the father of two boys and a girl, Simon, Jonathan and Sarah so he was now "on the rampage" again. In and out of trouble but that is just the way he was back then. He made the same mistake as me and Paula and got married before he was ready and for the same reason as me I think. At this time things were "a bit rough" for me especially. On one occasion I had gone out for a bit of fresh air and in Ma's words looked like death warmed up. The new local copper pulled up at the side of me, started the usual, who are you? What you doing? Where are you going? All the usual bullshit you got from those jumped up overgrown boys showing off their uniform and trying to wield a false sense of power on any susceptible member of the public they came across. After his inane questioning he just told me that, in his opinion, I was mentally deranged and should be locked up in a mental home. This comment I found extremely upsetting and by the time I got back home I was in a worse state than when I had gone out. Ma asked what had happened. I told her. She told Frank and he went to see his sister Grace who lived about a mile away. Now Grace at the time was a "big wig" on the local council so she reported what had gone on to the powers that be and the jumped up little "Mr Plod" never came near me again. Obviously he had been given a good talking to by his superiors. I was lucky to have my adopted family around me at this time . . . Really lucky!!!

Time passed. I started to get stronger, physically and sometimes mentally. I would sit for hours drawing, in pencil, pen and ink now as I had no paint. It took my mind off things. An escape from reality for a while. Frank was now a self-employed chimney sweep, gardener, odd job man and on a good day I would go to work with him. Just like being a boy again. I also spent the odd day or two with Donald out and about in his lorry. Just like being a late teenager / early young man again. I was on the mend again . . . at last. My horizons were beginning to widen. I could see light at the end of the tunnel so much so that I applied for a job as a kitchen porter at The Manor Hotel just down the road at the end of the village. This proved to be a significant move. It got me back out "in the public domain". The start of a new journey, or 2 or 3 or 4 or more.

Working at The Manor was good. It got me out of the rut I had dropped into. I met new people and made new friends. It was a biggish kitchen. Six or seven chefs, two wash up ladies and two "pot wash boys". Me and a lad called Bill. Bill had gone there as a homeless and got a job plus accommodation. There was a staff residence building where all the chefs lived. Well those that were single anyway. The head chef was a chap very short in stature. He always wore clogs. Most kitchen staff wore clogs back then as a safety measure in case any sharp knives landed on the floor unnoticed. I loved my clogs. You could always tell when "chef" the head chef, was about because he would clonk his footwear down so hard that he reminded me of an approaching cart horse. He was a nice sort of little fella so much so that he took Bill and I into his office one day to tell us "Not to take any shit off that lot in the kitchen because our jobs were just as important as theirs. More so because if we did not keep the place clean the kitchen would be shut down and they would all be out of a job". I thought that was a nice thing for him to do. The chefs were a cosmopolitan bunch. The most noticeable was a black lad called Jeff (Jeff the Chef as he called himself). He was as "black" as the ace of spades, stood about 6'6" (2 metres) tall and was literally addicted to sugar. So much so that he reckoned he would not drink a hot drink until there was enough sugar in it to enable him to stand his spoon up in it unsupported. Eventually he had to be medically weaned off this habit. Martin was half Italian with dyed blonde highlights in his hair. The biggest womaniser on the premises. Allan was the sauce chef. A quietish sort of lad when at work but not as much so after hours. "Milky" was a very white skinned (hence his nickname) with ginger hair. The pastry chef was a lad called Keith. He was "Chefs" brother but they obviously did not see eye to eye. Always bickering. Commis chefs came and went on a regular basis. I can only really recall one of them. Another young "black" lad who just wanted to be a professional footballer. He would spend most of his spare time and energy in the car park just "playing" with a ball. He was good at that. More so than he was at the cooking because he was not there for long . . . good luck to him anyway.

Summer arrived and Milky was off on holiday from the kitchen. We were talking about his vacation and where he had gone and off the top of my head I just said he had told me he was going off to get married. He hadn't, of course. I just said it from nowhere. A few of the chefs ears pricked up so I just carried on with the yarn. I did let "Jeff the Chef" into my "blurb" and he agreed to go along with it just for a bit of fun. Now with the two of us spinning this yarn the rest of the staff in the kitchen, the restaurant, and the hotel were all "sucked in". So much so that we even arranged a collection for "the happy couple" but things started to get a bit sticky when the assembled donors wanted to know more. Who was she? Where did she live? Etc. etc. So Jeff and I decided that although we did not know her name we did know that she was a Chinese/British. She had originally come over here from Hong Kong where her parents were in business in a big way and that she and Milky had got married over here and gone off to Hong Kong on honeymoon. He would be coming back alone and due to family reasons she would be following later. The only problem with this "scam" was that "Milky" did not know anything about it and in those days there were no mobile phones so we could not let him in on it all. Jeff and I decided, because we knew the date he was due back and at what time then we would "hi-jack" him outside the hotel up in the village and enlighten him on the facts. This we did and he was happy to go along with it all. That was all good until patience was wearing thin in the kitchen and everybody wanted to see her. Now previously I had told my sister Beryl what we were doing. She agreed with us to pose as "the wife" just for a laugh but we had previously said "the wife"was Chinese/British. This scuppered our plans so after a couple of weeks of "getting away with it" the fairy story had to be revealed as "a bit of a wheeze" and all donations to the happy couple had to be returned from whence they came. Never mind it was fun while it lasted.

Christmas was now on the horizon and time for the annual Christmas "do" for the staff and friends. Apparently over the years this had become a bit of a "stuffed collar" affair. This was due to the fact that the hotel's general manager, Mr Portman, was a bit straight laced. The idea of the staff letting their hair down and maybe getting "a bit out of hand" did not sit well in his world. So much so that he had decreed he would only employ front of house receptionists who, for want of a better phrase, would not actually win any beauty contests. He had implemented this policy ever since the day one of the hotel guests went back to his room only to find one of the young chefs in his bed with the receptionist. Fair comment I suppose. Anyway back to the forthcoming festivities. We, in the kitchen, had decided to see how much we could get away with when the time came. We decided that I should dress up as a sort of New York gangster type and that Jeff the Chef would dress up as my "Moll" for the night. My costume was no problem to cobble together but when it came to Jeff it proved to be a bit more difficult. He was well over 6' (2 metres approx) tall. As black as the ace of spades with big feet. We got him a blonde wing. Lin donated one of her old long dresses which one of the waitresses adapted to "fit" the big fella. We made his face up and got him massive cheap earrings and bracelets etc. We managed to squeeze him into a pair of fishnet tights. We "Tattooed" his arms with pale lipstick and slung a "cape" for want of a better word over his shoulders. It was decided that as Mr Portman had always taken up his post at the doorway (on top of the stairs) of the ballroom to greet the guests then Jeff and I would walk up the stairs arm in arm. On reaching the top I would take off Jeff's cape, hand it to the ever respectable Mr Portman with the words "Thank you my man". As this whole charade had been kept reasonably secret (just basically confined to the kitchen) then the whole scene came like a "bolt out of the blue" to our esteemed manager. I think he was in a bit of a state of shock. He did not smile or laugh but then again he did not reprimand us either. Not at the time or afterwards. Both of us stayed in character for the whole of the evening and the whole affair was a bit of a talking point around the place for a day or two afterwards. It was good fun and made the assembled congregation laugh. That was the main idea anyway so you could say it all went well.

Back to normality for the next few weeks until about 10.30 p.m. on a busy Saturday night. The head waiter came rushing into the kitchen shouting that a customer in the restaurant was refusing to pay his bill and demanding to see the chef. He was from the public health department of the local council and he was not happy with the way things were. Chef immediately despatched the waiter to go and get this man and bring him to his office. This was adjacent to and in full view of the kitchen. The head waiter returned with a very smartly dressed gentleman in his 60's. At this point Chef went "off on one" to say the least. He knew the man. It turned out that he was "a gentleman of the road" who had worked in the kitchen as a pot wash some years earlier. It seemed he was at a bit of a loose end at the time so he thought, as he was in the area, he would pop in and see what he could "blag" for a day or two. This was my introduction to "Tiffy" who turned out to be a proper old fashioned English eccentric who during the winter months had a permanent lodging place in St. Ives in Cornwall but, when the holiday season started, he was cast out until the next winter. He just wandered about between places he knew living off his wits . . . and what wits he had!! He "installed" himself in one of the empty rooms in the staff block. Chef said it was easier to go along with him than it was to argue and that he would move on anyway when he got bored. I remember he used to lie in the bath for hours singing Land of Hope and Glory at the top of his voice. Now Tiffy was a bit like Marmite. You either loved him or hated him. Whatever you thought, he

240

was not going anywhere until he was ready, like it or not. I was bloody fascinated by him. It soon became apparent that he was nobody's fool and was very well educated. He spoke in a very aristocratic way and was always clean shaven, well groomed and well dressed. He would talk for hours displaying his copious knowledge of a whole kaleidoscope of subjects. You either sat and listened and learned or just walked away. I feel into the former category. I was enthralled by this man. What made him "tick"? Would I ever find out? I was chatting to him one day and I told him that I had come to the conclusion that he was basically just a "con man". This comment triggered a very bluff reply that went word for word as follows:- "My man, I am not a confidence trickster. I have merely acquired the art of taking advantage of the amenities intended for the rich and illustrious when I have ne'er but one penny in my pocket. One day I will show you have it is done." I have never forgotten those words, obviously, or I wouldn't be writing them down now would I? Over time I managed to be able to understand and see a bit of what he was about. On one occasion I asked him how he had ended up as he was. He told me that before he went into the forces he was a journalist but he had gone through the war. Again in his words "When I joined the army I was A.1. When I left the army I was Z.26". Enough said!! He had come to the conclusion that, again in his words, "If you dress well and can speak the King's English you can go anywhere in this country". By this time I had received a lump sum of a couple of thousand pounds as a pay off for life, as they called it, for my still on going back problems so I bought a little car, a Morris 1100, in fact. It allowed me to get about and in my spare time I would be back sniffing around farms and animals again. I had just got back one evening from one such excursion when Tiffy knocked on the door. It was pissing down with rain. He was soaked and because I had just come in from outside so was I. He wanted me to take him into Coventry so he could get a bus to Leamington Spa where he had managed to arrange himself "a parking spot" with a friend of his from the past. A parish priest no less. I agreed - no problem. We got to Coventry and he said to me "Come with me and I will show you how it is done". Now we were both soaked to the skin and although, as ever, he was well dressed, I had on an old army great coat, a trilby hat and a pair of wellies. This was no problem to him. We went into The Hotel Leofric and sat in the reception. He drank their coffee, and I drank their tea. We ate their biscuits. He used their phone to contact his reverend friend in Leamington. He then stood up and as he walked past reception he doffed his hat and uttered the immortal words "Thank you my good man and goodbye". Never even offering to pay. I do not think the thought had even crossed his mind . . . I just followed . . . innocently. That was how it was done!!

Months and months went by. Lin and Mandy had got a flat in Coleshill and we were basically back together again. One evening there was a knock on the door and there the old bugger stood. He had found out where I was and had come round to see us before he went off again. He came in, had a bath, some bread and soup and stayed the night on the sofa. He coughed all night long on and off. Morning came and he was ready to go. He asked us if we could lend him £2 for a day or two and when he got his pension he would pop it in an envelope and put it through the door. True to his word, a couple of days later, an envelope landed on the mat with £2 inside it. That was the last time our paths ever crossed but what a man to meet, to listen to and learn from. Thank you Tiffy!!

In those days all the waste food from the kitchen and restaurant was put in pig swill bins and collected, usually, once or twice a week. In the case of The Manor Hotel the swill man was a chap called Maurice. A bloke about 5' 6" (1.75 metres approx.) tall and about the same measurement wide. He had a balding head, a gaucho moustache and arms like small trees. Each steel swill bin, when full, probably weighed over 1 cwt (50 +kg). He would pick one up with each hand, walk out to his pick up with them and put them straight on without placing them on the ground first. He was a strong man. He made this plain one Sunday, early evening. He had loaded his swill up and come into the break room for a cup of tea. There were 3 or 4 of us in there. Sunday early evening was time for a break and to listen to the Top Ten for the week. Anyway one of the chefs was sat down at the table with his back against the wall. He must have said something to Maurice that didn't "hit the right note". So our friendly swill man did no more than grab this lad by the throat with one hand, pick him up, slid him up the wall and clouted his head on the ceiling. No more out of the way remarks from that young man.

As I said earlier Lin and Mandy had got a flat in Coleshill and our relationship was basically back on track but I had got "itchy feet" again. I just wanted to go up the road, stick my back to the wind and see where it blew me. I had ideas of going back round Evesham way. That way I could earn money and get my head back on properly (or as properly as it had ever been). So that's what I did. (Lin and Mandy stayed at home because Mandy was in her last year at school now and wanted to take her exams). I earned money and sent most of it back home. I lived mostly on Ryvita, processed cheese, digestive biscuits, marmalade, and copious amounts of sweet tea plus the odd "treat" from time to time. I had set off from Coleshill on foot, with a flask of tea, some buttered bread rolls, some pencils and a drawing book and an urge to "find something". I did not know what I was looking for or where it might be. Anyway I walked the 20 or so miles to Evesham and ended up sharing a lad's tent. I had met him not long after arriving. I had got work sorted out to start next morning. Up, off and running again. New places to see, new people to meet . . . better times ahead.

Strawberry picking time now. Luckily enough the piece was just over the road from where a few folks were "camping" in a field behind a pub at Norton. This would prove to be less than desirable. When it came to throwing out time then the odd piss head or two would decide it would be good fun to come round the camp and just do what pissheads do . . . be a bloody nuisance!! The work was good, all piece work (paid by weight). The wages were paid at the end of every day so cash was never a problem. Pickers came and pickers went as usual but a rather "crusty" looking girl turned up one day, on her own, just with a bag of bits and a pair of hands. That is all you needed really to get by. She did not speak to anyone. She kept herself to herself but she intrigued me so after a day or two I started to try and chat to her when we were in rows that were next to each other. I could not get a name out of her at all "Just call me Girl" was as far as that avenue of curiosity led. After a while she began to "open up" a bit and it was only a bit. It turned out that she was partaking in a self- imposed life experiment, or something similar. She would live totally, and that included her food and anything else she might need, out of skips. Shops were definitely off the scene. She would not drink anything that she regarded as "addictive". That included anything, including tea and coffee. She drank only water or, on a good day, milk if she could find any. She told me she never washed herself or combed her hair. When she got too "crusty" then she would relent and go to the doctors for head lice treatment and then got cleaned up a bit for a while. People either ignored her or took the piss out of her. So far as the latter is concerned somebody was having a go at her one day and they happened to mentioned peanuts . . . yes, peanuts. She immediately responded with a river of facts about peanuts. Their latin name and where in the world grew most peanuts, its position on the planet in degrees of latitude and longitude . . . the full works. She had exposed a tiny chip in her armour of secrecy. She was obviously no fool!! After the first day in the strawberries I realised I had lost my bag containing my pencils and drawing books. It turned out that I had left them at the farm's head office about six miles back up the road. The first evening, after work, I spent walking the twelve miles there and back to retrieve my mislaid parcel. I needed it really. You never know when a hand drawn picture can buy you a bit of food and drink.

Days went on. We had all been thrown out from behind the pub at Norton so my mate (I can't remember his name sadly) but I can remember we both had the same sense of humour. We had a good laugh anyway. We decided to take his tent and our bits and bobs off down a long, old, track that ran between two more pieces of strawberries that we were now working in anyway. It was about now that a beaten up old transit van turned up on the piece one morning. Out got a middle aged travelling man, his wife and ten kids. They descended like a bunch of locusts. Where ever the good picking was then that is where they went. The old man would walk around looking for the best picking. He would whistle one or two of his kids and put them in there even if it was right in front of somebody else in their row. They only stayed a day. The foreman would not let them back on again. Little did I know it, at the time, but the family would become and still are (those that have not died in the meantime at least) our very good friends. Indeed the eldest lad is still my best mate. As I write this meet Rocky Price. He will turn up again later along with all his family.

Strawberry time was now coming to an end. Time to move on but it had been good. I had managed to earn a few quid and send some back to Lin and Mandy. I had met some new people and had a laugh all at the same time. My mate and his tent decided to move back to Bristol but I had heard about pea picking up in the Cotswolds at Chipping Camden. It was a long old walk. A lot of it uphill to get there. I arrived anyway, found the work, got permission off the boss man to start and so I did. You could work for literally as long as you liked. All piece work (as usual) and paid at the end of every day. It could not be better and lo and behold, who had also made their way up there? Only "Girl". She must have had the same idea as me. The piece we were working in was right behind all the shops and houses on Camden High Street. It was a big old piece with plenty of work for a while. Most of the pickers were travellers or locals who came every morning and went every evening but a few of us, including me and Girl, had nowhere to go so we just lived in the field.

We would have a fire of an evening to boil water for drinks. When it came time to sleep we would just dig a good scrape in the ground, lie in it and cover ourselves over with pea straw. What more could we want. Luckily it stayed dry all the time we were there so there was no reason to do anything different was there? We just kept working as long as we were able, well into the night at times. I have never been the world's best pea picker but something is better than nothing. I could earn enough to keep going and still send a bit back to Lin. No problems.

A gap in the pea harvest was imminent so a few of the people that had been living on the piece moved on to pastures new. It got down to just me, Girl and a couple of Scotsmen who were the only four left actually living on the piece. One evening the Scotsmen had gone down to the pub and came back late one night a bit the worse for wear and a trifle mouthy. It was a really dark night, too dark to really see enough to pick peas, so Girl had gone off to her "bed" and I had done the same and gone to my scrape in the ground. Anyway, as I said the Scotsmen were a bit mouthy and when they got back they shouted out in broad Scots accent "Hey up Girl. Are you up there with your boyfriend Nick?" To which she replied as sharp as a knife. "Nick is up here, he is a boy, he is my friend but he is NOT my boyfriend". That shut them up for the rest of the night anyway.

Time came to move on again for more work. I do not know where Girl went. I often wonder but I have never seen her since. I got a lift on the back of a pickup to Evesham late one afternoon. I arrived, probably looking a bit on the scruffy side, with a couple of bags, a flask, a couple of bottles of water, a saucepan, my pencils and paper and a couple of quid in my pocket. I found an old shed to stop in. It was in the middle of an old abandoned orchard a mile or so away from a farm where I had managed to get work on the plums. It was a bad year for the plum job so most of the travellers had decided to follow the peas or go on to the spring onions. It turned out to be more by luck than judgement that I had dropped straight into more work straight away at Twyford Fruit Farm. A fruit farm with its own farm shop and café. Could not be better. There was not only the plums but also apple picking, late in the season, alongside a few days on the Blackcurrant harvester. This machine always surprised me in how gently it picked the fruit. So gentle in fact that at times the odd baby bird would appear at the far end of it, completely unharmed, after its brush with mechanisation. The plum picking was good. As I said earlier it was a bad season but this place had got a decent crop that they sold well in their own shop. So much so that at one time me and another lad were put into a piece on our own. The plums, Victoria's, were bloody massive and we got paid 30p a chip (one of the old cardboard mushroom baskets with the metal fold down handle). We were picking on average 30 chips an hour each. That amounted to £9.00 an hour . . . Cash in hand. Can't be bad!! This only lasted a couple of days, worst luck, before we had picked the piece out so we were put back with the main gang but it had been a good couple of days. It was at about this time that "a bit of a character" turned up in the orchard. A man, a job to say how old he was. He was so crusty, a mop of rank dreadlocks that seemed to have been planted on top of his head and left to their own devices. A bit like a very unkempt, ungroomed, unwashed Old English sheepdog. He walked or, should I say, shuffled around most of the time with his trousers basically at half mast revealing the crack in his arse. Not a pretty sight at the best of times. There was an old local travelling woman who had been a fixture on this place for years called Topsy Smith who was disgusted by this newcomer and refused to work anywhere near him. In fact she admitted she was a bit scared by him. I just thought he was an interesting sort of chap. He did not say much even when he decided to communicate with anybody. By now I had christened him "Trogg". Nobody knew where he went after work. He just wandered off through the trees never to be seen again until the next day. By now I had invented the "fact" that he must have a burrow somewhere that he retired to. On saying that I did stumble across him one evening in an old picked out piece of strawberries. He was boiling up old fruit in a tin can over a bit of a fire he had lit. Not doing anybody any harm was he? Good luck to him I said!! Usually after work 3 or 4 of us, including Trogg, would go on to the site café and sit with the tourists and customers for an ice-cream. Trogg would do the same but he did not sit down with us. He would just get his cornet or whatever and shuffle about trying to keep his locks from getting entwined in his daily ice cream treat. His trousers still at half mast and mumbling to himself oblivious, or at least, uncaring of the weird looks and comments that were being directed at him. These were given by the "respectable" clientele who were busily munching away on their cream teas, fancy cakes and buttered scones. One early evening a beaten up old yellow Renault car turned up in the yard and out got the driver. A chap similar to Trogg but a bit taller and just the tiniest bit tidier. They both got in the motor and off they went. A couple of days went by before the man himself, Trogg, re-appeared. It seems they had been on their way to Hereford, had been stopped by the police and had the motor taken off them. He said the police tried to search the vehicle on the side of the road but it was in such an unhygienic state that they had taken it away to be fumigated before they had dare delve into its contents – legal or otherwise. Hence the return of Trogg on foot!!

The lady that ran the café was chatting to us about herself and her husband. The latter it turned out was one of the last surviving bare knuckle boxers around. Hence he used to get invited every year to some big boxing dinner, or other, in London. In the previous year he had apparently decided to give it a miss because Cassius Clay (or maybe he had become Mohammed Ali by then) was due to attend and he had not got a lot of time for Mr Clay or Mr Ali. He did not rate him at all. He said he was no more than a big mouth with a big head – or words to that effect. Anyway in the end he relented and decided to attend and when, on his return, he was questioned by his wife about the occasion he admitted that his first opinions of "The Greatest" were wrong. In fact he was one of the most polite, intelligent, people had had ever met. So he, along with millions of others worldwide also became a fan of Mr Clay (or Mr Ali) whatever he was calling himself at the time.

Plum time was by now coming close to an end particularly in a year like this. As Mandy was going off on a horse riding holiday Lin and I decided to have a break ourselves and spend a week in Torbay. Lin would go down on the train and I would get there by hitch hiking. This I did and the first lift I got was on the junction with the M5. A truck pulled up and lo and behold I knew the passenger in the cab. It was Rose, the youngest daughter of Tom and Dora, our ex-neighbours from Pailton. It turned out she had married a lorry driver and here they were. Talk about a small world!! They gave me a ride so far down to the point where they had to turn off anyway. I do not know where it was . . . somewhere the other side of Bristol I think. From here I gradually worked my way down and eventually arrived in Paignton in the early evening. I wandered about a bit. Had a cup of tea and a bit of food but I seemed to be creating a bit of interest within the local police force. They kept driving past and giving me "the evil eye". I suppose I looked a bit like an illegal immigrant come to think of it. Long black hair, well tanned after the summer, very unkempt and scruffy. I decided the best thing to do was to vacate the town and go and find somewhere to bed down for the night. I came across a big detached house, set well off the road, with a big old yew tree in its grounds. That will do till morning. Nice and dry and sheltered at least. The following day I met Lin at the train station. It turned out she had managed to rent a caravan on a holiday park between Paignton and Brixham so we settled in for the week. We had not got a lot of money but I recall that we treated ourselves to a cream tea every evening. During that week we decided to go and have a look at Brixham. We both loved it. Just something about the place. I said to Lin "Bloody hell, you could walk round this place with a fuckin' horse on your head and nobody would take any notice!" In years to come, unbeknown to us at the time, this observation or idea would indeed turn out to be true.

The week was soon over and the time came for us to split up again. I remember it was a painful experience at the time. Anyway I managed to get myself back to Evesham one way or another. I got there, no money, no food to speak of and I was really hungry. I remember walking past a bakers shop on the High Street. There was nobody behind the counter but there was a slab of fruitcake just sat there on top of the display cabinet. I could not resist it so I slipped in, robbed the aforementioned piece of culinary delight, and shot off a bit quick back up the orchards to the old shed I had spent time in before. I lit a fire and ate the cake . . . all of the cake in one go!! That was the wrong thing to do really. It just resulted in me spending a sleepless night interrupted by bouts of colic but I would be alright the next day. I had arranged to go back to what few plums were left at Twyford Fruit Farm and therefore got paid the same evening . . . back on track. A couple of new pickers had turned up during the week I was away. They had not got anywhere to stay but they had got a tent so they came back with me to my shed and set up next to me. I can recall one evening we had been sitting around the fire. They went back to their tent but as it was a nice evening I just lay down and went to sleep by the fire . . . Mistake!! You see I had an old Afghan coat that I used as a blanket, perfect, until that evening at least. I must have laid down a bit too close to the fire. I was woken up abruptly when the old coat caught fire. It must have been a spark or something but I lost my "blanket" in the end. A few of us itinerant pickers used to meet up at a café sometimes after work. A right kaleidoscope of humanity but two people stuck in my mind. The first was an Australian lad who seemed to survive purely on "Scrumpy" cider. He would work all day, get his money, and then walk up to "The Cider House" at Elmleigh Castle with a plastic gallon container, get it filled up and walk back to his camp again. Now apparently this "Scrumpy" was only one step down from rocket fuel in the alcohol stakes. It was beyond a liquid. It was almost like a weak treacle. It was extremely potent so much so that the Landlord of The Cider House had a rule that stated any regular was only allowed 2 pints (1/2 litre) and anyone else would only be served it on the basis it had to be diluted with lemonade first. Our Aussie friend seemed to thrive on it. Every evening he would go for a refill and every evening he would drink the lot!!. It turned out that he was stopping, along with a few others, in an orchard a couple of miles away. We went back there one evening just to socialize and for a change of scenery. The camp consisted of a few tents and random shelters but the best one of them all was this monstrous construction made entirely of bender poles and clear plastic secured to the frame in random places by bits of baler twine. It was the home of a single girl. She had built it in the style of a maze. It must have taken her bloody ages!! She lived in the centre of it. Takes all sorts!! Back at Twyford it turned out that while I had been away Topsy's nemesis Trogg had appeared with a girl for a few days. Then the girl had vanished much to Topsy's concern. Had he killed her? Had he sold her? Had he eaten her? In Topsy's mind all of these were possibilities so I said to her" Well have you asked him where she is? " She hadn't. She was too scared of him to go anywhere near so I asked him anyway and his answer to my question "Where is your lady friend?" was to reply in a drawn out lazy American accent, with a shrug of his shoulders and upturned palms "Couldn't decide whether she wanted to work or travel. I guess she travelled " . . . Classic quote.

Plum time was basically now at an end. Really sparse pickin. I was working next to Trogg one day and I noticed that he seemed to be more "away with the fairies" than normal. He was looking at each plum, individually on the tree, before deciding to pick it or not. I asked him why he was doing this and being so particular the reply came in the same American drawl " Taking it easy man, looking for the real best" . . . another classic!!

Apple picking time came. Trogg vanished but a few of us stayed on. We thought we would make good money because unlike the plums the place was dripping with apples. Hanging on the trees like bunches of grapes and as the going rate, at the time, for apple picking was £12.00 a ton we thought we had got it made . . . Wrong!! The apples were all "eaters" and were to be kept in cold store until sold through the shop then, because of their delicate skins, the job would be paid at the day rate. That was not a lot but it was work. Everybody's bins were given an individual mark, so that if anyone's apples had been bruised then this would become evident over the storage period and anyone's fruit that fell below the required standard was noted and they would not be employed next season. Fair enough!!

The weather was now going down hill fast. My shed leaked and one of the other lad's tent had become a bit the worse for wear so we two decided to relocate to an old brick barn, right on the side of the road, about a mile nearer our work. It was dry. There was a fair bit of dry wood in there for a fire. I had managed to get the pencils and paper out and had drawn a few of the local old fashioned dwellings and managed to sell one or two of them to the owners. The rest I kept and used them in work I was to do in the future.

Apple time came to an end. It had been a good season. I had earned a few quid. Met some interesting people and had a good laugh along the way but now it was time to go home and embark on another chapter of my life. Maybe the down days had gone. A new journey on the horizon. Well, Lin and I had come through our bad patch. There had been a few hiccups and obstacles to negotiate on the way but we had got there. Time to earn a living somehow, anyhow. I started to do a bit of driving for young Phil Upton, Donald's son. He had now started his own business with two 30 cwt flat beds and two trailers. The money was not good. £10.00 a day, cash in hand, but I enjoyed going up and down the roads here, there and everywhere. We, Lin, Mandy and I, also started selling pet food in the markets. We just stood on Birmingham Rag Market and Henley in Arden. It was good fun really. Plenty of banter and interaction with Joe Public. I also used to sell the odd piece of my artwork, especially at Henley. I had gone through of phase of doing dog portraits in pen and ink. Drawn one hair at a time. Very labour intensive. I recall one Sunday I had some pictures out on the stall, including one of an Afghan Hound, and this very upmarket aristocratic wannabee woman came along with her husband in tow like a pet poodle. She examined this drawing and then proclaimed in a very upmarket plum in your gob accent "Oh that looks nothing like my Afghan Hound" to which I replied "No, and your husband looks nothing like me but we are still the same breed!! She tutted and walked off. No sale, but it put her in her place at least. Lin and I were sat in the café at Henley Market one day when we got into conversation with a Sikh stallholder and he told us that us English would never beat his people in this business. We asked him why. He said that in his opinion we were too greedy. "We all wanted to be the boss". We spent too much time concentrating on this aspect rather than all pulling together with the same end he explained. In his culture maybe 5, 10, 20 or more individuals would get together. The oldest man present, no matter who he was, would be "the boss" . . . end of story. He said that if you had 20 people all with the same aim and they all put, for example, £1,000.00 in cash each on the table then with the £20,000.00 they held the upper hand when it came to buying whatever they decided to trade in. He said that if, for example, they decided to trade in jewellery then they could go to the Jewellery Quarter in Birmingham and in his words "We would not ask how much things were but instead we would tell them what we were prepared to pay." If they did not like it we would just go home and make our own. All this done with no arguing, just total respect for their elder . . . there's a lesson in there somewhere!!

Mandy and I had been working Birmingham Rag Market one Saturday but because it started to rain torrentially, and our pitch was outside, we decided to pack up and go home early. We loaded all the stuff into the motor and off we went. No problem, until we got outside what was back then the main entrance to Elmdon (now Birmingham) Airport. Then there was the blue flashing lights and sirens. We were pulled in by The Plod and what a pair of wankers they were as well. They made both Mandy and I get out, stand in the pouring rain, while they totally emptied all our stuff out of the motor on to the side of the road. They proceeded to "test" the floor of the vehicle with a small jemmy bar. They even inserted it between the seat mounts and the floor pan and levered it. Obviously trying to find a weak spot but to no avail. They just shrugged their shoulders, told us we were free to go, got in their motor, and drove off. By now all our stuff was more than a little wet and it was still on the side of the road. This little "flush of power to their heads" really pissed me off so I put in a formal complaint about their behaviour to "the powers that be" but I doubt they were ever reprimanded. We will never know.

Winter was now beginning to set in. I really was not enjoying standing still behind our stall waiting for a customer I may be able to take a few quid off. By now it was freezing cold on some days As luck would have it a new hotel was just about to open on Coleshill High Street. This was just a few hundred yards away from where we lived and they were advertising for staff, including kitchen porters. I wrote them a note, telling them that I had done the job before, and where, and that I was the best kitchen porter in Coleshill and that they would be wise to employ me. Nothing wrong with a bit of "front". It worked anyway. I got the job along with another local man, a certain Ronnie Limm, a well known local man in his 50's but "as queer as a fishes tit" as they say. He was broad Lancashire and spoke with the relevant accent. He was a laugh. It turned out he had spent a lot of time in the past working as a Redcoat at Butlins Holiday Camps and to him Billy Butlin was only one step down from God. He carried a picture of himself and the erstwhile Mr Butlin around with him at all times. He showed it to anyone who would stand still long enough. The other pot washer, apart from Ronnie and myself, was a lady of portly build called Rita. It turned out she was the mother of Lin's brother's (Brian) best mate. So it was all local in the cleaning department at The Coleshill Hotel. The place had not officially opened yet but everyone was rushing around "tweeking" things. It was, however, to be officially opened by another local character, a homeless man who lived rough, either at the bottom or at the top of the town. He kept all his belongings in an array of prams which meant that when he moved from one end to the other it was a major operation. This could take a couple of days to achieve because he would push one pram so far, leave it and then walk back to get another one . . . and so on and so on. He was "the guest of honour" for the opening ceremony and was immortalised on a wind vane on top of the hotel. He hung around for years after I believe . . . up and down . . . up and down but hurting no-one.

Trevor Locke was the man behind The Coleshill Hotel. A local businessman/entrepreneur from Shustoke. Apparently he owned a factory in Birmingham. He had decided to expand his portfolio by buying Blackmores old garage/filling station together with the adjoining Cameo sweet shop and the, now defunct, picture house that all adjoined each other. Basically, he turned it all into a small hotel complex. He was not the "nicest" man on earth. In fact he was a bit worse than that. In my eyes and in the eyes of a good many other he was little more than a bully, a show off and a "bread head". Just the kind of person I did not like but it was a job. He was not going to walk all over me. In fact a few months down the line I said to Bobby Daniel (who had become a regular patron of the hotel bar) that I wished Trevor would sack me but Bobby said "He'll never do that". I asked him why? He said "Because he likes you because you stand up to him" Ah well, but I did stand up to him. He came to me one day with a toilet seat and told me it was a present for me and I said to him "The best place for that it over your head and around your neck the amount of shit that comes out of your gob!!". He just walked off taking "My Present" with him . . . Plonker!!

The head chief in the kitchen was a friend of Trevors, a West Indian chap. A very rotund sort of fella called Barry. Barry was a lovely bloke but he was really a "banquet chef". He would spend hours making petite fours and crafting roses out of tomatoes and flowers out of apples and spiral turning potatoes and mushrooms. At times the pressure of a full on restaurant service would get the better of him and like most chefs I have ever met he was a temperamental bloke. Most of the time he was a big placid loveable man but he could snap. When he did everybody knew about it but once he had "gone off on one" he would calm down again as if nothing had happened. Such an occurrence arose one service when a commis chef called Tony (who was not the sharpest knife in the box at the best of times) had been performing well below par and too often. He had messed something up. Barry went off on one, chased Tony into the break room and hit him over the head with a panful of hot ratatouille!! Within minutes of this "blow out" Barry was sat in the break room crying and overflowing with remorse.

Regularly it would get to about 6.45 pm (15 minutes before the restaurant was due to open) and Barry had got hardly anything prepared ready go to and he would start running about the place, shouting out in a broad West Indian accent "De Chefs in da shit, De Chefs in da shit!!" I really liked Barry. I was sat talking to him on one occasion and I said to him "I don't mean to be rude, in anyway, but why is it that most of you West Indian blokes seem to be inherently lazy?" and he answered "Where I come from there is fish in the sea, fruit on the trees and as much ganja as anyone could want . . . we don't need to work" . . . fair comment. Around that time one of the main T.V. channels bought out a weekly sitcom called "Chef" about a black chef and his white wife (Barry's wife was white) who bought a hotel and just did banquets. It turns out this series was based on Barry and his wife. Lenny Henry played the part of Barry. I think it only ran for one series and then it was taken off. A bit like Barry in real life because he was soon to leave the hotel and move on.

A new head chef was employed. A man called Malcolm, a divorced chap, who "liked to socialize" to put it bluntly. We got on well, so much so, that when it came time for a break and a meal he used to say to me "Are you eating here or are you taking it home?" and winked at me several times. I would plump for the latter option and because I used to take a black bag full of basically fresh veg waste home every night for Mandy's horse (more of that later) he would secrete some liberal assortment of culinary goodies in the said "swag bag".

Trevor employed his eldest son, who was a chef, and his middle son, also a chef, in times of need. The rest of the kitchen staff were a lad called Andrew (the son of a local Insurance Brokers) and the aforementioned Tony, poor sod. They did take advantage of him. There was also a girl chef called Suzy whose main claim to fame was that she used to go out with one of the two main members of the band 10 c.c. From time to time the youngest son Wayne would also give a hand. A lad after his dad's heart. A proper "Chip off the old block" . . . Jumped up little shit bag!! The turnover of staff at the hotel was massive. Trevor would decide, at any time, that he did not like somebody and they would be out of the door on the spot. He even terminated his own mother's employment!! Maxine, his daughter, was like her Dad in most of her ways. She was employed as the receptionist but like her father she was someone who liked to throw her weight about whenever she saw fit. Again like her father she was not well liked among the staff except for Chef Malcolm. They got together and the last I heard still are together. About the only member of staff on the "domestic" side of things that managed to stay on the right side of "He who must be obeyed" was a lady called Margaret. She was telling me that one morning when she was cleaning in the bar she found a beer soaked £1 note underneath a tray. She thought it might have been "planted" there so she showed it to Trevor. He did no more than peel it off the table, hold it up to the light and mutter the immortal words "Look at that. That's a pound note you know. I'll take that off and dry it out" . . . Bloody bread head!! This, and from him, a man who was not exactly short of a few quid!!.

While I was there I designed a few "special" menu boards for them and I also had a few bits of my art hanging around the place. I had done a pen and ink drawing of the outside of the hotel and it was hung in the entrance foyer. Anyway a message came down to the kitchen one Saturday night saying could I go up to reception as someone wanted to buy it. Now it was summer, it was hot outside, but it was even hotter in the kitchen. All I had on was a sleeveless T shirt, and pair of flip-flops. Thinking about it I might even have been barefoot. I had a pair of jeans and an apron tied around my waist. Rather than going on a scenic tour of the ground floor to reach reception I took the quick route, out of the kitchen, and straight through the restaurant. Not a pretty sight I suppose when you are sitting there, tucking into your very expensive a la carte meal but there you go. I sold the picture, that was the main thing, but my little excursion had come to the notice of "He who must be obeyed" and he was not a happy chappie to say the least. I just told him that if I was good enough to do the customers washing up then I was good enough to walk through the restaurant when it was busy. He just "tutted" and walked off.

Ronnie, the other pot wash, was a proper nutcase. As I say, a proper gay boy but loveable with it. He was a mate of Trevors and after work he would stay on in the bar drinking with the management and a few favoured locals. He was married, despite his sexuality, and had a daughter. He was well known in the town for his "parties" at home. His wife suffered his indulgences but apparently during one of his "get togethers" an argument and a fight occurred and someone got stabbed and died so that was the end of those little happenings. I was chatting to him one day and apparently he and his wife slept in different rooms at home. Anyway, he was telling me he had got home one night, a bit worse for wear, got into bed but had forgotten to turn his light off. He lay in bed, and in his own words, started to shout "Woman, woman get in here". His wife duly entered the room and asked him what he wanted to which he replied "Switch light off in here will ya?" . . . enough said.

The fact that most evenings "after hours drinking" became the norm soon got around. This fact had started to attract a few undesirables. This was not really a good thing so Trevor employed a "doorman" in an attempt to keep these types away but unbeknown to said doorman one of the regulars was none other than the musician Roy Wood. His uncle and aunt, part of his management team, only lived in Water Orton about 5 miles away and were regulars at the hotel. Indeed they commissioned me to draw their house for them but that's "by the by". Roy turned up one evening in his purple Range Rover and multi coloured long hair only to be turned away at the door . . . oops!! The doorman was soon re-educated . . . say no more!!

The time had come for Mandy to finish off her schooling. She had never asked for anything over the years really. She was happy with Megan, her corgi, that we had got her years earlier in Hampshire but she had always let it be known that she would like a horse. We decided that as she had helped us on the markets then we would buy her a pony when we could find a place to keep it. I asked Reg Wright if we could graze it on his place but he said no because in his eyes a horse had got 5 mouths, one on the end of his head and one on the end of every leg. In other words they made too much mess of the ground. He kept sheep anyway. Horses and sheep are not the best bedfellows ever invented. However, I knew there were two little adjoining paddocks down by the river, a couple of miles beyond The Cuttle. My old childhood home. They belonged to John Plumb who, along with his father Sir Henry, farmed the ground on the other side of the road from the Levi's place where Frank had worked years earlier. Because, at odd times, Frank had done a bit of work for them "on the side" and I had always gone with him then John and I were already acquainted with each other. He agreed to rent us this ground for £40 a month. It was already well fenced and because of the river it had water laid on so grazing sorted. Time to buy the pony. We had been going to Henley in Arden horse sales at odd times for years so this is where we headed next and ended up paying £40 for a 14hh/14.2hh dark bay gelding. Supposedly "ride and drive". The former claim was true but the latter proved to be a bit questionable. No matter Mandy loved the pony. She called him "Conker". We scratched together enough tack to get her going with him but she only ever put a saddle on him if she took him on the road. Otherwise she just rode bareback. The pony, it turned out, had got a bit of a mind of his own and when he thought he had had enough of being ridden he would try and get her off. He would rear and buck and all that tantrum stuff but she rarely came off until he worked out that if he lay down while she was still on him, and rolled, then he would get rid of her that way . . . scheming bugger!!

We had bought the pony at the back end of the year. Not an ideal time really but there you go. Before we decided to give into Mandy's desire to own a pony I had absolutely insisted that either she or I must go and check on him every single day without fail. Not necessarily to feed him but just to . . . well check he was O.K. Mandy would go every non-school day on her bike or by foot. I would go every other day. The problem was going to be feeding him through the wintertime. At the hotel there was always a lot of vegetable waste. This I would collect up and take home in a black bag every day. This habit turned out to be a good thing in more than one way as Trevor Locke, the boss, was now becoming more of an arsehole than normal. I decided to relieve him of some of the more tasty morsels kept in the kitchen and fridges. This swag I smuggled out hidden in a bag of "vegetable waste". Barry the head chef knew what I was doing and why. He went along with it whole heartedly. In fact at break time he used to ask me "Are you eating in or taking a bit home with you?". He would then wink his eye which meant he had some goodies for me. Seafood platter, steaks, passion cake and black forest gateau. This list went on and on. We had never eaten so well. Free food day after day. In fact it got to the point that if I did not smuggle anything out I would get upset. All this under Trevor's nose. He had not got a clue. In fact one evening he was in reception at the end of my shift and he shouted across "Haven't you forgotten your black bag for the pony?" I had indeed. I had left it in the kitchen. There is more than one way to skin a cat. This free veg was all very well but as the year wore on and the grass got less then our next problem was being able to afford to buy hay. We could not really afford it so I just went out at night and stole a bale or two every week or so from various farms in the area. I carried these across the fields on my back. The furthest source was at least a two miles walk away from its intended destination. All across fields except for the last hundred yards or so. I have always said that if you cannot look after your animals properly then do not have them in the first place. That is a mantra that I have always applied right up to this day. I will carry on abiding by it as long as I keep, or look after, livestock of any sort.

Winter was now on us. A wet winter indeed. Over the years I had never known the river, where we kept the pony, to flood right out and completely cover the ground he was on. One night, after a long spell of wet weather, it absolutely chucked it down so I shot off in the car. I got as close to the paddock as I could but had to wade the last bit of the way to find Conker stranded on a little piece of high ground completely surrounded by water. I got him out on to dry ground. What to do with him now? I knew old Bren had got an open sided pole barn where he used to have a few cattle from time to time. Luckily it was vacant. He said I could put the pony in there until the river went down. Now this pony had never, ever, been under a roof in his life. Understandably he was not the happiest little horse in the world, even with hay in front of him at all time, but needs must. Over the short time of his incarceration the weight absolutely fell off him. Rarely have I seen an animal lose so much weight in such a short time. Obviously he just did not like the situation. Fortunately the river went down pretty quickly so he was able to go back home, to his ground and feel the weather on his back again. He soon got back to his old self.

Winter was now upon us and that meant snow. Not a problem but one evening it really blew up a blizzard. I remember Lin and I were having a bath at the time and we could hear the wind and snow outside. I decided we had best go and check on Conker even if only to make sure he had enough hay until morning. It was a walk of about three miles to get to him against the wind and snow. I recall I walked in front of Lin to shield her from the worst of it. We got down to the grounds only to be greeted by the sight of Conker standing under some trees with his back end shoved under the hedge as far as he could get it and resting one leg. He looked at us as if to say "What are you silly sods doing here in this weather?" So all was well. However, if we had not gone down and checked on him I would never have been able to sleep that night!

Life at the hotel was beginning to really get on my nerves. I just wanted out of the place but work is work. There was a glimmer of a chance to remove myself from there and get back to working outside again. It presented itself when the farmer who owned the paddocks where we kept the pony found himself without anyone to milk his cows especially in the mornings. He asked me if I would have the time to do it before I started work at the hotel. I jumped at the chance. All I had to do was go in and milk in the mornings and the odd afternoon if I could fit it in. Just the milking nothing else . . . lovely!! John had a decent sized herd. I cannot remember exactly how many but he was milking well in excess of a hundred cows and all in a new fangled "tri bone" parlour. A new concept but it was just a triangular herring bone. He had it put in when his father Sir Henry Plumb (who had always kept some of the best Ayrshire cattle in the country) retired. Now Sir Henry, in recent years, had decided to have what was, at the time, a rotary parlour installed. This, on the drawing board at least, entailed the cows stepping on to a rotating surface. They then had the milking machines put on them to enter. By the time they had done one full revolution they should be milked and could then step off and so on. BUT apparently the whole set up was a constant headache. The main problem being the whole thing was powered by belt driven mechanism. As soon as those belts became anything less than perfect, through wear and tear etc., then the whole thing would grind to a halt. One of the workers told me that it had got so bad they had an alarm fitted. Every time it malfunctioned this would be sounded. Whoever was around at the time had to drop everything and go and help to get it going again. I do not think this "rotary" concept ever got over its teething troubles. John told me the instant his dad retired he had this monstrosity removed and replaced by the tri-bone parlour.

Mandy had by now basically come to the end of her time at school. She decided she was going to come and help me with the cows. By the time she was fifteen years old she could milk on her own . . . to a point. She was keen and a big help to me. To fit the milking in before starting work at the hotel meant we had to be up and running with the cows by four in the morning at the latest. This was not a problem. Mandy was up and ready to go before me some mornings. Now at the time we did not have a car or bikes so it meant walking the mile or so to the farm. One morning, between three and four, we were doing just that when the police pulled up at the side of us. They quizzed us as to what we were doing wandering about at that time of the day. I told them where we were going. That laughed at this so I just told them if they did not believe me to get on the phone to Sir Henry and check right now. This ultimatum proved too much for them to get their heads round and they shoved off and left us alone. I cannot recall how long we were milking for at John's but it was a few weeks or months. I can recall that everybody said John and I would never get on with each other. I am a total non-believer and he is a devout churc-goer but we agreed never to discuss this subject and we never did. Even now we still never do. We are still friends to this day and often speak on the phone. John was well impressed with our Mandy. She had told him she would like to carry on with the cows as she got older. Now concerning this point. At that time the Terling and Lavenham herd of British Friesians were generally regarded as the best herd in the world (sadly now dispersed). John, being the son of Sir Henry, moved in the right circles and knew the right people. He revealed, one day, that he had been in touch with Terling and Lavenhams regarding Mandy and they had agreed, on his recommendation, that when she was old enough then they would give her a job and see how she went. This was a chance in a million if she was going to be serious about it. I told her that when I was her age I would have paid them just to go and lick the floor clean with my tongue. More of that later.

John eventually resolved his labour problems, so it was just the hotel again now. Then, out of nowhere, Conrad Levi (the farmer Frank had worked for and I had spent hours trailing after as a boy years earlier) wanted someone to go and lamb his flock of sheep for him. Conrad had always been affected by some sort of lung disease he had contracted from the sheep and was now in failing health. Julie, the daughter, was married and gone to Wales. The youngest son, Mervyn, was not really old enough to do an awful lot. Now sheep had never have been, and never will be, my favourite animal to work with. In my eyes when their tail drops off then their brain falls out at the same time. Most of their time seems to be spent trying to find the most economical and painless way to die. It is just the way they are. A sheep man is a sheep man and a cattle man is a cattle man. I definitely did not fall into the former category. It would be a full time job so at last I could say goodbye to Trevor Locke and his Coleshill Hotel. I knew from past experiences, as a kid, how the Levi farm worked. What to expect with lambing, sheep etc. It is not exactly brain surgery. Off we go. Mandy used to come and help whenever she wanted but like me sheep were not her favourite animal either. Jack's sheep were, as they had always been, dealer's sheep. In one door and out the other. A lot of them had come off the Welsh hills and mountains and did not know what a fence was. Basically a reasonable percentage of them were little more than woolly nut cases. They only wanted to know you where food was concerned or if they had lambs. Unless any ewe was in trouble lambing then they never came inside. Everything was done out in the fields as it always had been done. Mandy and I spent a few weeks with Jack and his sheep but both Mandy and I noticed that he had been adjusting our wages. She mentioned it to me a few times. I just told her not to worry about it I would sort it out. By the time the job came to an end old Jack had managed to "milk" a fair bit off what he owed us. I had seen it all before, off him, when I was a kid. Mandy was still wittering on about it and I just told her to forget it and I would sort it.

Now I was jobless again but not for long. I knew there was a local man called Ken Thomas who ran a little agency for relief cow men and farm workers so I got hold of him and he took me on straight away. No problem. The relief milking was not really my scene. I always said it was a good job for a kid to cut his teeth on. It was one farm one day, another farm another day but Ken gave me a regular round. A seven day week round most of the time. Most of the clients were nice enough folk. No problem at all. I, and sometimes me and Mandy, would go in and milk the cows. We would then go home again but one place we went to we stayed all day. We did everything not just the milking. The farmer's name was Dawson I think. Me and him did not really get on that well but a day's work is a day's work!! We went there one day a week for a fair while. One morning he got on my nerves and I was close to walking out from there but decided to stay for the rest of the day as we were already there. Mandy and I were sitting on the motor, having our dinner, when a big old Muscovy drake (a breed of duck) started to waddle across the yard. By now I had become a bit of a dead eye Dick with the catapult. I told her to open the window and lean back. "Smack" I got the feathery bugger straight on the side of the head. He went down like he had been shot at point blank range. Thank you Mr Dawson. The only good thing about going to the Dawson farm was that on the way home we drove past an old brick barn on the side of the road that was full of hay bales. Every week we would stash a couple in the car for the pony.

As I said we would probably go to five or six different farms a week. We used to go to this one place. Nothing to speak of but one afternoon, when we switched the electric motor on to run the milking machines in the parlour, it blew the trip switch and all the power went off. This did not happen once. It happened time after time. After several hours literally of isolating different things, one at a time, it was decided the best course to take would be to get professional help. It was by now nearly evening. The farmer and his wife fed and watered us. By the time an electrician turned up it was late evening. Not one cow had been milked but finally, after going though the whole system with a fine tooth comb, it was discovered an earwig had managed to get into the wiring. It was shorting out nothing more than a light bulb. By the time everything was sorted, and the milking done, it was well after midnight before we got home.

Luther Kelsey was another client of Ken Thomas. I had got to know Mr Kelsey during my days riding around with Don Upton in his cattle lorry. He was the area's number one cattle and sheep dealer. He kept a flying herd of dairy cattle. This meant he would buy cows in as fresh calvers, milk them for as long as they were most profitable, then sell them again. He did not have a purpose built parlour, just an old cow shed. Here you could tie so many beasts up, milk them, let them out and then get some more in. In those days the odd kicker still managed to find her way on to the market. Inevitably, because Mr Kelsey bought and sold so many milking cows, one of these kickers would end up at his place from time to time. So it turned out to be. We arrived one morning to see a few new faces in the herd. As soon as I went to put the machine on one of them "Smack"!! Thank you very much!! Now we knew why she had been sold. However, I had seen worse and been kicked much harder in the past. Mandy went to put the machine on her a few days later and this cow had not got any more receptive to the whole idea of being milked. I told Mandy to watch this cow and be careful to which she replied "I am O.K. I know what I am doing". I just thought go on then get on with it then . . . "Smack". Mandy stood up rubbed herself down and stated "It did not hurt anyway". What can you do? I was like that at her age. She would learn. I was always told as a kid there was no such thing as a fat cowman or a cowman with no scars on him somewhere.

One thing that did happen at the Kelsey place, on one occasion, was something I have never forgotten either. It was a late Autumn morning, dark, very dark. The fog so thick you literally could not see more than a few steps in front of you. At that time of the year most dairy herds would have been inside in the yards for the winter. Not here. They were still out and had the run of two or three fields adjoining each other. Really the only way to find them was to use your ears. In fog like that you might just as well have shut your eyes anyway. We did find them after a while as far away as they could get. We started to drive them home but by now Mandy and I were so disorientated we just had to follow them and hope they knew their way back. They definitely had no problem with that. They started to form a single file and passed through a gap. This was, maybe a metre (three feet) in the hedge. They then went on towards home. I was gobsmacked!! Somehow they all knew where this gap was even in almost zero visibility. They had not looked for it. They had not wandered about a bit lost. They knew exactly where this hole in the hedge was. I have never forgotten that and we think we are clever!! Most of us these days cannot go two miles down the road without a bloody Sat Nav!!

A few months went by, on the same old circuit, with the odd extra job thrown in when Ken was short of staff. He turned up, at home, one evening to say he had been asked to send a man down to Ripley near Guildford in Surrey for a couple of months. This was to get a pedigree herd of Friesians ready for a dispersal sale to be conducted by no less than Hobson's Auctioneers. Now Hobson's Auctioneers were to the dairy cattle scene what Christies and Sotherbys are to the fine art market. They knew, or at least had access to, every available official breed and milk production records of every vaguely important herd right to the very top pedigree dairy herd in the country. They had obviously had this herd submitted to them for sale. They had gone through all the relevant records etc. and decided that the job would be good enough for them to put their name to. It is just a shame that they had not visited the place and looked at what they had been asked to do. They had just accepted the job based on paper records alone. Say no more.

Over the previous few weeks Mandy had been wittering on about how Jack Levi had short changed us. To be honest it was still niggling at me as well but I had a plan to get our own back. I knew his farm like the back of my hand. After all I had spent enough time round there, with Frank, as a kid. I just kept an eye on things and knew where the ewes and lambs were being grazed. Patience has never been my strongest virtue but slowly, slowly, catches the monkey as they say. By now the lambs, although still running with their mothers, were old enough and big enough to only warrant a quick daily visit for a count and check up from a vehicle. A job which, I suppose, Jack or Conrad had been doing. The lambs had now been moved to the far end of the farm, well out of sight of the house, yard and buildings. I knew exactly how to get them across the fields without being seen especially very early in the morning. The grass on the ground where they had been grazing had seen better days. However, the adjoining field, belonging to the neighbour farm, had obviously been put aside to let the corn grown and was fenced in by large square mesh sheep netting. The mesh was just big enough for the lambs to put their heads through and graze on whatever was in their reach. The grass is always greener on the other side!! I could see they had discovered this fact. Every morning, very early, I would walk from home across the fields and lift this fence up off the ground. This was just enough for the odd lamb to be able to get out and graze away to its hearts content. Every morning I went the lambs had been put back where they belonged and the wire put back down again. This went on for a few days. Every morning the same. Time to strike now!! Off I go and got to the sheep and the fence. I made sure they saw me and what I was doing. I just lifted the fence in the usual place. Sure enough, before long, a couple of lambs had liberated themselves and were heads down grazing away in "the promised land!". I got between them and the fence, put the fence back down on to the ground and then got behind them. At this point they tried to get back but on doing so got their heads and necks stuck fast in the large square mesh. Sheep being sheep were a bit thick to say the least. The harder they tried to escape the more wedged they became. The easiest thing in the world to get hold of. I just grabbed the best looking one and held it by the leg I let the other escape back and put the fence back down. I slung my captive over my shoulders and just walked off keeping well away from any chance encountering. Even though the chance was remote I did not want to see anyone out for a very early morning stroll across the fields. I had my prize. I turned it to my advantage and Jack Levi had now got one less lamb than he thought he had. When Mandy was going on about us not being paid properly for the work we had done (lambing those ewes) I told her I would sort it. The job was sorted now and so was the outstanding pay. This episode, or at least the effect of it, would rear its head in times to come but that is not for now.

Back to the farm at Ripley in Surrey. At the time we had an old V.W. Beetle. This barely managed to get me there but it did. On arrival I almost turned straight round and went back . . . from whence I had come. What an absolute shit hole I had landed. Shit everywhere. The cows were no more than a herd of bony old rakes. Obviously Hobsons had not actually seen them in the flesh. If they had they would not have taken the sale. It came to light, instantly, that the place was owned by a business man who had bought it as an investment. He had put a manager herdsman in there and left him to it, hoping to reap the rewards, but it had all gone badly wrong as the place was about to go under. The only option was to sell the whole place and the herd. The actual owner was a nice enough man but he had bitten off more than he, or his appointed manager, could cope with. The aforementioned "head of operations" was a big, fat bloke in his mid-forties who would not walk anywhere if he could get there on his motor bike. To me that was a "No No" straight away. How can you see, hear or get the feel of an animal when you are astride a noisy machine. I was really beginning to wish I had not even bothered travelling there never mind agreeing to the job "sight unseen.". One of the first things I said to the actual owner of this whole cock up was "Do you expect me to make a silk purse out of this sow's ear". He replied "Well if you think it is too much for you then just say so". That was it. That was like a red rag to a bull to me. I agreed to stay on the agreement I would do what I thought was for the best. I would explain my reasons why as we went along. He would definitely know I had arrived and that I was going to go through the job like a knife through butter. We had an agreement and shock hands on it. That was good enough for me. This was the biggest challenge of my life so far but I would give it a go. Head on . . . No holds barred. The resident herdsman stayed on for a few days just to show me where everything was and then left for good. I was given his cottage to live in during my stay. I had been left a bed, a table, two chairs, a cooker, T.V. and a kettle . . . but what more do you need? This was not going to be a holiday. The place had a nice garden which was good because back home we had taken on an allotment. Apart from growing stuff we kept two ducks on it as well. To save Lin or Mandy having to care for them every day I took them with me. They travelled loose in the back of the Beetle.

The only other member of staff on the place was a young lad, an agricultural student who came in at weekends and whenever he was not at college. A cocky little bugger who thought he knew it all but really knew very little but he was a help. Time to get down to business. We spent days cleaning the yards, milking parlour and dairy. The cows were literally standing ankle deep in shit when they were in the yards. Once done this problem was alleviated. The parlour and dairy were so filthy the only way to get them clean was to take them to pieces bit by bit. Thoroughly clean them and then put them back together again. As long as all was functional twice a day then that was the plan. It took us two or three days to do the job. Once done everything could be kept clean on a daily basis quite easily and in no time at all. The herd was well over 120 strong but what a sad looking bunch of cows they were. So time to get into it. Who was who and who was doing or had done what. It was an officially milk and performance recorded herd so everything was down on paper, along with all the pedigrees etc. in the office. It just needed dredging through and getting to the bottom of it. I explained to the owner when sale time came he had either got to present the cows as either well in milk or dry, in calf or barren and fat. Everything giving less than 10 lb (4 kilo) of milk a day was dried off and allowed to get fat and fit at her leisure. Everything over and above that would be kept on and improved on through the parlour. They would either get to be well in milk or fit and healthy enough. That would be a good base to carry into the future. That being either to be milked again or otherwise. Looking at the records it became obvious at one time this had been a reasonably decent herd with some well bred cattle but they had been let slide almost into oblivion. A real shame. I was really beginning to feel for them and take them into my heart by now. I had decided to milk them every twelve hours. This proved to be a good move in earlier years with John Gray at Rugby. Milking would be at 3 a.m. and 3 p.m. whether the student liked it or not. He would get bought down a peg or two anyway. This job was not going to be a quick fix, at the best of times, and the sale was scheduled to be held in about three month's time. So let's get on with the job now. I had the bit between my teeth.

The boss had stuck to his word, as long as I explained the reasons why, he went along with everything. It would be to his good in the end. Previously it had been agreed that I would have every other weekend off once things were up and running. That way I could go home and the student would stay in the house while I was away. The old V.W. Beetle was struggling more than a little bit now and on its first return journey back home it just about managed to struggle its way back to Ripley before finally giving in. So time for a new motor. I just bought the first one I saw. This turned out to be an Audi 100 LS. What a motor! The best second hand car I have ever owned. We christened her Audrey. I remember she cost £300 with tax and a full M.O.T. but this turned out to be £300. well spent. Everything was going to plan. The place was clean, the cows looked a lot fitter and were milking better but more than that they were a happier bunch of girls now. About two months before the due sale date things began to get a bit more intense. It was decided the whole herd would have their feet pared and tidied up. A sub-contractor was bought in with a specialist crush that turned the cows on their side. A professional bovine chiropodist. It took him about two weeks to do the whole lot but a worthwhile job well done. They used to say in those days "No hoof, no horse". Or in our case "No hoof, no beast". The student was now on holiday from college so he was available a bit more often but at times his attitude used to get on my nerves a bit. One day, when I was milking, I had to leave the parlour and go into the office for some reason only to be greeted by the sight of this little know-all sitting in my chair with his feet on the desk, papers and milk records at liberty. He was showing off to his parents. I was not in the best humours at the time anyway. This just rubbed me up the wrong way and I went through him like a dose of salts in front of his parents. He was as good as gold after that. Sorting him out had been on the cards for a long while.

The sale was now less than a month away and there was a lot to do. As luck would have it Mandy had now left school and was keen to come down and help me see the job through. She and Lin moved down into the scantily furnished residence. I just needed a bed for Mandy and this would be our home until it was time to go. Mandy's friend had agreed to look after her pony while they were away so that was sorted. The allotment would have to look after itself. We still had "Megan" Mandy's dog so, of course, she came as well. The ducks were still part of the family and enjoying themselves in Surrey. Now was the time to get all of the paperwork, pedigrees, milk records etc. into some sort of order. Hobsons were now regularly on the phone with queries they had and vice versa concerning entering the right information into the sale catalogue. It always amazed me the amount of information they had at hand. On one occasion there was one beast that seemed to be floating about who, at that time, appeared to be unaccountable for. In those days every pedigree dairy cow had its own I.D. card which was basically a card with blank silhouettes of the animal on to which its individual marks would be filled. For the animal in question, although we had her card, there was no relevant information. The birth date, sire and dam had been filled in. The card was posted to Hobsons Head Office in London. They duly phoned back with her full pedigree, etc. They could put their hands on any paper work. That amazed me. The cows had by now all been sorted into different groups, milking, dry and in calf or barren. All that was left now, apart from daily tasks, was to tidy them all up one at a time. This meant clipping tails, back and heads (around where the horns once were) and shampooing them. A long old job indeed. A maximium of three an hour but usually only two. There was over one hundred of them to do but the three of us got stuck into the job. Every day after the morning milking and chores. Either Mandy or I would milk in the afternoon while Lin and whoever was available (including the student) would carry on as beauticians. A long drawn out old job but we got it all done in the end. The trouble was that some of them were now beginning to look a bit dirty again so a couple of days before the sale we decided to keep them all in and feed them in the buildings. These we had furnished with copious amounts of clean deep straw. They would all have a quick rinse over again and then be confined until sale day.

Mandy used to help me milk every morning. This meant her getting out of bed at 2.30 a.m. every day. One day I thought I was asking a bit much so decided to let her have a lie in that day. Wrong!! When I went home for breakfast she was still fast asleep. Lin went and woke her up. She appeared with a face like thunder. When I asked her what was wrong she bit my head off and asked me why I had not got her up and basically told me not to do that again. We had come to an agreement with her that we would pay her for all the time she worked at the end of the job. By now she had decided that she wanted another pony. It would be her money and she would do what she liked with it. She had earned it and she was a big girl now.

During the last few weeks before the sale day the next door farmer had been coming round for a bit of a sniff around. A bit of inside information with the view of buying a few cows when the time came. I thought no more about until, with only a couple of days to go, I had run out of fly spray for the milking parlour so I jumped in the motor. I drove round to his place to scrounge some off him. A fair exchange for his past privileges.

No problem, but he followed me back to the car and offered me a job. A permanent job as his herdsman. He said he had been keeping an eye on what we had been up to while we had been there and he was well impressed. He offered at least £10,000 a year plus bonuses, plus a house. That was a lot of money back then . . . a proper lot of money. I explained to him that since being down there and getting back into the grove I had started having trouble with the old back injury. With this in mind I did not want to expose myself to more wear and tear. More importantly I did not want to take on a job that I might not be able to do to the best of my abilities or expectations. This with or without Mandy's help. Anyway I had not even talked it over with her. He said he appreciated my honesty and pride. He thanked me and we left it at that. He did attend the sale and he did spend money.

The sale day came and went. Some cows made more money than expected and the odd one or two did not live up to expectations but at the end of the day the whole job was done and dusted. The boss man came round with food and wine (the latter being no good to me) and a nice cash bonus on top. What moved me the most was the young student lad. He appeared with a piece of paper feed sack he had torn off. On it he had written words to the effect of "Thanks Nick for the last few months. I have learned more in that short time than I have ever learned in college". That bought a tear to my eye I must admit. That had taken a lot for him to write. Such a nice thing. All's well that ends well. Time to put Megan, Lin, Mandy and the ducks back into Audrey and go home. Wait and see what would turn up next. Something would no doubt. Another new journey. It just depended on which way the wind blew.

Back home now and as soon as the first horse sale came round at Henley-in-Arden we were there. Mandy was after her new pony. She eventually bought a young gelding. A chestnut with a flaxen mane and tail. A pretty fine boned young fellow. Pretty enough to be a mare I always thought. She called him Copper. She was happy enough now. She had earned the money herself so be it. Things had by now got back into the old groove. One farm one day . . . another farm another day. Not my ideal way of earning a living but needs must. The only break from the regular circuit was, every so often, I would be sent down to Bedfordshire for a few days or a week at a time to look after a small herd of Dexters. The smallest breed of cows. Whilst I was there the owner was off at all the main agricultural shows competing with the best of her stock. Dexters were not my favourite breed I must say. Very small and could be like most small animals a bit full of themselves. They reminded me of circus animals. They would come into the parlour and literally jump up on the standing to be milked as if they were jumping through hoops or something. At home we decided to move out of the flat and into a post war prefab at the bottom of Coleshill. There were still a lot of them about although they had only meant to be temporary housing originally. There they were some forty odd years later. This was much better as it had a garden, back and front, and an open fireplace. I like an open fire so it was back to burning wood but there was plenty of it about. Ever since I was a kid, right up until today, I have never been without an axe. The universal tool so no problem there.

The relief milking job was beginning to become more than a bit of a grind. When I saw a job vacancy for an urban farm manager on the outskirts of Birmingham (Small Heath) I applied for it. I went for an interview and got the job. It was under the umbrella of the Princes Trust (Prince Charles). It was a year only contract but it would make a change and give me something to get my teeth into again. Holy Trinity Farm was the name of the place. It was adjoined to Holy Trinity School so whatever went on there was overseen by them. I suppose the place, including access to the playing field, was just over two and a half acres. It had a series of small paddocks, a garden area and a wildlife corner with a pond. There were a few old sheds and a lovely bank of purpose built rabbit hutches. However the place smacked of neglect and disinterest. It had a few chickens, a few ducks, a goat, a pig and a few rabbits. It was supposed to be, basically, self-supporting as far as the animals were concerned. It had its own bank account at the school but all of the wages would be paid by The Princes Trust. Most of the animal feed, at the time, was scrounged from local grocers. It literally was a case of hand to mouth but I could not see the need for this scenario. Money was available but it seemed the attitude amongst the staff was well it is just a job, it keeps me off the dole for a year so let's just bumble on. No foresight, no interest, no ambition. This place was in the right position. It was not only an educational asset it was also capable of generating a big enough income to facilitate growth. More animals, a better environment for them and the children expected to attend. It just needed to be more or less farmed in some sort of way. Not only to let the kids experience the livestock but also to show them where some of their food actually came from. These were inner city kids. The majority of them Asian, Indians,

Afghans, Pakistanis etc. For most of them their experience of the world began and ended within the boundaries of a short bus journey. The school Headmaster, his senior staff and I agreed that I would be given "free rein" to try and get this place up and running. As far as everything was concerned (excluding wages) these would be self supporting and profitable. To run it more as a very small farm rather than a kids' petting zoo. The latter would still go forward and expand but only if it could stand on its own two feet.

I was still doing milking a one day a week with a small herd about 10 miles away from home for a man called John Mathews. This was on my one day off from Holy Trinity. I liked this family and Mandy enjoyed going there with me. Keeping her on the ball ready to eventually de-camp to Terling and Lavenham herd when the time was right. We had now got a small two wheeled trailer for Audrey (the Audi) and this proved useful to me in more ways than one. Every time I went milking I would buy enough hay and straw, at cost price, from John and Ingrid. About 2 or 3 miles away was a farm that had a side-line wholesaling all forms and variations of animal feed, both domestic and agricultural, so this business was patronised. We could buy broken bags of food, end of line food etc. at very competitive prices and sometimes even free rates. Having the trailer meant we could bag up all of the muck from Mandy's ponies and take it to Holy Trinity for the garden area. I was really enjoying myself in this job.

The staff were all part time, on a year contact, for The Princes Trust. Claire and Margret were already in situ when I arrived. Claire was a young lady in her late twenties and very short in stature. Margaret was a middle aged lady who was on her second stint at the farm. I think you could work for the trust for a year, leave for a year, and then return on a new Contract. The amount of staff you could employ was not set in stone as it were. It was a way of keeping unemployment figures down after all. We decided to take on two more part timers as things were now starting to move forward. The first lad was Nigel. A lad in his late teens and an out and out punk. Obviously well educated with an interest in gardening and very handy with electrics. His job would mainly be the garden area (which also included a fairly big duck pond). He was pleased with the opportunity. Within couple of days had come up with, and put down on paper, his plans for the area under his command. After Nigel was installed he introduced a friend of his called Sally an 18 year old young lady also a bit of a punk. I recall she had a mass of blue and purple hair. She was also well educated. She came along with her boyfriend Cameron, a tallish lad, with a mop of hair crowned by an old trilby. He wore a long coat almost down to the ground. He had not come for a job. He just came along with Sally for something to do. As before another well educated young person. Nigel who now lives in Wales runs hedge laying and stone wall building courses. Sally is now a teacher and married to Cameron who is an area manager. They both live only ten miles up the road from me. We are still all friends to this day well over 30 years later. I like to keep my old friends. The next person to come along (Claire had come to the end of her contract) was Dave or David as he insisted on being called. He was a chap a bit younger than me. So tall he walked with a permanent stoop. He had long shoulder length hair and a beard. A bit Jesus looking. He lived on his own on a canal boat that he had moored up a mile or so away. He was another well-educated chap. A former teacher who had opted out. He said that the only thing that spoiled teaching was the kids .... not for you then David! So we now had me as full time with Margaret, David, Nigel and Sal all part time. The school had a porta-cabin on the farm that they would use from time to time in conjunction with the wild life area for nature lessons. These were run by a part time teacher called Mark. He always struck us as a bit of a weirdo. Put it like this I would not have trusted him around my kids. Apart from the Headmaster, an extremely nice, understanding and amiable man, the only other input from the school was in the form of Tom. A short curly haired Irish man with an attitude problem . . . say no more.

Things were looking up. I had started going to Henley-in-Arden livestock sales on a Wednesday. I had been going there on and off since my late teens. Now I would buy a few more chickens, rabbits and the odd goat. We had now got two milking nannys and we sold the milk to locals along with a few eggs. Our older hens were still managing to lay from time to time. This small growth in the amount of animals we had got had come to the notice of the local community. Before long we were being asked for more eggs than we could produce. Also the Asian community wanted old boiling hens and ducks and male goats. All to go into their food chain. No problem. Here was a chance to raise much needed funds to improve the place. We needed to fence the garden and have wooden animal housing. Any permanent building plans had to be submitted to The Princes Trust and as long as all criteria (self-generating and cash mainly) was in place then they would partially fund any new brick built building. We applied for a new permanent hand milking parlour for the goats and this was eventually installed. Getting enough eggs to supply demand was no problem. We got rid of all the old, past it, hens and replaced them with youngsters and more of them. Still demand was outstripping supply so I just bought eggs from a chicken farm near home, took them to work and sold them. In the end we were selling 300 dozen eggs a week and these supposedly from less than a couple of dozen hens. It all put money in the bank. As far as the old boiling hens were concerned then Henley sale was a great source. Quite regularly they had quantities of ex-deep litter hens. Hardly a feather on them. Some carried more meat than others but in the main you could buy them for as little as twenty pence apiece. The Asians would queue up for them back in Small Heath at 50 pence each. No more, no less. It was a good job. I had a big car and the trailer. Sometimes if I was a bit late getting to the sale they had already booked me down a few pens of these birds. I would turn up to be told "Those are yours". Garden plants were also sold on a Wednesday and we had arranged a decent sized plant stall at the farm. A mini garden centre that we replenished every week. I would take either David, Sally or Nigel with me to the sale every week just so as not to miss anything. If we had a customer for a goat we would get them one and deliver it, via Holy Trinity, to their door.

Now a regular visitor to the farm was a Sikh named Jaswan. He would visit weekly mainly to try and persuade us to grow poppies…. Opium poppies for him!! No chance mate!! He came one day, a Saturday, with a couple of his mates. There was to be a wedding and they wanted male goats for the festivities. We had only one available at the time so a deal was done on the condition I took it back in the motor to his house. No problem at all. We put it into the motor along with him and his mates. The goat with its head out of the back seat window. To get to Jaswan's house, quickly, meant driving through the centre of Birmingham along New Street and Broad Street on a busy Saturday afternoon. By now the goat was getting a bit fed up with the situation. Head stuck out of the window making as much noise as it is possible to make. A sight for sore eyes. A beat up old Audi containing me (a long black haired young man resembling some sort of mixed race person) two or three Sikhs and a very noisy goat. Jaswan was by now getting more that a little embarrassed by the whole situation. "Can you make it be quiet". He kept going on and on about it. I just turned to him and asked him if he would rather take it on the bus. If not then he should shut up and get on with it.

Another regular pair of visitors to the farm were a Rastafarian couple. Very well spoken, very quiet and polite but who, it turned out, had all of their children taken off them at birth. Indeed the lady was pregnant at the time. She had the baby but again it was taken straight off her. I never enquired why but we did all think it was strange. Anyway they wanted a goat initially to keep at home until its time came and could I deliver it please. They lived in a row of old terraced houses with a really big garden. It was painted black, red yellow and green. Everything, even the edging bricks up the side of the garden path, the fence, and stairs. The wallpaper consisted of one stripe of each colour in sequence. Everywhere you went black, red, yellow, green . . . the Rasta colours. I dropped the goat off. He had plenty of room and a shed for shelter if needed. Weeks went by before their next visit. When they turned up I asked how the goat was. To which came back the reply in a really broad Jamaican twang "Hmm – HIM eat all me plants (cannabis) him ain't come down yet". Classic . . . loved it!!

Birmingham Nature Centre was like a mini wild life park on the other side of town. I had got to know the manager there. He contacted me one day to say that they had 2 or 3 wild Barbary sheep that they wanted rid of. They needed the space. The space it turned out was like a small man-made mountain within an enclosure. I said to leave it with me and I would see what I could do. Anyway, I knew an Asian gentleman who would be keen on them but basically he just wanted their horns (some sort of ceremonial thing) because there would hardly be any meat on them anyway. They had to be Halal slaughtered. I had a deal with the man and I was to deliver them to their place of despatch. That was the easy bit. The hard bit was catching the things. Talk about wild. The only thing they could not do was fly. It took two or three of us all morning to catch them. They went up and down their mountain. Up and down the fence. Leaping 6 or 7 feet (2 metres) over our heads. In the end they got tired thankfully. We got them loaded in my trailer which I had to put a roof on specially for them and off we went. Deal done, happy customer and a few more quid for Holy Trinity Urban Farm.

We had managed to get enough cash together by now for the Princes Trust to foot the rest of the cost of having a new small brick building erected. This was solely for the purpose of milking the goats. We had now got three milking nannies. When mating time came round I managed to buy a big, and I mean big, black and white Alpine billy goat. We called him Jason. When he went up on his back legs he was a tall lump of a fellow. He stood a good 6 feet (2 metres) tall and he liked to use his head as a cudgel. When coming down from that height he could hurt more than a little bit if he managed to catch you. He was just a typical teenager. A show-off.

As I said earlier the little farm was in the Small Heath/Hay Mills area of Birmingham. The resident population were, and still are, mainly Indian, Pakistani and Afghans so the bulk of the retail premises around the place were Asian Supermarkets. Open all hours and sold everything. Mainly fruit and vegetables including a lot of exotic produce. We had gradually built up a rapport with many of these businesses by relieving them of their out of date fresh produce. We had a regular little circuit which we would go round at least once a week. If the shop was reasonably close then wheelbarrows were used to fetch the stuff back. If the distance was a bit too far we would use Audrey and the trailer. We had got to the point where we were getting too much stuff at times but any excess just went on the compost heap for the garden. I recall that one place in particular always seemed to have an abundant supply of bananas. The trouble was the only animals we had got that relished this delicacy were the ducks. They loved them but you can get too much of a good thing. Whenever we were in the proximity of the shop that always seemed to be overwhelmed with this fruit the owner, a little bald headed chap, would come out shouting "You want Bwananna. You want BWANANNA?" Sadly for him we had to pull the plug on this one. There is only so much you can do with a seemingly unending supply of bananas!!

The place was now generating a respectable amount of income, all in cash, that it became necessary to keep this fact a bit quiet. After all the farm was in a very under privileged area and at times needs must. It had become obvious over the last few months we had been having night time visitors every now and then. Nothing really serious. It just seemed like bored youngsters playing about. The place had got more popular with the local younger generation. A bit like a mini youth club at times. Most of them could be trusted but a few, just the odd one or two, did not fall into this category. It was decided that, probably, the best course of action to take was to get a guard dog. He could have the run of the place over night. It would be mine, Lin and Mandy's dog but we would lend it to the farm as long as we were connected to it. Lin and I went off to Barnes Hill Dogs' Home in Birmingham and acquired a young 18 month old dog. He looked a bit like a cross between an Irish Wolfhound and whatever else had been thrown into his creation. He was big and tall. About 37 or 38 inches (1 metre at the shoulder). He was rough haired, prick eared and sporting a sandy/fawn coloured coat. He wasn't really nasty. He was just big and noisy. We called him Groucho. He suited the job well because back in those days most Asians seemed to have an inbred fear of any dog. We built him a big kennel next to the staff room/office. He would be tied up in the day and have the free run of the place over night. As I said earlier we were now beginning to accumulate a fair bit of cash on a daily basis. This would usually be left at the school in the secretaries' office overnight. This was all very well during term time. Otherwise I had to take it home with me just to be on the safe side. On my days off it would be kept or hidden in the locked staff room the keys to which were kept on a nail in the back of Groucho's kennel. Now we thought only the staff were endowed with this knowledge but apparently this was not so because one night the cash went missing. For some reason, I know not what, Groucho had not been let loose. This meant that whoever had stolen it not only knew where it was hidden but also where the keys were kept. Above all that person was friendly with Groucho when he was tied up. In view of these facts members of staff became suspects but they all denied it. Even a lad called Floyd. More about Floyd later. I believed them. The Police were called in even if only as a visible gesture/deterrent. Of course, as usual, they were not interested. After a time and more chit chat and rumour two suspects came to light. A brother and sister about eight or nine years old. Afghani children. They had become regulars at the farm. I always remember that on one of their visits they had been eating crisps someone had given them. It turned out these crisps were smoky bacon flavour. By the time they had eaten them and found out what was supposedly contained in them … bacon …. it was too late. The little girl, especially, became absolutely distraught. Being Muslim then any form of pig meat was definite a No No. She was petrified, genuinely petrified. It took Sally a long time to explain to her, as best she could, that there was no pig meat in the crisps. Just a flavouring that tasted like bacon. In the end, with the help of her brother, she eventually calmed down. Back to the case of the missing money. The guilt must have got the better of them and allied to local know how they admitted that they were the culprits. They had been spending so much time with us they had made good friends with our guard dog and knew exactly where everything was. What to do with the little buggers now? I thought the best course of action was to take them home and confront their parents with the situation. Bad choice. Once the language barrier had been overcome and their father realised what they had done he made (as far as the kids were concerned) his authority in the family abundantly clear. He gave them (to put it nicely) a very severe physical reprimanding. He got it out of them that somehow they had managed, with the help of an acceptable adult, to open a post office account with their ill- gotten gains. They had not spent a penny of it! This impressed me. I just told their parents to forget about it now. The kids had suffered enough by their parental beating and the knowledge of the shame they had put on their family. We did not see them for a while after that but eventually they very soft footed re-appeared and no more was ever said about the matter.

I mentioned earlier a lad called Floyd. Floyd had come to work at the farm part time. A lad of about 18 years old. He had a Jamaican mother and an English father. A self confessed petty thief who was a typical poser. He had smart top of the range trainers. All of his clothes had all the right labels on them. He turned out not to be the most reliable or hardest working man ever born but he was a joy to have around. He had the biggest smile and most laughing eyes I have ever seen. I really liked the lad and he understood and respected the fact that (as far as I and the farm were concerned) he kept his hands in his pockets or he would be out. He already had a reputation as a self-confessed petty shop breaker and any deviation from that line would mean he would be in big trouble. He came to work one day not in the best of humours. Well, anyway not up to his usual jovial standards. I asked him what was wrong only to be told that in his room, at home, he had a wardrobe that he kept padlocked. This was where he stashed all of his swag until he could cash it in. Now he had a brother who operated on similar lines to Floyd. One day the brother had broken into Floyd's wardrobe and stolen all of his stolen goods .... work that one out if you can. It was a rare occurrence for young Floyd to ever get to work on time. He had probably been out all night either on the rob or on the pull. He liked indulging in the comforts offered by the opposite sex. He always called me "Boss" and never Nick. Anyway, it comes to pass he, as usual, was late for work one morning. I asked him why this was so to which he replied with words to the effect "Well boss I got chased and caught by two policewomen. They put me in the back of the car and raped me before taking me to hospital in an ambulance that they had called. The ambulance crew raped me too. That is why I am late". What could I say except just laugh. Whenever he was late he would just diffuse the situation by putting on his big grin and saying "You want a cup of tea boss?" The lad was a joy to have around.

Floyd, whenever he had a few days free, would quite often take himself off to London. Supposedly for the night life and all of its attractions. Nobody thought twice about it really. At odd times he would ask a different male member of staff and their male friends if he could borrow a copy of their Birth Certificates. Supposedly to give the impression that he was old enough to get into some of these more edgy night spots. Nigel agreed to do this, one weekend, for a small payment. Off Floyd went with relevant documentation in hand. He returned on the Monday complete with the borrowed document. No-one paid much heed to it. It was just Floyd being Floyd. It turned out that that was only half the story. His real reason for going to London was not the night life but to take part in marriages of convenience. He told us he had done it two or three times. Maybe this was why he borrowed copies of birth certificates. This would also explain how he could afford to dress himself in all the top of the range designer label clothes. For years afterwards Nigel always said he had been inadvertently married to some foreign women bidding for U.K. citizenship. That was Floyd, a real, proper, loveable rogue. That was what he was.

Back at the farm we had cultivated a bit of trade with the local pet shops for baby guinea pigs and baby rabbits. It was decided to build a four tier stack of wooden pens for the guinea pigs. It was the rule that all of the animals be locked in at night because of the area the place was in. This meant incorporating wooden shutters over the front of the rabbit and guinea pig hutches. These would be closed and padlocked during the hours of darkness. The new pens we built, because of the space available for them, had to be longer than they were wide. This jeopardized the amount of fresh air available during the time they would be shuttered off. The answer to this problem was to remove one complete side and replace it with a big sheet of the old fashioned perforated zinc that I had managed to get hold of. That would sort it. I gave this job to David, along with other jobs to do, one Wednesday, while I was off to Henley Market with Sally. On arriving back David proudly let it be known he had done the perforated zinc job along with all his other jobs. This announcement surprised me as I had given him a fair list of jobs to do. I went to look at the new improved ventilation of the guinea pig hutches. True he had put the zinc on but instead of removing the old solid side he had just nailed the latter on top of the existing wooden structure . . . Dumb and him an ex-teacher.

The livestock at Holy Trinity now included two donkeys that had been loaned by a local donkey sanctuary. We had plenty of room for them because the school playing field was, in most places, extremely well fence. Where it needed repair we now had enough funds to do just that. Like most residents of rescue centres these donkeys had an on-going problem. As usual with donkeys it was their feet. At some time in their past their hooves had become so overgrown that basically, in lay man's terms, they had been forced to walk on their ankles. This is a problem that, once it gets established, never goes away. The tendon behind the hoof becomes damaged, to such an extent, that it is almost impossible for the animal to walk on the soles of its feet again. The sanctuary had loaned us the animals but also passed on their problem.

At home, since we had been together, Lin had failed to get pregnant. As far as I could understand it was a combination of damage done to her interior lady works when having Mandy together with cervical cancer she had been diagnosed with during fertility treatment. The cancer had been successfully removed. If we were ever to have a child, between us, then it would mean going down the test tube baby path. We had gone through all the preliminaries at the local level and they had failed so we were referred to Sir Robert Winston's Clinic at Hammersmith Hospital in London. This meant driving to and fro in Audrey who was now feeling the strain. A breakdown seemed inevitable, at some point, in the near future. Not really a problem if it happened locally but halfway down the M.1. or in London was a bit of a worry. Jaswan, my Sikh friend, lent me his A.A. card every time we had to venture down to Hammersmith. His words were "If you have to use it they will never know the difference". Much to his father's disgust he had given up wearing his turban and had his hair cut. Indeed I visited him at his house one day to be shown into his best room where two children sat watching the television with their backs to the door revealing long jet black hair down to their waists. I said to him that I did not know he had girls as well as boys. He then told me the kids were not girls at all. Those were his sons that I had met many times before. They had the most beautiful hair I had ever seen on a lad. Of course it was always hidden when they were out in public.

When not at work I had decided, along with the art work that I was still fiddling with from time to time, I would like to have a go at pottery. I enlisted in a night school for a while but got bored with it. Too regimented for me so I bought my own clay and was hand making (I never could use the wheel) stuff at home. I took this to night school to get it fired in their kiln.   In the end I managed to get hold of a small domestic kiln and we had it installed in our bedroom.   No more need for night school for me. I could now go my own way and make what I wanted to make.   Learn by my own mistakes.   Over time I managed to get together a decent number of ceramics. I used mainly porcelain clay. Pieces which, when time allowed, I would sell at craft fairs etc. along with the pyrography (burning designs on wood). Another thing I had started to do.   In years gone by when my mental state was below par I had started to do a lot of pen and ink drawings. Mainly of dogs heads but basically one hair at a time. In recent years I had sold one or two through various galleries.

My contract at Holy Trinity had been extended by, I think, six months. This took a bit of negotiating with the Princes Trust but it went ahead and things went on as normal. Mandy and I were still going, once a week, to milk at Johnny Mathews place and the time was getting nearer for her to start thinking about moving out and going off to Terling and Lavenhams herd down South. She had got herself a little moped by now. This made it easier for her to get back and forth to her horses and she would be back in time to go milking. It was my day off and we were at home. She said she was just going to nip down and check the horses and she would be back. She didn't return. I went off to Johns, did the milking and came back home but Mandy had still not re-appeared.   Lin, understandably, was getting worried now. It was all before mobile phones etc. I just said to her "Not to worry. I think I know where she is. "   Over a period of time it had become noticeable that she and David had been paying a lot of attention to each other. Mandy, Lin and I had been down to his boat on the cut (canal) a few times.   This was the first place to look. I jumped in the motor and took myself off there. Lo and behold there was the young madam. Neither she nor David seemed surprised to see me in the least. I asked her what she was doing to which she replied "The same as you were doing at my age". No answer to that one was there! I explained that, fair enough, she must be free to please herself at her age but I told her Lin was worried about her and that she must come home and talk to her mom about it all. If she did not come of her own free will then I would come back and drag her back by her hair (which was now so long it reached her backside).   She had to do some talking to her Mom. We agreed that I would go and pick her up next morning and take her back home so that they could sort things out woman to woman. No problem all went well. They both seemed to have agreed what would be would be. Even though Lin was unwilling. What about her horses? This could well be the sticking point. They were now too far away for her to look after. I told her I did not want them so she must decide what to do. I gave her a week or two to sort them out. If, when the time was up, she still had not decided then I would decide for her and sell them. She did not come up with an answer so as promised I sold them. A shame really. She had not only lost her horses but she had also lost the chance of a lifetime. She had missed out on the chance of taking up the offer of the job at Terling and Lavenham. The one that John Plumb presented her with. It was her choice. A choice that in hindsight was always on the cards!!

I can recall one day Audrey the Audi had fallen ill so we had borrowed an old pick up off John Mathews. We were going up Coleshill High Street one afternoon. Lin and I in the cab, Mandy and her dog sitting in the back. I looked in the mirror and there she was face up in the air, hair blowing in the wind, a picture of freedom. I turned to Lin and said "Look at her, out there, she is never going to settle as long as she has got a hole in her bum". To this very day I do not think that she really has. At the time her Nan (Lin's Mom) was not happy about the state of things. She asked me why I had not stopped Mandy from leaving. I just asked her what was I supposed to do. Nail her feet to the floor. If she wanted to go then she would just go in the end.

David's contract at Holy Trinity came to an end. As soon as the time was up and he was free to go then that is exactly what they did. They untied the boat and were off to where ever took their fancy. David's boat was about 45 foot long (14 metres) and painted totally black. Hull, cabin, everything all black. It was called Jade. He had lived on it on his own for several years since quitting the rat face. He had originated from Buckinghamshire and he had spent most of that time with a group of like- minded folk, all on boats, around the Milton Keynes and Hemel Hempstead area. No doubt that was where they would head off to. Indeed they did but not before they came home to announce that Mandy was pregnant. No surprise. That was always going to happen. They stayed around the area for a while but moved more into the sticks away from the city and its downfalls. Good luck to them!!

I was still going to John Mathews, once a week, to milk and before going home I would go into their house for tea and cake. We were sat round the table one afternoon, doing just that, when a man whose main farm was about twenty miles away came in. This man used to rent land from various other farmers within a reasonable radius of his home place. He was one of the biggest operators for miles and miles around and he grew vast areas of corn, vegetables, potatoes, daffodils. He also kept a big flock of sheep. He was renowned for being a proper bastard who would shoot first and talk second. That was his reputation. Anyway, it seemed he rented some land close to John and Ingrid's place and as he was in the area he had decided to pop in for a chat. As soon as he appeared in the room it was plainly obvious that something or someone had upset him. He was not a happy man at all. It turned out that his home farm land came down to the canal. Apparently a fisherman had seen, during the hours of darkness, a man and woman in a black boat tied up nearby stealing one of his sheep. They put it in the boat and cleared off with it. Bloody hell!! I knew Mandy and David were in that area. It could only be them. The only all black boat around at the time. I made my excuses and left fast. Time to find them and warn them. If this maniac of a man got to them first he would make a mess of them and their boat. No questions asked. I knew roughly where they were. After a bit of searching I managed to find them. I told them to get the hell out of it and don't stop. Paint their boat any colour just not black. Within a couple of days we heard they had got to Milton Keynes and had been absorbed into David's old group of friends. I recall they painted the boat's cabin in red oxide paint. At least it was not black. That was a close one. It could have ended badly. Mandy, after a time, told me that they were hungry and had very little money. She remembered me relieving Jack Levi of one of his sheep a couple of years before. She decided to do the same thing.

Audrey had finally decided that enough was enough. She basically broke down to a degree that was not financially viable to overcome. Because she had been such a good car we decided to buy another Audi 100 L.S. A green one. I was never happy with it being green . . . Suspicious. It was O.K. but it was not the motor Audrey had been. She did her job . . . just about. At this time we really needed a reasonable, reliable, car. Lin had been accepted for infertility treatment at Hammersmith Hospital in London. This meant regular trips to and fro to accommodate this. Then disaster! We were due to be in London on the Monday but on the previous Friday the green Audi packed up. We had two motors at the time but neither of them worked. As luck would have it Lin's brother, Brian, had a very good, lifelong, friend called Richard Mills. This lad was a self-taught mechanic. A proper old-fashioned mechanic. He understood the whole job. He would rather mend something, if he could, than throw it away and replace it. He always said that some blokes were not mechanics they were fitters. Anyway, on that Saturday morning, after the green motor had given up the ghost, we managed to tow both motors to a space behind Richard's flat at the top end of Coleshill. To cut a long story short, by late Sunday night, he and Brian had managed to make one good car out of the two broken down ones. I did not then understand anything mechanical so I do not know how they did it. I can just remember going up there, late Saturday night/early Sunday morning, to see the two motors both in bits scattered all over the place. Richard had run lights on extension leads from his flat down to where they were working. This to enable them to work in the dark. By about two o'clock on Monday morning our new chariot was ready to go. Richard's place was only ten minutes away from where we lived. Unfortunately on the way home our new vehicle ground to a halt in the High street. Luckily Richard and Brian were following us just in case. It turned out that in the rush to get the motor ready for its trip to London in a few hours they had inadvertently left a wire in a position. This had got too hot and melted. Richard soon found the problem and fixed it but now for the big test. The drive to London and back but luckily I still had Jaswan's card . . . just in case.

In the meanwhile things at Holy Trinity carried on as always but now Mandy had left home a change was in the air. We had met a couple through David called Steve and Juliet and a bloke about our age called Derek. Steve or Stevie Weevie Pufty Woo as we called him was a bloke about our age. It was always a subject of debate as to whether or not he was gay. He enjoyed sewing and cake baking. He had all the mannerisms of, and spoke like, a lad who leaned the other way. Juliet on the other hand was the complete opposite. Small, wiry, loud mouthed, liked her drink and her dope etc. It turned out when David had come up from Milton Keynes he had towed these two and their boat up with him. They were both Brummies so they were, in fact, both coming home. Steve had got a job a few miles away and Juliet, well Juliet, was Juliet a total one off. Loud, brash, gobby. Hard but underneath all of this bravado she was, and still is, a person with a big heart. In the end Lin and I, especially, just regarded her as another daughter. A very wayward daughter. She would feature in our lives up until this day. Derek on the other hand was almost an old hippie or he definitely would have liked to have been anyway. A tall, lean, gangly sort of chap the same age as us. He was either extremely depressed or on a good day extremely funny. He worked in shop display and window dressing. He liked the girls but unfortunately could not stay in any form of relationship for long. By now Mandy and David had worked their way back into Birmingham. At times we would all get together for an evening/night on the canal. In the bowels of the hidden watery network that threads its way through Brum. We would have a fire and barbecue and a bit of a party. The whole new world was opening up to Lin and I so we decided to get ourselves a boat. We would give up the prefab and join in. As long as we could carry on with Lin's fertility treatment there would be no problem. It turned out that before this treatment could get down to the real nitty gritty she would need two operations to set things up. These she had in due course although it was a long protracted affair.

We had not got a lot of money but by hook or by crook we managed to get enough together to buy a little narrow boat only about thirty foot (9 metres) long. Very basic. It had no engine of its own but was powered by an outboard motor that had been installed inside the boat. A very basic, mass produced, little craft but it became home to us along with 3 or 4 dogs and, according to Juliet, a cat. Lin said he was called Santa Claus as she had him at Christmas. I cannot recall having a cat but what I can recall is a little smooth haired Jack Russell type dog. He had come into our lives after being dumped in a cardboard box one night at Holy Trinity. What a sight for sore eyes he was when he arrived on the scene. Almost totally bald and barely old enough to have his eyes open. He looked like a little pink rat. Lin took him home and got him up and running. He eventually grew his coat, pure white, except for a little bit of brown hair round his big black eyes. He looked as if he was wearing mascara. He never grew much but he made up for his lack of stature with his temperament. Nothing was too much for him to tackle. A feisty little character. A bit of a canine version of Juliet.

We kept the little boat "Gypsy Rose" until we saw advertised in the paper, one night, a seventy foot long, wooden, narrow boat for sale for £900. I rang the chap up about it and asked for details expecting at that price for it just to be a converted hull but it also had an engine. A ford tractor 40 h.p. engine. The whole boat just needed some love and attention. We agreed to go and look at it anyway. The chap who owned it worked for British Waterways and had rented a bit of ground at Lapworth off the B.W.B. He had moored and kept it here but over the years had begun to neglect and lose interest in it. He agreed if we bought it we could keep it on its mooring and live on it for as long as it took us to sort it out. We did the deal. The boat and mooring were now ours. We sold the Gypsy Rose and were now the proud owners of the Duke of Warwick. Another journey in our lives was about to begin. The mooring was perfect. It was on the opposite side of the canal to the tow path and separated from the road by a bit of woodland into which we could drive the car. Perfect because by now my tenure at Holy Trinity had finally come to an end. It meant we could spend all of our time working on the boat to get it into some sort of reasonable condition. It was perfectly liveable on but it was very sad to say the least. It had been spruced up back in the sixties in the days of chipboard and conti-board. This was before Brian, the man we bought it from, had got hold of it. This was most apparent in the surface of the cabin roof. All fifty foot (16 metres) or so of it. It looked like a field full of mole hills covered over with various layers and patches of roofing felt tar and gravel. It leaked in numerous places. This would be the first job. Let's just get the inside dry first. We decided to strip it all off, bit by bit, and replace it with heavy duty ply and new roofing felt. When we started to excavate, the said problem, it was revealed that underneath numerous layers of waterproofing was a layer of absolutely sodden conti-board. Gradually we worked our way through it piling all the old redundant material up in a big heap on the adjoining ground. We had a spell of dry weather. Me, in my wisdom, decided late one night to set fire to it. If only to get rid of all the tar and old roofing felt. I thought if we did it right, at night, then no one in the area would notice. Wrong. The fire got a good hold and fuelled by all the old tar etc. was now well underway. So much so that someone must have seen it and sent the fire brigade out. They arrived, looked at the situation, decided it was no threat to anyone and promptly went away again. By the time we had replaced the whole of the roof the boat had come up out of the water two and a half inches (6 cms). This meant the old roof must have weighed in excess of two and a half tons. That new roof must have been a weight off the old boat's back. The sides of the cabin were basically watertight and rain proof so we decided to tackle the inside. Under the front deck was a 300 gallon water tank. From this you went down steps into the lounge, followed by the kitchen, the bedroom, the shower, the toilet and finally the engine room. The most striking feature of the whole inside space was the kitchen. The walls were lined with thick slate and natural light was let in via a curved roof light the whole length of it. This roof light had probably been the most expensive part of the refurbishing the roof. The old Perspex was cracked and leaked. In those days big pieces of

Perspex were not cheap. Getting a good seal on it turned out to be more of a problem that we had anticipated but we managed to do it in the end. Brian would come down, from time to time, to see how we were getting on and he explained the reason the kitchen (which was in the middle of the boat) had been lined out with really heavy slate. This was to counter balance the weight of the water tank in the bow and the weight of the engine and the gearbox etc. in the stern. Otherwise it was feared the hull might bow in the middle. Indeed it always appeared the hull was bowed. It turned out the roof and cabin had originally been constructed on a slight bow to help it to drain away from the ever suspect sky light over the kitchen.

To do the interior meant stripping everything out and re-doing it all. Wiring, plumbing and fascias. As luck would have it Nigel from Holy Trinity loved messing about with wires and electrical things. This was all beyond me. Obviously the wiring was all 12 volt but Nigel understood this and how to do the jobs needed. When he was available I would go into Birmingham, pick him up, then take him back at the end of the day. The arrangement suited both of us. A few extra quid for him and one less headache for us. The plumbing was a totally different kettle of fish. Again, luckily, my foster sister Beryl had married a third generation plumber …… Tim. They, had by now, got two daughters Eve and Kelly and would all come down on a weekend. Over time Tim put everything right. The central heating, water pumps, all of it. By now Beryl had got married and Jackie had become a mother of a boy she called Wayne. They both still lived at home with Ma and Frank. Billy had also married and divorced and was the father of two boys Jonathan and Simon. He also had a daughter called Sarah. Billy had still not calmed down in any shape or form. Still as mad as a hatter, in a motorcycle gang, frequenting various abodes in Birmingham. Still Billy Whizz but at the time of writing he has now calmed down and has been in a stable relationship with his lady Kate for a number of years.

The plumbing in the boat was almost finished except the task of getting the water from the tank in the bow to a hot water tank in the engine room. This was heated by a stove fire. Tim managed to get hold of a second hand domestic water tank which he installed in its appropriate position and piped it to the tank in the bow. I had bought a 12 volt pump to get the water the full sixty foot (18 metres) down the length of its intended course. All done. Everything installed and piped up. Water tank filled up. Time to switch it on and give it a whirl. We sat in the lounge listening to the pump ticking away waiting for it to stop when the tank in the engine hole was full up . . . but no!! All we heard was the muffled banging and popping sound coming from that end of the boat. Tim bolted down there and shouted back "Switch the pump off". It turned out this little 12 volt pump was so powerful it had actually forced enough water somehow into the tank to actually pop out the bottom and it was sitting on a perfectly domed base. It reminded me of the little Kelly doll toys my Nan used to put in her budgie cage. So that job was back to square one!! Tim managed to replace the hot water tank and I traded in the old 12 volt pump for a less powerful one. It all worked well in the end thanks to my brother-in-law.

To finish the pretty bits inside, along with Lin's help, I thought I could manage to do this. There was also Tim to help from time to time. The supermarket B & Q had these very products on offer. Tongue and groove wall boarding at some insanely cheap price at some of its bigger stores. That was lucky timing. We struggled on with this job, alongside the re-cladding the outside, by putting ply over the top of what was already there thus achieving, by accident, a double skin. All this took time but we struggled through. I am no handy man at the best of times. My temper would wear thin. Sometimes too often. At one point Lin announced that "When we have done this I am never going to do another boat up with you". All that remained to sort out now was the engine and gearbox. This is where Lin's brother's mate Richard came into his own. This bloke absolutely, luckily for us, loved taking engines to bits. Although the engine did fire up and run, just about, he could not wait to get his hands on it. As, previously, with Nigel I would go and pick him up from his home and take him back again and bung him a few quid on top. He never seemed at ease with the work he had done or maybe he just loved what he was doing. This scenario came to light in time to come. Something trifling had gone wrong in the engine room so I went and fetched him to sort it out when he had the time. To someone, like Richard, it was less than an hour's job. Every man to his trade is what I have always said. Anyway, I fetched him over and he vanished, along with a cup of tea, down to the engine room. Lin and I must have both fallen asleep. We woke late at night and it dawned on us "Where was Richard?" I went down to see if he had fallen asleep, gone home, or whatever. I was greeted by the sight of him surrounded by bits of engine and all its relevant appendage. He was still working away under the light of a couple of 12 volt neon strips.

I asked him what was wrong. He said words to the effect "Well I started it up and it did not quite sound right so I thought I would take it to bits and have a look". Sadly the lad passed away a few years ago. A proper mechanic - R.I.P. Richards Mills – You are a star!!

The Duke of Warwick was now up and ready to go. The only thing we had not done was take it out of the water and check the hull. Being wooden it was a bit of a risk I suppose especially as it had not been moved for years. It did not seem to be letting in water. We thought for now we would give it a miss. A job for later. We went up to the middle of Birmingham to Gas Street Basin which was, and still is, the canal version of Spaghetti Junction. Steve and Juliet came up there with us although their relationship was now on the blink. Juliet had seen a little 15 foot (4-5 metre) wooden boat that she managed to get her hands on. We went round to Hockley Port. A sort of canal centre come educational experience for under privileged inner city kids. We chucked a rope on the little boat and towed it around to stay next to us. It seemed the move had unsettled its hull. This had been built using scrap wood and tongue and groove boarding. It did have a cabin that did not leak. Well it did not let in as much water as the hull. By this time my employment at Holy Trinity had run its course and we had taken Groucho to live with us. Juliet was now on her own and she spent most of her time with us. She just used her little boat "Banum" as a place to sleep. If she went out, at any time, she would leave Groucho on her boat in the cabin. Unfortunately at this point there was direct access from said cabin to underneath the little back deck. At times the dog would sleep in this space and he must have got a bit fed up at one point being left with just himself for company. He decided to liberate himself by chewing through the hull at the stern. He managed to make a hole big enough to get his head through before being discovered. Indeed I believe Juliet has a photo of her little boat with Groucho's head sticking out of the back hull. We patched Banum up as best we could and at least it was still afloat for now.

A couple of hundred yards from where we all moored and around a sharp bend was an ex- British Waterways yard that had been squatted by a man in his mid- forties. Meet Swoop as he was colloquially known. A name that, apparently, he had been tagged with whilst spending time at Her Majesty's pleasure. The story went that he would swoop on any fag or nub end that any of the other inmates dropped on the floor. I will return to this individual later in the story. Juliet was already mates with

Swoop and his right hand man a mixed race lad called Rowan. Another chap, called Phil, appeared from somewhere and was renting a little wooden sea going boat that Swoop had managed to get his hands on. This was not water tight so it was propped up on dry land in the yard. Juliet took a fancy to young Phil. A very quiet, inoffensive, little chap who had drifted around mainly in France just doing as best he could. To this day Juliet admits, in hindsight, that amongst her conquests he was the one she wished she had not let get away. I can recall Phil had a pet snake that lived with him. One day it escaped, hopefully, into the hull of the boat. It was a mad dash to try and find the thing before it got too cold or liberated itself completely. I cannot remember if it was ever found again. Probably was. We used to feed young Juliet every evening and soon she started to bring her beau along, as well, most evenings. Both Lin and I liked little Phil. In fact he used to call Lin "Auntie Lin".

Gas Street Basin, as I said earlier, is situate right in the middle of Birmingham City Centre and today is the main focal point for inner city living. Back then it was in a state of semi-dereliction waiting to be re-developed. One side of the canal was old Birmingham interspersed with pieces of land that at one time had been home to a thriving population. These were now just tidy enough to be used as public car parks. The other side was still complete with all its original buildings. One of these backed directly on to the canal and had been converted into a multi venue night club called Bobby Browns. This was O.K. but the biggest earache came on Friday and Saturday nights when all three of the venues would be in operation at the same time all playing different music. This situation soon became part of the furniture. Just a bit further up the tow path was the head- quarters for a trip boat company called Inner City Cruises. A total bodge job run by a young man called Mark. He had converted a full length steel boat into a kind of floating bar come disco. He would hire this out complete with steerer….. Rowan. He had been employed to perform this duty and they would go out, at night, for a set amount of hours. They would go so far down the cut, to a turning point, and then return. That was the plan but according to Rowan mechanical breakdowns were not uncommon on such trips. Indeed he would be sent out with enough money to get the punters back to base in a taxi. The inside of this boat had been decorated with, amongst other things, a mirror ball and plastic plants that Mark had salvaged from The Rum Runner night spot. This had recently been closed down and was in easy striking distance by canal anyway.

Amongst the little community of boat dwellers, based in the basin, was a middle aged man known as Railway Alan. He worked for British Rail and lived alone on a little boat that he had turned into a floating homage to the aforementioned Institution. The outside was painted in the various colours of different Railway Companies and adorned with railwayana as they call it these days. The inside was a revelation beyond belief. It looked like an inventor's laboratory. It was filled with a selection of belt driven wheels and pulleys that when in motion would perform various tasks. Thinking about it now I do not know what all this was for but Alan was happy. He would quite often chatter on about his experiences over the years working on the trains. One story that has always stuck in my mind was when, during one bad winter, a train had come to an emergency stop for, initially, no apparent reason. Staff were sent out to sort the problem out only to be greeted by the sight of the engine driver dead, in his seat, with a nasty wound to his chest. He was sitting behind a broken windscreen. Originally it was thought some sort of projectile had been thrown. Maybe off a bridge. It had smashed the windscreen and mortally wounded the driver but no such object was found in or near his cab. In the end it was decided by all of the relevant investigators that a large icicle must have fallen off a bridge, smashed through the windscreen, and speared this poor man in the chest.

Stephanie was also a resident alongside us. She was an extremely good looking young lady who lived, most of the time, alone on a full length wooden boat like ours called "Harlequin". Now Derek (the man we had met through Steve, Juliet and Dave) used to come and visit at various times. He was a single bloke, drove a V.W. Beetle and fancied himself with the ladies. He spent much time and energy trying to impress Stephanie but to no avail. She was hooked up with a lad who seemed to be quite involved with the drug scene at the time. Indeed her boat was raided by the Police one night but she managed to keep them out of the boat long enough for her fella to jettison all the contraband overboard. While refreshing my memory on this section of our travels I have been speaking to Juliet and she was on about how beautiful Stephanie was. Her remark was " If I had been a lesbian and Steph had been a lesbian then I would have been after her". Amongst Julie's attributes was then, and still is today, her honesty. She said it as she saw it.

Derek had managed to boat sit for somebody he knew. He turned up at Gas Street, one day, in this quite smart 50-60 foot (15-16 metres) steel boat. Apparently he had agreed to do a bit of internal tidying up on it for the owners. He had by now given up on trying to impress Stephanie and had hooked up with a young lady called Mary. We all really liked Mary. It turned out she had had a really rough childhood. I think I am right in saying she told us that her mother was "A lady of the night". She herself had gone into the work of looking after elderly people in care homes. Deep down she was as hard as nails. She had seen it all. At the time we were all basically penniless. One Saturday Lin, Derek and I decided to take our dogs (the number of which was now expanding for one reason or another) for a walk up the towpath. Whilst on this little excursion we stumbled across a briefcase. On opening it we found forty pounds of cash along with several papers etc. It must have belonged to some city gent because amongst the papers was a list of after dinner speakers and how much they charged. I remember discovering, via a document, that Jasper Carrot charged thousands of pounds to perform this task. Anyway back we went to the boats with £40 in hand. We gave Derek a few quid. The rest bought us a bit of food and tobacco. Derek had run out of cigarettes and was by now gasping for a fag. Mary, amongst others, was on our boat when we got back. The Duke of Warwick had by now become almost a community boat. Open to all and sundry. Mary had got some cigarettes so Derek was immediately on the blag but before we had gone out for a walk they had had a row so he was not in her good books. As I have said earlier Derek could be either extremely funny and witty or the exact opposite. The former state of mind worked well with the girls but on this occasion Mary was having none of it. He was being as witty and comical as he could be but she was managing to keep a straight face. So much so that he got down on his knees and offered her £1.00 for one cigarette. She just told him to fuck off. She had seen it all before. In his work Derek had been abroad a fair bit and he would try to blind his projected future girlfriends with tales of his travels but this never worked with Mary. She had obviously forgotten more about real life that he had ever known. At some time in the past she had started to take up hairdressing but given it up. One sunny Sunday afternoon she decided whoever wanted a trim she would do it for them. Sitting outside, on a lump of discarded masonry, I decided she could have a quick tidy up of my locks. They were down to my shoulders. This was fine but the top bit had got a bit out of control. She set about the job of making it look a bit more respectable. I told her just to do the top not the sides or back. This she did to the best of her limited ability. Lin says I ended up looking like Max Wall. Never mind who cared anyway!!

Derek started to do whatever he had agreed to do on the boat he was looking after. Fiddling about with one cosmetic thing or another. For some reason he decided to dismantle one of the fixtures only to discover a huge stash of cannabis hidden behind the fascia. I do not know what he did with it or anything. I was not, and am still not, into drugs or alcohol. I can get into enough trouble and have enough fun without going down that path. I remember the boat going back to its owners and dear young Mary going her own way leaving Derek lady less. We eventually lost touch with Mary which was a shame. We all loved and admired her. I quite often wonder where she ended up. Hopefully she has settled down with a good family of her own.

It was not long before Derek appeared with a new girlfriend. Another girl younger than him. A petite little thing, from Nottingham, called Sharon. Being younger than him he thought it would be in his interest to pull out all the stops on this one. He decided to ditch his ever reliable V.W. Beetle. This car was so reliable it never ever broke down. He did not even carry a spare wheel. All he did was put oil, water and fuel in it. It would go wherever, whenever. Because Sharon lived so far away, was very pretty, and so young he decided he needed a faster, more impressive, vehicle to impress this young lady. He did a deal to part exchange for some sort of M.G. Sports car. For some reason he decided he wanted the battery out of the old Beetle before he let it go. Derek had 'A' level battery knowledge. He knew where, when and how to relieve any large, usually industrial, vehicle of its battery. This, for all of us on the boats, was good because everything ran of 12 volt power. Anyway back to the point. He turned up at Gas Street, one Saturday, with a less than reliable battery. He was going to exchange this for the good one in his V.W. Now back in those days the battery compartment in the old Beetles was a kind of box with a lid on it. Well it was on his anyway. Out came the spanners. Time for the swap. We were all on our boats and we heard a bit of a bang coming from his direction. It turned out that because the battery was in a confined space a certain amount of gas or fumes, or whatever, had been able to build up around it. As he undid the terminals it just went up in a cloud of smoke taking off his eyebrows in the process. The old reliable Beetle was having the last word!!

Derek had known David, Steve and Juliet for a fair while before they came into our lives. As I said earlier Steve and Juliet were the original "odd couple". He could not seem to make up his mind whether or not he was gay or straight. She was more manly than he was. I think it just suited them both to live together. She got a roof over her head and he had got a boat sitter while he was at work. Their relationship was tempestuous to say the least. So much so Derek said he went to visit them one night and Juliet was on the towpath burning her clothes to keep warm. Steve had thrown her out again. In the years to come Steve did get married to a woman called Jan who, apparently, he had known for years.

Time went on and we all hung about the city centre. Derek had now got himself a vintage river cruiser. Only a small thing about 10-12 foot long. It had, according to him, been one of the little boats that went across to Dunkirk but that was never proven one way or another. He reckoned he was going to tart it up and re-sell it. He arrived one weekend in his new car with Sharon. He had been out and hired electric sanders. We had now got ourselves a small generator, drills etc. The trouble was Derek was not very hands on when it came to doing jobs like that. I always said that instead of using his hands to do anything he used his fingers. A bit effeminate really. He messed about with the job all weekend but did not really achieve much at all. That is the way it stayed until it eventually ended up in the big boatyard in the sky. He actually lived in a house at Sutton Coldfield right across the road from Rose, one of his ex-partners. Along with ex-partners Derek also collected large bric-a-brac. He had a bumper car he reckoned he was going to convert to roadworthy. Like his cruiser that did not happen either.

About this time he got it into his head that he wanted a real parking metre to put in his front room. This, for him, was lucky because just down the canal, a short distance from where we were all moored, were some of the old back streets which were all well adorned with examples of his desire. How to liberate one? Now that was the problem. He had tried hack saws etc. but to no avail so he decided to borrow a pair of industrial pipe cutters off my brother-in-law Tim. On a Sunday evening, after dark, he and I went down the street and very soon were able to return as the proud owners of a piece of street furniture in the shape of a parking metre. The complete thing from just above ground level. This was not good enough for him. He now decided he wanted to empty it of its cash contents. We could hear something rattling around inside. When it came to getting at it then that was a very different story. We tried hammers, chisels, screw-drivers but all to no avail. All we ended up with was an extremely disfigured artefact. After all this effort he had still got it in his head to get at the cash. To cut a long story short we reverted to the heavy stuff. The back of my axe. This was hardly a discreet method. We made a lot of noise at an unsociable hour. So much so that some sort of security guard from ATV studios, across the way, had his interest tweaked by the goings on outside our boat but he did not respond in any way. He just seemed satisfied to watch what was going on as best he could from a distance. Eventually we managed to get to the inner workings of the bloody thing and emptied the cash box onto the ground. It contained 40 pence. All that effort just to end up with a completely mangled parking metre and 20 pence each.

Since leaving Holy Trinity Sally, Cameron and Nigel kept in touch by visiting us at regular intervals while we were in town. Beryl, Tim and the girls also visited most weekends. A little "off the wall" clique was now beginning to centre itself around us and the Duke of Warwick. As it turned out this would only get bigger in the time to come. It seemed, in those days, there was an ample supply of youngsters like us about and from time to time a number of them would come our way. They would stay for a while then wander off again. It was all good fun. We did not have a lot to worry about really. We had friends and a roof over our heads but not a lot of money. Not a lot at all. We were now, basically, living off the disablement pension I had eventually been awarded after my accident at Pailton years before. It was enough as long as nothing went wrong. Juliet was now basically living with us full time. She just went to her bed at night and contributed as best she could.

Gas Street Basin was the centre of all the Birmingham Canal Navigations so over time boats of all sorts, shapes and sizes would pass through. None was so strange as "The Shed". This was just a wooden garden shed, sat inside an empty hull, and powered by an outboard motor. It was a little craft that would appear from time to time. The Shed towed a structure that was, basically, no more than a punt on top of which the owner carried a Reliant Robin Car. Apparently he would find a place that allowed him to get his motor on to dry land and vice-versa and would go about his business from there. Swoop was a regular passer-by. He had a little aluminium launch with a really oversized outboard engine attached. He liked to show off its power by, what seemed like, attempting to achieve the fastest speed obtained on an inland water way. He would come screaming around the bend from his yard, bow out of the water like a playful dolphin and creating enough wash to sink a small island. At this time he was also salvaging whatever goodies he could from the Old Rum Runner night club. This was a man who knew every inch of the Birmingham Canal Navigation like the back of his hand and this knowledge he put to good use. He knew where everything was, how long it had been there, where it had come from and where it was going. It was going into his little aluminium launch if of any use or value. Quite often, late at night, you would be aware he was out on the prowl. You would hear him come past the moorings and then return several hours later. At times he did illuminate us, sparingly, on his night time excursions. He did mention, at some time, he had found an old tunnel that had been sealed off because it was deemed unsafe. Somehow he had managed to overcome the gate problem and gained access. We always said this was where he kept some of his loot. A fascinating man. He will surface again later on in this story. It takes all sorts but everyone was happy and not hurting anybody else.

After a while Lin and I decided to take the Duke of Warwick, ourselves, and the dogs off for a wander down the cut. We headed out towards Knowle into the countryside. We had got enough diesel, dog food and gas to last for a while but not a lot so on the first night out we moored behind Birmingham University. The canal here was well wooded and it afforded direct access to the university grounds. This, as we had already noticed, was the base for most of the local Canada Geese that grazed on its lawns. Time to get a bit of meat. That night I just rode around the grounds on my bike. I thought this looked more student like than walking with a knob ended stick. On the ground near the geese I broke up some stale bread. They were used to people so were quite tame. Almost like the pigeons in town. If food was on offer then they would get really brave and come within range. It was just a case of waiting for one or two to put their heads down, to take the bread, and then despatching them with one good sharp blow to the back of the skull. Instant demise! I got a couple like this so all was well in the pantry department. I must say they were the greasiest fowl we have ever eaten.

We slowly worked our way down to Knowle, past the place where we had originally bought the boat. The top of Knowle locks was a handy place to stop for a while. We could moor up close to the water point and within walking distance of the shops etc. It was also close to Lidgates slaughter house. Over years gone by I had used this place a lot for the acquisition of dog food. In those days abattoirs were allowed to sell all the offal to anyone who wanted it. It was good cheap grub for dogs. Sheeps heads only a few pence and a whole tripe for about £1.00 according to size. Not a lot to worry about really. We spent a while there but then decided we would move through the locks and on to Warwick. No rush just a gentle wander. We moored up below the locks, tied the dogs up on the tow path, and in the evening fed them where they were. To help them get into the sheep's heads I would split each one down the middle with the axe. It was nothing out of the ordinary to us but after a while the local police were outside. Someone had walked past and seen the dog with their dinners and reported us for sheep worrying. I explained to Mr Plod where the heads had come from and told him to go and check if he did not believe us. I do not know if he did but we shifted the next morning anyway.

Luckily when we had done the boat up we had put a wood burning stove in the lounge. This was now brought into use for most of Lin's cooking. The trouble was we were now getting to the point where we had very little to cook at the best of times. This particular time was proving not to be too abundant in the old food department. By the time we had spent a few days at Warwick things were getting a bit on the wrong side of comfortable. We had no money at all and had to resort to putting icing sugar (we had some in the cupboard) in our tea and coffee. The next pay day, with the disablement giro, was not directly imminent. We moored up at the bottom of Lapworth locks. I took the dogs for a walk up the tow path only to discover a row of houses whose gardens backed down directly on to the canal. These were old fashioned post-war gardens designed to allow people to grow their own vegetables and keep chickens if they wanted to. Our luck was in. A ready-made supermarket on our doorstep and all for free. It just meant going shopping in the middle of the night that's all. It would be easier than gleaning the odd wild duck off the cut or wandering about at night with a catapult looking for a roosting pheasant as had been the need before now. We stayed around for a few days reaping the rewards of the nocturnal harvest but never too much in one place. A bit from one garden and a bit from another. I must say we ate well. Fresh veg, duck, chicken and even guinea fowl one night. Noisy devils they are. Not the easiest bird in the world to extract from its roost but enough was enough. We decided not to push our luck.

Time to wander off again. We thought we would go back through

Birmingham and up to Caggys yard in Tipton. I had been there before by road and it was a good place to stop for a while. Caggy was a complete one off character. More about this fellow later. An uneventful journey ensured. Well uneventful until we were almost in Brum. Then all of a sudden, and out of the blue, the old boat started to take in water at the back end. Not a serious amount but enough to worry about. Luckily, at this point, the bilge pump was managing to keep on top of things but it was not getting any better. We got to Gas Street and moored up. Steve and Juliet were still there and luckily for us the canal was just a bit higher than the ground we had tied up next to. Between us we managed to get enough pipes into the bottom of the hull to be able to syphon off enough water, and fast enough, to keep us afloat until we could get the boat out of the water and fix things. On inspection it was plain to see that the water was getting in through the stern gland. This is the place where the propeller shaft exits the boat. This point is usually fixed tight with the stern gland that is kept full of grease at all times thus creating a water tight seal. This had now worked itself loose somehow or another. Being a wooden boat it was more likely to leak at this point than a steel or iron hull. This is because on the latter the gland would be welded into place. While waiting to get into dry dock we contacted Richard Mills our number one mechanic go to. He came over and sussed the situation. He came to the conclusion that the Duke of Warwick was never intended to accommodate an engine because it was built and used as a butty. A butty is basically a trailer that would be towed by a boat with a motor. A bit like an extended articulated lorry but much longer. At least 140 foot (47 metres). Basically, on conversion to a motor boat it had been deemed necessary to have a prop shaft that was a good 5-6 feet (2-2 ½ metres) in length. It was only about 2 inches in diametre so Richard deduced that at a decent amount of revs this shaft began to whip. A bit like a frustrated skipping rope. Anyway, once in dry dock he would come back and dis-assemble things. He would take all the relevant parts away and try to fix the job. Juliet and Steve were on good terms with the powers that be at Hockley Port, the original home of Banum (Juliet's boat). Via these two we managed to get a slot in the dry dock on site there. We had now managed to scrape enough money together to pay for this time out of the water. Juliet left her boat at Gas Street and came along with Groucho and stayed with us for the duration of this exercise. Richard had been back and removed the prop shaft and taken it away to try and cure the problem. He, along with people he knew in the right places, had tried several cures but in the end decided the best thing to do was to weld the original shaft inside a steel tube, about 6 inches (2 ½ cms) in diametre. This they thought would stop the whip and it turned out they were right. While the boat was in dry dock it gave us a chance to look at the hull and bottom in all their glory. We were really pleasantly surprised. For its age it seemed to be reasonably solid. A few patches in places etc. It was a cheap boat to start with and we had spent money doing the cabin up before we had it out of the water. In hindsight not the best policy really but in for a penny in for a pound. The night before it came out of the water I had said to Lin, fingers crossed, the hull would not be in such a state that we may as well let it sink. Luckily that scenario was well into the future.

In time to come Caggy would reveal he knew the boat when it was a working boat. Caggy was a man in his late 60's, early 70's, and had spent his whole life on Birmingham canals. In years gone by he had his own fleet of working boats. He knew our boat had never carried loose loads. It had only ever carried wooden cases so therefore it had never been knocked about with shovels or sharp edges. He told us it used to work for a firm called G.K.N. that manufactured, amongst other things, nuts and bolts. It was lucky we had dropped on a good one. The next job to do, before it went back in the water, was to tar the hull. It had not been done for years and it looked as if it could do with a new raincoat. We had managed to get enough together to do the job. The three of us set about it and got done in good time before we were due out of the dock. Just a case of re-floating it now. To get the prop shaft out we had to take the helm (the rudder) off. This was, of course, made of wood, inch thick elm, so it weighed a fair bit. It was just a case of slotting it back into its couplings and off we go. It was so heavy we decided it would be easier to more or less float it back into place. To do this Lin and I would hold it up high enough, using rope, while Juliet stood on the fish plates. These are wooden plates fixed to the hull just above the propeller to help keep the flow of water in the right place. All was going well. Juliet was in enough water so as not to go over her wellies and Lin and I were on deck holding most of the weight. Between us we managed to re-locate the thing. Only one thing went wrong during the operation. By now I had surrendered all of my natural teeth to the rubbish bin and was now a denture wearer. Well half a denture wearer. I never could wear the bottom set. It was like having a bag of gravel in your mouth. The last time I saw them was when I had coated them in glitter and hung them on Lin's mom's Christmas tree. The top set were and are O.K. until this day.

297

During the re-location of the helm I had been leaning over the back of the boat above the water. I coughed and my teeth shot out hitting Juliet on the way down and they gracefully wafted way down to the bottom of the dock. That is where they stayed for a while anyway. They were retrieved a few days later. Job done on the boat. No more leaks and looking well in its new coat of tar.

We stopped off for a while back in Gas Street but as winter was coming we decided we would go back to Knowle for as long as the British Waterways would let us. It was out in the sticks. If and when things got a bit tight again we would be able to get on easier than in the city. We had never really been hungry in the city. I would not have known where to start if we became short of food. Out in the country it would not be such a grind. Steve and Juliet would eventually join us there. Steve towed Juliet down. He had a motorbike which he used to get to work on. When they arrived it was just a case of him mooring up, getting a train to Birmingham, and picking his bike up.

Hockley Heath would be the next stop for Lin and I. We moored up behind a pub, near to a shop and a wood yard, that we had used during our renovation days. We were not total strangers. This is always a help and raises less suspicion. After all we were not anything like the usual holidaymakers out for a jaunt on a trip boat. The roof of our boat was encumbered with all sorts of necessary bric-a-brac. We stayed a few days before moving off to Catherine-de-Barnes. A little one shop, one pub, village on a bridge over a canal. For a while we stopped close to the bridge but later moved on up a bit. Back into the sticks a bit more. I had watched pheasants coming into roost over the last few days so one or two of them would be ending up on our plates. The stop in dry dock had given our finances a bit of a smack. To help things along a bit I would go out early on my bike and follow the milkman around at a distance and relieve his customers of a few pints of milk and any other goodies he had left on their doorstep. Needs must. We got to Knowle locks, moored up and settled in for as long as we would be allowed. It was handy here, close to the shops and the slaughterhouse (for the dogs' food). From time to time we had to make the odd trip to London for Lin's treatment and we were within striking distance of the train. There was also plenty of firewood about just to top things off. We had been there a while when a little wooden boat appeared. I say boat it was really half a boat. It had a wooden hull. We had seen it floating about willy-nilly full of weeds and

The Duke of Warwick at a winter mooring near Knowle
with Vic, Juliet and Stevie

shrubs around Gas Street. It appeared that Nigel had noticed it when he had been visiting us in the basin and told his mate Vic about it. He had shown an interest in it and was asking around after it. This fact had come to Swoops notice. He immediately claimed it and sold it to Vic for £50 on the agreement that he got it out of Gas Street and out of the way. Nigel knew we had moved to Knowle so he, Vic, and a lad called John came to visit us. Another visitor was a lad with the name of Phil (who lived with his girlfriend Kerry). They lived in a converted lorry. When they were not in this country they would take it off to Portugal so we never saw a lot of them after that day. Vic had managed to find a very small outboard motor and strapped it on the back of his hull to help get it down the canal. This little motor had been designed for small deep water boats and its biggest enemy was all of the weed and rubbish in the canals. It was always getting wound up. In fact Vic revealed to us it was often easier to bow haul the boat by hand. Vic, Nigel, John, Phil and another lad Stan had been mates for years apparently. Especially Vic and Stan. They had got a little band together. John was the drummer, Stan the guitarist and Vic played or, as it turned out, strangled the harmonica. John would turn out to be the funniest lad I have ever met. Vic, to say the very least, was the scruffiest, crustiest bloke I had ever come across. A head full of greasy, tangled dread locks. His clothes, the jeans especially, held together by various coloured and textured patches that he had glued in place when needed. His plan was to remain living in Birmingham with his mate Stan until such time that he had at least constructed some sort of weatherproof cabin on his little boat. Until then he would travel to and fro on an irregular basis. This habit soon morphed into him stopping with us. At first, occasionally, for a few days but it was not long before he became our lodger. He told us he intended to do his boat up using only materials that he could either beg, find or salvage. He was really tight.

Mandy and David had wandered off down to Milton Keynes again. By now they had got themselves, amongst other things, two or three goats. Their only problem was how to move them apart when tying them up on deck. They managed to get hold of a little 'V' bottom steel boat about 20 foot (6 ½ metres) long that consisted of an empty hull, wrought iron lattice work sides and a roof. All complete with a little outboard motor. Apparently it had been built this way because, at one time, it had been used for tootling up and down selling ice creams to anyone on the canal who wanted one. We christened it "The Goat Boat". It was a good find and ideal for the job it was intended for. We did not hear from them a lot at this time except to be told that Mandy was pregnant. They spent their time during the pregnancy down around Watford and that area. She had a baby boy and they named the little fella Jax.

Things were running smoothly with our little clan at the top of Knowle locks. The weather had taken a turn for the worse and all three boats were now frozen in solid. Just at this time the B.W.B. decided we had got to be shifted. Somewhere, anywhere, as far as they were concerned. We told them that it was impossible due to the ice. We were stuck until it thawed. They left us alone for a few more days. Then one morning we could hear this cracking, banging, sound coming down the canal towards us. It turned out to be the B.W.'s, as we called them. They had sent an ice breaking boat all the way down from Birmingham. They cleared enough room for us to turn round at the top of the locks. These were still frozen solid but they told us that we could move now. We turned our boat round, first throwing a rope across to Vic, so that we could tow him. Steve and Juliet would bring up the rear. Before we set off we had to rescue Steve's cat "J.J". The silly sod had got stranded on a big piece of ice and was floating about shouting its head off. That's cats for you I suppose! I think we decided to make a dash back to Gas Street. We had enough wood for the stoves to last for a while anyway. It would be easier to sit it out up there. We would move on to the Black Country later.

On The Duke at Tipton.

If I recall correctly it was about this time that we got to know Vic's flatmate Stan. He was a very quiet, studious, sort of lad. A bit crusty but not as bad as Vic. None was a bad as Vic. What hair Stan had was red. It turned out he worked full time at a medical apparatus wholesalers in town but he never said much. In fact when he did come in our boat he would just sit, drink his tea or whatever, and basically stay quiet. A strange lad but he and Vic had known each other for years. Stan was the guitarist in their little band they had formed along with John. The latter of these three came along with his girlfriend Jackie spending more and more time with us all. John, also red headed like Stan, was the polar opposite to him. An extremely funny and humorous lad. Apparently he and Jackie had been part of the Old Goth and then New Romantic scene in earlier days. Jackie was a plump young lady with long dyed red hair. She always wore long dresses and Doc Martin boots, unlaced of course, as was the fashion apparently. Apart from John her main interest was sewing and making clothes. John had a strange habit of not smoking between the time of waking up in the morning and four in the afternoon. This was almost a religion to him. He could be gasping for a fag at 3.55 p.m. or even later but he would not light up until the allotted hour.

Steve had 3 dogs, two bitches and a dog. There were always pups about of some sort or another and we had one off him. A little male pup that was basically as thick as two short planks. Over the years we have had

Messing about on The Duke.

Kath, Dick-Dick, Lin and me on Stevie's boat: Falmers Bridge Locks, Brum.

The Duke at Falmers Bridge.

Me and Lin and in dry dock at Hockley Port.

Chrissy's boat in dry dock with David, Juliet, Chrissy JoJo de Bobo.

hundreds of dogs but he has got to be at the top of the pile in that respect. He looked like a cross between a Corgi and a Lassie Collie. Stubby legs and long bodied like a Corgi but with a long coat, ears and tail like a Lassie Collie. One of Steve's bitches had a few pups like him over time. He was a laugh. A really greedy little devil. He would eat so much his belly got so low to the ground that his manly appendage would touch the floor. He would then lie down and moan because he had given himself the guts ache. He acquired, for some bizarre reason the habit, every morning, of going into the bedroom and getting the pillows and cushions off our bed. He would bring them all into the lounge and then go up the steps that led to the front deck and lie on top of them until someone moved him. One morning he had gone, to his usual haunt, on top of the steps but he had not gone through the daily pillow routine. We were sat down in the lounge when, all of a sudden, he basically startled himself awake. He must have realised he had not done his daily task so off he trots into the bedroom. He made his usual 3 or 4 trips, back and forth, with the relevant soft furnishing. When he had fetched them all he just went back to sleep on top of the steps . . . strange little fellow but so loveable.

Vic had also got himself a dog now. A cross bred Collie bitch he called "Shroom". A yappy little devil. In the end he and his dog were our full time lodgers and stayed as such for not an inconsiderable amount of time. We charged him £5.00 a week for him and his dog with meals all round and a place to lay their heads. Juliet was now spending all of her time with us. It usually ended up with Vic towing her because she was engineless. Indeed her little floating home spent a fair percentage of its time trying to become a submarine because the hull was made only of tongue and groove board. It did not take much to create a leak. It became a regular occurrence to bail it out and patch it up. At one point it took on so much water it sank completely. When we finally got it re-floated there was actually live fish inside it. Nobody had noticed it was sinking until it was too late. It turned out a piece of ply wood had floated between it and the piling against which she was moored. A boat must have gone past. The wash caused by this had rocked Banum enough to push against the ply. This then just cut straight through the hull like a knife. We used to say the little boat spent more time under the water than on top of it.

Sally and Cameron had got in touch with us to say that they had got Groucho. He had always just wandered about from boat to boat. No more was ever thought about it. He just shared himself out. On this particular day he must have wandered off and Cameron had found him in Birmingham City Centre. Should he bring him back? Juliet had now got one of Steve's pups herself a black dog she called Shades. It was agreed that as Sally and Cameron had now got a house with a garden then he should stay with them. He did so until he passed away naturally years later.

We spent a while up Gas Street. Vic was managing to find enough material lying about, or floating about, in the canal to be getting on with his project. He was taking his time but circumstances forced this upon him. His work was meticulous. Once he had done something it stayed done but everything had to be perfect. A complete contradiction to his appearance. We all decided to make our way up to Caggys' yard at Tipton. The Duke had got a couple of weak points at the back end that needed fixing. Not big leaks but enough to give the bilge pump a job. To fix this I pinned ply wood between the struts. I then put screws through it into the hull, leaving enough room at the top to pour in hot bitumen and tar and at one point asphalt. I would get this really hot in the watering can over a fire. Pour it in behind the patch and then tighten up all of the screws. The hotter it was the better it was. At times it would actually be on fire. Juliet was helping with the job because we were also doing a few more running repairs to Banum at the same time. We had got the tar hot enough for it to be on fire. It then started to rain. We thought nothing of it until the time came to pour it into its allotted space. Red hot tar and rain water do not mix. As I was pouring the tar the rain came into contact and started to spit. Like sausages do when you put them in a frying pan. I had my arms and feet covered but not my hands and face. It was not so bad until a few drops must have got on to my face and stuck my eyelashes together. Luckily nothing hit my actual eye. Lin and Juliet managed to pick the now, cold, tar off and liberate my lashes. That could have been a lot worse and to this day Juliet goes on about the hot tar "the hotter the better" she always says.

We left Gas Street Basin behind us and spent the next couple of hours heading up to Tipton. A straight run through the centre of town and off up the main Wolverhampton line. No locks . . . just a steady pootle. Vic towed Juliet and Banum. Me, Lin and Steve just progressed under our own power. Stevie's engine started to become a bit temperamental but it got him there. We had now landed outside Caggy's yard. A new little world peculiar to itself which was good. Nothing worse than being bored!! Caggy was a chap in his mid-sixties, rotund, portly, and red faced. He wore heavy rimmed glasses, a trilby hat, black and grey, striped, evening wear trousers and, most noticeable of all, a full length bibbed waterproof apron. This he revealed hid an absolutely huge hernia. He had refused to have it treated. He spent all day, every day, in his yard either walking about chatting or sitting in his tugboat drinking tea next to the stove on cold damp days. The yard was home to a collection of folks. All different in their own way. They all lived on boats, either in the water or on hard standing. Amongst the boats were the odd riveted iron hull butty boats in various stages of deterioration. There was also one or two of the same moored up outside near the bridge. This was the canal entrance to his yard but his main asset and money earner at the time was the dry dock. He rented this out to whoever wanted to use it. On chatting to the old boy he gave us a brief C.V. of his past life. He was, apparently, the last surviving owner and operator (not much done in the operating sphere those days though). He had spent all of his life on the canals with his own fleet of working boats. That was back in the heyday of the canals, and their traffic, being in full commercial operation. He had been at the job before there were many motor driven boats about. In his prime it was nearly all horse power. On this subject he told us a lot of the horses in those days were what they called "bad vanners". In other words horses that had worked the streets and roads but had the tendency to bolt with whatever vehicle they were working with. These were the horses that usually ended up on the tow paths. As Caggy said they would not bolt for long if they were dragging one or two loaded up to 70 feet (23 metre) boats. He told us he managed to get hold of a mare at one stage that came complete with the bolting habit. He said she tried it once but decided it was too much trouble. These horses were led by hands up the tow path and she had learned that if her handler was standing on the canal side of her then she would push him in. If he was on the land side of her she would just smack him up the wall as soon as a bridge hole came up. Clever old mare!!

In years gone by we were told by an old man that knew of Caggy when he was in his prime. He was a man not to be messed with. Apparently in his earlier years he had had a head full of red curly hair and a fear of no man. Because his business was basically a one man band, the bigger commercial canal carrying companies looked down on his much smaller set up. At times they tried, for want of a better word, to bully him away from work but apparently this tactic never worked. The old boy (who

David on Caggy's tug.

Grandson Jax: dry dock, Tipton

was enlightening us on the subject) said that he was sitting in a pub one day. At one end of the bar were employees of one of the big companies and at the other end were employees of another big company. Caggy walked in, stood right between the two gaggles of men, slammed his bull whip on the bar as if to say "Here I am, what you going to do about about it" or words to that effect. Caggy told us that, even at the time we knew him, he always carried a lump of chain in his pocket just in case. The bull whip, we were told by the same chap, was, at times, used to get his workers out of bed in the morning. Caggy Stevens was a living legend on the canals of Birmingham and the Black Country. He had been featured on T.V. on the Childrens' Programme "Rosie and Jim". He was quite often interviewed on local radio by a man called Tony Butler. One of Caggy's quirks and delights was to insist on singing to anyone in his presence at any time he felt like it. "Singing" being the operative word. Basically his utterances were no more than a noise delivered in some sort of rhythm. In the past he had tried to persuade Butler, as he called him, to let him sing on the radio but to no avail. Much to the old boy's frustration. In the end, in Caggys own words, "I told that Butler if he don't let me sing then I ain't going on his programme no more".

As I said earlier the yard was home to a mish-mash of people all paying Caggy a bit of rent to stay there. Caggys right hand man, who did not live on the yard, was a single chap in his late forties called Alan. Strange sort of bloke. Very quiet and very strong. He had apparently introduced himself to Caggy by jumping off a bridge on to his tug while the old boy was going through some locks, on his own, with a windlass in his hand. Alan asked if he could help. From that day on he became a permanent piece of the furniture. There was also another Alan residing there. We called him little Alan. He lived on a little wooden boat on the hard standing. Then there was fibreglass Phil who lived on a little cruiser also on dry land. Believe it or not he was a fibre glass fabricator. Another member of this little gathering was "Old Stan". A miserable old sod with a beard and glasses. He turned out, in the end, to be more than a bit of a shit stirrer. He lived afloat in the basin on an old wooden boat. Joe was Scottish and liked his drink. He lived on and steered a trip boat that operated out of the yard. Then there was Coffee John and his wife who lived on, probably, the most respectable and well equipped vessel present at that time. The trouble was that they knew it and let everybody else know it as well. Not the most popular couple in the area. We had been there a while when a couple who knew David, Stevie Weevie and

Juliet from their days in Milton Keynes turned up on their boat. Like us they had a 70 foot wooden boat. They were on their way up north at the time so had decided to use the dry dock on their way up. Meet Chrissie and Strawney (Paul) and if I remember rightly four kids. Two older boys called Amzil and Raven. A boy a lot younger called JoJo de Bobo and a little girl as well. Chrissy was a lady, a little bit older than Lin, and looked for all the world like a red indian squaw. Long black hair, tanned skin and she always wore long dresses. Strawnie was her present beau. A lad a lot younger than her and the father of Jojo de Bobo. The other kids were the children of Chrissy's previous partner. A lad who will make an appearance in time to come called Brian. Chrissy and Strawnie stayed long enough to do what needed to be done in the dry dock and then set off again. By now our presence outside Caggys' yard had come to the notice of the B.W.B. We were getting grief and so was Caggy so time to go.

On our travels we had noticed a piece of woodland near Knowle. It was on the opposite side of the canal from the tow path between the water and a residential cul-de-sac. We had found out that many years earlier it had been a dumping ground tip for B.W.B. rubbish etc. It was now completely overgrown and left to nature. Because it had been a commercial site it even had concrete piling to moor up against. It suited us very well. It was on the right side of the canal so was no hassle to anyone using the tow path. It had a walk-through from the residential cul-de-sac the other side of which allowed access for anyone in a vehicle. The boats would be completely hidden from the houses. A short walk across the fields to Knowle for the shops etc. Near to water and all the wood in the world for the stoves. We decided this would suit us for the winter as long as we were left alone. On the way down we stopped off for a day or two in Gas Street just for a social visit. It was, at this time, that Mandy turned up with Jax. She had split up with David. That's kids for you!! Not a problem but not ideal. We went out and got a cot for the little fella. We never did find out what Mandy had got planned. Anyway we were sitting in the boat when brother-in-law Tim came to visit. He told us that David was outside across the way. Mandy went out to him. After a while she came back to say she was taking Jax and going back with David. We were not best pleased about the situation and I let them know this in no uncertain terms. In other words I went off on one at the time! Anyway off they went. David was apparently moored up near his old stomping ground near Milton Keynes (or milk and beans) as we used to call it. Lin started to worry about young Jax so she went off, on the train, just to check all was O.K. That is all that mattered really. David and Mandy were old enough to make their own mistakes and sort themselves out. You cannot live your kid's lives for them.

Upheaval over we set off for our little haven near Knowle. We arrived, me and Lin on our boat and Stevie Weevie on his boat. Juliet on her boat. Vic and his boat and Derek's waste of time cruiser project. He only visited the bloody thing when the weather was nice at the best of times. Sally and Cameron and Groucho had by now got a house in Kings Heath, Birmingham. She had a job selling tickets for charities over the phone from an office in the centre of Birmingham and a vacancy had come up there. She told Lin about it. Lin went for an interview and got the job. She had to travel by bus and train. By now the nights were drawing in so, usually, Juliet would walk across the field in her wellies to meet her in the evening. We were well settled now. Steve had made arrangements to leave his motorbike near one of the houses on the other side of the wood. Vic was working on his boat. I was cutting wood for the stoves and by now I had taken up pyrograph (burning pictures on wood). The generator allowed me to heat the burning tool up so that was O.K. Juliet was being well . . . Juliet. A happy little peaceful clan. If anyone wanted to get on the tow path side for any reason it was just a case of making a bridge by untying the bow of our boat and pushing it across to the other side. Luckily it was long enough to reach all the way across. Job done! Just a case of hoping we would be left alone for a while now.

Winter came and went. It had been an easy winter. Lin and I had made another trip to Hammersmith Hospital for more tests and treatment. In those days I.V.F. on the National Health Service was a long drawn out job. It all had to be done in London. We had been going through the programme for a couple of years. They found that Lin had got cervical cancer. This had to be removed and healed before the real business could get underway. It all took time in the eyes of the N.H.S. and rightly so. There were more important things in their remit than infertility. John, Jackie and Stan had visited us over the winter during which time John had decided he wanted to join us. When John, being John, decided he was going to do something then he threw everything at it and went full bore. In this light he had found an old, riveted, iron boat. This was sitting in a field next to the canal up near Stafford somewhere. He took himself off to look at it. Bought it and arranged to get if off the land and on to the water somehow. I think he managed to get a crane out of hours to do it. All he had to do now was to get it back down to us. With this little job on the horizon we decided we would all head up back to Tipton. This suited Lin and I because I had managed to get a job working for Swoop in his yard whenever I wanted. The railway station at Tipton was only a few hundred yards away from where we moored so it was straight into town from there. No problem. John, Vic and Jackie decided once we got there they would go up to Stafford and pull John's new boat back down, by hand, and he and Jackie would tag along with us . . . sorted.

Within a couple of days John, Jackie and Vic arrived with the new boat. It was a cut down, riveted, iron hull. No engine or gear box and just the shell of a steel cabin. They decided to put an old stove in it, wooden pallets on the floor, and throw a tarp over the whole lot. They would just do it up slowly a bit at a time. John could weld metal after a fashion. Not tidy but functional. They lived on it, as it was, along with their three dogs Ley, Shroom's sister Willow and Astral Biscuit Tin plus John's drum kit. Jackie had found herself a little cruiser, plus engine, that she emigrated to when needs dictated. All was well. A happy little band all helping each other whilst going about their own business at the same time.

Enter on the scene Dick-Dick and his girlfriend Kath. They turned up via someone who knew someone etc. Nothing really out of the ordinary. They had got a little aluminium hull of an ex-war department lifeboat. Apparently these little boats were used during the war to be dropped from planes in emergencies and after serving their purpose were just thrown away. Dick-Dick and Kath had managed to get hold of one and had decided to put a wooden cabin on it and move in. They were all tied up a couple of hundred yards up the canal from Caggys' yard. That way it would be better for the old man as far as the B.W.B. were concerned. When they did come we just told them we were waiting to go into the yard to do jobs on our boats. They let this go. Life was a lot easier on the canals in those days. More flexible and accepting unlike the mantra of today.

Time came for me to start work at Swoops yard in Birmingham. Just a quick trip on the train, a short walk and I was on the job. Now then - Swoop. Swoop was a total one off. A force of nature. A very clever self-educated man. A self-taught steel boat builder who, when you could stop him from talking and verbally illustrating about what he knew, was a competent mechanic, come engineer, come steel fabricator. As I mentioned earlier he had squatted an ex-British Waterways yard just around the corner from the main basin at Gas Street. It had a waterfront of about 100 yards (60 metres). Also a big brick built, double story residence, plus a double storey workshop big enough to get a full sized boat in and much more. A gated entrance and a cobbled access leading down to the cobbled yard and moorings. It had been lying empty and unused for a long time. It came to light when Swoop had been released from prison he was homeless, but he knew of this yard and decided to move in and see how it went. It went very well as it turned out. He said when he decided to squat the place the water was on. In fact there was a hose pipe permanently, 24 hours a day, 365 days as year, disgorging the stuff straight into the canal. The whole place, cottage, workshop and yard was all wired up for electrics. With his knowledge of such things he managed to get a live feed into the place. He took advantage of this in no uncertain terms. The workshop was packed with industrial welders and drills. Everything a man of his profession needed. There was armoured cabling . . . live armoured cabling lying all over the ground. A bit like an unfinished spider's web. The one thing that always stuck in my mind, from the first time I saw it, right up until this very minute, was a very big industrial bench drill with a heavy duty food whisk attached. This was used permanently for trying to inject some kind of useable life into very old tins of paint. This machine was never switched off. The cottage was home to the man himself. He just used the kitchen and one room. The rest of the space he filled with second hand washing machines and heaters. The heaters were installed upstairs in what he called the drying room. This ended up more like an area better suited to the rain forest. These amenities he hired out to any waif and stray that wanted to use them anytime day or night. He had converted he area above the main workshop into a space for local bands to practice. It was also to be host to what I suppose, these days, would be called some kind of illegal rave. He had done the whole of this space out with the bounty he had liberated from the Old Rum Runner night club. Loads of black drapes, artificial flowers and foliage and copious amounts of anything that glittered.

Earlier, when introducing Swoop, I explained he was a total one off and a force of nature. He was well into his martial arts and the power of the mind. In the end I was convinced, that he was convinced, he had managed to harness some sort of out of body force. This fact was

313

illustrated, perfectly, when Dick said he had been up Swoop's yard one day. Swoop had come running straight at him in some oriental martial arts pose. He stopped two or three metres away from him and Dick-Dick felt a force strong enough that it knocked him over. Whatever . . . Dick-Dick was a bit spaced out at the best of times! I think in the past he had partaken in the act of infusing various chemicals into his body. Perhaps that explained "Being knocked off my feet" experience but who knows.

Swoop was in his mid forties, not tall, very stocky and bald headed. His number one regular habit was to run down the yard first thing in the morning, totally naked, and jump straight into the canal whatever the weather. The reason he had given me a job was because he had been given the job of building a full length 70 foot (23 metre) narrow boat. To start from scratch, including everything except the actual last minute cosmetics inside. I had not got a clue about anything like this. I was just a general dog's body and gopher. We got on well together. He was a man who interested me and he paid me at the end of every day. Perfect! In his yard he kept his road vehicle. An old ambulance, totally road illegal. He used it on the Queens Highway when it became absolutely necessary to do so. Its main purpose was to drag the finished boats out of the workshop and into the yard so that they could be craned into the water. This feat was achieved by gradually, bit by bit, dragging the boat on rollers one at a time out of the shed. To do this he would let most of the air out of the back tyres, fill the old ambulance up with anything heavy, including lumps of steel, anvils, and concrete, anything that had a bit of weight to it. He would then gradually edge the craft into its desired position ready for the crane. The whole business from the very start of the build to the launch was a long drawn out affair but I enjoyed it. We got a few quid behind us again which, let's face facts, was the whole point of the exercise to start with.

During our time up and down the canal, on odd occasions, we would see a couple and their two kids with a pair (a motor boat and a butty). Full length iron hulled boats that were dripping with all and sundry. They looked a bit like a floating boot sale really. While I was at Swoops they turned up looking for a place to tie up for the night and they were accommodated. They already knew Swoop so all was well. Meet Stan the Skip, his woman Jenna and their two boys Rush and Bim. Stan was a bloke about my age. Full beard and hair down to his waist. Jenna was a petite little thing and the two boys were about 12 or 14 years old. They both wore their hair in a bun on top of their heads. These two boats were absolutely laden down with almost anything Stan thought might come in useful one day or he might be able to sell at some point. He even collected old worn out discs from electric grinders in case he could get a few more useful revolutions out of them. Apart from the two boats Stan and Jenna had an old transit van. He said if it saw a skip it would stop on its own. This is how they lived. It was a vital piece of Stan's life was this old van. He told me he had originally got the money to buy his two boats when he called on a company that manufactured aluminium window frames. They had got the contract to manufacture a considerable amount of frames for some big developer or another. It also turned out they had got their measurements wrong and had made everything the wrong size. They had chucked them all in skips out the back of the factory. As long as he took them all away pronto then he could have them all. Talk about being in the right place at the right time . . . good luck to him!! I turned up for work, one morning, and Stan showed me inside his boats. They were full of half-dead house plants that he was trying to revive into a saleable condition by keeping them warm and humid. He had borrowed a couple of Swoop's heaters from the drying room and was using his free electric. It was like walking into the hot houses at the Botanical Gardens. He had apparently found a company that rented out indoor plants to offices and the like. When those plants began to come to the end of their days they just threw them all in a skip. Stan had found them, retrieved them, and was trying to inject new life into the plants so he could sell them. As I recall it was basically a lost cause. I said earlier Stan very rarely, if ever, threw anything away that had the chance of being remotely useful or saleable. This was demonstrated perfectly one afternoon. He had got back to his boats from some jumble sale. His van was full of whatever it was full of. Jenna was helping him unload and sort things out. She found a baby, plastic, spider plant about 2 inches (5 cms) long. She asked Stan if she should throw it away to which he replied "No somebody might buy that".

Back at Tipton all was going peacefully. No hassle or anything. By now, between us all, we had managed to get a basically weatherproof little cabin on Dick-Dick and Cath's boat. It was basically no more than a floating wooden and aluminium tent but they were happy enough with it. Dick-Dick decided to call it Sane because he said that if anyone ever asked where he was he could say he was insane. At times he definitely would be pointing that way. Certainly after a night out or a night imbibing in whatever he could get hold of at the time. They were an odd couple Dick-Dick and Cath. She was very small. A good job really considering the size of their dwelling. I think she was a trainee pharmacist. He on the other hand came across as a not unintelligent young man but the worse for wear. He sported a completely unruly shock of fair hair that over time had morphed into a mass of tangled short dreadlocks. When their boat was as finished, as much as it ever would be, Cathy came back from work one Saturday evening with a fair sized 12 volt television. It was dinner time, the next day, before Dick-Dick appeared into the light of day. I asked him what he had been doing there all that time to which he replied "I've been twiddling with Cath's controls".

We were a happy little band. We kept ourselves to ourselves. Just visiting Caggys' yard for a chat and change of scenery. Everybody got on well together except for Coffee John and at times old Stan. The former thought he was a notch above everyone else and Stan was just a miserable, shit stirring, old sod. It came to pass that Vic and Coffee John had fallen out in no uncertain terms much to Vic's distaste. He had got his revenge planned. Coffee John's boat was tied up in such a position that the stove pipe came out of the roof within touching distance of the foot bridge where it was moored next to. Now Vic had a bucket loo on his boat. The contents of which he poured down the stove pipe thus liberating it into the cabin below. Nobody ever owned up to it. Coffee John and his woman went mental. He got the public health department involved. He was not a happy chappie but it bought him down a peg or two. We all denied any knowledge of it. However it had been made clear that not everyone was going to stand for his "Better than thou" attitude.

Back at Swoops yard things were trundling on. The boat he was building was coming along slowly. Everything Swoop did came along slowly. He would spend a day talking about it and an hour or two actually doing it. According to those who knew about these things, when he eventually got round to exercising his hands rather than his mouth, then whatever he did was of a very high standard. Stan, Jenna and the boys had moved on. The odd one or two people came, tied up for a few days, and then moved on again.

One afternoon there was only the two of us in the yard. All of a sudden the sound of what seemed like a small explosion emanated from the cottage and all the power went off. We dashed up to see what had happened. We were greeted by the sight of the Heath Robinson junction box he had previously installed, now looking like a 3D model of the London Underground, hanging off the wall in a smoking lump of wires, plugs, connectors, etc. At this point he began to panic. I had never seen him panic before. "Quick hide everything electrical" he shouted. Hide everything electrical. He must have been joking! The whole place thrived on being electrical. We were trying to hide all the armoured cabling by throwing tarps and anything else that would cover them over. Covering all the static drills, welders and all that sort of stuff with, amongst other things, the black drapes from his illicit night club above. "If ever they find out what has been going on here I will be locked up again" he kept saying. Luck must have been on his side because, although the power to the couple of adjacent streets had been blown out, the electricity board, on inspection, found a fault outside in the street or somewhere. They never suspected anything underhand had been happening the other side of his gates. The lucky bugger. His only problem was now he had no power. They had totally isolated the supply to the cottage and yard and deemed the place to be without a supply . . . which now indeed it was!! This was a massive problem. He relied on the electric and he had got a boat partially constructed in his workshop. Inevitably it came down to the point where he would have to hire a commercial generator. So it was, but he was not happy. It was not a cheap alternative. Something needed to be done and sharpish. In the days that followed he would pop out from time to time in his ambulance. That was a risk in itself. It must have been one of the least road-worthy or legal vehicles in town. I thought no more of it until I turned up for work one morning. The rented generator had gone and in its place was a mobile industrial generator/compressor used on building sites and road works. He had borrowed it for a while. This is where he had been going when he went off in his ambulance. He had found it on a site somewhere. Had even been back a time or two to watch it working just to make sure it was up to the job. He had then gone back at night and liberated it.

Caggy still did a few commercial jobs on the canals from time to time. These he managed perfectly well with the help of big Alan. It turned out that Alan was as strong as an ox as they say. A contract had come his way to moor a couple of his empty hulls next to a demolition site. They would fill them up with rubble and brick waste and Caggy was tasked to take it all away and get rid of it. Now the old man was averse to paying for anything that he did not need to. In his wisdom he would just take his tug up, tow the fully laden boats a few miles up the cut, and chuck everything in. In his wisdom he knew the B.W.B. would probably hire a couple of his boats to get it out again. Unloading this cargo was too much for even Alan, strong as he was, to manage on his own. John and I were recruited for a couple of nights work, along with big Alan, to shovel all the rubble over the side by hand. A handy little earner. Caggy bunged us a few quid as he used to say. So all was good.

Back at our moorings we had begun to feed and water all and sundry. This had happened slowly over time. It had started with Vic and Juliet. No problem. Vic was bunging us a fiver a week and Juliet was basically becoming almost like a daughter. We helped her and she helped us. Gradually Dick-Dick began to expect to be fed. Anyone else around at tea time also got fed. Steevie Weevie would help us out with this by baking a cake or two from time to time. It had now started to get beyond a joke. It seemed the next thing they would want would be a menu. One evening Lin decided we would go out for a meal and leave them to it. For once we did go out. We went for our tea on Steevie Weevie's boat. We had made sure that Vic and Juliet had got food but as for the rest of the assembled gang . . . they could go and whistle!! I recall Dick-Dick got a bit grumpy over it but a word in his ear soon put an end to that.

Vic had now got himself a girlfriend. She still lived in Brum and he asked if she could come and stay with us on our boat, with him, for the weekend. His project had not reached, as yet, a state suitable to impress a member of the opposite sex. Of course, we said yes it would be no problem. She turned up on the Friday evening with her one leg in plaster. She was not too mobile. She either spent her time sitting or lying down. She stayed all weekend. We fed and watered her and when Monday morning came she got up and left without even a simple "Thank You" or anything of the sort. She even went back to Birmingham on the same train as Lin. This woman never spoke to Lin and did not sit by her. This whole episode really upset us. I said to Vic "I do not care who I help but a Thank You and a show of appreciation costs nothing. Do not bring that woman back on our boat again." The most ironic thing of all was the woman's name was, of all things, Charity.

Time went on. I stayed at Swoops until all of the main work had been done on the new build boat. To witness the actual launch had to be seen to be believed. The craning into the water was straight forward enough. Getting the actual hull and cabin (he had now fitted the engine and gearbox etc.) into the right position in the yard so as to enable the crane to get near enough to it was a sight to behold. As I said earlier this is where the old ambulance came into its own. It was now a job for more than two people so all available help was roped in. It was to come out stern end first. We jacked that end up enough to get a couple of scaffold poles under it to start off with. With the ambulance filled up with as much steel, concrete and anything heavy, and its back tyres well deflated, it was now time to put the chains on and gradually ease the boat out of the shed. Little by little, bit by bit, scaffold pole by scaffold pole. It took time, sweat and a lot of hard work for the old ambulance but in the end it was out in the fresh air, strapped up, lifted and floated. No leaks. Swoop was a good welder and he had tested it to be watertight as the build went on. Job done.

John had now got his boat reasonably liveable. He had sourced an engine and gearbox and fitted that, along with help, mainly, from Vic and Jackie. He really loved his boat. Jackie still says to this day that "He loved the bloody boat more than he loved me". Indeed every evening, before he went to bed, he would go and kiss the engine goodnight before covering it over with tarp. Vic's little boat was also progressing well. He had put the cabin on and was slowly fitting it out. It took time as he only used salvage materials. Vic, if nothing else, was tight where money was concerned. In days gone by we had run out of money so I had sold my old silver rings for six or seven quid. He, on the other hand, had walked for two hours there and back, just to relieve some allotments of a few veg, plus any nettles he could find on the way, just to see us over for a day or two. He liked nettle stew. All of this, as would be revealed later, while he had got in excess of £200 in his bank.

The back end of the year was just on the horizon. We kept shifting to and fro near Caggys' yard but the B.W.B. were beginning to get on our backs. Time to shift. I thought we would go back down to Knowle. Turn all of the boats around and spend another winter tied up at the old B.W.B. tip where we had stayed before. John and Jackie moved up to Swoops yard. I had stopped my work there now and John had taken it on. I think Vic stayed in or near Gas Street so it was just us, Steevie Weevie, Juliet and Derek's bloody useless cruiser that set off. We stopped off at Gas Street for a while on the way, just to spread ourselves out a bit, before moving out into the sticks for the winter. I do not like towns at the best of times, especially in winter. No wood for stoves, no free fresh food. Just dark, grey unfriendly old factories etc. Not my scene at all. Tied up in Gas Street, it was chucking down with rain when a knock came at the door. I opened it to be greeted by the sight of a young man wearing only a pair of jeans, flip flops and no clothes on his upper half. He had no hat but was wearing a Sketchley dry cleaning bag with three holes in it for his head and arms. It turned out to be Chrissy's ex-bloke and the father of Amzil and Raven. He was looking for them for some reason or another. He had hitched and walked his way from Milton Keynes in his quest. We told him which way she, Strawnie and the kids had headed. We dried him off and warmed him with tea and a bit of food. We gave him a shirt and off he went to who knows where.

People were always turning up whether we knew them or not. I came out of the cabin, one afternoon, to find a chap asleep on the front deck. I woke him just to make sure he was O.K. I took him inside and gave him a cup of tea. He asked if he could rest a while. No problem. He lay down on the settee and went back to sleep. I was doing some job or other at the back of the boat so I just left him to it. I thought no more of it and basically forgot about him. After an hour or two it did cross my mind to go and check on him. I went into the lounge only to find him gone. He had slept, put the cushions straight on the settee and made his way off never to be seen again. Ah well, what can you do?

Derek, me and Stan the Skip.

Juliet.

Big Allan.

Derek.

I suppose it was because we had the biggest boat and because the kettle was always on. That is why Duke of Warwick was getting to be more like a community centre than our home. This situation manifested itself to the extreme one Sunday. To cut a long story short by the time tea time came around there were 21 people either in, on, or next to our boat. We went through something like 200 tea bags and 14 pints of milk. Lin had to go out and buy more sugar and milk. We used in excess of a full bottle of gas. People were everywhere. If they wanted to smoke a spliff they had to go outside. I would not have drugs or alcohol inside. This whole day was pushing things to the limit. So much so that Lin and I had to go for a walk just to have a tiff . . . what the hell can you do?

Before we moved from Tipton en-route to Knowle, Juliet, Vic, John and Jackie had noted that most of the residents of Caggy's yard being Scottish Joe, Coffee John, Old Stan and Fibreglass Phil had vacated the premises one evening. Between them they thought they would start up the trip boat that Scottish Joe was looking after. They decided to take it for a little spin about. No harm done really. Nobody was any wiser for now. After a couple of days their nocturnal escapades were noticed and Scottish Joe informed of the fact. He did no more than get the police involved resulting in Vic, because he was at the helm, being done for taking without permission or something or other like that.

322

Sally.

Ginger John.

The lovely Mary 'cutting' my hair.

Derek's old faithfull V.W. Beetle.

Derek's cruiser did not have a licence to be on the canal and the B.W.B. were giving him grief over it. They threatened to impound the thing so we said we would drag it along behind us and take it to Knowle out of the way for a while. He agreed to this. After spending a while in Gas Street we thought we would set off for our intended winter stay. We had never been bothered there in the past so it seemed as good a place as any to head for. The idea was for us all to move on Sunday morning. Derek was supposed to come along and give us a hand because our boat was the only one of the four that now had a functioning engine. This meant we now had to tow the other three in one long line. We had agreed to stop off at Catherine-de-Barnes on the Sunday night so that Steve could get to work the following morning. Even allowing for the lack of communal engine power this little trip should not have been a problem. Wrong! Sunday morning came upon us only to present us with a howling wind and an utter downpour. We ummed and arred about whether or not to go but I had agreed to get Steve and Derek's cruiser to Catherine-de-Barnes before evening. As our boat was the only one with an engine we set off. The Duke of Warwick up front, towing Steevie Weevies boat Mison de Sante, Juliet's little boat Banum and Derek's cruiser. All in all from the front of our boat to the back of the cruiser (including all the tow ropes) we measured getting on for 300 feet (90 metres). Now the one thing canal boats do not like is a strong wind. This is because they only draw below the surface of the water between 1 and 2 feet. This day had served up just that. Because the three boats behind us had no power it meant they were more difficult to steer. The easiest way to travel, in a head or side wind, is to get your bow as straight on into it. You then avoid, as far as possible, getting caught side on. This would not have been so much of a problem if we had been a boat on our own but we had a 200 foot tail (60 metres). Every time we put our nose into the wind then this tail dragged us along to the tow path. Boats are supposed to travel on the right hand side of the canal. As the tow path was on the left we decided to do the opposite, enabling, through the use of poles and bare hands, to keep everyone off the side and as free as possible. The rain and wind were relentless all day. After almost 14 hours of struggle, strife, bad tempers and everything else in that vein we eventually arrived at Catherine-de-Barnes in the late evening.

Now Derek had been conspicuous by his total absence all day long. Not a sniff of him anywhere at anytime. As we had got his boat with us he had agreed to come and help us but his presence was not forthcoming until now. We were all sat in Steve's boat. He had got his stove on and had made hot drinks for all of us. We were all sat there like a bunch of tired, bedraggled, soaked to the skin drowned rats when Derek decided to make an appearance. Cheeky devil!! When confronted by the fact that he had not turned up to help he just started rattling out one excuse after another. All totally obscure and unbelievable. I had had enough of this bullshit by now and I said something to him, I cannot recall what, and he replied with a funny sarcastic answer. That was enough for me! I stood up, grabbed him in a headlock, dragged him out of the boat by his neck, and rammed him, arse end, into a thorn hedge. That was the last we would see of him for a while. Before all of this he had said that once his boat was at the B.W.B. tip he was going to smash it up, out of the way of the B.W.B. and its impending confinement.

I think we stayed at Catherine-de-Barnes until the following weekend and then all moved on to our destination still in a 300 foot line but we got there. We all got tied up safe and sound and settled in for as long as suited . . . we hoped! Derek never showed his face at any time but we still had his bloody cruiser along with us. It therefore, basically, became our responsibility. No thank you!! As he had said he was going to get it on dry land and break it up then we decided to do it for him...We took all the deck and cabin off just leaving the hull. We thought we would get this on to the side high and dry no problem. Just a couple of ropes we thought and a bit of man power. We would flip it over and out of the water. No chance! We made several attempts and almost succeeded on more than one occasion but to no avail. Luckily Lin's brother Brian and his mate Richard the mechanic turned up for a visit. They managed to rig up enough rope and a couple of block and tackles etc. to eventually render the little craft high and dry. Enough to meet its fate.

The winter went on with no problems for anybody from anybody. Vic had now pootled his way down and re-joined us all. Little Phil and Juliet had parted company and between us all we had managed to get Steevie Weevies engine going so he was now self-propelled again. We were a happy little band all round. Five or six people and over a dozen dogs between us. Lin and I got at least six. We had now taken on a little Spaniel cross bitch we called Cressy who had been trimmed at some time in the past and had been left sporting a top knot on her head. Lovely wave coated ears and her legs looked as if she was wearing flared trousers. A typical spaniel. Always happy and always a tail wager. Thumb was still under the impression that despite his lack of size. He weighed only about 4 or 5 lbs (1 ½ or 2 kgs) he was convinced he was indestructible. So much so that whenever we got fresh sheeps' heads for them all the little devil would collect them into a heap and sit on top of them defying any other dog to try and come and get one if they dare. This was a regular habit. One day he had harvested his stash and was as usual perched on top snarling and snapping at any of the dogs that ventured too near. I picked him up and tossed him on the top of a good sized clump of brambles. He just sat there looked around and looked at me with an expression that inferred that he was grateful because he wanted to be up there anyway. The stubborn little devil.

Vic continued working on his boat and was now applying the finishing touches. He actually spent money and bought wooden trim, stain and varnish. He had made a brilliant job of it. Turned out that despite his crusty looks and tight pockets he really was a very skilful chap when it came to woodwork and the like. Well done Vic!

I had talked Lin into agreeing to sell the boat and to go up the road with horses and a wagon. I had been out poaching pheasant one night and whilst out had been joined by a black and white cob horse who just seemed to want a bit of fuss. On my return to the boat Juliet was in with Lin and I just said words to the effect "Do you fancy going up the road with horses?" Lin eventually said we might as well give it a go but we would have to sell the boat first. I put it about that if anyone sold the Duke of Warwick for us then we would give them 10 per cent of what we got for it. In the end this proposition reached Dick-Dick and Cath's ears. They knew a young couple of teachers who were looking to leave their bricks and mortar, move on to the canals to live, and work from a permanent mooring nearer the city. Over time they came and visited a couple of times. They liked what they saw on the inside but, of course, wanted to see the boat out of the water and have the hull looked at. No problem. We contacted Caggy, booked it into his dry dock, and got him to give it a good going over . . . hull wise. So off we all set again to where we had come months before. Vic decided to sell his little boat as he had found a bigger one up in Runcorn, Cheshire. He fancied taking this on as another project.

In the mean-time he, John and Jackie went for a trip around Alvechurch. Vic had now got a new girlfriend, a red headed girl called Grace. A pretty

327

little thing. Talk about Beauty and the Beast. Lin and I went to visit them in the motor one evening. We lit a fire outside their boat and, by hook and by crook and many devious moves, we actually managed to get his long suffering, much patched, and severely unwashed jeans off his body and put them on the fire. They were in such a poor state they put the fire out anyway. At least he was now forced to wear fresh garments on his lower body. Vic and washing were not the best of friends at this time. At times he would dye his beard along with, according to him, his pubes. From time to time he had to wash his hair because he would get head lice. On one such occasion he decided he would get rid of his little cranial visitors by treating his head and hair with white spirits He only ever did that once. It shifted the lice alright but it also caused severe aggravation to his scalp. On the night we visited them and relieved Vic of his beloved Jeans an old Asian chap had also turned up, from somewhere, and was hanging around with them. He was, or seemed to want to be, a bit of a Sharman. Dressed in old Pakistani type clothes, wearing a hood, prancing about bare footed and chanting. When not doing this he would make birds out of grass stems. I have always remembered his grass birds but we only met him once. Vic managed to sell his boat to someone down Milton Keynes way. He delivered it down there and came back with his money clenched tightly in his fist. For safe keeping he asked Lin to look after it for him while he went off and did whatever he had to do.

Time went on, nothing much going on except that Dick-Dick's friends had been to look at our boat and liked it. Of course they would not commit to anything until they had seen it out of the water and had a good look at the hull. We had arranged to take it back up to Caggys yard. If he said it was sound they would buy the boat once they had sold their house in Birmingham. Not a problem because if all was good then we would need time to sort ourselves out anyway. Horse drawn wagons were not the easiest things to find in those days. We had arranged a date for the inspection so we, Steevie Weevie and Juliet de-camped back up to Tipton. We got the boat into Caggys' dry dock. At the first weekend our potential customers came and met up with us there. Boat out of the water and time for Caggys' verdict. We all sat inside the boat whilst the old man descended into his dry dock armed with a 7lb (3 kg) lump hammer and a heavy duty screwdriver. From inside it sounded as if he was trying to beat and gouge his way through the hull with his chosen tools of torture. After a while he declared it fit for purpose. No real weak spots or anything to worry about in the short term at least. A deal was done. We agreed we would give the Old Duke a fresh coat of bitumen. Shook hands on the job and the deal done. Just a case of waiting for the couple to sell their property. They had been assured by the estate agents this would be no problem.

Time for us to find a wagon or two and a couple of decent cob horses. Vic had now re-emerged and come to collect his money. Lin decided she would wind him up a bit and told him that while he had been away we had had an emergency and had to borrow some of his cash. Now as far as money is concerned Vic, by his own admission to this very day, is ultra tight. As tight as anyone I have ever known. Now being under the impression that his stash of cash had now shrunk Lin said the colour just drained from his face. He went white with shock. She let this little farce run for a few minutes before she told him that she was just winding him up. He was reunited with the object of his desires…. …his money. As mentioned earlier he had found himself another boat up in Runcorn but it had no engine. He decided that if I took him and Jenna (Stan the Skips wife) up there in our motor then they would bow haul/hitch a tow back down with it. Not a short journey at the best of times. Never mind taking the job on as they intended.   Both of them, and anything they thought they might need for the journey, were piled into our motor. I drove them up to what was known, back then, as the wooden board yard in Cheshire.   It was basically a similar version of Swoops yard in Birmingham but more legal and more orientated towards wooden craft. I dropped them off with all their stuff, wished them good luck, and left them to it.

Time to sort ourselves out now. I thought the best thing to do was to stay in the area until our exchange took place. The Black Country is home to a lot of families that are basically traveller/semi traveller bred folk. A lot of horse drawn carts. Basically the old fashioned rag and bone men. There would be a coloured horse tethered out on most vacant pieces of ground that could support the growth of even the slightest hint of grass. Good old fashioned half legged types. In fact they used to say if a horse could work the Black Country it could go anywhere in the country due to the abundance of short, sharp, hills around the area. I found out later in years gone by it was thought the border with Wales began around the Dudley area and west of it. During the time we had been tied up in the area I had taken the dogs out for a run across some of these council owned grounds. The council suffered the fact this grassy ground was a magnet for anyone in the area with a horse. The whole horse tethering ethos was suffered by but not encouraged by officialdom in the area. So much so that Tipton, at this time, even had its own horse pound into which any stray animals would be shut up for the duration of their excusions until re-claimed by their owners. Joe was a bloke I had befriended on my dog walks. He and his brother were tatters come horse dealers like the majority of this small area around Tipton, Great Bridge etc. Everything revolved around the horse and whatever vehicle it could pull. I recall there was a small council estate tucked away near Tipton that was the nucleus of this way of life. It had got the nickname of "The Lost City" because local folk lore said if any stranger dared to venture in there then they might become lost. Through my acquaintance with Joe and his brother I had met one or two of the lads down there. Horses were everywhere, stabled in back gardens and grazed on any piece of green that was suitable. For some reason I had gone up there, one day, to see a chap I had met called Jackie Brookes. I pulled up outside his place to find him with a hose pipe running from his back kitchen, through his house and out of the front door. He was washing his horse down on the front lawn. In this area (well at least with all of the people I was interested in) if it was not a horse, a dog, a bird, a chicken, scrap metal or a horse drawn vehicle then no one was really interested in it. Joe lived in a council house with his family and like a lot of others he had built stables in his back garden. His wife Angie was a typical Black Country woman. Built like a brick shit house and would fight with anyone. There are no airs and graces anywhere in this part of the Midlands. It is what it is! You say what you think regardless of the outcome. It is either black or white, right or wrong, and no messing about.

Angie reminded me of a woman we had met months and months before. We had been tied up on the canal when we needed to go and fill up with water. However the water level had dropped overnight and the Old Duke was sitting on the bottom in the mud stuck fast. Lin and I were the only people home. We had struggled to try and pole, rock and power our way free but it was no use. We had got three or four car jacks knocking about and we were tied up against concrete piling. I thought we might be able to use the jacks and the engine to gradually ease ourselves free but it was not really working. Help was at hand! A young couple were going past on their boat and offered to tow us free as soon as we had a rope between the two boats. This broad Black Country lad just touched the throttle on his boat and we were floating again. The ease at which this had been achieved made me wonder what engine he had got. He invited me on board and introduced me to his wife. She was sitting on the bed which was built on top of the water tank in the cabin. She was a young lady of ample proportions. He then proceeded to show me his engine. He lifted up the back deck to reveal a six cylinder ex-lifeboat engine. A huge great thing. No wonder he had pulled our boat off so easily. I mentioned the size of it to him to which he replied with, his bulky wife perched on the bed a few feet away, "Arr well if youm goin' to 'ave one 'ave a bloody big un that's what I say". In his broad Black Country way. It turned out he had built the boat himself by welding steel round an old wooden hull and then burning the wood out leaving him with the steel replacement.

Back to the matter in hand. Time to find a wagon or two. The horses would not be such a problem. I had already agreed, in words, to buy one of Joe's horses when the time came. A cob about 15 hands. A good strong amiable sort. I am not, nor never have been the world's number one horse fan but I could recognise a good sort when I saw one. That little deal was on the back burner. I had managed to find a man in Wales who renovated old horse drawn living wagons so we went to visit him. A man called Mervyn Jones at Hollywell. He did the woodwork and his wife did the painting. He had got a nice little square bowed wagon there. It seemed pretty sound. The wooden wheels were all good, that was the main thing and a nice paint job. What really took our eye was the little wood burning stove/oven. It was a pretty little thing. Small fire box, small oven. Just about big enough to squeeze a small chicken in and two hot plates. It had been enamelled in white with enamel images of violets and ribbons. Apparently it had been originally commissioned by a very rich man for his daughter's Wendy house. How the other half live!! We explained our situation to Mervyn Jones. As with the horse we pencilled in the deal and left it at that for now. Originally we thought we would get two wagons and two horses even if we only kept the one wagon. An extra horse was no problem. The idea of getting two wagons was we would live in one and use the other as a bit of a travelling art gallery. By now I had got enough art work and ceramics for sale to give it a go. Anyway, something would turn up. It always had in the past so why not now! Our search for another driving horse led us back to Henley-in-Arden horse sales. One month, when we attended the sales, there was nothing there for us but we got talking to a woman who dealt in horses and had a riding school near Warwick. She reckoned she had got an animal there that might suit us so we went to have a look. I recall when we arrived in her yard work was on going. This involved a compressor and a pneumatic drill. Anyway she had been giving us the usual dealer's yarn. (We had used it ourselves often enough in the past). This horse was bomb proof. On hearing this I immediately replied, that in my eyes, the only bomb proof horse was a dead one. Off she went to bring him into the field. As she got in the yard I asked her to walk him past the compressor and, by now, the active pneumatic drill. She did so and he never even flinched. Apparently he had originally come to her with four messed up feet. It seemed he had been neglected and his hooves had actually grown over his shoes but he moved well enough now. The old saying goes No hoof, No horse but he was O.K. His name was Joe. A gelding cob about 15 hands high. A good long tail and mane and plenty of feather on his legs. He gave the impression you could knock a nail in his head and he would not move. We were told that once he was in the shafts he was a different animal. His idea of life, at work, was to get where ever you were going as fast as possible to get back out of the shafts again. We liked the horse and despite him having a roman nose he was sound enough and moved well. We decided to buy him on the same agreement as the Cobb in the Black Country and the wagon in Wales.

Now just a case of waiting for the cash from the sale of the Duke of Warwick. We had been in touch with the intended new owners and they had sold their house. They were just waiting for it all to go through. We had sold the boat for ten thousand pounds. Apart from it being our home we had made six thousand pounds profit from it after the costs of purchase and renovations. Dick-Dick was eagerly awaiting his 10% as agreed. Lin was looking forward to new horizons and all that went along with it. Me not so much in hindsight. We had agreed with John and Ingrid Mathews that while we were getting sorted out with wagons, horses, tack, etc. we could park up in their yard and give them a hand whenever they needed it. I would still milk the cows whenever necessary. We would just generally help around the place in times of need. Summer time was on us by now so there was always some kind of help needed. Although I was still in receipt of a small disability allowance I decided to register with The Small Business Scheme out of which the government gave you a weekly allowance of £40. a year. This was, supposedly, to help subsidize the setting up of a new first time enterprise. This would come in handy because Lin's infertility treatment was now almost in its final few stages. The travelling to and fro to London was not cheap. This was the only slight niggle I had in the back of my mind about going horse drawn. We would have to be available at extremely hard and fast set times. As was my usual mantra "It will be alright in the morning" with fingers crossed behind my back. We were not young but we were not old either.

Looking back on things today in a way I was selfish to a point. I just presumed whatever bright idea came into my mind then Lin would go along with it. She always did . . . bless her!! True to their word our customers for the boat had come up with the cash and were ready to move. We agreed, before we vacated the Duke, they would give us enough money to go off to Wales and fetch the square wagon. We would drop it off in John and Ingrids's yard so that at least we had got somewhere to move to. They would then pay us the rest on completion of this task. Donald Upton borrowed one of his son's motors and a trailer and off we went to Wales. We picked up the wagon and dropped it off ready to move into in a few days. The last night before we left the Duke we spent on Juliet's boat so the new owners could get settled in. All of the money had been paid. Dick-Dick had got his 10%. We had paid for the two horses as well. The one we had bought from Joe at Tipton was a good sound sort of an animal named George. Just the slightest bit taller than his new mate Joe but a completely different character. He had a twinkle in his eye and liked a bit of mischief from time to time.

We had got ourselves the square wagon, two horses, 6 dogs, Thumb, Brains, Cressy, Toby and a ginger coloured dog we had got from the rescue centre a while earlier. A lovely happy dog. A bit bigger than a whippet and probably the best hunting dog we had ever had. If he thought there was a rabbit down a hole then he would dig, literally, for however long it took until he was proved right or wrong. On the odd occasion he would come home with bleeding front paws. Very rarely, if he thought he had a chance, he would climb 6 feet (2 metres) up a tree after a squirrel. Another ex-inhabitant of a Dogs Home was Rooky. A black dog we had originally got for Mandy. A bit bigger than Toby but a lot finer built. We used to nickname him Brian Ferry. You could just imagine him in a quilted smoking jacket, cummerbund around his waist puffing on a tortoiseshell cigarette holder. A cool dude! Mr Suave! Although he had only been blessed with one testicle he certainly knew how to use it and did so whenever the chance arose. If such a chance did not present itself then he would take himself off, sometimes for days on end, looking for

George.

Joe.

A couple of our old wagons.

Up the road.

Lin, Juliet, me and the dogs Thumb and Cress somewhere in Leicestershire.

Eve, Kelly and Wayne. Neices and nephew.

On the move.

Juliet, Wayne, me and George

Getting ready to move.

a fair maiden. Everywhere he went he left pups behind. Grubby was a half-bred Staffordshire Bull Terrier. A brindle (dapple colour) with a white chest and blaze. He too came from the Dogs Home. When we got him he was so full of puppy fat that when he got excited his whole body seemed to wobble. Hence the name Grub or Grubby. He was a typical Bull Terrier. Faithful to the extreme. He followed me everywhere. To the toilet, into another space, onto another chair. Everywhere. So much so he would become a nuisance because sometimes I would trip over him. Apart from me his main love in life was a car. Any car, anytime. If the chance to get in a car did not present itself then if you were not careful he would get on a bus. He was never on a lead. He would just walk right behind me anywhere. Through the centre of Birmingham or out in the sticks. At least once when we were in Gas Street he vanished. Either to be brought back by the owner of the car he had got into or he would end up as a stray in the Dogs Home. If he saw a vehicle with an open window he would be in there in no time. On more than one occasion, when out with me in a busy place, and a bus stopped (within a few feet of us) and the door opened he would be in there. We were lucky we never lost him completely. He just loved vehicles.

Apart from the dogs we also had a cat. A sort of half Persian type. Black in colour and very un-cat like. We called him Santa. He acted more like a dog really. We had him a fair while. Over time he learned what to do if we moved while he was out and about. If he waited at the last place we had been then we would come back and fetch him. He was Lin's cat. She liked and still does like cats. I put them more on a par with horses. Take them or leave them. We got him for her one Christmas from a pet stall in the Bull Ring. Hence his name. He would travel with us for years to come as it turned out.

Just one thing to do now. Find another wagon. Then we could be off. The only worry, that was still in the back of my mind, was Lin's fertility treatment but I was sure we would work something out. My old Mantra– it will be alright in the morning – fingers crossed. In a tight knit community word travel fast. It was not long before we were introduced to a chap from Chesterfield, Chris Thorpe, and his right hand man Sunny. As part of making their living they built and decorated horse drawn living wagons. We made arrangements and went up to see them and their place. This was at the end of a well surfaced single track road. A collection of sheds and bigger buildings all connected to a bungalow.

Most of the dry outside space was used for re-cycling clothes, cloth, light metal and jumble etc. What we had really come to see was in the main building. This was where the wagons were built. On entering Chris and Sunny showed us an almost complete project. A good, big, wagon that, when being built, had more or less ended up as an almost copy of a Bill Wright's wagon. Bill Wright being generally regarded as one of the best, if not the best, of all wagon builders from days gone by. Chris said he needed a few days to finish the job. Just bits and bobs, left to do, including a bit of painting. I told him to forget the painting because I would do that. We agreed a deal. We gave him £2,500 for this brand new wagon on new wooden wheels. This amount included a black horse and its tack and delivery to John and Ingrids' yard. These days the wheels and lock-turntable, would cost that on their own. I suppose that bundle of goodies would set a man back the best part of £20,000 these days. Back then nobody really wanted such things. It was a buyer's market. I decided we would look at it as the wagon costing £2,000 and the horse, his tack and delivery as the rest.

Within a few days the wagon, horse and tack arrived. We put the horse, Jack , out with George and Joe on a piece of ground next to a brook at the far end of John's farm. It was big enough for them, for a while, but not really big enough to be a lot of use to the farm. Chris had told us that Jack had been in harness but never done a lot of work in that respect. He had been used, in the past, for trekking and was known to be a plodder. He would just keep plodding on forever as long as life did not get too strenuous. He was cheap enough to give him a go. He would learn. We would ease him into the job gently by just using him as a side horse, with George, on the big wagon and leave Joe with the smaller square bow top. Well that was the plan. We decided we would slowly work our way down to Milton Keynes. Mandy was still on the boats in that area and it would be easier to get to and from Hammersmith Hospital if and when needed.

It was a Sunday morning. We yoked the horses up and put them in their respective shafts. Jack seemed perfectly happy just twaddling along at George's side. Lin drove Joe and the little wagon as close to the back of my wagon as possible. Joe had the reputation, once he was in the shafts, of wanting to get where he was going and get out of shafts and chill. As long as he was right behind, just following, no problem. Easier for Lin. Our plan was to cut across via Warwick and Northampton but maybe this was wishful thinking. We had gone 2 or 3 miles down the road. Down a reasonably steep hill and we were about to go up the other side when John overtook us in his motor pipping his horn. He was waving, what at first I thought, was a clutch of yellow Liquorice Allsorts. It turned out he had decided to follow on behind us, for a while, just to check everything was O.K. He had noticed little bits dropping off Lin's wagon and stopped to pick them up. They were nuts that had come undone, from their relevant bolts, under the works of her vehicle. Time to have a look at what was going on. To cut a long story short we had been done!! Basically most of the wagon was putty and paint. All that had been holding the nuts in place, alongside other pieces of ironwork, was the paint. Of course, being on iron rimmed wooden wheels, the first decent amount of vibration just started to shake things part. No way was this wagon ever going to make it to Warwick never mind Milton Keynes. I came to the conclusion the best thing to do was to re-trace our tracks, back to John's place, and take it from there. We turned the wagons round at the bottom of the hill we had just come down. A decent sized mound in the road to say the least. Because Joe liked to get everything done as fast as he could we put him in front and let him fly to the top. This, he had no problem with but George was a totally different sort. He liked to get his collar head down and just keep going. A proper old fashioned Black Country tatters sort. This would have been O.K. as we had got Jack hooked up at his side. If the job got a bit too much for George, on his own, then Jack should get his arse in gear and share the job. Wrong! As soon as Jack felt his traces tighten he stopped. This was not for him and no amount of persuasion was going to convince him otherwise. He was O.K. in a harness until the going got a bit tough. At this point he would just say "Sod this" and dig his heels in. The best thing to do was to unhitch him, walk him up the hill, and bring Joe back down to side up with George. Joe installed and off we went. We basically trotted up the rise from a stand still. Two young cob horses just showing off to each other. A bit of friendly one upmanship.

Back in the yard. Horses back down the field. Time to assess the situation. The wagon, on really invasive inspection, turned out to be no more use than a garden ornament. I confronted Mervyn Jones with the fact that he had sold us something that turned out to be unfit for its intended purposes. I said we wanted our money back and as soon as possible. To which he replied "I have spent the money putting a new floor in my kitchen so you will have to take me to court and I will pay you back in dribs and drabs". That was no good to us. We decided to take the really pretty stove out and put it into the big wagon and then sell the pile of putty and paint as a Wendy house/ornament. It was at least painted nicely and looked proper chocolate box inside and out. We advertised it and sold it to a place called The Baby Farm at Pailton (just down the road from John Grey's farm where I had worked years before). A small world. The Baby Farm was situated in a few old farm buildings just on the edge of the village. They traded in second-hand baby and toddler clothes and accessories. They wanted the wagon just to stand at the entrance of their premises. Not only as an eye catcher but also as a place for any visiting children to play in if they wanted. Job done.

We wanted but did not really need another wagon. We got in touch with Chris and Sunny again. As luck would have it they were in the process of building another one at the time. I told them we would buy it and go up with the horses and the big wagon and fetch it when it was ready. I told them to leave it as an open lot. Just canvas curtains on the front and this would save time. As soon as the time came we slowly worked our way up there. The only fly in the ointment now was Jack. A nice enough horse but not cut out for our job. We sold him to a lady who went long distance pony trekking at regular intervals. She just wanted a good reliable plodder and that would suit Jack down to the ground. Indeed she contacted us, a fair bit later, to say she was over the moon with him. Just what she wanted. A good stead horse that would walk on forever. It had turned out well for all concerned. We had got a spare set of driving harness and Jack had found his place in life.

While we were staying in John and Ingrid's yard my foster sister Beryl and her husband Tim and their two girls Eve and Kelly would come and visit on a Sunday most weeks. They would also bring foster sister Jackie's boy Wayne. The kids loved it. Indeed Kelly (now married and mother herself) always remembers when they used to go off and play with the horses in the brook. Apparently George used to go in the brook with them and intentionally splash them with his front feet. He had these odd habits. If he saw you coming he would gallop right up to you and stop dead about 3 foot (1 metre) away. Look you in the eye as if to say. "I bet that worried you". Another quirk of his was when it was time to have his collar on. He would stand, as tall as he possibly could, head and neck right up in the air. Often this habit resulted in his collar having to be thrown on him like a hoop-la. Once it was in place he would just stand, with his head held normally, while he was tacked up. Those silly little habits just made him more loveable. A proper child of a horse.

With Jack and that bloody square wagon now gone up the road we did the same. We trundled off through Tamworth, Measham, and Ashby. All around that way. With the two horses in the same wagon it was easy work for them. Once Joe had realized that George was not going to go shooting off, first thing in the morning, then they got used to working together. It was a lovely sight to be sitting on the wagon, both horses in a trot, their manes wafting around in the breeze. It is one of the sights in my life that even now, after all this time, still makes me smile and give me a moist eye.

Towards the end of one day we were on the look-out for somewhere to stop, for at least the night, when Joe dropped a back shoe. What a pain. Time to look for a blacksmith now. As luck would have it we passed a riding school who gave us the number of a blacksmith and pointed us towards a good little place to pull in for a while. No problem. We phoned the Smith from the riding school and told him where we would be. He said he would be along later that evening. True to his word he arrived. Took all of Joe's shoes off, trimmed his feet and put them all back on again. He said he could see by looking at his hooves that at some time or other, in the past, they had been badly neglected. True, they had. Job done. We were sat drinking tea, coffee in Lin's case, when Brains, our little Corgi x Lassie Collie look alike, appeared from somewhere. He had obviously been off having a mooch about. By now he had become a very capable rabbiting dog. He would wander off on his own. Come back covered in dirt and whatever but invariably with a rabbit in his mouth. To look at him he was the most unlikely candidate to ever achieve such things but he did. We told the blacksmith about this. He said he also had a dog you would never think could catch a rabbit as long as he had got a hole in his bum. Like Brains this little dog had worked out the job for himself. He told us, quite often, he took this little fella into the pub to have bets with the blokes that his dog could get more rabbits that any of theirs. Usually he was right. The little dog had won him money on more than one occasion. It just goes to show "You cannot judge a book by its cover". In years to come this saying would again be proved to be true by another little dog that came our way. More of that later.

Time to shift again. The horses had run out of grass where we had them tethered. Eventually we ended up near Long Eaton. I decided to

343

stop next to a traffic island opposite to McDonalds. An easy stop and, more importantly, close to water so we could fill up the butts. It was a well-lit place but a lot of hassle. All night there was hassle from mouthy youngsters, driving past, hurling abuse. Par for the course really. People were either really friendly or total gob shites. There were only the two of us and a few dogs so the axe was always next to the bed at night time . . . just in case. Morning came and an old boy turned up in a pick-up. He had got a place further down the road. He suggested to move down closer to him just to be on the safe side. This was an old travelling man called Donkey Ball. He lived in a little wooden bungalow with his mother. A really old, hard, skinned lady. She was proud to show us her original angel lamp that, in days gone by, had been in her wagon. "You do not see many of these about now lad" she said. She was just clinging on to her memories . . . bless her. Donkey Ball was, as his name suggests a dealer who concentrated mainly on donkeys and mules. Not so much the horses. He told us he had been asked to go to some Wild West style theme park up in Derbyshire to buy all their mules. He said he had never seen mules as big. He reckoned the odd one was 16 hands high but they were now getting more difficult to find at the best of times. Funny how these little things stay in your brain! I only ever met them twice. Once now and, as it turned out, once again a couple of years later. All part of life's rich tapestry I suppose.

We stayed for a couple of days near his place but grazing, or the lack of it, dictated another move. I cannot recall where we were, in a definitive way, but we ended up down some lane or other and we found ourselves at the top of an extremely steep hill. It was, and probably still is, one hell of a drop. Should we risk taking the horses and wagon down or turn round and go somewhere else. We decided to give the descent a go. Joe was in the shafts and George on the side. We started to venture down. The brake wound full on. Joe, as far back in his breaching as he could go. George being on the side had no breaching. He was sticking his bum as far back as he could, looking for the breaching, to try and stop the wagon running away. Lin and I can remember this hill was so steep it felt as if we were both going to topple off the wagon on top of the horses. To this day Lin says she has never been so scared. However, our two trusty black and white friends did not let us down. With the help of the brake we got safely down. I remember at the bottom there was an old pub with a big car park. We pulled in there and gave the horses and ourselves a drink. Those two lads had earned it and a bit of a rest.

Burton-on-Trent was the next significant place ahead. We had never been in that area before so we decided to stick to the main road, right through the centre of town, and get out of there as soon as possible. We would then find somewhere to stop for the night. We had had a long day and we and the horses were tired. They needed to get out of the shafts, get some food down their necks and have a good rest. We got out of town but, for love nor money, we could not find a verge big enough to stop on. Eventually we came across an old quarry, or sand hole, or something like that. We pulled in there. There was enough grass and enough space to last until the next day. Everybody fed and watered. The horses and dogs all tied up. Santa the cat in residence. Time for a sleep. The next morning a car turned up, driven by a lady, bearing gifts of tea and a bit of food. Apparently she had noticed us go past, the previous evening, and thought we all looked a bit the worse for wear. She decided to bring us some breakfast. She asked if all was well. When she discovered Lin only drank coffee she did not more than get back in her car reappearing with the desired beverage. This little happening was nice in itself but what really stood out was the fact that she served it all out of a silver tea and silver coffee pot on a silver tray. Within a few days we had seen both sides of humanity. The loud mouthed gob shites at Long Eaton and now this very benevolent lady somewhere near Burton-on-Trent. There is nowt as strange as folk!

Time to get out of there and find somewhere better to stop. Neither Lin or I can recall these days except we can recall going past Twycross Zoo and seeing really big terrapins swimming about in a big ditch/ natural water course outside the place. Nothing noteworthy occurred for a while but things were starting to come together. The new wagon was ready to be picked up in Chesterfield and Juliet wanted to come and stay with us for a while. I think we arranged to meet her somewhere and we would all set off along with her dog Shades and head towards Chris and Sunny's place. We would put Joe in the new wagon with Lin and Juliet. I would have George in the big wagon. We all three lived and slept in the big wagon with Juliet and Shades on the floor. There was no stove in the new wagon but we had the spare we had left in John's yard. The plan was to go back down, put the old stove into the new wagon and take it from there. We took our time trundling up to Chesterfield but we got there. We stopped down the lane leading to the place, let the horses loose on Chris's land for a good leg stretch, and then settled in for a few days. Apparently Chris and Sunny used to go out for a drink together one night a week. As Juliet liked a drink they took her along. Now Juliet was no shrinking violet. Although we had now known her for getting on for forty years, on this occasion, Chris actually made her blush. Something we had never seen before or since. As they went off to the pub Chris said to her with no airs and graces "Aye up Juliet, how do you fancy havin' a curly haired babby?" in his broad Derbyshire accent. Of course, he was only teasing her but just for a moment she was embarrassed . . . bless her.

Time to pull away now. Chris had told us several times that if a horse could pull a wagon up the hill leading out of his lane then it would go anywhere in the country. I took this with a pinch of salt. It did not look that steep really. We put the horses in. Checked everything was present and correct only to find Santa the cat was missing. Usually if we left before he returned home he would eventually return to the last place he saw us. The horses were in and ready now so we would get out of the lane and go back and look for him afterwards. The not so steep hill (in my opinion) proved Chris to be right. It got the better of both the horses. It was just a case of the wagons up, one at a time, with both of them sided up. This hill really was a trick to the eyes. Job done. Time to go and find Santa. Before we had left we had tied the horses back up, on their chains, for a day or two just to get them back in the right frame of mind after their few days of free roaming. Sure enough there was Santa waiting for us next to where the horses had been pegged out. It was back to his place, tied up on the bed, while we were on the move.

The plan now was to pull up back at John and Ingrid's place and put the stove in the wagon. As it was now harvest time we would all three stay for a week or two and give them a hand with the bale carting. A bit of tractor driving and a bit of milking. They employed no staff. It was just them and their two kids. Joanne who worked away and Julian who was just finishing his school days. Any help they could get would be appreciated. We stayed until all of the bale carting was finished. The plan was that Juliet, who now lived near her sister in London as well as in Birmingham, would go back home. Lin and I would work our way back down towards Milton Keynes. Juliet went on her way.

We set off late one afternoon, stopping that night only a few miles away. We set off in earnest the following morning. We had got as far as Dunchurch near Rugby and had come a fair old way. The horses were getting a bit lack-lustre. We had come to the bottom of a long steady rise

346

in the road. Me, feeling a bit sorry for George, broke the number one rule. Never lead the horse by the head unless someone is on the wagon holding the reins. I decided to jump off and lighten his load a little. Joe was quite happy with Lin. He had his nose stuck in the usual place right up the back end of my wagon. Where ever that went he just followed. It was a good thing he had got into that habit. I was walking on the inside of George, holding his bridal and telling him what a good boy he was when out of the blue he startled, pricked his ears, and was off. I tried to pull him back on his bridal but because I was up the side of him I just pulled him into me. He tripped me up. I went under the front nearside wheel and out under the back off side wheel. When I came to my senses I was lying in the road. Joe, Lin and her wagon were about as close to me as they could get. Joe had got his ears up looking at my turn out just a bit up the road. Luckily George had come to his senses and stopped, but Joe was used to travelling as close to the back of my wagon as he could comfortable get. Now his usual leader was up the road. In sight and the other side of me. I can recall lying there looking up at him and thinking "For fuck's sake stay where you are". I cannot recall a lot after that except the police had arrived. I was still prostate on the road with this policeman standing astride me. He was obviously protecting me. I can remember looking up at him and thinking to myself "If you say two words out of place then I can get you straight in the bollocks from here". Luckily someone had got hold of George and my wagon and brought them back to me. Joe was now more at ease anyway. We were waiting for an ambulance. I was still unable to move so I asked the policeman if he would ask Lin to make me a cup of tea please. He said he did not think that was such a good idea in this situation. I just wanted a cup of tea and a fag.

Next stop, hospital, St. Cross, Rugby. Exactly the same hospital I had been in when I had the back injury at John Gray's years earlier . . . small world! I was in casualty, unshaven, and covered in horse hair, dog hair and horse shit. The nurse came along and asked me where it hurt. I pointed to the top of my head and to my toes and said "Well it starts here and ends there". To which she replied "Do not be so funny, where does it hurt the most". I pointed to my right leg below the knee. She had a look and found a big cut across my shin area. She decided to get that X-rayed. It turned out it was broken. She got it plastered and said I could go now as the police were outside ready to take me back to Lin and the wagons. I stood up and immediately collapsed again. This action prompted the response of "Do not be such a baby, you have only broken your leg", from this, not over caring, nurse who had treated me. At this point I can remember the policeman getting me to his van. He more or less poured me into the passenger seat. While I had been in hospital a nearby small-holder had, apparently, heard what had happened and let Lin move herself and everything into his field. I could not get up the steps into the wagon so Lin bedded me down on the ground outside for now. I recall it was a boiling hot day but I was lying there absolutely freezing. Lin got all the bedding, all the coats and everything out of the wagon that might help me keep warm. I even had the dogs stashed under all of this stuff in an effort to stop shivering. Things were not looking too promising right then. Lin decided to ring the police again and luckily, when they arrived, it was the same man that had fetched me back from the hospital earlier. He decided to do no more than get me back into Hospital St. Cross. It looked as if I could now be in Shit Street or words to that effect.

So here we go again, back to A & E for the second time in a few hours. This time the nurses were bypassed and it was straight on for the attention of the doctor who duly arrived. He decided to lift my shirt up to have a good look etc. and, lo and behold, this action revealed a big diagonal cut across my left hip area. He asked when I had done that? I just said "Well, I haven't done it since last time I was here". So down to X-ray and more was revealed. It seems I had either broken or fractured a couple or three vertebrae. It was decided that the best thing to do was for me to stay in hospital for now. After a couple of days it was noticed that my right knee was swelling up so back to X-ray where it was seen that I had done my knee in as well. It seemed one of the wagon wheels, at least, had run over my left hip and right leg in a diagonal track which explained why my tobacco tin (which I always carried in the left hand pocket of my jacket) was basically flattened. They say smoking is bad for you but that baccy tin certainly helped avoid any more serious injury. When I thought about it the wagon weighed over a ton and all that weight was spread over an area of 2 or 3 square inches (5 or 8 square cm) on each of the four wheels. If it had gone over my chest area then things would have been a lot worse than they presently were. Next stop the operating theatre to sort my knee out. They put a couple of screws in it and supported it with a plaster type slab up each side of my leg to allow for swelling. I recall coming round and Lin and Juliet being at the side of the bed. The pain was horrendous. The worst pain I had ever been in, or ever have been in, so they decided to put me back to sleep again. I do not know how long for but, anyway, next time I awoke things were a lot better at least. I was now confined to the prone position for what turned out to be well over two months to allow my back to heal. Luckily I do not mind hospitals as long as I know all is well at home. Luckily word had got back about everything and John Matthews got in touch with Lin and said if she could get the wagons and horses back to his place then we could stay there until things got better. He got hold of Donald (Upton) and took him out to Lin and Juliet. On that Sunday he helped them take the whole turn out back to the safety of the farm. At least the women were off the road and in a safe place. I never did meet the man who took Lin and the horses, dogs, cat and wagons on to his place after the accident but, if by some bizarre set of coincidences he, or any of his family, should ever read this book then I would like to take his opportunity of doing so now . . . thank you Sir!!

The days dragged on in Hospital, St. Cross, Rugby. Lin, or Lin and Juliet, would visit whenever they could but it was a long way and an awkward journey by public transport. Lin was by my bed one day when the Orthopaedic Consultant (a big tall "black" man) came for an inspection along with the surgeon who, apparently, had done the operation. I can remember today, as plain as if it happened yesterday, Lin was standing on one side of the bed and the two surgeons on the other side. The consultant lifted the relevant X-rays up to the light to have a look and did no more than to turn to his subordinate and utter the words "You'll have to do better than this you know". That was not a heart-warming thing to hear. Lin was shocked. She was already thinking about reporting the nurse who had originally treated me. The nurse that had decided that I had "Only broken your leg" . . . quote. I said just to leave it. I was stuck in there for the foreseeable future and I did not want or need the aggravation of going through all that procedure.

The ward I was on contained "three long stay patients". Me, another lad called Nick and a lad who had been originally treated in Warwick Hospital for a bad ankle injury. It turned out that one day his visitors were at his bedside in Warwick when they noticed a strange smell originating from beneath his bedcovers. It turned out his injury had gone gangrenous while he had been in their care!! He had been duly transferred to Rugby to get it sorted out. In the end, if I recall correctly, he ended up having his foot amputated . . . poor bugger. The other Nick was a lad about 19 years old. A big, tall, strong type who had been in an accident on his motorbike and gone through the windscreen of a car resulting in multiple injuries.

He had apparently been in there for ages and ages. I remember that because he had got pieces of windscreen glass imbedded in his arms they had decided to let them work their way out. Quite often, in any quiet time, the nurses would occupy their time by sitting down and picking out any of these pieces that had been accessible. Nick's girlfriend would visit him. My God was she a funny woman or not? She was hilarious. In all my life I have only ever met three naturally "funny" females and she was one of them. The other two being Sally the girl from Holy Trinity Farm in Brum and the other a young semi-disabled friend of my foster sister called Fran. Late one Saturday night a new patient arrived on the ward. A chap called Laurence. A bit of a hippy type. Long hair, beard . . . the usual thing. He had his hand and arm below the elbow supported in an upright position. It turned out he had shot himself through the hand. I asked him how he had managed to do that? He replied "Missed my fuckin' head man!!"

After a couple of months, lying on my back, it was decided that as soon as I could lift my injured leg off the bed (standard par for the course for knee injuries apparently) then I could sit up and eventually get up, but I was having trouble doing this. I do not know why I just was. I realised that if I put my hands under the covers then I could lift it up like that. I remember the nurse sitting at the end of the ward so I thought I would give it a go. "Nurse, watch this", I called to her and proceeded to perform my "trick". She just looked, smiled and said "Now do it with your hands and arms on top of the covers". She had seen it all before hadn't she? One day, when I was not really thinking about it I just did it. No problem at all. Must have been some kind of mental block, but at least now I was allowed to lay more upright until it was time to try and stand up again. This was a slow process starting with just sitting up on the bed and gradually working my way onwards bit by bit. Apparently if you have been lying down for a long time it takes a while for your body to re-adjust to being upright. This process usually involves several fainting episodes but in the end I got there and on to crutches. The doctors had decided that the time was now right for the other Nick to attempt to do the same thing. All went well for him during the sitting up on the bed stage but one lunch time three nurses decided to try and get him to stand up. Now he was a big lad, over 6 ft (1 ¾ metres) tall and well built. They positioned themselves around him for support and up he stood and DOWN he went. He had fainted and collapsed in a big heap on his bed taking the nurses with him!! Slowly he too managed to stand on his own, two feet, unaided. The only concern for me now was that my knee seemed to be locked solid even when the plaster slabs were loosened. It would not move at all but the doctors said it would start to move eventually. "Eventually" it turned out would be the operative word. I had been in hospital for over 3 months by now. It was decided I could go home at last. John bought Lin to the hospital and took us back to the wagons. Juliet, bless her, had stayed with Lin all this time. When we got back she had already got the kettle on. You cannot beat a good cup of tea in time of stress and she knew it. So back home at last with strict instructions to spend most of my time in bed and whatever I did do NOT fall over. Easier said than done after a while. At this present time I was not really that keen to go anywhere anyway.

John and Ingrid had taken a couple of adult men lodgers while I had been in hospital. A chap called Clive, who drove an MG sports car, I recall, and an older local man called Pete. Between them all they had managed to rig up a plant walkway for me to use when I wanted to get outside. For the first couple of days I was a bit wary of using it. In the end with the help and support of all present I managed to get outside again at last. I spent a lot of time laid on the bed, as instructed. Because the bed in a wagon is, at the very least, above waist height off the floor we had placed a square pouffe type box (that we used to sit on) below the bed for me to use to get in and out during the time I was confined to this position of repose. Little Thumb our white terrier, that we had had since he had been dumped a few days old at Holy Trinity Farm, would lie in bed with me. Lin would put him outside a few times a day to do whatever he had to do. I noticed after a few days how, when he had gone outside to go to the loo, he rushed straight back and waited to be lifted back upon the bed with me. It turned out the little fella had not been eating. We always made the joke that because he was white (as in wearing a white coat) he thought he must be the doctor around the place. He needed to be in bed, looking after me, at all times.

John and Ingrid used to go into Nuneaton every Friday to do their shopping and Lin would go with them. On one such occasion they were all out. I was on the farm on my own in bed. No problem but all of a sudden I wanted a cup of tea. The kettle was always on the stove so it was just a case of getting down, putting a bit more wood on the fire, and boiling the kettle up. No problem I thought . . . Wrong! I managed to get my good leg down on to the pouffe box but slipped off it in the process of getting my bad leg down. I ended up in a heap on the floor and in a lot of pain. I had done exactly what I had been told NOT to do. I had fallen over. I must have passed out for a few seconds because I was now on the floor, head spinning, feeling faint and being sick. I managed to get hold of the milk and drank it all to fresh myself up a bit. The next problem was getting back on the bed. After much struggling and effort I eventually managed it. When Lin got back with John and Ingrid all was revealed. I was chastised in no uncertain manner. I would not try that again for a while. I gradually got stronger and more mobile but still the knee would not bend. We had now got to decide what to do next. I was not strong or stable enough to handle the horses. As far as Lin was concerned, seeing the accident unfurl only a couple of yards away from her in the first place, she had got scared and wanted rid of it at all. Very understandable. She had witnessed her husband almost getting killed in front of her very eye . . . time to change course . . . again what next? I still could not bend my leg so driving a vehicle was out of the question, at least, for a while. We decided to try and buy another boat. Every so often the B.W.B. held a sale, in London, of boats that they had impounded and taken ownership of for one reason or another. We thought Lin could go down on the train and see what she could find. This mission proved pointless and to make it worse she had her handbag "dipped" on the underground and her purse was snatched. Luckily she had got her return ticket in her pocket so at least she could get back to Coventry. John went and picked her up from there. Time to re-think things. It was a waste of time keeping the horses any longer so we sold them both . . . Sad really. I am not really a "horseman" but I loved George as much as I have ever loved any horse. I have always said that "If a horse isn't serving a purpose then the best place for it is inside a good dog" but that is just my view. A travelling man called "Bacon Rind" turned up at the farm one day. We had seen him about over the last few years from time to time at various places. He was out "calling" and he had stumbled across us again. We drank tea and chatted. He had heard what had happened with the accident and was interested in what was going on. In the past he had given us a "driving whip" as a gift. Something in all the years to come he would bring up in conversation from time to time. We told him the wagons that were for sale. Well at least the small one and off he went. Time went by and a chap called Siddy Riddle turned up to look at the wagon. His daughter was courting Bacon Rind's son so word had passed on. We already knew Sid. Again like Bacon Rind our paths had crossed in the past. In fact we used to make little ornaments out of sea shells, feathers and dried flowers that we would sell to his mother who hawked them on again. They were travelling people but we had originally met them years earlier at Henley-in-Arden Auctions. They were staying in a wood yard just up the road at that time. Anyway we sold them the small wagon. It was unusual in that it was built on a Burnley Dray that incorporated a wooden brake bar. Quite an unusual thing. This was what he liked. One of his other kids lived and travelled in it for a while but I think he told me it ended up in America so it was just the big wagon to go now. Until his death a few years ago Bacon Rind always said that this was the best wagon on the road at the time. We were obviously living in it at the time but John said that if we sold it then his son Julian had got a 12' (approx. 4 metre) long caravan that he used for fishing. He would fetch that in to the yard for us until we could get mobile again. This we did because we sold the wagon to an Equestrian Centre who had a brick plinth built for it at the entrance to their premises. That was the last we ever saw of it but Bacon Rind said he passed it from time to time and always reported back. Usually with the words "Waste of a bloody good wagon that is!" My leg, by now had been liberated from its plaster slabs etc. but it still would not bend much more than an inch (2 ½ cm) and I had been told by the hospital that I must stay on crutches and I must not damage it in any way. We had settled in the little trailer (caravan). It was small but it was dry and with the cooker on it stayed warm because it was now Autumn/Winter time. Lin had to go back to Hammersmith for a couple of days for more treatment so Juliet came over to stay to help me/us out for a while. I remember that my hair needed a wash and she offered to do it for me but I refused. She still jokes about that to this day. Lin had had to have surgery so she would be "on the blink" for a while and I was about as useful as a wet rag. Mobility or the lack of it being the problem. I kept trying to bend my leg and it had now reached the point that I could just about bend it enough to drive a tractor at least.

We knew of, and had seen and been inside of, a vintage showman's wagon up near Nottingham. A big old lump of a thing. Well over 20' (almost 7 metres) long. A four wheeler with a pull out kitchen. All the original mahogany veneer and mirrors inside but minus the cooking range. We decided if we got that and a tractor then we would be able to be off up the road again. We got a lift up to go and have another look at it but sadly it had been sold the previous week so that idea had been blown away.

The semi-frozen knee joint had now become a problem. Firstly due to the very fact that it was almost still unbendable and secondly it had always been my "good leg". It did most of the work thus relieving the pain in the left leg that had always been there since the accident in the cattle crush at Rugby years earlier. By now my thigh on that side had shrunk by about an inch (2 ½ cm) in circumference simply because I had been favouring the, what was, the good leg. The surgeons decided to have me back in, put me to sleep and try and force it to bend. I woke up after the procedure fully expecting to have a fully functional knee again but this proved not to be the case as it turned out. I did have a little bit more, and I mean "a little it" more flexibility in it. Just enough to drive a motor if I pushed the seat right back as far as it would go. At least that was a positive anyway. Time to get a bigger trailer and a motor and off we could go again. We found an old Leyland Red line, otherwise known as an F.G. lorry with a horse box mounted on it. Donald took me to have a look at it. He said it was O.K. but why was the engine running when we first got there? He was dubious, but me, being me, a bull at a gate, overruled him and bought it. Mistake, big mistake. I knew nothing about motors and hadn't listened to a man who did. If I decided to do anything then I wanted to do it yesterday!! Life is too short!! The lorry was now part of our furniture but it was an awful thing to start. Hence the fact that it was already running when we went to look at it. Frank came over several times. He was used to messing with engines, especially diesel engines, but it was always a massive job to fire it up. Time to get it going and park it up somewhere. John Plumb said I could park it alongside his farm machinery at his place. We dropped it off there until we could decide what to do with it. As luck would have it Phil, a friend of Vics, was a lorry man and he and his girlfriend were on the hunt for a motor to go to Portugal in so we told him the story. He bought it. Sorted all its problems out. Next thing I heard was that he and his girlfriend and the old F.G. were in Portugal where I think they are to this day.

An old Bedford C. F. van was the next vehicle to enter our lives. At least it started out and ran when we needed it and I could just about get my legs in well enough to drive it. Just a case of getting a trailer now. This we found at a travellers site back up in Tipton. A 20' (6 meter plus) Astral. Chrome flashing, double axle, end bedroom, stove cooker, the lot. We bought it off a man we knew called "Buzzer" Rafferty. A man who was known for his horses. Especially his stallion. A red and white fella with a tail that touched the floor. A mane that reached half way down his front legs and the longest leg feathers (hair) any man had ever seen. We bought the trailer and it was delivered by Buzzer to the farm next day. At the time we had not got a tow bar on our C.F. van so Clive, one of John and Ingrid's lodgers, had taken me across to Tipton to look at it in his sports car. That was a squeeze. I had to get in and out through the roof but anyway the job was done. I think we gave £900. for it at the time and on putting our stuff in the drawers we found a few pennies. Maybe a bit of "luck money". In another drawer we found a doll of a baby about 6 or 7" (15cm plus) long wearing just a nappy . . . could this be an omen because the infertility treatment was now reaching a critical point. Lin had bouts of having to go to hospital every day for 3 or 4 days for injections etc. When these times came around we would take at least one dog, usually Toby, with us. Park up in a car park behind the hospital and Wormwood Scrubs prison for a few days at a time and live in the back of the van. Finding something to do to pass the time. Most evenings a game of Irish Hurling would take place on the playing field next to us. We found out years later there was a bird farm nearby. If we had known that, at the time, then we could have spent time visiting there but we did not know so that was that. The advice from the doctors was that once the embryo was placed into Lin she must not exert herself more than was absolutely necessary for the duration of the, hopefully, pregnancy. Mandy and her new bloke Jim had got themselves a boat and were moored up at Coggy's Yard. They had already got one boy, Tym, and she was pregnant again so we agreed with Coggy that we would pay him rent to stay up his yard in the trailer until, fingers crossed, a baby was born. Because we had used Lin's parents' address this would take place at Marston green Hospital. About an hour away. The very hospital where both Mandy and Colette had been born. We hitched up and shifted and at this point I would like to take the chance, on behalf of both of us, to sincerely thank John, Ingrid, Julian and Joanne for all the hospitality they showed us and all the help they gave us in our times of need . . . thank you all!!

Time for the final trip to Hammersmith Hospital. Three embryos were put in place. They said that they did this because if one did not survive we would have twins, and if two did not survive we would still have one left. Just a case of waiting with fingers crossed now. During the pregnancy we spent our time not doing much at all really except chatting and visiting people. We would go over and visit Ma and Frank and Lin's parents and brother. We would just pop in to see people we knew. At odd times we would see John and his family. By now they had got rid

Ralph.

Marg.

of the milking herd through a government scheme and gone into buying calves and rearing "bull beef" – beef from un-castrated cattle. John was showing me a bunch of his adult beasts one day when I started to climb the gate, along with my crutches, to go in and have a look at them much to John's dismay. "You can't go in there with that lot. You can hardly move at the best of times" he said. No wonder I used to get knocked about a bit!! On one such visit I was walking across the yard and could see Joanne, who was probably in her mid twenties, getting changed in her bedroom. Anyway we went inside for tea and she came into the room and I told her that she ought to close the curtains when she was getting changed. She blushed and got all embarrassed, to which I just blurted out "Don't worry I've seen bigger tits on a goldfish" and we all laughed, embarrassment over . . . Bless her.

Back at Coggys, Mandy, Jim and Tym (Jax was now living full time on the boats with his dad David) were going to hang about for the time being until Lin had the baby. They had got a 50' (15 metre plus) long wooden narrowboat called Ironside. It turned out they had got it cheap and by pure chance. One day down near Watford, apparently, Mandy was walking down the towpath when she came across a chap in a very irate state looking at his boat that was partially submerged, sitting on the bottom. Poor bugger. He was at his wits end. He told her he had spent ages with it out of the water, repairing the hull. Almost as soon as he had got it back in the canal it started to leak again and sunk. Well of course it had. The wooden planks had shrunk and dried out while it was in dry dock. According to Mandy she said that "She'd give him a quid for it". Something she had grown up with hearing me say the same thing. She said to which he only bloody well agreed!! She gave him the pound, made him give her a receipt and just left it where it was for a few days until the planks swelled up again. She then took Tym down to it, and phoned the fire brigade up. She made out she was a single mother and they pumped it out and re-floated it for her. Cheap boat, good girl!! It turned out that since we had last seen her she had met Jim, had a baby and been living in an old "hippy motor". They had been up to Scotland and basically got thrown out back over the border. She said they were parked up one night when the police raided them, searched the motor and found spices in jars in the cupboard. These were suspected to be herbs of questionable nature. At this point Jim had "Gone off on one" and confronted them with a Samarai Sword. This did not go down too well and he was carted off to cool down. Jim was, and still is, a man not

357

much younger than me. A Geordie chap, the spitting image of Charles Manson and who walked with his head thrust forward at an amazing speed. He regaled everyone with the fact that in his youth he had been a steam powered crane driver up in Newcastle. He had joined the original "Hippie Convoy" back in the 60's and had not gone back. I really liked Jim. A bit mad headed and fiery but who am to talk? He could "bodge" or mend anything mechanical. When Mandy was with him we never worried about her at least, he was wild, so what? He could, again "bodge" his way out of things. The reason they had moved away from down South was that social services down there had told them they were not happy about her having the baby on the boat and were being "a pain in the arse" about the whole thing. She and Jim decided to get out of it and come up North. Whatever, it had turned out well as both she and Lin were pregnant and staying within a few hundred yards of each other. Mandy duly gave birth to another boy they called Wolfe.

Lin, by now, was extremely rotund around the middle and in due course decided the time had come to go to Marston Green for the baby to be born. I always said that it was a baby girl and although she was not due until January/February I said she would be born by Christmas, and she was . . . on the 20th December 1988. Welcome to the world little Fleur. A tiny little thing, 6 weeks premature. Just like Colette, also born within a few days of Christmas. As a matter of fact so was Mandy. Three girls all born at the same time of year. From now on my life would never be the same again. I phoned round everyone to give the news and within an hour Sally and Cameron had arrived complete with a cigar. I kept this for years and years until Donald became not too well and I gave it to him. He always liked a cigar and Sally agreed to be little Fleur's godmother. I was smitten by the little bundle. In years to come Lin would always say "Look at you, you just melt whenever you look at her". It had all been worth it in the end . . . Where will the wind blow . . . now three of us . . . next?